World War Two Legacies in East Asia

How to remember World War Two in East Asia is a huge source of friction between China and Japan, causing major diplomatic and political difficulties right up to the present. As this book shows, however, there is also disagreement within these countries as to how to remember the war, which in the case of China began immediately after the war and lasted with varying degrees of intensity. Based on extensive original research, the book explores how China's remembrance of the war has evolved over time. It not only explores the roles played by the national as well as local state actors in the formation of the Chinese war memory, but also pays attention to individual Chinese people. It considers particular aspects of commemoration in China, explores the corresponding situation in Japan and discusses the continuing impact on the relationship between the two countries.

Chan Yang is a Lecturer in the Institute for International Studies at Wuhan University, China.

Routledge Studies in the Modern History of Asia

For a full list of available titles please visit: https://www.routledge.com/Routledge-Studies-in-the-Modern-History-of-Asia/book-series/MODHISTASIA

World War Two Legacies in East Asia

China Remembers the War

Chan Yang

LONDON AND NEW YORK

First published 2018
by Routledge
2 Park Square, Milton Park, Abingdon, Oxon OX14 4RN

and by Routledge
711 Third Avenue, New York, NY 10017

Routledge is an imprint of the Taylor & Francis Group, an informa business

© 2018 Chan Yang

British Library Cataloguing in Publication Data
A catalogue record for this book is available from the British Library

Library of Congress Cataloging in Publication Data
A catalog record for this book has been requested

ISBN: 978-1-138-30370-6 (hbk)
ISBN: 978-1-315-14249-4 (ebk)

Typeset in Times New Roman
by Taylor & Francis Books

Contents

List of illustrations

Figures

Tables

Note on Chinese and Japanese word usage

Chinese and Japanese words, including names of places and people, have been romanised using the Hanyu Pinyin system and Hepburn system in most cases. However, other transliterations will be used when a word in Pinyin is unfamiliar in English: for example, Chiang Kai-Shek (Jiang Jieshi). Except in the case of Pinyin and Romaji, Chinese and Japanese scripts and English translations will be given when necessary. Following the conventions in the two countries, Chinese and Japanese names will be given with the family name first, followed by the given name.

Note on the terminology used to refer to the war

Different names have been given to the military conflict that was fought between China and Japan in the 1930s and 1940s, which merged into the greater conflict of World War Two after the Battle of Pearl Harbor in 1941. Different periods in time are also referred to. The most internationally recognised name is the Second Sino–Japanese War (1937–1945). In China, people normally refer to this as the War of Resistance against Japan or Anti-Japanese War (Kang Ri zhanzheng, 抗日战争, 1937–1945), or the Fourteen-Year War (Shisinian zhanzheng, 十四年战争, 1931–1945). In Japan, several names are given to the conflict, like the Great East Asia War (Daitoua sensou 大東亜戦争, 1941–1945), the Fifteen-Year War (Juugonen sensou, 十五年戦争, 1931–1945) and the Pacific War (Taiheiyou sensou, 太平洋戦争, 1941–1945). This book prefers to call this conflict the Fifteen-Year War. However, at times different names will be used in this book, according to the context.

Preface

Almost seventy years have passed since the end of the Second World War. However, unlike in Europe, no consensus has been reached as to how to remember the war between East Asian countries, and even within each East Asian country consensus is hard to reach. What is more, the remembrance of the war is often a source of diplomatic controversy in East Asia, especially between Japan and China. Exploring how the Fifteen-Year War (the military conflict between Japan and China from 1931 to 1945 – the main conflict in the Second World War in the East Asian theatre) has been remembered in mainland China and Japan is an essential step towards understanding the origin of the currently explosive Sino–Japanese 'history problem'. There is an extensive literature on the evolution of remembrance of the Fifteen-Year War in post-war Japan, but there is just a sprinkling of literature on the Chinese side.

Thanks to several recently published books, such as Rana Mitter's *China's War with Japan, 1937–1945: The Struggle for Survival*, readers outside China and Japan have gradually come to know the Fifteen-Year War from the Chinese perspective, which has previously been overlooked. However, despite its importance, there is no effective discussion about how Chinese people have remembered that war. A domestic tradition of discussing the evolving history of remembrance of the war is lacking in mainland China. Discussion of the topic is dominated by a few scholars from outside of China, who are mainly interested in Sino–Japanese relations and individual war-related controversies.

Most of this research on the Chinese side argues that before the 1982 'Textbook Incident' there had been a 'benevolent amnesia' with respect to the Fifteen-Year War, and the current problematic remembrance of the Fifteen-Year War in China can be attributed to the patriotic campaigns sponsored by the Chinese Communist Party (CCP) regime since around 1982.[1] Nevertheless, there are two major shortcomings in the research examining the pre-1982 period: a lack of thorough first-hand research, and a strong government-centric view, which renders these studies overly simplistic and partial.

Thus, this book primarily aims to overcome the shortcomings of the existing literature and to present a new picture of Chinese remembrance of the Fifteen-Year War prior to 1982. It does so by incorporating a great deal of fresh empirical data generated through fieldwork conducted in mainland

China and Japan, such as national as well as local archives, and interviews. In addition to the top-down perspective, it also probes the pre-1982 period from the perspectives of ordinary Chinese people and non-governmental actors. As the book reveals, the remembrance of the Fifteen-Year War was substantial in China before 1982, although not on a scale as large as today. Central as well as local authorities and various unofficial actors interacted with each other to shape a relatively unified remembrance of the war. Furthermore, since the issue of remembrance of the war has been entangled with Chinese international relations and various domestic affairs, this book also aspires to bring previously overlooked aspects of post-war China to attention. Ultimately, this book intends to explore the formation of the Sino–Japanese 'history problem', and to contribute to solving the problem.

Chapter 1 provides an introduction, which sets the context for the study. Comparison can render invalid purely national explanations for what are in fact universal phenomena, and can also help to identify those phenomena that are genuine peculiarities of a particular nation.[2] A comparative perspective, using European experience to shed light on the study of East Asian war remembrance and comparing Chinese and Japanese experiences, is adopted in this chapter and is threaded throughout the rest of the book.

Chapter 2 examines pre-1982 Sino–Japanese relations to uncover the correlation between remembrance of the Fifteen-Year War and China's relationship with Japan. Chapter 3 explores how martyrs of the Fifteen-Year War were glorified before 1982. Chapter 4 examines aspects of Fifteen-Year War remembrance constructed by the Chinese government (the national anthem, school history textbooks, and history museums) and pays attention to the central–local dimension of remembrance. Chapter 5 examines aspects of remembrance constructed by unofficial actors (Fifteen-Year-War themed arts, scholarly works and grassroots memories) and emphasises the interaction between the state and unofficial actors in constructing remembrance of the war in the People's Republic of China (PRC).

Chapter 6, the concluding chapter, summarises the original research contained in the book and answers the three overarching research questions: namely, how was the Fifteen-Year War remembered in China and how did this remembrance evolve before the 1982 Textbook Incident? What was the relationship between national and local Fifteen-Year-War remembrance activities before 1982? How did official and non-official agents interact with each other to shape remembrance of the war before 1982? The epilogue will also answer several unresolved questions that are posed in the introductory chapter – for instance, why did the 1972 Sino–Japanese normalisation not lead to a Sino–Japanese post-war reconciliation? Why and how have Chinese and Japanese Fifteen-Year-War memories clashed with each other?

As a Chinese person born in the late 1980s, I was brought up to believe stories of the 'Japanese devil' (*Riben guizi* 日本鬼子). I then got a chance to stay in Japan for a period, and to meet 'real' Japanese people, as an undergraduate learning the Japanese language. It was this experience that made me realise that the perception, which is common amongst Chinese, that Japanese society as a whole denies its wartime misdeeds is wrong. Also, there is a mis-understanding amongst the Japanese that the Chinese aggressively and end-lessly accuse them of past wrongdoings merely for pragmatic reasons.[3] Both countries are demonised by the other to some extent. It was a wish to con-tribute to resolving this unfortunate situation, and to bring about a real reconciliation between China and Japan, that led me to start conducting my doctoral research – from which this book emerged.

Over the course of writing this book I have incurred many debts, both academic and personal, that I wish to acknowledge. I would like to begin by offering my sincere thanks to my doctoral supervisors, Professor Robert Bickers and Professor Tim Cole, for all their support, advice and encourage-ment during the past three-and-a-half years. Professor Rana Mitter, Dr Juliane Furst, Professor Ronald Hutton and Dr Josie McLellan also gave extremely helpful advice as examiners of my doctoral thesis. I would like to thank the staff of the Department of History and the Centre for East Asian Studies at the University of Bristol. I am also grateful to my fellow post-graduates at Bristol, my friends, and my family, for all their love and support.

I would also like to thank the friendly staff at all the libraries and archives I have used in China, Japan and Britain for their assistance. I was invited to attend the workshops of the Sino–Japanese Relations Research Network at the University of Leeds several times. This provided me with valuable insights into the wider context of the Sino–Japanese history problem and the legacy of the Fifteen-Year War.

Funding for my research trips to China and Japan came from the British Inter-University China Centre and the Sasakawa Peace Foundation. I would also like to thank the Graduate School of Arts and Humanities at the Uni-versity of Bristol and the Bristol Alumni Foundation for their logistical and financial support.

I am extremely grateful to the staff in the Department of History at Nanj-ing University, the Faculty of International Studies at Hiroshima City University, and the School of Political Science and Economics at Meiji University. I would also like to thank the individuals who were kind enough to be interviewed for this project, as well as the people who have helped me at various time, in these two countries.

Finally, I have been privileged to work with several rigorous editors and members of staff from Routledge, including Peter Sowden, Lucy McClune, Becky McPhee, Paola Celli and Andy Soutter.

Notes

1 The phrase 'benevolent amnesia' originated from James Reilly, 'Remember history, not hatred: collective remembrance of China's War of Resistance to Japan', *Modern Asian Studies*, 45 (2011), 463–490.

2 H. William Sewell, 'Marc Bloch and the logic of comparative history', *History and Theory*, 6 (1969), 211; V. E.Bonnell, 'The use of theory, concepts and comparison in historical sociology', *Comparative Studies in Society and History*, 22 (1980), 156–173.
3 The gap between the current Chinese and Japanese memory is also discussed by several scholars, see, for example, Sun Ge, 'Nicchuu sensou – kanjyou to kiokuno kouzu' [Sino–Japanese war – composition of sentiments and memories], *Sekai*, 673 (2000), 158–170 孫歌, 日中戰爭 – 感情と記憶の構図, 世界, 673 (2000), 158–170.

1 Introduction

A new approach to the Sino–Japanese history problem

On 24 September 1972 a Japanese press group that was visiting China was guided to the Marco Polo Bridge in Beijing. This trip was not included in the official schedule but was arranged at the delegation's request.[1] Most of the journalists, who were reporting the forthcoming negotiations on Sino–Japanese normalisation, experienced a moment of catharsis in this place on the outskirts of Beijing that, in 1937, had witnessed the beginning of an eight-year full-scale war between China and Japan. The next day, Tada Minoru 多田実, a senior journalist from the group and an ex-student soldier who had fought on Iwa Jima island during the Pacific War, wrote a sentimental article in *Yomiuri Shinbun*, just before the Japanese prime minister, Tanaka Kakuei, arrived in Beijing.[2] He retraced the Marco Polo Bridge Incident and pointed out the importance of the legacy of the Fifteen-Year War in the relationship between the two countries, stating that an equal, peaceful and friendly Sino–Japanese relationship could only be achieved if the Japanese could truly repent of their wartime wrongdoings and overcome the wartime past. He thus suggested that, as a representative of the Japanese people, the first thing Premier Tanaka should do when he arrived in China was to sincerely apologise to the Chinese people.

On 29 September 1972, China and Japan signed the Joint Communiqué of the Government of Japan and the Government of the PRC, which normalised diplomatic relations between the two nations. Although not quite in the way that Tada had wished, Tanaka did offer a sort of apology in the communiqué: 'the Japanese side is keenly conscious of the responsibility for the serious damage that Japan caused in the past to the Chinese people through war, and deeply reproaches itself'.[3] Furthermore, the Chinese side renounced its claim to war reparations to show that they accepted the Japanese apology. By sealing the communiqué, Japan and China normalised their relationship. However, they did not achieve a true post-war reconciliation.

Both Japan's apology and China's forgiveness eventually became mere formalities. The legacy of the Fifteen-Year War, which has still not yet been properly overcome, became a hidden problem in the 1972 Sino–Japanese normalisation, as Tada had warned. Since then, disputes surrounding the history of the Fifteen-Year War have frequently, and sometimes destructively, disrupted the relationship between the two nations. In addition to various chronic war-related controversies, like the Nanjing Massacre debate, the issue of remembrance of the war has sparked large-scale protests and disturbances: for instance, the textbook incidents and the anti-Japanese demonstrations by Chinese students in the 1980s. The 1982 Textbook Incident is generally considered to have been the first large-scale diplomatic conflict to arise between Japan and China (also involving several other Asian countries) over the wartime history. It occurred in the summer of 1982 when the governments of the PRC and other East Asian countries strongly upbraided the Japanese government for its alleged attempt to distort the history of the Fifteen-Year War in Japanese school textbooks. Although the incident was settled by the Japanese Ministry of Education's compromise, as reflected in its new textbook authorisation criterion (widely known as the 'Neighbouring Country Clause'), which was adopted in November 1982, similar conflicts continue to arise.[4] In the new millennium, these conflicts have become increasingly two-way: anti-Japanese and anti-Chinese movements have both broken out (for example, the dispute over the Diaoyu/Senkaku Islands in 2010).

Disputes like these are often referred to as manifestations of the Sino–Japanese history problem. More exactly, the Sino–Japanese history problem is the clash between China and Japan over 'the history of Japanese aggression against China during the half-century before', and especially during the Fifteen-Year War, which 'has developed into a vicious cycle of emotional outbursts'.[5]

The 1982 Textbook Incident was a watershed moment, in terms of the nature and scale of the Sino–Japanese history problem. Since then, it is observable that the war history-related problems have developed into a special, yet serious, element of Sino–Japanese relations. Contemporary Sino–Japanese relations exist on a number of levels: the military level, the diplomatic/political level, the economic level and the human/individual level. The history problem overshadows all of these factors, and at the same time it is affected by these factors. The problem, needless to say, is not only seriously damaging Sino–Japanese interaction, it is also tangibly affecting East Asian stability.

Why did the 1972 normalisation not lead to a Sino–Japanese post-war reconciliation? How has the Sino–Japanese history problem arisen? The history problem between China and Japan was first studied academically by a number of political scientists dealing with Sino–Japanese bilateral relations. The approach taken by these academics to probing the origins of the Sino–Japanese history problem has been insightful. However, by only examining a few influential diplomatic conflicts over the wartime history issue, and focusing exclusively on the decision-makers – as if they are the only decisive factors in causing or resolving the problem – these studies have paid little attention to the social and historical soil nurturing the problem.[6]

A relatively new kind of scholarship, which applies the Western concept 'collective memory' or 'collective remembrance' to the East Asian context, and which sees the current Sino–Japanese history problem and memories of the Fifteen-Year War as inseparable, has been developed by a few researchers, mainly working in the fields of political science, history and philosophy. The concept 'collective memory' emerged in early twentieth-century France, as a radical response to cognitive psychology, which posits that memory is a 'solitary act' and is independent from the social context. Collective memory can be defined as the memory of a group of people, typically passed from one generation to the next, which is greater than the sum of individual memories.[7] It took a long time for this concept to be applied to the study of war memory. The pioneer of collective memory studies was sociologist Maurice Halbwachs.[8] One of Halbwachs' assertions is that individual memory only reflects the viewpoint of the collective memory, which is continuously subject to innumerable criticisms. This approach overemphasises the collectiveness of the memory, and fails to recognise sufficiently an individual's ability to remember. Thus, speaking about collective war memory is problematic, as collective war memory is 'not what everybody thinks about war; it is a phrase without purchase when we try to disentangle the behaviour of different groups within the collective.'[9] Although this remains unresolved, several imperfect strategies for coping with the dilemma of how to bridge collective memory and personal memory have been developed.

One of the strategies adopted in this book is to shift the focus from the content of 'collective memory' to the action of 'collective recollection', by integrating the findings of cognitive psychology and sociology.[10] Specifically, the book distinguishes 'collective remembrance' from 'collective memory'. The former refers to public recollection, which means the action by groups and individuals in public of gathering bits and pieces of the past and joining them together. The latter is considered to be the product of collective remembrance. (These two terms are used interchangeably in this book: I use the term 'memory' normally when I discuss other scholars' works which have used this term, or when I talk about 'memory' itself – the product of 'remembrance'). The actions of agents are the linkage between individual memory and socially determined memory. Individuals, associations, state governments, and even inter-state institutes – and anyone who has input into the national memory – are defined as agents, in the sense of *homo agens* (man as an acting being).

The perspective of the new scholarship as regards the formation of the history problem can be summarised as follows: due to an evolutionary process since the end of the Fifteen-Year War, the Chinese and Japanese versions of the war have become divergent and problematic for each other. The divergence between the two nations' current problematic forms of remembrance of the war gives rise to conflict between the Japanese and Chinese over the war history – and, ultimately, gives rise to the frequent manifestations of the 'history problem' that take place. What, then, are the problematic aspects of current Chinese and Japanese Fifteen-Year-War remembrance? How have the different forms of Chinese and Japanese war remembrance evolved into the current problematic versions? Why and how have these two memories clashed?

The numerous atrocities committed by Japan during the war, and the heroic wartime resistance, make up the major part of current Chinese war remembrance. The problems with this perspective are the prevalent feelings of hatred towards the Japanese, as well as the condemnation of the 'Japanese devil', as a result of Chinese suffering during the war, and the exaggeration of Chinese heroism (such as in unrealistic portrayals in Chinese TV dramas of the Chinese resistance as super-hero-type characters and Japanese soldiers as very cruel but also weak invaders – a portrayal that is now often criticised by Chinese audiences themselves). One thing worth mentioning in this context is the relativity of the word 'problematic'. The PRC's remembrance of the Fifteen-Year War is problematic for the Japanese, but it is not necessarily problematic for other countries, such as, say, South Korea.

Meanwhile, the current form of Japanese war remembrance is more complicated because of its 'contested nature'. Namely, in Japan there is no unified or dominant theme of war remembrance, as there is in Germany (overcoming the past), or in China (resistance, hatred and condemnation). In his empirical research within Japan, Seaton identifies five primary groups and their versions of war remembrance: progressives, progressive-leaning groups, the 'don't knows and don't cares' group, conservatives and nationalists/revisionists.[11] The problematic aspects of the nationalists' war remembrance (glorifying the 'Great East Asia War') and the revisionists' war remembrance (denying the atrocities) are easily seen by outsiders as the dominant theme in Japanese war remembrance. The problem manifested by the 'don't know and don't care' group – amnesia – is often criticised as well. However, the real worrying problem with respect to Japanese war remembrance is the victim mentality – a mentality that is demonstrated by most Japanese people. Shimazu implies that by placing the burden of war responsibility on the shoulders of the military and others, the Japanese can be anointed forever as victims of the war. Moreover, this intensely myopic victim mentality has come at the cost of ignoring the real victims of Japanese aggression, especially in Asia.

To uncover how the Chinese and Japanese war remembrance have evolved into the current problematic versions, it is necessary to pin down the origins of the formation of these problematic war memories, by examining the historical evolution of Japanese and Chinese war remembrance.

Several distinctive phases of Japanese war remembrance before 1982 can be identified. During the war, ordinary Japanese people did not learn of the various atrocities committed by the military in China – not only as a result of the state's censorship, but also because the nation as a whole was unwilling to learn about them due to the ultra-nationalist education and propagandistic mobilisation conducted by the Japanese authorities.[12]

After the end of the war on 15 August 1945, there was a short period during which most Japanese started to reflect on their wartime behaviour and to discuss the issue of war responsibility in a very diverse yet progressive way.[13] The democratic reforms and war tribunals established by the General Headquarters (GHQ) (the US-led occupation authority in Japan) – especially the International Military Tribunal for the Far East (IMTFE) – are considered to be the most important contributor to this trend. Nevertheless, the IMTFE's decision not to put the Emperor Hirohito on trial and to use the punishment of a few military leaders to 'clean up' the crimes committed by the Japanese nation 'reinforced a strong popular inclination to ignore what the men of Yamato had done to others in their frantic quest for empire and security'.[14] That is, the formation of the most worrying problem of the Japanese war memory – victim mentality – can also be attributed to the GHQ. Still, some scholars consider that although the IMTFE inculcated the victim mentality in Japan, this mentality was not imposed on the Japanese but was willingly accepted by them, because such a perspective suited Japan, as a country that desperately wanted to break with its past.[15]

After 1947, with the onset of the Cold War, there was an obvious reversal of the GHQ's reformative policy, which returned the conservatives – who favoured a form of war remembrance that asserted great national pride – to power.[16] In April 1952, the foreign occupation was ended and Japan regained its independence. The Japanese conservative government embarked in earnest on its policy of nurturing Japanese patriotism. Education was targeted and in October 1956 the Ministry of Education issued a decree on textbook certification to curtail leftist textbooks. The government also started to use war commemoration days to construct a national community with a shared form of remembrance of the Fifteen-Year War. At the same time, the Japanese victim mentality became further entrenched – especially after Hiroshima and Nagasaki entered the national narrative and became a symbol of national suffering, bolstered by the 1954 *Lucky Dragon* incident (a Japanese fishing boat, the *Lucky Dragon*, was contaminated by nuclear fallout from an American hydrogen bomb test at Bikini Atoll).[17]

Despite this conservative state hegemony in the area of war remembrance, the second half of the 1950s actually witnessed a new era, in which intellectuals tried to overturn the views of the war that were promoted by the GHQ and to reflect on the war according to their own perspectives. Various progressive views of the war were developed by these intellectuals, such as Takeuchi Yoshimi 竹内好, who emphasised Japan's responsibility to the East Asian countries.[18]

In 1960, large-scale destructive demonstrations occurred throughout Japan to oppose the extension of the Japan–US Security Treaty.[19] After the 1960 crisis, Prime Minister Ikeda replaced his predecessors' aims of constitutional revision and rearmament with the aim of economic expansion. In this phase, the state, which immersed itself in material development, stayed relatively small in terms of shaping Japan's remembrance of the Fifteen-Year War. However, a move to stir up nationalism among Japanese by preaching the 'righteousness' of the 'Great East Asian War' was initiated by several revisionist intellectuals, such as Hayashi Fusao 林房雄.[20] Furthermore, the economic prosperity created by the LDP (Liberal Democratic Party) in the so-called Japanese post-war miracle period, brought stability to Japan and diverted people's focus from political activism to the pursuit of economic success. The public's sympathies with the progressives and their views on the war gradually evaporated due to the rapid economic growth of the 1960s.[21]

In the 1970s, their economic achievements made Japanese people feel more secure about their national identity, which encouraged them to look more openly at their wartime past. Several events further encouraged the Japanese to reconsider their own atrocities against East Asian nations: the Vietnam War, the return of Okinawa, the diplomatic normalisation with China and the Emperor's visit to England in 1971 as well as his visit to the US in 1975.[22]

On the other hand, the LDP's hegemony was severely threatened in the 1970s when the economic miracle was hit by the Nixon shock and the oil shock. What is worse, several scandals involving LDP politicians were exposed around the same period, such as the Lockheed scandal in 1976.[23] In the early 1980s, after recovering from a leadership crisis, the LDP re-adopted the nationalism and the aim of constitutional revision that had been emphasised by its pre-1960 predecessors, to cope with various domestic and international problems. Consequently, patriotic education, with the Fifteen-Year-War history as an important component, was again promoted by the LDP.[24]

In short, before 1982, remembrance of the Fifteen-Year War was an important part of Japanese society. The Japanese state and various non-official agents, with different views of the war, as well as different wartime/post-war experiences, often competed with each other in shaping the Japanese remembrance of the war. Also, remembrance of the war was different from place to place. As a result, Japanese remembrance of the war was contested and multi-layered. Still, it has been mentioned again and again by Japanese as well as foreign observers that there was one thing which was shared by almost all groups in post-war Japanese society (even the progressives who reflected on the issue of war responsibilities): a victim mentality.[25]

After the 1982 Textbook Incident, pressure from outside countries completely changed the atmosphere in Japan in terms of the discussion of the war. Upset by the foreign criticisms and the compromise made by the Japanese government, the problems of Japan's war remembrance – such as the victim mentality and the nationalist views – were aggravated even further.[26] Various patriotic education programmes continued to be implemented by conservative politicians, like Nakasone Yasuhiro's *Sengo seiji no* soukeisan (Settle all accounts on post-war political issues 戦後政治の総計算) movement.

Meanwhile, patriotic campaigns were also launched by the Chinese government from the end of the 1970s, especially after the 1982 Textbook Incident. The role of these campaigns by Japan and China in making Japanese and Chinese remembrance of the Fifteen-year War problematic, and ultimately causing the Sino–Japanese history problem, has been often discussed. For instance, in a monograph exploring why Poland and West Germany achieved deep reconciliation while China and Japan failed, one author suggested that this was because the gap in respect of memories of the Second World War between the former pair has been narrowed down through their governments' de-mythification initiatives – a joint textbook project is singled out. By contrast, the gap between the latter pair has been widened by their governments' national mythmaking during the 1980s. Namely, in Japan, the conservative government promoted 'self-glorifying' and 'self-whitewashing' myths through patriotic/nationalistic campaigns; while in China, 'other-maligning myths' about the Fifteen-Year War were also promoted by the CCP regime.[27] Are these patriotic campaigns the origins of the two countries' problematic war memories?

Recent studies have begun to question the effectiveness of Japan's government-sponsored patriotic campaigns from the late 1970s onwards.[28] These studies have revealed that those campaigns failed to instil patriotism or nationalism among the Japanese: instead, they led to cynicism or indifference to the past war. Sometimes, these campaigns, especially the patriotic education received in school, even met fierce opposition from the public.[29]

As a result of examining the history of the evolution of Japanese war remembrance, as outlined above, I contend that the 'contested nature' and the various problems of Japanese war remembrance have been an established aspect of post-war Japanese society for a long time, rather than a consequence of the state-sponsored patriotic campaigns since the late 1970s. What about China? How has Chinese remembrance of the Fifteen-Year War evolved? Were the patriotic campaigns in China the origin of that country's problematic war remembrance?

War remembrance in China

Although there seems to be no single work exclusively concerning the pre-1982 period, an 'imperfect' picture of pre-1982 Chinese war remembrance can be pieced together based on several relevant works.[30]

Immediately after the end of the Fifteen-Year War, Chiang Kai-Shek formed a policy of *yide baoyuan* (returning good for evil 以德报怨) towards the defeated Japanese, in order to gain the friendship of Japan. The Kuomintang (KMT, Chinese Nationalist Party) administration is also alleged to have used Japanese soldiers to fight against the Communists. Furthermore, the Fifteen-Year War gradually faded out of sight as the Chinese Civil War broke out: even the KMT's trials of Japanese war criminals had to be brought to a rapid halt due to the devastating situation of the Civil War. Against this background, the KMT administration has been accused of starting a 'tradition' of 'benevolent amnesia' in respect of the Fifteen-Year War in China.[31]

The main theme of the Maoist era, especially during the Cultural Revolution period, was permanent revolution, and the main task was economic reconstruction and class struggle. Also, the country's external enemies were the United States (USA), the KMT government in Taiwan, and the Union of Soviet Socialist Republics (USSR).[32] Against this historical backdrop, it has been argued that remembrance of the Fifteen-Year War, and especially the recollection of Chinese suffering and Japanese aggression, was discouraged and even suppressed by the revolutionary and isolated Communist government.

Generally, three explanations have been given for this phenomenon. First, it is argued that the CCP regime 'suppressed' recollection of Japanese wartime atrocities since friendship with Japan was important to the CCP. Reilly has argued that 'the Communist Party applied a similarly lenient approach [to the KMT's]' to Japanese wartime atrocities.[33] He Yinan has further identified a period of illusory Sino–Japanese friendship created by the CCP regime after it normalised its relationship with Japan in 1972. During the period, she has implied, young people could not learn about Japanese atrocities in state-controlled textbooks, and ordinary people were not able to learn about Japan's revisionist treatment of the war history through the state-controlled media. As Kosuge has pointed out, the lenient stance of the CCP regime did not reflect public opinion among the Chinese. The regime suppressed the domestic anti-Japanese sentiment, and its generous policy towards Japanese war criminals was imposed from above.[34]

Second, according to Mitter, as the KMT played a leading role in the Fifteen-Year War, even talking about victory in the war was inconvenient in the PRC, since 'any positive or even nuanced mention' of the KMT's role in victory over Japan would be toxic. Similarly, Wang has also suggested that the CCP regime discouraged detailed discussion surrounding the War of Resistance during the Maoist era, as it did not want 'their people to find out there had been no Communists there at all'.[35] Finally, any victimhood narrative with respect to the Fifteen-Year War was 'discouraged' by the CCP regime, because it was considered that such a narrative would have a negative impact on Chinese people's morale.[36]

After Mao's death, the CCP inherited a contradiction between commitment to communism and desire for modernisation. China experienced a short period of political turmoil, as well as sharp economic decline, often accompanied by violence.[37] Deng Xiaoping returned to power in July 1977 and introduced 'reform and opening up' as the party's new line in the Eleventh Central Committee in 1978. Nevertheless, Deng's leadership was not uncontested and his new political line brought the party several problems. One of these was an increasing lack of respect for the government, as well as for the socialist ideology. To cope with this problem, from 1979 onwards the CCP leaders started to call for 'socialist spiritual civilisation', and a series of socialist spiritual campaigns were carried out until 1984. China's uncompromising response to the Textbook Incident in 1982 was affected by the development of these campaigns.[38] In addition, it is inferred that Deng also saw the Textbook Incident as 'a good opportunity to shore up his own and the party's prestige and also prepare for the upcoming Party Congress'.[39] After a month-long deliberation, the CCP regime gave the officially controlled media permission to report Japan's revisionist content in Japanese textbooks, and lodged a formal diplomatic protest against Japan in relation to its wartime past.[40]

After the Textbook Incident, the wartime atrocities committed by Japan re-entered Chinese public discourse on an unprecedentedly large scale. Consequently, the diplomatic as well as grassroots conflicts between China and Japan over the history of the Fifteen-Year War also dramatically intensified.[41] It is argued that behind this was the CCP regime's decision to institute Fifteen-Year War-related patriotism in the PRC, which was necessary for the CCP to legitimise itself as well as to mobilise the people in an increasingly polarised society where communism was losing its attraction, in addition to being useful in regard to moving towards reunion with Taiwan.[42]

Here is a glimpse of this series of patriotic campaigns after the Textbook Incident: in 1984, in one of his speeches regarding the socialist spiritual civilisation campaigns, Deng emphasised the necessity of 'encouraging patriotism and a sense of national dignity and self-confidence', in the mission of 'opposing the tendency to worship capitalism and to advocate bourgeois liberalisation'.[43] In 1985, the government re-instituted a 1950s patriotic education project – 'Five-love Education'.[44] Deng felt it necessary to instil Chinese youth with patriotism after the 1989 Tiananmen Square incident, and patriotic education was intensified thereafter. Under the Jiang Zemin administration, more patriotic education movements were further promoted and systematised by the 'Patriotism Education Policy Framework' issued in 1994. As a legacy of the 'Framework', hundreds of sites, books, films and songs were selected by the Chinese government to foster patriotism among Chinese people – youngsters in particular.[45] On 27 February 2014 the seventh session of the 12th National People's Congress (NPC) passed legislation to ensure the status of September 3 as National Memorial Day of the Victory in the Chinese People's War of Resistance against Japanese Aggression, and December 13 as National Public Memorial Day for the victims of the Nanjing Massacre. The military parade held by the Xi Jinping administration on 3 September 2015 expressed an extreme form of this Fifteen-Year-War related patriotism.[46]

On the other hand, unofficial actors also played an increasingly important role in shaping Chinese war remembrance after 1982. For instance, the Chinese media, which consistently replicates the image of Japan as a wholly cruel nation, has had a huge influence on nationalist intellectuals in China. The latter are convinced by the image shaped by the media and are inclined to ignore leftist Japanese intellectuals' efforts to reflect on the war.[47] In the mid-1990s, an autonomous popular patriotic historical activism emerged, which was 'not fully supportive of the CCP policy and was expressed in various independent mass movements'.[48] It was no longer easy for the state to manipulate public consciousness after the mid-1990s, when it faced the expansion of a more liberated commercial media and the internet, as well as an increase in international engagement. A group of dedicated 'history activists' – such as campaigners for the victims of the Japanese 'comfort women' system – seized upon the patriotic campaigns to demand compensation for wartime victims, to seek official commemoration of wartime anniversaries, to oppose economic cooperation with Japan and to publicise Chinese wartime suffering.[49] Over the years, these history activists have even challenged the 'mild' official narratives and have undermined the Chinese government's pragmatic diplomatic and domestic objectives.

Prominent studies of Chinese remembrance of two individual misdeeds committed by wartime Japan – Japanese biological warfare atrocities and the Nanjing Massacre – also fit into the above picture of the evolution of Chinese Fifteen-Year-War remembrance. The post-war tribunals distinguished between these two misdeeds, in regard to how they treated them. In particular, the most influential one, the IMTFE, treated the Nanjing Massacre differently to how it treated the Japanese biological warfare atrocities.[50] Nevertheless, according to these prominent studies, after the post-war tribunals ended their activities, the ways in which these two misdeeds were remembered in China were similar: remembrance of the misdeeds evolved along the same lines. There was a 'silence' about these atrocities until the 1982 Textbook Incident, when Japan's biological warfare and the Nanjing Massacre were internationalised. After 1982, these events, and their memory, became highly contested Sino–Japanese controversies.

The major contributors to the silence regarding Japanese biological warfare were the Allied countries, which had possessed some knowledge about the atrocities during the war, and, ultimately, the Cold War structure. Thanks to the valuable scientific data that biological warfare generated, it was deliberately excluded from the US-influenced tribunals. The USSR's show trial of the biological warfare-related prisoners of war (POWs) in 1949 was fiercely attacked by the 'capitalist camp'. Meanwhile, in wartime China, the mysterious outbreak of plague in areas like Ningbo, Changde, were well documented, and the strategies for dealing with them were developed by the medical teams in the KMT Army. However, after the end of the war, the Nationalists failed to pursue justice on behalf of the Chinese victims. The Communists' treatment of Japanese biological warfare criminals was also unsatisfactory. About nine such Japanese prisoners (out of around 900) transferred from the USSR in 1950 were prosecuted in the Taiyuan and Shenyang military tribunals in 1956. During the tribunals, the CCP government repeatedly emphasised the humane treatment of the prisoners and 'failed to rigorously investigate Japanese BW [biological warfare]'. Nie suggested the issue had long become a political tool for the PRC, and that the need for Japanese friendship explains the CCP's lenience.[51] After this period, it is generally considered that discussion of Japanese biological warfare disappeared until 1982.[52]

In contrast, the prosecutors in the IMTFE and the KMT's Nanjing Tribunal exposed the Nanjing Massacre as a major war crime committed by the Japanese military in the China theatre.[53] Nevertheless, during the war, the Nanjing Massacre was not as 'famous' as Japan's air attacks and chemical warfare, which were emphasised by the KMT on many occasions, including at League of Nations meetings. This was mostly because the KMT thought the latter issues would generate greater attention in international society and would thus help the KMT to gain assistance and to secure punitive measures against Japan. Consequently, although the Nanjing Massacre was important in terms of local awareness, it was only considered to be one of many Japanese atrocities.

After the CCP came into power in 1949, it is argued that Nanjing was still not a symbol of Japanese atrocities in the PRC, a situation that remained for a long time. The Nanjing Massacre was sometimes manipulated by the government to denounce other enemies. It was also used to attack the KMT regime in Taiwan, for example after the memoirs of some KMT generals were allowed to circulate in mainland China in the 1960s, recollecting that the KMT had not done enough to protect the capital. During the period of Sino–Japanese illusory friendship in the 1970s, it is argued that the Nanjing Massacre, together with other war legacies, was eradicated from the public consciousness. As the CCP regime started to promote patriotism among Chinese people, many previously 'classified' archives concerning the Nanjing Massacre became publicly available and the Nanjing Massacre memorial hall was built in 1985.

Nevertheless, the above picture, which is derived from the existing literature, is flawed. Most of the literature behind this picture gives much greater weight to the era after the 1982 Textbook Incident, when the Sino–Japanese history problem became increasingly contentious, and deals with the period before that merely as a 'preface'. Inevitably, this literature's examination of the pre-1982 period has not been sufficient – and, consequently, its argument as to the pre-1982 'amnesia' is suspect.

The argument concerning the pre-1982 amnesia did not result from a thorough study of available sources. For example, Reilly coined the term 'benevolent amnesia' for attitudes during the period between 1945 and 1982, based only on an examination of a few leaders' speeches, the results of the Shenyang and Taiyuan military tribunals in 1956 and some secondary literature. However, between 1949 and 1982, some CCP leaders' speeches seriously condemned the Japanese atrocities. Furthermore, Japanese biological warfare and the Nanjing Massacre were not really ignored in the pre-1982 PRC – in fact, they were widely presented through platforms like memoirs, academic research, museums and so forth.

Furthermore, this literature touches upon some important themes, such as the CCP's clear differentiation between the small handful of Japanese militarists and the majority of ordinary Japanese people, the roles of the war legacy in Sino–Japanese diplomatic interactions, and the anti-Japanese sentiment among ordinary Chinese people. Unfortunately, this literature failed to explore these themes any further.

What is more, most of the discussions in this literature on the evolution of Chinese remembrance of the Fifteen-Year War are too government-centric, suggesting that the legacy of the war was either rejected or promoted by the Chinese ruling regime for pragmatic purposes.[54] Similarly, scholars working on the legacies of Japanese biological warfare atrocities and the Nanjing Massacre also pay most of their attention to the top-down aspects and suggest that remembrance of these two war legacies has been manipulated by the ruling regimes throughout China's post-war history, either for diplomatic gain or domestic mobilisation.

This government-centred view is especially conspicuous in these scholars' discussions of the Maoist period. They imply that during this period the official control of Chinese people's minds was absolute. Although ordinary Chinese people have occasionally been the main characters in these discussions, they are portrayed as pawns that are mentally manipulated by the CCP regime. The fact that different memories of the past can be constructed by different social groups is acknowledged to a certain extent. However, in the PRC's context, it is believed that the CCP government institutionalised its official memory as the national war memory, and built up dominant state control over war memory, with its 'totalitarian control of state power and thorough penetration of social life'.[55] One study on the role of veterans' activities in influencing war memory in mainland China also alludes to the CCP's monopoly of the war remembrance issue. According to this study, veterans' voices were regarded as weak in China, and the field of national war memory was dominated by the intellectual elites in various cultural and propaganda offices.[56] Was the CCP regime really so powerful that it could persuade all Chinese people to accept its official national war remembrance – and, furthermore, persuade all localities to adapt to it? Was the CCP regime really too authoritarian to tolerate any non-official input in Chinese remembrance of the Fifteen-Year War, whether these inputs were in line with the official stance or not?

In conclusion, a lack of sufficient examination and a strong government-centred view renders the discussions contained in the prominent relevant literature on the pre-1982 period unconvincing. I contend that there is a huge gap in our understanding of Fifteen-Year-War remembrance in mainland China before 1982. Without filling this gap, it is difficult to judge whether the patriotic campaigns promoted since the end of the 1970s are the origin of China's problematic war memories. Most importantly, if this gap is not filled, understanding the evolution of Chinese war remembrance and the formation of the Sino–Japanese history problem, and, ultimately, resolving the problem is extremely difficult. Thus, the primary aim of this book is to fill this gap.

Approaches

Two practical lessons can be taken from Western collective memory studies. First, the present book takes into consideration a range of agents in relation to Chinese memories of the Fifteen-Year War. 'Agents' are positioned in the centre of the concept of 'collective remembrance'. Two tiers of agents have been identified: the first tier consists of the (individual) witnesses, who are 'involved in memory work, that is, public rehearsal of memories, and quite often *not* in order to create social scripts or schemata for the interpretation of the war'.[57] The second tier consists of social agents, including the state apparatus, whose activities have other objectives, like profit, artistic expression and so forth. The efforts of the two tiers sometimes overlap, and social agents can sometimes be witnesses as well. The distinction between these two tiers of agents lies in whether or not they deliberately recollect the past publicly.

The agents' acts do not always follow instructions from above – much commemoration goes on spontaneously within civil society, particularly after significant events. Furthermore, agents construct collective remembrance within a given geographic scope through a 'multi-faceted negotiation': this is sometimes described as a battlefield where incompatible groups advocate confronting memories.[58] In addition to the account of post-war Japanese war remembrance in Chapter 2, this argument is also supported by the empirical studies on the evolution of European war remembrance.

Studies of the evolution of European World War Two remembrance deal with all kinds of agents. The manipulation and reinterpretation of elites as social agents is often overemphasised in these studies but they do not see the state as a united apparatus, which exclusively controls the war remembrance in its society – efforts are made in these studies to consider the importance of unofficial social agents.[59] According to these studies, various forms of war remembrance sustained by different agents have always co-existed with official war memories, and various individuals have challenged mythologised war memories, even during the Cold War when the arena of war remembrance was highly influenced by the ideologised official version.

In Western Europe, the contestation of war memory was visible. Even in the East, where the civil society was weak and authoritarian regimes could and did try to manipulate their people's understanding of the war, the input of private discourse in the national collective war remembrance was still powerful. Not only were there private remembrances that were not drawn into national remembrance, but also there were individual narratives that shaped the public cult and national mythical memories of the war to a large extent, as a case study about the siege of Leningrad and the war memory of the USSR has indicated.[60] Those efforts gradually led, when the Cold War structure started to loosen, to changes in the national memory and to reinvestigations of the dark side of the war history. Therefore, in addition to the totalitarian CCP regime, other agents' inputs into the national war remembrance in China, and the interaction among all these agents, will be thoroughly examined throughout this book, especially in Chapter 5.

The larger a group is, the harder it is to find a memory that is common to all. Research on local European World War Two remembrance thus provides an important methodological inspiration for this book in regard to exploring national war remembrance by studying war remembrance in a smaller area – an area which reflects the nationwide war remembrance culture and at the same time differs from it. We can assume that a shared World War Two memory exists in local communites, due to the various features of a particular locality, such as the intimacy of residents' relations with each other and with the local organs of power, and the confluence of languages, narratives and idioms which circulate locally.[61] The contributors to the collection *Beyond Berlin* pointed out another rationale for analysing the memory culture in various towns outside the German capital: that is, it is possible to achieve a 'more nuanced understanding of the dynamic interaction between local and national trends within [Germany's] broader culture of memory', and 'a deeper understanding of how post-war [German] society has dealt with the [Nazi] legacy'.[62]

It is also an operable method to capture the intangible Chinese national war remembrance by using one Chinese local area as a case study of war remembrance activities in the whole of China. Therefore, the war remembrance activities conducted by both government and non-government actors in a local area of China – Nanjing city and the area surrounding it – will be used as a case study in this book. Nanjing offers a typical and mostly ordinary case; nevertheless, in order to provide a relatively comprehensive picture of Fifteen-Year-War remembrance in pre-1982 China, other local areas with various types of wartime past will also be occasionally brought into the discussion.

Nanjing, a city in eastern China, has been the capital of the country on several occasions. In 1927 it was taken by the KMT under Chiang Kai-Shek and chosen as the capital of the Republic of China. Through its military campaigns and various reforms, the Nanjing-based KMT regime did bring a certain stability and prosperity to China, and the period of its rule in China between 1927 and 1937 is often referred to as the Nanjing decade.[63]

On 7 July 1937, full-scale war between China and Japan broke out. After several defeats in the battles against Japan, the KMT government left Nanjing in early December and gradually relocated itself to the southwestern city of Chongqing to continue the Chinese resistance. On 13 December 1937 a poorly-defended Nanjing was captured by Japanese troops. During the subsequent six weeks, the Japanese soldiers committed a number of shocking crimes in the city, including mass killing, looting and rape – collectively known as the Nanjing Massacre. According to the verdict of the IMTFE, between 200,000 and 300,000 Chinese were killed during the Nanjing Massacre.[64]

After Nanjing fell in 1937, collaboration with the Japanese was not unusual among officials and residents in the city. In 1940, the 'Nanjing Nationalist Government' – a puppet government of Japan – was established by Wang Jingwei in Nanjing. On the other hand, the CCP also established several anti-Japanese bases on the outskirts of Nanjing.[65]

After the end of the war, the KMT returned to Nanjing in 1946 and a grand ceremony was held for this occasion. Nevertheless, the KMT regime soon suffered defeat at the hands of the CCP during the Chinese Civil War, and it had to give up Nanjing again on 21 April 1949, when the city was conquered by the CCP's People's Liberation Army. During the era of the PRC Nanjing has been the capital city of Jiangsu Province.[66]

This book's first-hand research primarily concerns the period between 1949 and 1982. However, the wartime period and the immediate post-war period (1945–1949) are also touched upon where necessary. The overarching research enquiries are: how was the Fifteen-Year War remembered in China and how did this remembrance evolve before the 1982 Textbook Incident? What was the relationship between national and local Fifteen-Year-War remembrance activities before 1982? How did the official and non-official agents interact with each other to shape Chinese remembrance of the Fifteen-Year War before 1982?

This book explores the general situation as to how the Fifteen-Year War was remembered in China by studying how the war was presented in a series of 'realms of memory': memoirs, martyrs' memorials, the national anthem, war memorial days, textbooks, museums, songs, films, scholarly works and so forth. According to the French historian Pierre Nora, 'realms of memory' arise as a way to preserve the memory when there is no longer any environment in which the memory is a real part of everyday experience. The memory preserved by various realms is already a kind of history (which is objective and emotionless); however, it has the feature of the memory – the emotional attachment – which distinguishes it from factual history.[67]

Each chapter in the book explores the pre-1982 Chinese remembrance of the Fifteen-Year War through the examination of certain fields/realms, and also responds to one or two of the 'myths' regarding a 'generous amnesia' (the reasons given by the existing research into Chinese war remembrance as to why the Fifteen-Year War was 'forgotten' in the pre-1982 PRC).

Chapter 2 examines pre-1982 Sino–Japanese relations. It responds to the 'myth' that due to the CCP regime's pursuit of Sino–Japanese friendship, remembrance of the wartime Japanese atrocities was discouraged in pre-1982 China. In addition, the chapter explores how remembrance of the Fifteen-Year War was positioned within the diplomatic practice of the CCP regime in relation to Japan during the period. Two questions are asked: what was the correlation between the Fifteen-Year War-remembrance and Sino–Japanese relations? What was the CCP's stance as to how to remember the Fifteen-Year War in the context of its diplomatic conduct towards Japan before 1982?

Chapter 2 first introduces two events that occurred in Nanjing in the autumn of 1965: the Sino–Japanese Youth Friendship Get-together and the commemoration of the 20th anniversary of the victory in the War of Resistance – as well as some bizarre situations relating to these two events. The main body of this chapter first looks at the CCP's activities of bashing/ condemning Japanese militarists that took place when Sino–Japanese inter-governmental relations were hostile. It then moves to discuss the remembrance of the war by CCP leaders, the Chinese people and Japanese visitors during friendly encounters between China and Japan.

This chapter argues that the war had never in fact been ignored, regardless of developments in Sino–Japanese relations, thanks to the idea promoted by the CCP regime that 'we should distinguish a handful of evil Japanese militarists from the majority of kind Japanese people'. This notion could also indicate the CCP's stance that one requisite condition for Sino–Japanese friendship was remembering the war past rather than forgetting about it.

With the exception of Chapter 2, all the following chapters deal with Fifteen-Year-War remembrance in the Chinese domestic sphere. Chapter 3 examines the activities that honoured the Fifteen-Year-War martyrs. It responds to the 'myth' that because the KMT had played an important role in the Fifteen-Year War, talking about the war was not convenient. This chapter argues that there were two interlocking necessities for both the KMT and CCP regime before 1982: the necessity of honouring the Fifteen-Year War martyrs, and therefore the necessity of remembering the Fifteen-Year War. Chapter 3 explores these necessities. The chapter begins with a story about a KMT pilot killed in 1938 and his family, as well as how this anti-Japanese martyr was glorified by the KMT and CCP regime before and after 1949. The main body of the chapter discusses, in turn, the prehistory of the PRC's activities of honouring the Fifteen-Year-War martyrs, and the activities during the first seventeen-year period of the PRC (1949–1966). The activities during the Cultural Revolution period and thereafter will be briefly introduced in the Conclusion.

Chapter 3 concludes that both the KMT and CCP regime glorified the Fifteen-Year War martyrs in earnest, which in turn promoted Fifteen-Year-War remembrance in mainland China before 1982. The chapter also suggests that the fact that the KMT played a vital role in the Fifteen-Year War did not prevent the PRC government from honouring the Fifteen-Year War martyrs. Many KMT members killed in action during the war were recognised as 'martyrs', and their families were taken care of by the PRC government (apart from during the Cultural Revolution period). Moreover, once they had been recognised by the PRC, there was no big difference between the state's treatment of the KMT's martyrs and their CCP counterparts.

Chapter 4 examines the realms of Fifteen-Year-War remembrance constructed by the agency of the state: the national anthem, school history textbooks and history museums. It investigates the central–local dimension of Chinese war remembrance and it responds to the 'myth' that because the memory of victimhood during the Fifteen-Year War was too negative for the national morale of the PRC it was discouraged.

By exploring the history of the 'March of Volunteers' (a famous national salvation song produced during the Fifteen-Year War, and the current Chinese national anthem), this chapter shows that the CCP regime made the Fifteen-Year-War remembrance a focus of attention. I argue that because Fifteen-Year-War remembrance has been useful, it has been placed in such an important position by the CCP. Moreover, the CCP-centric and tragic but heroic part of the Fifteen-Year-War memory was specifically useful for the CCP's leaders. The first part of Chapter 4 further demonstrates this argument. By various means, the CCP regime promoted its version of the war as the 'national' memory of the Fifteen-Year War. Was this national memory embraced throughout China? The second part of this book examines the complicated picture of local war remembrance through the case study of Nanjing.

Chapter 4 concludes that Fifteen-Year-War remembrance was a very useful political tool for the CCP regime and thus was used by the regime for various diplomatic as well as domestic purposes. Moreover, by using the war remembrance, the regime actually helped consolidate the memory of the war among Chinese people. Furthermore, to foster a new socialist identity and to justify its claim to legitimacy, the CCP regime even promoted a stable version of the Fifteen-Year-War memory nationwide, which was characterised by its CCP-centric narrative and tragic but heroic tone. This national war memory was embraced by local people. Nevertheless, as long as it adopted the essence of the national war memory, in local areas it was the war memory that was identified by the locals that thrived most. Finally, this chapter also shows that both the central as well as local governments did use the miserable aspects of the war history to serve their various aims.

Chapter 5 goes beyond the state and examines the realms of war memory constructed by unofficial agents – Fifteen-Year-War themed arts, research and grassroots memories – and emphasises unofficial agents' interactions in constructing war remembrance in the PRC. This chapter explores the influences on the unofficial agents' efforts to mediate the Fifteen-Year-War remembrance in the PRC.

Three different efforts, made by a scholar, a group of farmers, workers and a writer, to bring something new to the mainland Chinese memory of the Fifteen-Year War will be introduced at the beginning of this chapter. The chapter first researches the influence of the CCP regime, mainly from three perspectives: the regime's attitudes, its direct initiatives and its indirect impact. It then goes on to explore other influential factors apart from the state.

Chapter 5 argues that, when recollecting the Fifteen-Year War, unofficial agents were constrained by the CCP regime; nevertheless, they were also influenced by their own motivations, each other, their professional traditions, the availability of funds, audiences' preferences and so forth. In short, these people were not merely pawns who were mentally manipulated by the CCP regime during the Maoist period. In addition, this chapter also responds to two myths related to domestic affairs in the PRC, from the standpoint of unofficial agents. It shows that remembrance of the Fifteen-Year War related to the KMT was not absolutely poisonous and that a victimhood narrative substantially existed in the realms of memory constructed by unofficial agents in pre-1982 China.

Chapter 6 concludes that the Fifteen-Year War was very much remembered in China before 1982, although not on a scale as large as nowadays. The central as well as local authorities and various unofficial agents of the war memory interacted with each other to shape a relatively unified remembrance of the Fifteen-Year War in China. The core part of the national memory promoted by the central CCP regime, as reflected in school history textbooks and national history museums, was the series of heroic and tragic wartime events, which justified the CCP's wartime leadership. On top of that were various memories that thrived in local areas and that were remembered privately by individuals. The PRC's war remembrance after 1982, then, is seen as a relatively natural continuation of that before 1982. Similarly to Japan, the origin of the current problematic Chinese memory of the war (exaggerating the heroic resistance and the prevalence of the victimhood narrative) comes from the pre-1982 period.

Finally, this chapter reflects on the 1972 episode and discusses why and how Chinese and Japanese memories have clashed. As I have contended in Chapter 1, the underlying characteristic of the Sino–Japanese history problem is a clash between problematic Chinese and Japanese remembrances of the Fifteen-Year War. Therefore, it will help to resolve the history problem if both the Chinese and Japanese can perceive the other side's problematic war remembrance calmly, and if they are able to understand objectively that this war remembrance was shaped in a particular international and domestic setting. This book's contribution to resolving the history problem, thus, lies in its examination and presentation of the historical settings which nurtured Chinese and Japanese war remembrance.

Notes

1 Anonymous, 'Rokoukyou kengaku imawa heiwa sonomono' [Trip to Marco Polo Bridge, 盧溝橋見學 今は平和そのもの], *Yomiuri Shinbun*, 25 Septenber 1972; Tada Minoru, 'Sensou Shazai, Socchoku' [Sincerely apologize for the war, 戦争謝罪、率直], *Yomiuri Shinbun*, 25 September 1972.
2 Tada Minoru, 'Senso Shazai, Socchoku'.
3 See, Ministry of Foreign Affairs of Japan. 'Joint Communique of the Government of Japan and the Government of the People's Republic of China'. www.mofa.go.jp/region/asia-paci/china/joint72.html, 29 September 1972, date accessed, 5 March 2014.
4 See, B. Kenneth Pyle, 'Japan besieged: the textbook controversy: introduction', *Journal of Japanese Studies*, 9 (1983), 297–300; Caroline Rose, *Interpreting history in Sino–Japanese relations: a case study in political decision-making* (London: Routledge, 1998); Tim Beal, Yoshiko Nozaki and Jian Yang, 'Chosts of the past: the Japanese history textbook controversy', *New Zealand Journal of Asian Studies*, 3 (2001), 177–188.
5 D. Yang, 'Mirror for the future or the history card? Understanding the "History Problem"', in Marie Söderberg (ed.), *Chinese–Japanese relations in the twenty-first century: complementarity and conflict* (London: Routledge, 2002), 11.
6 For scholarly works adopting the 'diplomatic approach', see for example, C. Johnson, 'The patterns of Japanese relations with China, 1952–1982', *Pacific Affairs*, 59 (1986), 402–428; H. Ijiri, 'Sino–Japanese controversy since the 1972 diplomatic normalisation', *The China Quarterly*, 124 (1990), 639–661; Rose, *Interpreting history*; Yang, 'Mirror for the future or the history card', 10–31.
7 The definition and the development of the concept of 'collective memory' is based on Whitehead's work, see, A. Whitehead, *Memory* (London: Routledge, 2009).
8 Some scholarly works especially contributed to connecting the war with collective memory, see, for example, J. E. Young, *The texture of memory: Holocaust memorials and meaning* (New Haven, CT and London: Yale University Press, 1993); J. M. Winter, *Sites of memory, sites of mourning: the Great War in European cultural history* (Cambridge: Cambridge University Press, 1995); J. Winter and E. Sivan, *War and remembrance in the twentieth century* (Cambridge: Cambridge University Press, 1999).

9 Winter and Sivan, *War and remembrance in the twentieth century*, p. 9.
10 Discussion about this strategy is based on Winter and Sivan, *War and remembrance*, pp. 6–40.
11 P. A. Seaton, *Japan's contested war memories: the 'memory rifts' in historical consciousness of World War II* (London: Routledge, 2007).
12 Yoshida Takashi, *The making of the 'Rape of Nanking': history and memory in Japan, China and the United States* (Oxford: Oxford University Press, 2006), p. 24.
13 Ishida, Takeshi, *Kioku to boukyakuno seijigaku – douka seisaku, sensou sekinin, shuugouteki kioku* [Politics of remembering and forgetting: assimilation policy, war responsibility and collective memory] (Tokyo: Akashi shoten, 2000) 石田雄, 記憶と忘却の政治学 – 同化政策 戦争責任 集合的記憶 (明石書店, 2000).
14 John W. Dower, *Embracing defeat: Japan in the aftermath of World War II* (London: Penguin, 2000), p. 27. Shin also pointed out the US's role in the formation of problematic Japanese war remembrance, through the IMTFE, the San Francisco Peace Treaty and Americans' crimes, see, G. W. Shin, 'Historical disputes and reconciliation in Northeast Asia: the US role', *Pacific Affairs*, 83 (2010), 663–673.
15 F. Seraphim, *War memory and social politics in Japan, 1945–2005* (Cambridge, MA and London: Harvard University Press, 2006); Carol Gluck, 'The past in the present', in A. Gordon (ed.), *Postwar Japan as history* (Berkeley: University of California Press, 1993).
16 B. Cumings, 'Japan's position in the world system', in Gordon, *Postwar Japan as history*, 34–64.
17 See, Yoshida, *The making of the 'Rape of Nanking'*; Ishida, *Kioku to boukyaku*.
18 Ishida, *Kioku to boukyaku*.
19 Mikiso Hane, *Eastern phoenix: Japan since 1945* (Oxford: Westview Press, 1996).
20 Nakamura Tetsu (ed.), *Higashi Ajia no rekishi kyoukasyou wa dou kakareteiruka* [How the history textbooks have been written in East Asia] (Tokyo: Nihon Hyouronsya, 2004) 中村哲, 東アジアの歴史教科書はどう書かれているか (日本評論社, 2004), pp. 5–6; For Hayashi's representative work, see, 'Daitoua sensou kouteiron' [Argument of affirming the Great East Asian War 大東亜戦争肯定論], which was published serially in *Chuuo kouron* [中央公論] between 1963 and 1965. This work argues the war was not an invasion war, but a war for liberating Asia.
21 Ishida, *Kioku to boukyaku*.
22 Ishida, *Kioku to boukyaku*.
23 R. Vietor, 'Japan: deficits, demography, and deflation', *Harvard Business School Case*, 2005.
24 Hana, *Eastern phoenix*; K. Ide, 'The debate on patriotic education in post-World War II Japan', *Educational Philosophy and Theory*, 41 (2009), 441–452.
25 See, for example, Kiichi Fujiwara, *Sensou wo kiokusuru: Hiroshima, Horokousuto to genzai* [Remember the war, Hiroshima, Holocaust and the present] (Tokyo: Koudansha gendai shinsho, 2001) 藤原帰一, 戦争を記憶する 広島 ホロコースト と現在 (講談社現代新書, 2001); Ienaga Saburo, *Senso sekinin* [War responsibility] (Tokyo: Iwanami Shoten, 2005) 家永三郎, 戦争責任 (岩波書店, 2005).
26 Nakamura Masanori, *Sengoshi* [Postwar history] (Tokyo: Iwanami Shoten, 2005) 中村政則, 戦後史 (岩波書店 2005).
27 He Yinan, 'Remembering and forgetting the war: elite mythmaking, mass reaction, and Sino-Japanese relations, 1950–2006', *History and Memory*, 19 (2007), p. 45; He Yinan, *The search for reconciliation: Sino–Japanese and German–Polish relations since World War II* (Cambridge: Cambridge University Press, 2009), p. 206.
28 Ide, 'The debate on patriotic education'; H. Tanaka, 'Kyouiku houki kaisei nimiru "aikokushin kyouiku"' [Review 'patriotic education' from the perspective of changing education law], *Ryuukyuu daigaku kyouiku gakubu kiyou*, 76 (2010), 67–76 田中洋, 教育法規改正にみる「愛国心教育」, 琉球大学教育学部紀要, 76 (2010),

20   *Introduction*

67–76; Che-po Chan and Brian Bridges, 'China, Japan and the clash of nationalisms', *Asian Perspective*, 30 (2006), 127–158, at 133.

29 See, C. Rose, 'Patriotism is not taboo: nationalism in China and Japan and implications for Sino-Japanese relations', *Japan Forum,* 12 (2001), 169–181.

30 There is no equivalent idea to 'post-war' Japan in the historical study of contemporary China, as China has fought several other wars since 1945. Furthermore, the pondering of China's intellectuals over the war has not been as deep as their Japanese counterparts. Consequently, unlike in Japan, a domestic tradition of discussing how the Chinese remember the war is lacking in China. Although Chinese language literature looking at the Fifteen-Year War memory has started appearing recently, most of it focuses on individual testimonies of the war rather than the evolutionary history of the Chinese war memory as a whole.

The discussion of the latter topic is actually dominated by a few scholars from overseas, who are mainly interested in Sino–Japanese relations and individual war-related controversies (e.g. the Nanjing Massacre, the Comfort Women system, and Japanese biological warfare). For works from the perspective of Sino–Japanese relations, see, for example, He Yinan,'Remembering and forgetting the war', He Yinan,'Ripe for cooperation or rivalry? Commerce, realpolitik, and war memory in contemporary Sino–Japanese Relations', *Asian Security*, 4 (2008), 162–197; He Yinan, *The search for reconciliation*; James Reilly, 'China's history activists and the War of Resistance Against Japan: history in the making', *Asian Survey*, 19 (2004), 276–294; James Reilly, 'Remember history, not hatred: collective remembrance of China's War of Resistance to Japan', *Modern Asian Studies*, 45 (2011), 463–490. Also, see other articles in the special issue of *Modern Asian Studies* entitled 'China in World War II, 1937–1945: experience, memory, and legacy'.

31 This section is based on He Yinan and Reilly's works. Japanese POWs continued to be used in post-1949 Taiwan, see, Barak Kushner, 'Pawns of empire: postwar Taiwan, Japan and the dilemma of war crimes', *Japanese Studies*, 30 (2010), 111–133.

32 This general history of the Maoist period is based on Maurice Meisner, *Mao's China and after: a history of the People's Republic* (New York: Free Press, 1999).

33 Reilly, 'Remember history, not hatred', p. 469.

34 Nobuko Kosuge, *Sengo wakai* (Tokyo: Chuukou Shinsho, 2005) 小菅信子,戦後和解 (中公新書, 2005), p. 178.

35 Rana Mitter, 'Old ghosts, new memories: China's changing war history in the era of post-Mao politics', *Journal of Contemporary History*, 38 (2003), 117–131; Rana Mitter and Aaron W. Moore, 'China in World War II, 1937–1945: experience, memory, and legacy', *Modern Asian Studies*, 45 (2011), 225–240; Wang Zheng, *Never forget national humiliation: historical memory in Chinese politics and foreign relations* (New York: Columbia University Press, 2012), p. 88.

36 See He Yinan and Yoshida's works.

37 Kwan Ha Yim, *China since Mao* (London: Macmillan, 1980). Yim suggests, in addition to purges, violence in factional conflicts was also widespread, mainly between Chairman Hua Guofeng and the Gang of Four.

38 More information on the difficulties and instabilities caused by the reforms, faction struggles as well as the international environment, see, Michael Y. M. Kau and Susan H. Marsh, *China in the era of Deng Xiaoping: a decade of reform* (New York: M. E. Sharpe, 1993); Rose, *Interpreting history*, p. 70.

39 He, 'Remembering and forgetting', p. 54.

40 Rose, *Interpreting history*.

41 From the political scientists' angle, apart from the Fifteen-Year-War related patriotic campaigns, there were other elements which have caused the Sino–Japanese conflicts over history issues: the CCP regime's increasing disputes with Japan over the economic frictions, the Taiwan issue (e.g. the student dormitory incident in 1987), the deepened Japan–US security arrangement, the revisionist

behaviour of conservative Japanese politicians, et cetera; see, Rose, *Interpreting history.*

42 See He Yinan, Reilly and Mitter's works.

43 Deng's speech (1984) is included in Rose, *Interpreting history.*

44 He, 'Remembering and forgetting'.

45 Suisheng Zhao, 'A state-led nationalism: the patriotic education campaign in post-Tiananmen China', *Communist and Post-Communist Studies*, 31 (1998), 287–302; W. A. Callahan, *China: the pessoptimist nation* (Oxford: Oxford University Press, 2010); Z. Wang, 'National humiliation, history education, and the politics of history memory: patriotic education campaign in China', *International Studies Quarterly*, 52 (2008), 783–806.

46 Anonymous, 'Woguo sheli Zhongguo renmin kang Rizhanzheng shengli jinianri he Nanjing datusha sinanzhe guojia gongjiri' [China set up the National Memorial Day of the Victory in the Chinese Peoples's War of Resistance against Japanese Aggression and the National Public Memorial Day for the victims of the Nanjing Massacre, 我国设立中国人民抗日战争胜利纪念日和南京大屠杀死难者国家公祭日 2014年02月27日]. www.gov.cn/jrzg/2014-02/27/content_2624727.htm, 27 Feb 2014, date accessed, 22 Aug 2016.

47 Sun, Ge, 孙歌, 'Zhong Ri chuanmei zhongde zhanzheng jiyi' [The war memory in Chinese and Japanese media, 中日传媒中的战争记忆]. www.frchina.net/data/personArticle.php?id=126, November 2003, date accessed, 8 March 2014.

48 Chan and Bridges, 'China, Japan and the clash of nationalisms', p. 133; Reilly, 'China's history activists'.

49 For more on the Comfort Women issue, see: G. Hicks, *The Comfort Women: Japan's brutal regime of enforced prostitution in the Second World War* (New York: W. W. Norton, 2011); Y. Yoshimi, *Comfort Women: sexual slavery in the Japanese military during World War II* (New York: Columbia University Press, 2000); M. Levin, 'Case comment: Nishimatsu Construction Co. v. Song Jixiao et al., Supreme Court of Japan (2nd Petty Bench), April 27, 2007, and Ko Hanako et al. v. Japan, Supreme Court of Japan (1st Petty Bench), April 27, 2007', *American Journal of International Law*, 102 (2008), 1–6; H. Mitsui, 'The politics of national atonement and narrations of war', *Inter-Asia Cultural Studies*, 9 (2008), 47–61; Su Zhiliang, *Weianfu yanjiu* [Research on Comfort Women] (Shanghai: Shanghai Shudian Chubanshe, 2000) 苏智良, 慰安妇研究 (上海书店出版社, 2000).

50 For studies on the Tokyo Tribunal, see, A. Casses and B. V. A. Roling, *The Tokyo Trial and beyond: reflections of a peacemonger* (Cambridge: Polity Press, 1993); Arnold C. Brackman, *The other Nuremberg: the untold story of the Tokyo war crimes trials* (London: Collins, 1989).

51 See, Jing Bao Nie, Nanyan Guo, Mark Selden and Arthur Kleinman (eds), *Japan's wartime medical atrocities: comparative inquiries in science, history, and ethics* (London: Routledge, 2010), pp. 42 and 129.

52 S. Harris, *Japanese biological warfare experiments and other atrocities in Manchuria, 1932–1945, and the subsequent United States cover-up: a preliminary assessment* (Dordrecht: Kluwer Academic, 1991); Tsuneishi, Keiichi, 'Unit 731 and the Japanese Imperial Army's biological warfare program', www.japanfocus.org/-Tsuneishi-Keiichi/2194, date unknown, date accessed, 16 March 2014; Materials, *Materials on the trial of former servicemen of the Japanese Army charged with manufacturing and employing bacteriological weapons* (Moscow: Foreign Languages Publishing House, 1950); Nie et al., *Japan's wartime medical atrocities;* Jinteng Zhaoer and Luo Jianzhong, 'Mei Su Ri sanguo dui "731 budui" de yanjiu zhuangkuang' [The research of the US, USSR and Japan on 'Unit 731'], *Wuling xuebao*, 35 (2010), 53–55 近藤昭二, 罗建忠, 美苏日三国对 '731部队' 的研究状况, 武陵学报 35 (2010), 53–55.

53 Research on the evolution of Nanjing Massacre is scarce; this section is based on articles in Mark Eykholt, Yoshida and Fogels' articles in Joshua A. Fogel (ed.), *The Nanking Massacre in history and historiography* (London: University of California Press, 2000) and Bob T. Wakabayashi (ed.), *The Nanking Atrocity 1937–1938: complicating the picture* (Oxford and New York: Berghahn Books, 2007).

54 Reilly suggested that both the KMT and CCP benevolently forgave Japan and forgot the Japanese aggression, by analysing Chiang Kai-shek's and Zhou Enlai's public speeches. Reilly, 'Remember history, not hatred'.

55 He Yinan, 'Remembering and forgetting the war', p. 48.

56 N. J. Diamant, 'Conspicuous silence: veterans and the depoliticisation of war memory in China', *Modern Asian Studies*, 45 (2001), 431–461. For another work about veterans, see, A. W. Moore, 'The problem of changing language communities: veterans and memory writing in China, Taiwan, and Japan', *Modern Asian Studies*, 45 (2001), 399–429.

57 Winter and Sivan, *War and remembrance*, 6–40.

58 Winter and Sivan, *War and remembrance*, 6–40; M. Evans and K. Lunn (eds) *War and memory in the twentieth century* (Oxford: Berg, 1997), p. xvii.

59 Winter and Sivan, *War and remembrance*; R. N. Lebow and W. Kansteiner, *The politics of memory in postwar Europe* (Durham, NC: Duke University Press, 2006); Jan-Werner Müller, *Memory and power in post-war Europe: studies in the presence of the past* (Cambridge: Cambridge University Press, 2002).

60 F. Biess and R. G. Moeller, *Histories of the aftermath: the legacies of the Second World War in Europe* (New York: Berghahn Books, 2010).

61 N. Gregor, *Haunted city: Nuremberg and the Nazi past* (New Haven, CT: Yale University Press, 2008), pp. 20–21.

62 G. D. Rosenfeld and P. B. Jaskot, *Beyond Berlin: twelve German cities confront the Nazi past* (Ann Arbor: University of Michigan Press, 2008), p. 2.

63 For more information on the Nanjing decade, see, Charles Musgrove, *China's contested capital: architecture, ritual, and response in Nanjing* (Hong Kong: Hong Kong University Press, 2013); Zwia Lipkin, *Useless to the state: 'social problems' and social engineering in nationalist Nanjing, 1927–1937* (Cambridge, MA: Harvard University Press, 2006).

64 M. Yamamoto, *Nanking: anatomy of an atrocity* (Westport, CT: Praeger, 2000); Wakabayashi, *The Nanking Atrocity 1937–1938*; T. Brook, *Documents of the Rape of Nanking* (Ann Arbor: University of Michigan Press, 1999); Fogel, *The Nanking Massacre in history and historiography*.

65 See, Timothy Brook, *Collaboration: Japanese agents and local elites in wartime China* (Cambridge, MA: Harvard University Press, 2005); John Hunter Boyle, *China and Japan at war, 1937–1945: the politics of collaboration* (Stanford, CA: Stanford University Press, 1972); Gerald E. Bunker, *The peace conspiracy: Wang Ching-wei and the China war, 1937–1941* (Cambridge, MA: Harvard University Press, 1972).

66 For the postwar history of Nanjing, see this book's Chapter 3.

67 See, Whitehead, *Memory*; Pierre Nora, *Realms of memory*, abridged translation (New York: Columbia University Press, 1998).

2 Remembrance of the war and Sino–Japanese relations

Nanjing in 1965

In 1965 Nanjing was allocated the mission of receiving a Japanese delegation, consisting of Japanese youths from many different interest groups. They had come to China for a quasi-diplomatic event, the Sino–Japanese Youth Friendship Get-together, and their tour passed through Beijing and fifteen other big cities starting on 21 August 1965. The get-together was sponsored by the China–Japan Friendship Association, the All-China Youth Federation, the All-China Student Federation, and many other 'friendly' Japanese groups.

Because of a passport problem caused by the Japanese government, some members of the delegation only arrived in November and the get-together was therefore repeated for those members. Both occasions were vast events. There were around 600 Japanese delegates. In Beijing alone they were welcomed by around 10,000 Chinese youths.[1] The aim of this diplomatic mission for Nanjing, and probably for other cities in general, was to improve Sino–Japanese relations, to support the anti-American movement among Japanese youths, to introduce China's revolutionary situation and Maoist theory, and to show China's achievements in agriculture, industry and education, as well as the new ideological outlook of Chinese youth. Also, it was thought that this event itself would give 'American imperialists' and 'Soviet revisionists' a shock.[2]

According to official propaganda, the get-togethers in Nanjing went well. Ninety-six Japanese delegates arrived in the city on 7 September and left on 11 September. Another delegation consisting of seventy-five Japanese youths came to Nanjing from 14 December to 18 December. The press was full of reports of Sino–Japanese friendship during this period. Also, souvenirs such as stamps were produced to commemorate the event. These souvenirs have reminded several generations of Chinese and Japanese people of this event. The event was the first among many Sino–Japanese Youth Get-togethers in the post-war era, and has been considered by scholarly works as well as by some memoirs as being representative of Sino–Japanese friendship.[3] However, if we look carefully at the inside stories and the wider background of this particular event, scholars who believe that the CCP discouraged the recollection of Japanese wartime atrocities for the sake of Sino–Japanese friendship may be surprised to learn by how bizarre the situation actually was.

Inside stories

From the very beginning, this quasi-diplomatic mission was queried strongly by Nanjing citizens. The cadres of the Nanjing branch of the Chinese Communist Youth League made a painstaking effort to mobilise Nanjing citizens. The mobilisation was very thorough, especially in terms of educating the citizens to be friendly to the delegates. The cadres tried to indoctrinate Nanjing citizens with messages such as that there was a need to distinguish between the kind Japanese people and evil Japanese militarists. According to this message, Japanese militarists committed many crimes in China, conducted a 'three-alls' policy (kill all, burn all, loot all) and owed the Chinese people countless blood debts, but the Japanese people should not be held responsible for this: they too were the victims of Japanese militarism.

Also, the cadres emphasised that, 'in the past, we called Japanese military invaders "east ocean devil" (*dongyang guizi* 东洋鬼子), "Japanese devil" (*Riben guizi* 日本鬼子) or "Little Jap" (*xiao Riben* 小日本); please don't use these words to swear at our guests this time. We invited them to influence them and win them over, not for venting anger at them.'[4] Still, the cadres realised that there were citizens, especially those who had been the victims of Japanese atrocities, who could not accept the idea of receiving Japanese guests in the city. Examples of the citizens' complaints recorded by the cadres include the following:

> Our house was burned by the Japanese devil, how can you have a get-together with them? You should learn properly this time and settle this bloody debt with them!
>
> Why do we not receive other kind people, but receive the people who killed us?
>
> If I see a Japanese person, first of all I will go and slap him in the face.
>
> The Japanese did a lot [of] bad things in China, and the Chinese all know Japanese swear words. It will be really awkward, if we say *baka yarou* [a stereotypical Japanese swear word among Chinese, meaning 'idiot'] to the Japanese.
>
> How can we forget the old hatred? We should not forget the past ... the hatred of the nation.[5]

Nevertheless, thanks to the hard work of local cadres, many Nanjing citizens did change their attitudes towards Japanese people, at least according to a few well-documented episodes. Their hatred was still there, but only against past and present Japanese militarists. For instance, a Japanese delegate (Fujimori, an artist) was painting alongside the Yangzi River, when an old boatman came to him and pointed out some scars on his head. He gesticulated emotionally towards the delegate and told how he was chased and slashed by about four Japanese solders around twenty years previously. The delegate was shocked by this unexpected visitor. The accompanying translator immediately told the boatman that this Japanese man was a guest at the get-together. In this very tense moment, unexpectedly, the boatman smiled. He answered: 'I knew, the government had already educated us about this', and at the same time shook the delegate's hand – the hand of one of the perceived 'kind Japanese people' – in a warm way.[6]

Interestingly, the cadres were also not shy about showing the delegates the Chinese people's experience of the brutal war; in fact, they actively engaged in doing so. A revolutionary opera, *The Legend of the Red Lantern* 红灯记 was performed for the delegation on the evening of 16 December. The piece is a classic anti-Japanese themed contemporary Peking opera. The father and grandmother of the heroine – a 17-year-old girl called Li Tiemei – are killed by the Japanese occupiers due to their underground anti-Japanese activities. To get revenge and to save her fellow countrymen, Tiemei completes her father's unfinished job by sending a secret telegraph code to the anti-Japanese guerrillas. Many scenes show how the Japanese occupiers bullied and oppressed the Chinese. For example, in one scene an injured rickshaw puller complains, 'I pulled a Japanese devil, he did not pay me any money and beat me.' Also, the hatred of the Chinese people towards the invaders is manifest in the opera. For instance, after members of Tiemei's family are killed, she sings, 'the bottomless fire of my anger will burn down the dark earth and sombre sky'.[7] The cadres carefully observed the reactions of the delegates. According to their observations, some delegates were interested in the opera, while others were not comfortable with it. One delegate (who was considered to be a rightist) said, 'we let Tiemei down and I apologise for this'. Then he added 'we have nationalistic feeling. After watching this opera, we can understand. It's unnecessary to show our stance'. He also asked 'did you create this opera for this get-together?'[8]

The Japanese delegates were aware of the atrocities committed by their wartime government and communicated frankly with Nanjing citizens about it. For instance, shortly after arriving at Nanjing railway station, one of the delegates said 'the Japanese military slaughtered 300,000 innocent people in Nanjing, thus we came to Nanjing with grief and remorse. When we saw the friendship and enthusiasm conveyed by the Nanjing people, we felt really uneasy.'[9] Also, many delegates were keen to know more about the Nanjing Massacre. Forums with victims were hastily organised for the first delegation. During the second get-together, in accordance with instructions from the central government and demands from the delegates, a formal exhibition and presentation on the Nanjing Massacre, utilising careful wording (mainly to avoid offensive words like 'Japanese devils' and to emphasise the distinction between Japanese militarists and people) was arranged for the delegation. As is clear from the script of the presentation, many details of the massacre were collected and revealed to the delegation. Three aspects of the atrocity were introduced: inhumane massacres, brutal acts of rape, and robbery and destruction. Most of the delegates were shocked and apologetic.[10]

Some delegates even requested to talk with victims of the Massacre. Jiang Genfu 姜根福, who was often invited to give his testimony in public, and two other victims, met with a journalist from *Shinbun Akahata* (the newspaper of the Japanese Communist Party). After listening attentively to their testimonies, the journalist reportedly replied: 'thanks for helping me understand the crimes committed by Japanese militarists ... I will reveal these crimes to the Japanese people'. He also promised that he would publish their testimonies in *Akahata*. [11] Throughout the get-togethers, especially when the topic of the war was touched upon, the cadres reassured the Japanese delegates by emphasising the distinction between the Japanese people and Japanese militarists. Still, after being taught of so many horrors committed by Imperial Japan, one of the delegates commented, 'you suggest that the military and the people should be distinguished; for me it is not that simple. As Japanese, we should be responsible'. [12]

The Nanjing cadres were proud to have fulfilled this quasi-diplomatic mission successfully. [13] In their view, the true contributor to this success was not the friendship activities portrayed by the official media, but the activities of exposing the crimes committed by Japanese militarists. This was because the latter was 'closely related to the current anti-American movement, and directly targeted the American and Japanese plot to revive Japanese militarism, as well as revealing to the Japanese youths the spurious nature of elements of their education'. [14] The cadres adopted a strategy of scheduling these activities of exposing the atrocities in the middle of the get-together, and gave the delegates a chance to encounter the strength of warm feeling on the part of the Nanjing citizens before and after the activities. The contrast between the cruelty of Japanese wartime atrocities and the kindness of Nanjing citizens made most of the delegates, including left-wingers, right-wingers and neutralists, feel guilty about the crimes committed by imperial Japan. Some of them also started to concur with the attitudes of the Chinese by criticising the militarists in their own country. For instance, they criticised the problems of Japanese education, such as the fact that Tojo Hideki's picture was once again included in primary school textbooks, and that the Japanese invasion was taught as a 'national liberation activity'. Furthermore, after returning to Japan, 'many of the Japanese youths' started to 'advocate Chinese-style revolution and launched activities against the Japanese government'. [15]

Twentieth anniversary of the end of the war

In the background of the youth get-together, from August 1965 onwards, a nationwide campaign to commemorate the 20th anniversary of winning the 'Anti-Japanese War' was launched.

In Nanjing, a mass ceremony was held on 3 September (the Chinese V-J Day; see Figure 2.1). Many articles were published in Nanjing's local newspapers. Some of them were written by the CCP leaders, such as Vice-President Lin Biao 林彪. [16] Apart from introducing the basic historical facts of the war,

Figure 2.1 'Ceremony for celebrating the 20th anniversary of the victory in the great Anti-Japanese War' (middle); 'Global people's struggle against imperialism will certainly triumph !' (left); 'Long live the victory of the people's war!' (right)
Source: Xinhua Ribao, 4 September 1965.

most of the speeches at the ceremony and in newspaper articles were rather routine.[17] However, other commemorative activities took place which provided the people with more direct opportunities for remembering the merciless war. Many forms of commemoration were utilised for this 20th anniversary. Events, including those organised by the Art and Literary Circle, were organised and broadcast nationwide through the Central People's Radio Station. Commemorative stamps were issued and war memoirs were released.[18] For instance, between August and September, many memoirs of famous battles and stories during the war appeared in Nanjing's local newspapers or were published separately as books.[19] He Bingyan 贺炳炎, who commanded the army that participated in the battle of Yanmen Pass, wrote in his memoir:

> When we were marching towards Yanmen Pass, we could see the brutal scenes left by the Japanese bandits everywhere: many villages and towns were burned and reduced to rubble, many fellow countrymen were slaughtered. Just in Ningwu Town, countless people were killed; the vegetable cellars of almost every family were transformed into pits for burying living people; all the wells were filled up by the bodies of men and children who were stabbed by bayonets, as well as the women who were raped and killed ... the blood debt must be returned by blood! ... I will never forget the monstrous crimes carried out by the [Japanese] devils.[20]

Exhibitions of photography, paintings and historical materials were held in national venues like the National Art Gallery. Many items on display revealed the atrocities committed by the Japanese army, which 'stimulated Chinese people's hatred towards imperialists.'[21] A group of Nanjing veterans organised an exhibition of the history of their own battalion. Visitors to this local exhibition commented that the displays took them back to the period of the War of Resistance.[22] Jiangsu Provincial Art Gallery in Nanjing also held an exhibition, and pictures of the Nanjing Massacre could be seen there.[23] Classic Fifteen-Year-War themed films, such as *Little Soldier Zhangga* 小兵张嘎 and *Five Warriors in* Langya *Mountain* 狼牙山五壮士, were shown in Nanjing from 15 August to 25 September. Concerts of classic war songs, which were popular during the Fifteen-Year War, were also organised.[24]

The Chinese did not try to stop this massive war remembrance campaign for the sake of the large-scale Sino–Japanese friendship mission. During the first youth get-together, commemoration activities for the 20th anniversary went on uninterrupted. For example, one article describing how around 3,000 youths in Nanjing welcomed their Japanese friends was printed on the front page of *Xinhua Daily* on 9 September. However, advertisements for Anti-Japanese-War themed films and concerts were also printed in the same issue.[25] Also, according to the press, during the get-together period, despite the reports of a deep Sino–Japanese friendship, Nanjing citizens still swarmed into the cinema to see *Long Live the Victory of the People's War*, a documentary film made for the 20th anniversary. The audiences were very moved when the scenes showed the invading Japanese army trampling Chinese territory and slaughtering Chinese people.[26]

* * *

To make sense of the bizarre situation in Nanjing in 1965, it is necessary to understand how the remembrance of the Fifteen-Year War was positioned in the CCP regime's diplomatic practices in relation to Japan during that period. This chapter will discuss this by addressing two questions: what was the correlation between Fifteen-Year-War remembrance and Sino–Japanese relations? What was the CCP's stance as to how to remember the Fifteen-Year War in the context of its diplomatic conduct towards Japan before 1982?

China's relationship with Japan between 1949 and 1982 has always been simplified by the existing literature dealing with the Sino–Japanese history problem as 'pursuing (1949–1972) and maintaining (1972–1982) friendship with Japan'. However, the picture of China's relations with Japan at this time is far more complicated than this. Before Sino–Japanese normalisation in 1972, the inter-governmental relationship of the two countries was negative overall. Without a peace treaty, the two countries were legally at war. Also, due to the East Asia Cold War system, the CCP regime and the various Japanese administrations were hostile towards each other. Any amity that existed involved friendly Japanese people and groups only. Furthermore, as the CCP government constantly pointed out the danger and evidence of a resurgence of Japanese militarism, friendship was only manifested in fragmented moments, as against the wider background of the negative inter-governmental relationship. Between 1972 and 1982 China's relationship with Japan was good overall, but, still, there were bad moments, when warnings of a resurgence of Japanese militarism were voiced.

Consequently, the main body of this chapter is divided into two parts: one part discusses remembrance of the war when Sino–Japanese inter-governmental relations were bad, and the other part discusses remembrance of the war during moments or periods of friendly relations with Japan. The CCP's stance on war remembrance is dealt with in the final section. As the chapter will show, the situation in Nanjing in 1965 was not exceptional; rather, it represented the usual way in which remembrance of the Fifteen-Year War and the CCP regime's conduct towards Japan were played out together in pre-1982 China. As the chapter argues, the war was always remembered regardless of the status of Sino–Japanese relations, thanks to the slogan of the CCP regime that 'we should distinguish a handful of evil Japanese militarists from the majority of kind Japanese people'. This slogan may also reflect the CCP's position that a requisite condition for the Sino–Japanese friendship was remembering the war past, rather than forgetting about it. This argument lays the foundation for the following chapters, which focus on Fifteen-Year-War remembrance in China's domestic spheres.

Remembering the war when inter-governmental relations were poor

Numerous activities of bashing Japanese militarists were launched by the CCP regime when it was on bad terms with the Japanese government. This was either because the CCP leaders' genuine caution regarding Japanese militarism doomed the bilateral relationship or because that militarism was a convenient pretext for criticising Japan and its allies' actions, which infuriated the party leaders. It is worth explaining here that, if we look carefully at the contents of the CCP's Japanese militarist-bashing activities, 'Japanese militarists' consisted of two groups. The first group consisted of those who had invaded China or supported the invasion, and were referred to in the party's official discourse as (old-style) Japanese militarists, Japanese imperialists, Japanese invaders and so forth. The second group consisted of those who were charged with reviving militarism in post-war Japan. Hitting out at past and present Japanese militarists was not confined to empty sloganising. Many larger-scale campaigns, which directly or indirectly caused Chinese people to remember the cruelty of the war, were initiated by the CCP. Furthermore, these campaigns exposed many atrocities committed by previous Japanese militarists, as well as providing evidence (which was kept updated) of how the wartime ideology and practices were being revived. Apart from Japan's military build-up, the most frequently shown evidence was surprisingly similar to what we often hear about today, such as textbook revision, the Yasukuni Shrine, right-wing films and so forth.

In order to demonstrate this point, Figure 2.2 is based on an analysis of the headlines of the CCP's newspaper *Renmin Ribao* (People's Daily 人民日报) from 1946 to 1982. '*Rikou*' (Japanese bandits 日寇) is a very negative term for the Japanese.[27] It was used substantially in the article titles of *Renmin Ribao* before 1952 but use of the word in headlines stopped almost completely from 1953 onwards (Figure 2.2, chart 1). On the other hand, the use of '*junguo zhuyi*' (militarist 军国主义) in article titles in *Renmin Ribao* shows a completely different trend (Figure 2.2, chart 2).[28] At a glance, these two charts are at odds with each other. Actually, both of them reflected the Sino–Japanese inter-government relations very well. The decline in use of abusive language like '*Rikou*' to refer to the Japanese since 1952 implies that Japan was officially redefined, from its status as a disgraceful foe to a foreign nation. Nevertheless, this does not mean official accusations of Japan as a past or potential invader were disappearing.

According to the second chart, there were three phases of continuous yet fluctuating growth and decline in terms of the CCP's Japanese militarist-bashing: these were, approximately, 1947–1955, 1957–1962 and 1964–1972. Associating this chart with the broader background between 1945 and 1982, the peaks and troughs (the years without any article title using '*junguo zhuyi*') of the CCP's Japanese militarist-bashing were generally in line with the ups and downs of Sino–Japanese inter-government relations. In what follows, I

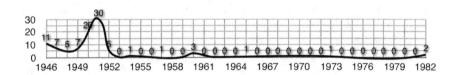

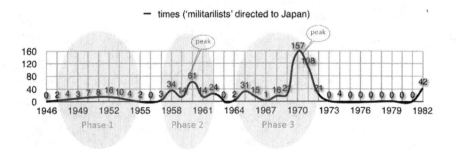

Figure 2.2 Chart 1 (above) shows the number of times '*Rikou*' appeared in *Renmin Ribao* article headings; Chart 2 (below) shows the number of times '*jun-guozhuyi*' appeared in *Renmin Ribao* article headings.

Source: Drawn by the author.

will discuss in chronological order how the two charts can indicate the CCP's war remembrance activities centred around Japanese militarist-bashing against the background of Sino–Japanese inter-government relations.

From undisguised accusations to undisguised courtship

Immediately after the end of the Fifteen-Year War, for the CCP the main theme related to the war was the issue of Japanese war criminality. Its propaganda sector reported in-depth on the IMTFE, and distributed articles revealing Japanese atrocities. In addition to the aim of accusing Japanese militarists, this propaganda had other purposes.

The first purpose was to accuse the KMT regime of colluding with America and Japan to bully China during and after the 'Anti-Japanese War'.[29] The second was to criticise the KMT's domestic rule in China. The CCP alleged that the KMT was corrupt when taking over the Japanese properties, that its behaviour towards the Chinese people was as brutal as that of the Japanese military, and that it even employed Japanese soldiers to kill Chinese people during the Civil War.[30] Thus, many articles deprecating the Japanese military also attacked '*Jiangzei*' (Chiang Kai-Shek the thief 蒋贼), '*Meidi*' (American imperialists 美帝) and '*Maimo*' (MacArthur the demon 麦魔). The third purpose was to praise the friendship offered by the Soviet Union and its assistance during the war.[31] Finally, this propaganda aimed at building a 'just' image of the CCP by reporting the abnormal lenience shown to the Japanese by the IMTFE and the KMT's military tribunals, whilst at the same time, promising that the Japanese war criminals would be punished in the CCP-occupied area. For example, a *Renmin Ribao* editorial described how Qin Dechun the Vice-Minister of KMT's Ministry of Defence failed to condemn the war criminal Kenji Doihara, at whom the Chinese 'will gnash their teeth to hate 莫不切齿痛恨', and criticised Qin as being 'wretched and impotent 猥琐无能'.[32]

From October 1949, when the Chinese Communist Party established the People's Republic of China, until October 1952, the CCP's narrative relating to the War of Resistance and its extra propaganda aims were similar to those in the previous period.[33] As before, accusations and revelations of atrocities committed by the Japanese Imperial Army were open and undisguised. According to the first chart, abusive language was substantially used to refer to this group of Japanese. The primary reason, I would argue, was that the CCP government still saw Japan – governed by right-wing politicians – as an enemy.

Formerly, the CCP had not trusted Japan. How to defend China against a potential attack from Japan and its allies was considered by Mao to be one of the fundamental purposes of the Sino–USSR Treaty of 1950, which was considered to be the most important treaty for the newborn PRC.[34] Later, the Yoshida Shigeru government (22 May 1946–22 May 1947; 15 October 1948–10 December 1954) signed the San Francisco Treaty and the Japan–US Security Treaty, which confirmed the image of Japan among the CCP leaders as the 'running dog' of the US. Yoshida and Chiang Kai-Shek also concluded the Japan–Taiwan Treaty and institutionalised Japan's pro-Taiwan stance, which further enraged the CCP.[35] Furthermore, when the Korean War erupted, there was widespread fear that a third world war would take place: the CCP also believed that there was evidence that Japan had helped American soldiers on the battlefield. By this point, Japan, as a potential danger had become a real enemy (although this time as an accomplice). The combination of all this suspicion, indignation and hostility meant that the CCP regime refused to be on friendly terms with the Japanese government, although the party still embraced kind 'Japanese people'.

During this first phase of the CCP's Japanese militarist-bashing (as shown in chart 2 of Figure 2.2), three mass campaigns to encourage the Chinese people to recall Japanese atrocities were implemented. The first two were related to Japanese war criminals. One was to 'protest against the release of Japanese war criminals by America': this was started around March 1950 and stopped around December that year.[36] Another campaign was to 'expose Japanese biological warfare atrocities'. The Chinese media followed the Khabarovsk trial conducted by the Soviet Union from 25 to 30 December, which revealed significant details about Japan's biological warfare atrocities. The Soviet Union sent a diplomatic note concerning the trial to several governments, including that of the PRC, on 1 February 1950. The note described in detail the brutal conduct of the Japanese biological warfare unit, as found by the court, and made a suggestion that other Japanese biological warfare criminals should be tried, including the Japanese emperor and Ishii Shiro 石井四郎, a prominent figure in the implementation of the biological warfare.[37] The Chinese Ministry of Foreign Affairs (MFA) replied formally on 8 February and expressed its support for the Soviet suggestion, as well as its wish to participate in the potential international military tribunal as the new government of China. Not surprisingly, with this wish in mind the party cadres embarked on their own investigations as well.

The correspondence between the two countries and the initial investigations were publicised, triggering a great wave of investigation, exposure and condemnation of Japan's biological warfare in relevant Chinese cities and towns. For instance, the Soviet diplomatic note was published on the front page of the *People's Daily* on 5 February 1950. Published on the same day were articles describing the site of biological weapons production in Anda, Heilongjiang Province 黑龙江安达, and describing the residents' suffering as a result of biological weapons use in Changde, Hunan Province 湖南常德. In the following days, more articles soon emerged, with experts' testimonies and victims' accusations, from places like Nanjing and Beijing.[38] After March 1950, this wave gradually ceased, and a pause ensued that lasted until the alleged discovery of America's attempt to use biological weapons in the Korean War in February 1952. Newspaper articles criticising the American attempt and tips for surviving in a biological war were published extensively thereafter, and gradually wound down in 1953.[39] Naturally, memories of

Japan's biological warfare and other atrocities were brought back in this later wave. A retired member of staff at Nanjing University recalled the exposure of Japanese biological warfare in the 1950s, and commented that it led to this atrocity being stamped on the memory of his generation ever since.[40] The CCP expanded its accusations regarding Japanese war crimes, particularly biological warfare, on various international stages. At an international conference on 6 September 1951, Sheng Junru 沈钧儒 listed some influential examples of how the US had since 1948 covered up for Japanese war criminals, including Ishii Shiro and the Japanese emperor Hirohito.[41]

The theme of the third campaign can be summarised as remembering the bitter Anti-Japanese War and protesting against the American plan to rearm Japan. This started around February 1951. All kinds of memories from the masses of Japanese atrocities were discussed constantly in the media.[42] According to the records of the labour union in Nanjing, dating back to February 1951, this campaign had been started late in the previous year as part of a movement to mobilise for the Korean War. Establishing patriotism and hatred of the US was the main aim. However, the movement did not go down well with Nanjing's workers. Thus, some new guidelines were created. The new core task was to protest against the American plan to rearming Japan and the American act of concluding peace with Japan on its own. Why was Japan set at the centre of this campaign? The document explained: the US had been smashed in the battlefield but was not willing to admit defeat. Thus, they had made some disgraceful moves to stay afloat. Sending John Foster Dulles to Japan in order to conclude a peace treaty and rearmament was among these moves, which outraged workers: '300,000 Nanjing people were killed by the Japanese invasion army during the Anti-Japanese War. The people and workers will never forget this huge debt of blood'.[43] Thus, the Japan-centred task was not only necessary to destroy America's plan but it was also in line with the sentiments of the workers. To fulfil the task, mobilisation of the masses was planned, by means of organising accusations, mourning ceremonies, petitions and so forth.

The campaign was not only carried out in Nanjing's factories but also in other sectors. For example, at a conference on 24 February 1952, Nanjing's industry and commerce sector decided to 'protest against American rearmament of Japan' as their current priority. Apart from organising a mass assembly to condemn the atrocities of the Japanese Imperial Army, other strategies were also planned, like organising small-scale discussion groups on each street.[44] Women were especially valuable in organising the campaign. Their demonstration against the American rearmament of Japan on International Women's Day was a highlight of the campaign in Nanjing. The result of this renewed campaign was notable, as the sentiment of Chinese people was aroused. In late April the central government started to warn that the campaign had miscarried in some places, as the local people were only expressing their hatred of the Japanese – they did not know that they should transfer their anti-Japanese sentiments to the Americans, and that they should be expressing a passion for constructing the motherland. This indicated that this campaign, originally designed to attack the US, was out of control and had become increasingly anti-Japanese due to the fact that the painful memories of Japanese atrocities were still deeply rooted among the Chinese people. Gradually, the media reports of this campaign became more devoted to routine discussions of how local people could successfully transform their anti-Japanese sentiment into anti-American sentiment.[45]

There was no official contact between the CCP government and the Japanese government until three members of the Japanese Diet came to Beijing and signed the first bilateral trade agreement on 15 May 1952.[46] Following this initial visit, thirteen Japanese delegates came to Beijing to participate in the Peace Conference of the Asian and Pacific Region 亚洲及太平洋区域和平会议 in October 1952. A series of resolutions were passed, including the Resolution of the Japan Issue.[47] Although Chinese people's sentiment regarding the Japanese and the war can still be observed, the undisguised condemnation of the atrocities of the Japanese Imperial Army gradually disappeared in official media after the conference.[48] Articles about biological warfare were still written, but they only criticised American conduct. Also, as reflected in Figure 2.2, '*Rikou*' has rarely been used to refer to Japanese people in official Chinese discourse since then. In brief, the CCP regime gradually changed its hostile stance towards the Japanese government after some semi-official communication between them, which may explain the vanishing, to a large extent, of the CCP's undisguised Japanese militarist-bashing. Still, rational criticism of Japanese militarism or its resurgence continued, despite increasing communication between the two governments after the end of the Korean War (27 July 1953). This was because the Chinese side still considered the Yoshida administration to be a right-wing government that represented the wishes of Japanese militarists, and was unwilling to build a proper state-to-state relationship with that administration.[49]

Nevertheless, as the USSR started advocating peaceful relations with the Japanese government and a change of leadership took place in Japan, China cautiously changed its attitude. Khrushchev visited China and discussed the joined change of Japanese policy in late September 1954.[50] Scholars noticed the fundamental change in China's Japanese policy from the statements at the Sino–Soviet summit meeting: previously the CCP regime only pursued friendship with 'kind Japanese people'; now they did not mind making friends with the Yoshida government.[51] Hatoyama Ichiro assumed the premiership on 7 December 1954, and the CCP publicly welcomed his government's statement on Sino–Japanese normalisation.[52] It was now that the two countries entered into the period of what I would like to call the first Sino–Japanese illusory friendship. In contrast to its tough stance on Japanese war criminals, the CCP actively engaged in repatriating Japanese POWs (and nationals), and it also conducted lenient military tribunals. Also, quasi-diplomatic communication between the two countries increased greatly. This is reflected in the second chart in Figure 2.2: once the first phase of the CCP's militarist-bashing ends, there is no instance of the word '*junguo zhuyi*' in *Renmin Ribao* during the tenures of Hatoyama and Ishibashi Tanzan (10 December 1954–25 February 1957).

The CCP's grudge against the Kishi-Sato brothers

These good times did not last long, however, and the next Japanese prime minister, Kishi Nobusuke (25 February 1957–19 July 1960), soon upset the CCP with his series of pro-US and pro-Taiwan actions. In particular, his unprecedented visit to Taiwan in June 1957 – the first by a Japanese prime minister since the end of the war – and his support for Chiang Kai-Shek's speech about reclaiming the mainland angered the CCP.[53] Around this time, the discourse surrounding Japanese militarism and Japanese imperial atrocities reappeared once more, on a small scale. Still, the CCP regime did not give up hope of normalising its relationship with the Kishi government. Its Japan affairs team devoted itself to preparing the negotiations on the fourth bilateral trade agreement, which was considered an important step towards normalisation.

Against this background, Liu Lianren 刘连仁, who had been a forced labourer brought to Japan by the Imperial Army during the war, was found in Hokkaido, Japan on 8 February 1958. Many reports about Liu's story, and how the Kishi government refused to acknowledge the responsibility of the Japanese Imperial Government, were printed in *Renmin Ribao*. However, it seems that these reports restrained their criticisms of a militarist resurgence and did not directly target the Kishi cabinet (although, technically, Kishi himself was a 'resurgent' member of the former militarist government). It appears that the CCP regime did not want to fall out with the Kishi cabinet by including its members on the list of blameful 'Japanese militarists' at this point. It was only when the Kishi government refused to acknowledge the fourth bilateral trade agreement, on 9 April, that the Chinese government started to directly criticise the Kishi government for a resurgence of Japanese militarism. On 2 May 1958 two Japanese youths damaged a PRC flag in a department store in Nagasaki, in what the CCP believed was a Tokyo–Taibei plot.[54] After the Nagasaki PRC flag incident, China ended its official relationship with Japan, and criticisms of both imperial militarists and resurgent militarism increased quickly, reaching a peak in 1960.

The justification given for the 1960 wave of Japanese militarist-bashing was to support the Japanese people's movement against the Japan–US Security Treaty, which was reported in China from 1958 onwards. The theme of this wave was a protest against America's attempt to revive Japanese militarism. The nationwide campaign started in Beijing on 9 May 1960. By 15 May there were assemblies and demonstrations launched in thirty-three cities and various counties, with around 12 million people reportedly participating in these activities. Japanese atrocities were recalled repeatedly by party leaders and participants. For example, Liao Chengzhi 廖承志 said in a Beijing meeting on

May 9: 'Chinese and other Asian people's memories of atrocities committed by Japanese militarists are still vivid.'[55] The citizens were very emotional during the 700,000-participant assembly in Wuhan – a city that had been ruled by the Japanese occupiers for a long time. For example, a woman whose husband was shot by the Japanese army expressed to the media her outrage regarding resurgent Japanese militarism.[56]

In Nanjing, two assemblies were organised on 13 May (with 400,000 participants) and on 22 May (with 1 million participants). According to the records of the Nanjing municipal government, the assemblies were carefully planned. It planned to mobilise 105,000 people across Nanjing to participate in the first meeting. The participants were required to be energetic and spirited, to set the mood for the demonstration. All the physical and intangible elements of the demonstration, such as banners, slogans and songs, were prepared by the government. To avoid any accident resulting from an overexcitement among the mass demonstrators, for example, the Public Security Bureau carefully checked the security measures as well.[57] Although it rained on 13 May, 400,000 citizens showed up for the demonstration – nearly four times more than the authority anticipated.[58] From the party head to the farmer's representative, those who gave speeches all mentioned how Nanjing had suffered since December 1937 at the hands of wartime Japan.[59] The meeting heard many testimonies from the victims of the Nanjing Massacre and from veterans who participated in the war.[60]

This series of activities and mobilisations carried on in Chinese cities until Kishi approved the renewed security treaty with the US and resigned in July 1960. However, criticism of past and present Japanese militarists did not stop after Ikeda Hayato formed a new cabinet (19 July 1960–9 November 1964). Not until the Liao–Takasaki Memorandum Trade Agreement was signed in November 1962 was the relationship between the two governments repaired again, for the first time since relations had broken down publicly after the Nagasaki flag incident. One can observe that accusations regarding Ikeda's resurgence of militarism ceased at this time.[61] Jailed Japanese war criminals were released ahead of schedule during this period as well.[62] This is reflected in Figure 2.2, where we can see that the second 'phase' of Japanese militarist-bashing ended at this time. Compared to the first phase of Japanese militarist-bashing, the second phase was more moderate – and not only in terms of the party's discourse. Chinese people were thoroughly and widely mobilised to condemn the crimes of the Japanese militarists on any possible occasion during the first-phase campaigns. Although they were still encouraged to speak out about their hatred in the second phase, this was confined to big assemblies, which were carefully controlled by the authorities.

Although Ikeda, as a low-key and pragmatic politician, found himself a balanced position between mainland China and the US/Taiwan, he still belonged to the latter's camp. Time bombs, with the potential of damaging Sino–Japanese inter-governmental relations, were buried during Ikeda's tenure, and exploded soon after his successor Sato Esaku took office (9 November

1964–7 July 1972).[63] China carried out a nuclear test successfully on 16 October 1964, which led Japan to worry about its safety. This in turn urged Japan to enhance its own military capability and its military alliance with the US. Other emerging problems also affected the mutual relationship, like the Japan–Korea Treaty and the Senkaku/Diaoyu Island issue. More importantly, Sato, with the ultimate political aim of regaining Okinawa, implemented a pro-US and pro-Taiwan policy much more openly, and the CCP regime struggled to tolerate this. As early as November 1965 he made comments that were considered to be supportive of 'two Chinas'. Unsurprisingly, criticisms of the Sato administration's resurgence of militarism appeared in headlines in *Renmin Ribao* for the first time in a relatively long period.

As all of the elements mentioned above took effect, tension between the two governments ran high; the CCP's Japanese militarist-bashing continued throughout Sato's tenure and reached a peak in 1970. However, compared to the previous two phases, the third phase concentrated on revealing the evidence of present Japanese militarist resurgence, rather than exposing the atrocities perpetrated by former Japanese imperialists, and castigating them. Although evidence warning of Japanese military resurgence was presented throughout the post-war period, the revelations in this phase were more thorough, dense and systematic (I discuss only that evidence which is not directly related to military build-up here).[64]

In terms of newspaper coverage, articles or special columns often analysed, item-by-item, how the Sato administration used cultural and educational tools to whitewash Japan's history of invading other nations.[65] For example, one article started by criticising Japan's annual memorial ceremony for the war dead, held on 15 August that year.[66] Sato's praise of those killed in the war was reproved, with an article indicating that this was a sign that he wanted to 'learn lessons from senior militarists and fight hard to expand abroad'. After criticising the enhancement of Japan's military production and military training, the article continued to express its outrage that the Sato administration had authorised cinemas to show the film *Turbulent Showa History: Warlord* 激動の昭和史:軍閥:

> This film reversed the verdict regarding the Japanese invasion by means of turning the history upside-down … it also brazenly called back the spirit of the major war criminal Tojo Hideki, [who was] a Japanese militarist leader of countless crimes, and whose hands were full of the blood of Chinese and other Asian people.

It was also revealed that Japan's notorious Mitsubishi A6M Zero fighter aircraft, as well as the uniforms and swords used by Tojo and Yamamoto Isoroku, had been exhibited alongside the film.

In conclusion, the article warned that a lot of 'poisonous weeds' were being produced to propagandise militarism, and it listed many examples. One of these weeds was the fact that, encouraged by the Japanese right-wing government, there was a wave of reprintings of the wartime primary school textbook in Japan, which encouraged people to expand abroad and to sacrifice their lives for the Emperor and the militarists. This textbook also denied the crimes perpetrated by the Imperial Japanese military by describing the Manchuria Incident as a military operation between the Japanese and Chinese armies. The article also revealed that the Tokyo National Museum was preparing an exhibition to celebrate Japan's military successes, and many paintings, photo albums and memoirs to commemorate the past militarists were produced, such as Okamura Yasuji's memoir, which was published in newspapers and in hardcopy. The article concluded that all of these facts indicated that Japanese militarism had come to life again, like dying embers that were now flaring up 死灰复燃. New Japanese militarists were reviving the old dream of a 'Great East Asia Co-Prosperity Sphere', and targeting the people of China, North Korea, Indochina and other Asian countries.

Individual pieces of evidence were revealed separately as well. Artistic works, especially Japanese war films like *Gateway to Glory* and *Men and War*, were attacked. A book that focused on condemning the Japanese militarist resurgence shown by Japanese war films was published.[67] Commemorative activities on the war-related memorial days, like *shuusen kinenbi* (the Anniversary of the End of the War, 終戦記念日) and *kenkoku kinenbi* (National Foundation Day, 建国記念日), were also a target.[68] Revisionism in Japan's education was also watched closely by the CCP regime.[69] Honouring militarists especially triggered the party's anger.[70] The Japanese Emperor had been seen as the spiritual mainstay of militarism since the early PRC period. Thus, any encouragement of the Japanese people to worship him was criticised by the CCP as a sign of the continuity of Japanese militarism. For example, even a mourning ceremony for the writer Mishima Yukio – who started a coup due to his belief in *bushido* (loyalty towards the Emperor and extreme patriotism) and committed hara-kiri after the coup failed – was denounced.[71] The Chinese media also warned that the Sato government and the US were following the old road of Japanese militarists – a road to destruction.[72] Apart from attacking the resurgent militarism, atrocities perpetrated by the Japanese invasions of other Asian countries were discussed.[73] Interestingly, the Japanese left-wing's exposure of the evidence in this regard provided a great avenue for China's Japanese militarist-bashing. Evidence of resurgent Japanese militarism exposed by the Japanese and their protests against militarism were reported in detail.[74]

Just as had happened ten years before, in 1970 the Japanese people's protests against the renewal of the Japan–US Security Treaty and the resurgence of militarism were substantially reported by the Chinese domestic media, as well as by journals targeting foreign readers.[75] The actions and speeches of the Japanese Socialist Party, pro-China groups and individuals (for example, 'we won't let the Marco Polo Bridge Incident that occurred 33 years ago happen again'), which took place on 7 July, 15 August and other Fifteen-Year-War related memorial days, were widely reported.[76] However, as regards the activity on the Chinese side, in contrast to ten years previously, in 1970 a propaganda campaign – as opposed to a physical mass mobilisation campaign which empowered bottom-up collective condemnation of Japanese militarism – was launched by the CCP regime. In other words, in each phase the mass character of Japanese militarist-bashing diminished. In addition to seeing the revelation and discussion of a large amount of evidence relating to Japanese militarism, this year also saw a vast commemoration of the 25th anniversary of the end of the war, on 7 July and 3 September. Chinese war memorial days usually had more domestic meaning and were not always used to serve the CCP's purpose of Japanese militarist-bashing but 'against resurgent Japanese militarists' was clearly included in this year's slogans for the memorial days. [77]

* * *

Criticisms of Japanese militarists declined swiftly around the time that Sato was replaced by Tanaka Kakuei as Japan's Prime Minister, on 7 July 1972. As is reflected in Figure 2.2, the third phase of Japanese militarist-bashing came to an end around this time. After the two nations normalised their relations in September 1972, China's inter-government relations with Japan prospered. Chinese leaders' public remarks about Japan now mostly related to how to learn lessons from Japan's economic reconstruction.[78] Still, the CCP leaders did not see Japan, which was considered as a pragmatic partner in the second camp of capitalist countries, as a completely trustworthy friend.[79]

Thus occasional warnings of Japanese militarist resurgence can be observed. For example, a Japanese right-wing organisation, *Seirankai* 青嵐会, founded in 1973 by a group of pro-Taiwan Diet members, held several national meetings in places like Tokyo (26 January 1974) and Nagoya (10 March 1974). Apart from quickly reporting on these meetings, Chinese media also revealed the organisation's connection with past Japanese militarists like Class A criminal Kaya Okinori 賀屋興宣, and criticised its members as resurgent militarists.[80] Similarly, in the same year it was reported that the House of Representatives passed the Yasukuni Shrine Bill, which also alerted Chinese officials to the danger of Japanese military resurgence.[81] Nevertheless, these reports would normally suggest that these were the actions of a small group of right-wing Japanese, acting against the will of the Japanese people, left-wing parties and even the LDP regime.

Remembering the war when China's relationship with Japan was good

Many historical sources show that the topic of the Fifteen-Year War was also frequently mentioned during those moments of Sino–Japanese friendship before normalisation in 1972. This section first discusses the CCP leaders' position as to whether the war should be forgotten. Then it talks about three occasions when the Fifteen-Year War was recalled during the moments of

Sino–Japanese friendship. The CCP leaders were not shy about discussing this topic with their Japanese visitors and were not afraid of defending Chinese memories of the war. Also, if any friendship event went too far and hurt the Chinese people's feelings, they reacted strongly. Chinese people were able to publicly express their animosity at this time: such feelings were not suppressed but were faced squarely by the CCP leaders. However, it was sometimes the Japanese who initiated the topic, as many of them were aware of the horrors committed by their wartime troops. Above all, when China and Japan were still legally at war before 1972, talking about the history of the war and dealing with its legacy was inevitable when Chinese and Japanese met. Finally, this section explores the situation of the war remembrance in the second period of Sino–Japanese illusory friendship between 1972 and 1982.

Should we let the war past go?

When receiving friendly Japanese groups, the CCP leaders sometimes remarked that they would like to let the war past go and build up a friendship with Japan. Proponents of the theory that the CCP regime discouraged remembrance of the Fifteen-Year War for the sake of Sino–Japanese friendship have frequently quoted these kinds of remarks to support their argument. However, these fragmented quotations do not represent all the remarks as to whether the war should be forgotten or not that were made by the CCP leaders throughout the period from 1949 to 1982. The party's position on the question actually evolved throughout this period, and changed as a result of the circumstances.

In the initial stages of the PRC, the CCP regime showed a firm determination to defend the Chinese nation's memory of the Fifteen-Year War. For example, Zhou Enlai drafted a statement on 15 August 1951 to protest against the draft of a peace treaty with Japan approved by the United States and Great Britan and the forthcoming San Francisco conference.[82] He devoted a lot of time to denouncing America and Britain's determination that the war lasted from 7 December 1941 to 2 September 1945. Zhou called this determination 'illegal' and 'insolent' (*manheng* 蛮横), and said the Chinese could not tolerate this and would oppose it firmly. Why was Zhou so uncomfortable with this periodisation? Because:

> Japan started to invade China from 1931 and started an all-round invasion war with China in 1937. The Pacific war only started in 1941. In this war of resisting and defeating [the] Japanese, Chinese people experienced the longest tough effort, sacrificed the most and contributed the most. This decision [regarding the period of the war] was to obliterate the period of Chinese people's independent resistance against the Japanese before 7 December 1945.[83]

As the CCP's Japanese policy was changing in the late 1950s, and the party's public statements that Japan should be responsible for the war in terms of paying reparations and trying Japanese war criminals was gradually disappearing, the status of the once cherished war experience became awkward. Comments by party leaders, such as 'we should forget the war' and 'the Chinese no longer hate the Japanese', started appearing in the period from the end of 1954 to 1955.[84] If one carries out a discourse analysis of these comments, one finds that it was not the case that 'the war past had been forgotten', and one realises that 'forgetting the war past' was not unconditional.

For instance, on 11 October 1954 Zhou Enlai stated to a Japanese delegation consisting of scholars, artists and members of the Diet, that 'during the past sixty years Sino–Japanese relations were bad, but this period has passed'.[85] He continued, 'we should let it go. History should not be repeated. I think this can be achieved.' However, he actually chose his words carefully and avoided saying something like 'this can definitely be achieved', or 'this has been achieved'. This suggests that what he actually meant was: 'We are trying to forget the war past, but this has not been achieved yet, and we do not know when this could be achieved.' Furthermore, Zhou also told the delegates how Chinese and former Japanese Imperial solders as well as Japanese nationals remaining in mainland China were harmoniously working together in northeast China, which he considered to be an example that showed that Chinese people had forgotten the hatred. Still, the Japanese people he talked about were 'friendly Japanese people', who voluntarily participated in the PRC's construction. For the Chinese to forget their hatred it was a precondition that the Japanese should be friendly to them. Whenever the Chinese thought the Japanese were not friendly enough, they were not timid at all about criticising them for their past wrongdoings, as shown in the previous section. More importantly, many historical facts suggest that, in reality, Chinese people, and even the CCP leaders, remembered the war past very clearly.

As communications between China and Japan increased, the CCP realised not only that animosity towards Japan existed among Chinese people, but also that not all Japanese people reflected on the war in the way that they might have assumed. The CCP leaders' remarks as to whether the war should be forgotten therefore became more rational compared to the previous two extremes (i.e. either of thinking the war should never be forgotten, or that the war should be forgotten entirely). To illustrate this, let us look at the following example of the famous lenient military tribunals conducted by the CCP in Shenyang and Taiyuan in 1956. The CCP cadres prepared carefully for the tribunals, as the regime wanted to prove its ability to conduct such tribunals according to international norms. Before the trials, the CCP regime carried out extensive investigations, including finding witnesses and collecting testimonies.[86] Also, to educate POWs, the CCP even organised for the suspected criminals to visit various places and to interact with a wide range of Chinese victims, which was publicly reported.[87] In the trials, the witnesses always gave testimony in tearful voices and listed the atrocities of these criminals one by one and in detail. The two trials, as well as the atrocities revealed in them, were vividly recorded on paper, tapes and film and were publicised domestically and internationally through newspapers, magazines and cinemas.[88] After the grand tribunals gradually disappeared from the media, reports about how the criminals, who were released or re-educated by the CCP, were grateful to the Chinese people emerged occasionally to remind the Chinese people of the trials and the war.[89] To demonstrate its leniency, in order to impress the Japanese government and Japanese people, it was reasonable for the tribunals to reveal extensive details of the war atrocities. However, these revelations also stirred up anti-Japanese sentiment domestically in China.[90] As I pointed out in Chapter 2, the events of 1956 took place during the first period of illusory Sino–Japanese friendship. I believe the CCP regime did not wish to see anti-Japanese sentiment prevail among the Chinese people at this time.

One can interpret the CCP's behaviour in the following way: stimulating Chinese people's memory of the war was an unplanned side-effect of these show tribunals. However, the CCP regime could have avoided this simply by not publicising the details of the tribunals in its domestic media, especially the revelations of Japanese atrocities. The fact that the regime chose to allow the Chinese masses to learn of the details of Japanese wartime atrocities suggests that, in its diplomatic conduct towards Japan, the regime's stance on how to remember the Fifteen-Year War was to firmly remember it and then generously forgive it, rather than to generously forget it.

One statement that perhaps reveals best the CCP's mature and rational stance throughout the post-war period was that made in the toast given by Zhou Enlai at a banquet welcoming Prime Minister Tanaka on 25 September 1972:

> in the half-century after 1894, owing to the Japanese militarists' aggression against China, the Chinese people were made to endure tremendous disasters and the Japanese people, too, suffered a great deal from it. The past not forgotten is a guide for the future. We should firmly bear the experience and the lesson in mind. Following Chairman Mao Tsetung's teachings, the Chinese people made a strict distinction between the very few militarists and the broad masses of the Japanese people.[91]

Sometimes, however, comments made by CCP leaders on other diplomatic occasions might deviate from this mature and rational stance. For example, Mao once complained emotionally to Burmese Prime Minister U Nu that in the past Japan wanted to be the housemaster in Asia, in the same way that the US was behaving at the time in North and South America. Japan said it wanted co-existence and co-prosperity, but actually it wanted to exploit and invade other Asian nations. And countries like China and Burma had 'been bullied' (受气 *shouqi*) by imperialist nations, like America and Japan, for a long time.[92] Many Chinese decision-makers had participated in the war and experienced in person the pain and humiliation when their country was occupied. It was almost impossible for them to forget the war completely, let alone ordinary Chinese people who did not have much 'diplomatic awareness'. Thus, when the CCP leaders suggested that Chinese hatred of Japan no longer existed on the part of the Chinese people, this was only being diplomatic, or was merely wishful thinking by the CCP – it was not the truth. Just like Japanese politicians' remarks that Japan was reflecting on its wartime wrongdoings, this did not represent their private thoughts or the opinions of all Japanese and Chinese people. A more realistic evaluation is that memories of the war were not 'taboo' during friendly moments between China and Japan.

Chinese leaders

When the CCP leaders spoke to Japanese delegates face-to-face, they sometimes brought up the topic of the Fifteen-Year War. These 'friendly moments' were the first occasions when the war was recalled. Often, they only briefly mentioned the war, to remind the delegates of it, for the following possible reasons. First, CCP officials wanted to dispel the misgivings of the Japanese people who felt guilty about the war, by expressing that although they had an unfortunate past, the two peoples could still build a friendship. Second, the CCP wanted to unite pro-PRC Japanese against the conservative Japanese government, which was accused of representing militarists. Nanjing cadres' actions of showing the Japanese youth delegation the details of the Nanjing Massacre and the *Red Lantern* were examples of this. Third, the CCP could give less 'friendly' Japanese a lesson by reminding them how huge a debt Japan owed to China, which was usually very effective. For instance, just before the negotiations on Sino–Japanese normalisation, Prime Minister Tanaka sent a delegation consisting of some hardcore right-wing LDP Diet members to Beijing in September 1972. Zhou Enlai received them on 18 September. He started an obviously planned conversation by asking the Japanese delegates 'what day is today?' The Japanese delegates could not answer Zhou's sudden inquiry. Zhou then explained: 'The September 18 Incident broke out 41 years ago. Forty-one years later, China and Japan are holding each other's hands firmly. This is a turning point in history; a new era finally arrives.' These Diet members were in fact not supportive of Sino–Japanese normalisation and Prime Minister Tanaka hoped their opinions would change after this trip. After Zhou's sudden words, they were moved. They did change their minds and further expressed that they would devote themselves to developing a Sino–Japanese friendship.[93]

Whenever the Japanese side did not show repentance for the war atrocities, CCP leaders would 'make a fuss' about it, although usually not publicly. One episode occurred during the Sino–Japanese normalisation negotiations, which exemplifies this well.[94] Many Chinese people were (and still are) disappointed that the Chinese government did not insist on a sincere apology from Japan for pragmatic purposes in this instance, which should have been an occasion on which to resolve war legacy issues, such as the issue of an apology and reparations. However, according to the memoirs of the cadres who were involved in the negotiations, as regards the war history issue, the CCP leaders tried their best to make the Japanese side compromise. In his first meeting with Zhou Enlai on 25 September, Prime Minister Tanaka commented that 'we gave the Chinese people trouble' during World War Two. Considering that Tanaka had just arrived that morning and the priority was to set the negotiation agenda, Zhou did not point out clearly that the comment was problematic. He only hinted at this by responding that the Japanese militarists' half-century invasion of China inflicted a huge disaster on both the Chinese and Japanese people.[95]

However, in the welcoming banquet that evening, Tanaka made a similar statement during his toast: 'what was regrettable was that the Sino–Japanese relationship had experienced an unfortunate process in the past decades during the period that our country gave the Chinese big trouble; we express our willingness of reflection'.[96] After the comments were translated into Chinese, they were immediately jeered by the Chinese attendees in the dinner hall.[97] Consequently, in the second summit meeting the next day, Zhou made his feelings, which had been hinted at in the last meeting, much clearer. He said:

> we understand the result of Japan's invasion war brought disaster to Japanese people as well, and Chairman Mao emphasised repeatedly that we should distinguish a small group of militarists from Japanese people. Thus, we can accept that you only used ambiguous words like 'regrettable' and 'reflection' instead of a formal apology. But the phrase 'gave trouble' caused our strong antipathy, since it could be applied to any common thing.

When meeting with Tanaka on the evening of September 27, Mao raised the issue about the problematic phrase again. 'In China we could say "gave trouble" when we messed up a girl's skirt', Mao said.[98] The result of this dispute was the much more sincere phrase that was used in the China–Japan joint statement: 'the Japanese side is keenly aware of Japan's responsibility for causing enormous damage in the past to the Chinese people through war, and deeply reproaches itself'.[99]

The CCP leaders talked about the history of the war with friendly Japanese groups – in part, driven by many other practical concerns. When negotiating with Japanese delegates over bilateral trade, the CCP leaders sometimes complained that old imperial ideas – for example, getting raw materials in China and developing industry in Japan 工业日本,原料中国 – still existed in Japan.[100] Also, when discussing the Taiwan issue with the Japanese delegation, the CCP leaders made the criticism that some of the Japanese affection for Taiwan was in fact nostalgia for Japan's previous imperialism and was an expression of gratitude to Chiang Kai-Shek by old militarists.[101] Nevertheless, generally speaking, the only occasion on which Chinese leaders strongly emphasised that the war could not be forgotten was when they felt under threat from a resurgence of Japanese militarism. In other circumstances, as mentioned above, the CCP regime's tone was generally soft.

Angry Chinese

The second occasion when memories of the war were recalled during friendly events involved the Chinese people. According to the memoirs of some of the cadres who were in charge of Japanese affairs, the Chinese people's resistance to friendship with Japan was fairly strong. For instance, Wu Xuewen 吴学文 recalled that in Shenyang, when some citizens saw Japanese delegations, they would stare at them with angry looks. When the Japanese casually used words like '*shina* 支那' and '*manshuu* 满洲' (Japanese words for 'China' and 'Manchuria' used during the war), the Chinese people felt resentful. Sun Pinghua 孙平化 also observed that:

> The long-term occupation and governance by Japanese militarists left countless painful memories among the people. After the foundation of the PRC, the party did much to provide explanations and provided an education in internationalism. [Although Chairman Mao said] we should distinguish the imperialist governments from their people and distinguish the government officials who make decisions from normal government staff … people's image of Japanese was still negative. They were not trusting of the Japanese. The jobs of explanation and education were especially difficult to carry out in the rural areas, which were devastated by the iron heel of Japanese militarists.[102]

A vivid example that illustrates this was the trouble caused by the Japanese flag. A Japanese products exhibition was held in Beijing in 1956 (Figure 2.3). Zhou Enlai recalled 'A very big Japanese flag was hung in the exhibition hall in Beijing Hotel … which gave me a strong impression. This was the very first time Chinese people saw the Japanese flag after the foundation of the PRC.'[103] The image of the flag was equally strong for Chinese people, whose painful memories of the misery inflicted by the Japanese invasion were triggered by its appearance. Many Beijing citizens made violent objections to the office which was in charge of the exhibition. The posters with Japanese flags were torn down.[104]

According to the record of a Japanese member of staff, similar scenes occurred in Guangzhou and Wuhan in 1958, where exhibitions of Japanese merchandise were also held. Many citizens deposited their queries and complaints regarding the Japanese flag in the message box at the event or submitted them to a news agency. A factory cadre who was obliged to visit the exhibition lost control of his emotions when he saw the flag and started to describe through his tears how his brother was killed by the Japanese Imperial Army.[105]

The CCP leaders were, of course, aware of Chinese people's sentiments and the potential danger from them. Zhou Enlai once again instructed the cadres:

Figure 2.3 The Japanese flag and PRC flag hanging together outside the exhibition
      hall in Beijing
Source: Anonymous,'Japanese goods on show in Peking', *China Pictorial*, 1956.

'we should distinguish between Japanese militarists and Japanese people', and the
cadres, in turn, made a great effort to educate the masses. Also, the People's Liberation Army (PLA) was deployed to guard the exhibition halls in case the public
made any physical threat.[106] When Prime Minister Tanaka visited China in 1972,
paper flowers instead of Japanese flags were used to greet his delegation, the
purpose of which was to avoid triggering people's emotions.[107] Nonetheless,
the CCP never attempted to forcefully suppress the people's sentiments and
consistently showed an understanding of them. Also, the CCP did not attempt
to conceal Chinese people's animosity from its Japanese counterparts.[108]

Raising the subject of the war from the Japanese side

On the third occasion, it was the Japanese who first raised the topic of the war.
During meetings between friendly Japanese delegates and Chinese leaders the
stance adopted by the Japanese was frequently apologetic. In particular, those

Japanese who had participated in the war had a kind of urge to apologise when they revisited China as friendly envoys. For example, when Endo Saburo 远藤三郎, who was a former lieutenant-general of the Japanese air force, met his old opponent Chen Yi, who was famous for leading an anti-Japanese guerrilla force, he repeatedly apologised.[109] To re-assure the Japanese, Chinese leaders repeated that the Japanese people should not be held responsible for the war launched by Japanese militarists. The Japanese, who were taken care of by the CCP regime (particularly those who were repatriated from mainland China), were inclined to publicly contrast the terror of Japanese invaders with the humanitarianism of the CCP regime.[110] Sometimes the Japanese people would make a great effort to express their remorse. During the Fifteen-Year War, Japanese people from Gifu prefecture made up the army that occupied the Hangzhou area. After the war, many Gifu citizens felt very guilty about this. From 1957 onwards, they overcame many difficulties imposed by the Japanese government in order to organise several delegations to Hangzhou. The two cities decided to build anti-invasion war monuments, in both Gifu city and Hangzhou, and they presented each other with epigraphs in October 1962.[111]

Furthermore, the atrocities carried out by the militarists during the war were often used by Japanese leftists in their struggle with the conservative government. As a consequence, some atrocities committed by the forces of the Japanese empire but which had been unknown to the Chinese – were investigated, causing a huge sensation in China. The best example was the Hanaoka Massacre, which was initially investigated and reported in a newspaper run by Chinese nationals residing in Japan, *Huaqiao Minbao* 华侨民报, on 11 January 1950.[112] The report, which also accused the Yoshida administration and the occupation authority of covering up this incident, appeared in the Chinese media in late 1950. Emotional memories from former forced labourers were soon recalled. For example, Ma Zixin 马子馨, who was working at a high school in Nanjing, wrote to *Xinhua Ribao*, in response to its reprinting of the report, about his own experience as a forced labourer in Fukushima prefecture and Hokkaido. However, this episode was soon submerged in the flood of accusations which took place in the early 1950s regarding Japanese atrocities, and it was not until 1953 that it was unearthed again.[113]

In response to the request of friendly Japanese groups, the Chinese government released an announcement on 1 December 1952 about their generous policy of repatriating Japanese nationals.[114] In return for China's favour, Japanese groups like the Japan–China Friendship Association and Japan's League of the Red Cross promised to repatriate Chinese nationals and the remains of those who had died in Japan, especially in Hanaoka. However, the mission was frustrated by the Yoshida government. The Japanese Communist Party published a statement in which it criticised this, and publicly mentioned the Hanaoka Massacre for the first time after a long silence on the matter, which made a great impression among Chinese people who were eager to know more about it. Consequently, the Chinese media started to educate the masses about the Hanaoka Massacre in graphic detail.[115]

On 7 July 1953 the remains of the victims of the Hanaoka Massacre were returned to China and a grand ceremony was held in Tanggu port. The friendly action of repatriating the remains of Hanaoka martyrs (those who had died in the massacre were seen in China as anti-Japanese martyrs) was covered widely in China and so was the massacre itself.[116] The Japanese side continued to compile a list of the names of Chinese forced labourers, to collect the remains and to return them to China in batches. The handing-over ceremony for the ninth batch of remains received renewed attention, for example in 1961 and 1964. Interest in Hanaoka among Chinese people gradually faded but was reiginited by Japanese leftists during the movement against the renewal of the Japan–US security treaty in 1970. The Chinese media narrated in depth how friendly Japanese groups had investigated the crimes of the militarists in Hanaoka.[117] In 1981, the original copy of the epic Japanese woodblock 'Hanaoka Story' (*Hanaoka monogatari*, 花岡ものがたり), produced in the 1950s, was rediscovered in Japan. Reported by the Chinese press, this once again caused a sensation in China.[118]

* * *

After the 1972 normalisation, Sino–Japanese friendship in both the official and non-official spheres became mainstream. Nevertheless, as shown in the previous section, warnings of Japanese militarist resurgence could occasionally be observed. As I will discuss in the following chapters, remembrance of the Fifteen-Year War was not only related to the Sino–Japanese diplomatic relationship, but was also entangled with various domestic affairs in China. For example, a campaign aimed at criticising Lin Biao was launched by the CCP in 1974. One of his doctrines, 'Self-restraint and return to the rites' (*keji fuli* 克己复礼) (its originator was Confucius), was particularly criticised. This doctrine was interpreted by the party propagandists as seeking a 'restoration of the past' that was full of ruthless exploitation of the weak. In order to demonstrate the darkness of the past, and ulmately to rebut the idea of bringing about 'restoration of the past', a great number of accounts about past horrors emerged. Terrors experienced under the iron heel of the Japanese Imperial Army were once again widely revealed and decried by the Chinese people. In short, September 1972 was a watershed in the Sino–Japanese relationship, but it was by no means as significant in terms of remembrance of the Fifteen-Year War. After 1972, Fifteen-Year-War memorial days continued to be celebrated, war monuments continued to be built or rebuilt and war stories continued to be told.

The slogan

The main body of this chapter has presented certain situations that are, like the circumstances of the Sino–Japanese Youth Friendship Get-together in Nanjing, confusing. As is discussed, the memory of the Fifteen-Year War was not only used by the CCP regime when its relations with the Japanese government were bad, but it was also frequently recalled during friendly Sino–Japanese moments, as well as during the period of the Hatoyama cabinet and the second half of the Ikeda cabinet – at which points Sino–Japanese inter-governmental relations were healthy. What is more, the history of the war was not a forbidden topic after Sino–Japanese normalisation in 1972.

The key to comprehending the bizarre situation in Nanjing in 1965, and how remembrance of the Fifteen-Year War was positioned in the complicated picture of China's relations with Japan, is a message that was used by the Nanjing cadres to harness its citizens' resentment towards Japanese youth delegates: that 'we should distinguish the majority of kind Japanese people from a handful of evil Japanese militarists'. This message is actually a famous slogan that was promoted by the top CCP leaders and was used on various occasions by the party cadres to deal with Chinese people's negative feelings towards Japan, and to relieve 'kind Japanese people' of their misgivings, as discussed throughout this book.

The slogan has two equally important layers. The implication of the first layer is that those who were defined as Japanese militarists should be blamed. When CCP leaders used the memory of the Fifteen-Year War to attack the Japanese government and right-wingers, as shown in the second section this layer could justify their Japanese militarist-bashing actions. Nevertheless, during friendly moments and periods when Sino–Japanese inter-governmental relations were good, how did the CCP regime manage to remember the Fifteen-Year War and at the same time to retain friendly relations with the Japanese? This contradiction was solved by a 'secret' weapon of the party: the second layer of the slogan, that 'kind Japanese people should not be blamed for the misdeeds done by a small group of evil Japanese militarists'.

Before Sino–Japanese normalisation in 1972, this layer meant that no matter how extreme the CCP's Japanese militarist-bashing was, its business of developing and maintaining a friendship with friendly Japanese individuals and groups would not be affected. Furthermore, there were occasions when the popular response to the CCP's militarist-bashing mobilisations seemed to have threatened to overwhelm events, such as the Nanjing rally in 1960 where hundreds of thousands more citizens came than was planned.[119] This layer thus also helped the cadres to tread the fine line between tapping into memory of the war yet keeping it under control. On the other hand, when organising friendly events, thanks to this layer, the party managed to confine the sentiment to a small group of Japanese militarists and convince its people to accept its diplomatic missions with kind Japanese people, as illustrated by the example of the Youth Friendship Get-together in Nanjing and the controversy related to the Japanese flag in Beijing and Guangzhou. After 1972, this layer was still useful for the CCP regime. It enabled the regime to criticise the behaviour of a handful of 'Japanese militarists' without affecting the overall friendly atmosphere, as shown by the *Renmin Ribao*'s criticism of the *Seirankai* and the Yasukuni Shrine Bill in 1974.

With these two layers, this slogan gave the CCP regime great diplomatic flexibility, as when attacking the conservative Japanese government, remembrance of the war was an asset; and when pursuing friendship with Japan, remembrance of the war was not a barrier. Ultimately, the slogan became a useful tool for the CCP to maintain a good relationship with its Japanese friends and at the same time to utilise the memory of the war for various aims.

I particularly want to point out here that this slogan, especially the second layer of it, was not merely created with the pragmatic aim of winning over the Japanese people and reining in Chinese people's animosity.[120] The Chinese view (including the CCP leaders) of the Japanese was largely shaped by the Fifteen-Year War, and even by the earlier period from the first Sino–Japanese War (1894–1895) onwards.[121] Consciously or not, they associated the Japanese with being brutal invaders. However, the CCP's idea of 'the majority of kind Japanese people' was shaped during the same period.

Based on the ideology espoused by the international communist movement, the CCP formed an abstract idea of 'Japanese people': they assumed that many ordinary Japanese people were poor people, such as workers and farmers, and were exploited by the Japanese imperialists. Thus, similar to Chinese people, these Japanese people would be 'against the Japanese imperialist invasion and war from the standpoint of internationalism, and against Japanese militarist politics from the standpoint of democracy'.[122] So, from the beginning of the full-scale war between China and Japan, the CCP leaders urged the Chinese people not to forget the distinction between Japanese invaders and Japanese people. Also, they continued to make an appeal to Japanese people on the home front and Japanese soldiers fighting overseas that they ought to unite against the invasion launched by their country's imperialists. They also believed a united front of Japanese people was forming, which would be a very important force to help China win the war of resistance.[123] Furthermore, many Japanese leftists and pacifists, such as the communist leader Nozaka Sanzo, came to China in the name of the 'Japanese people' and fought shoulder-to-shoulder with the Chinese resistors, which provided many CCP members with a real experience of support from 'Japanese people'.[124]

The idea and experience of the distinction between brutal Japanese invaders and kind Japanese people during the wartime period underpinned the CCP's basic principle of dealing with Japan in the post-war era. The basic principle reflected in the diplomatic field was the policy that one should 'distinguish conservative Japanese government from revolutionary Japanese people'. In the area of war remembrance, the policy was that one should 'distinguish evil militarists from the kind Japanese people'. The post-war political connotation of the term 'Japanese people' referred to Japanese individuals and groups who were friendly to the PRC (not Taiwan) and were truly remorseful regarding the Fifteen-Year War.

Post-war development in Japan also testified to this idea of a new 'Japanese people'. First, in the opinion of the CCP leaders, Japan had become similar and closer to China. Japan was no longer a colonial country as it had lost all of its overseas territories after the war. Furthermore, as China had, Japan was suffering occupation by a foreign country – the US. The CCP leaders also believed that ordinary Japanese people had suffered as much as Chinese people had. By exposing the crimes committed by the militarists, they thought they could evoke a positive response among the Japanese.[125]

Second, the pacifist movement in Japan showed the Japanese people's power and determination to resist militarism, which in turn confirmed the CCP's image of a revolutionary Japanese people. Third, most of the visiting Japanese, who were mainly pro-PRC or friendly people, apologised to the CCP's leaders. These visitors claimed to represent the Japanese people, which led the CCP leaders to think that the majority of Japanese people also felt guilty about the war. The offer of a sincere apology from the people of a nation, even without the slogan I have discussed, would, I expect, have been graciously accepted by the CCP. Also, Mao had a slightly unusual belief that he should be grateful for the Japanese invasion, not because the invasion had weakened the KMT while strengthening the CCP, as is wrongly interpreted by many Chinese internet activists nowadays, but because the Japanese invasion had 'educated' Chinese people by stimulating their nationalist tendencies.[126] Thus, it was not out of blind generosity that the CCP leaders made comments like the following: 'You have already apologised. You cannot apologise every day, right?'[127]

In short, the slogan was rooted in the Communist Party's ideology of internationalism and its message was given credence by the friendly support and revolutionary actions of 'Japanese people' during and after the war. Nevertheless, the slogan, with its two layers, was not a CCP invention. In fact, Chiang Kai-Shek also emphasised the distinction between cruel Japanese militarists and Japanese civilians during and after the war.[128] This kind of slogan was not merely a Chinese notion either. The distinction between the evil fascists and ordinary people in fascist-controlled countries was also emphasised by the Allies' post-war tribunals.[129] In terms of the first layer of the slogan, for example, the PRC seriously committed itself to the international anti-imperialist movement and often linked the Japanese invasion of China with the involvement of American 'imperialists' in countries like Vietnam and Cuba in the 1950s and 1960s.[130] This link between the past fascist invasion and the current American 'imperialist' behaviour could be observed elsewhere, such as in Hungary, where the connection was also used in relation to activities supporting the international de-colonisation movement.[131] As regards the second layer of the slogan, similarly to the PRC, ordinary people were distinguished from the Nazis during the reconciliation process between East and West Germany and their former enemies in Europe.

In general, the slogan was one part of a group of CCP policies that were based on Mao's philosophy of dichotomy. Among this group of policies were the diplomatic policy to 'distinguish between the conservative government and progressive people in a capitalist country', and the united front policy to 'unite the good majority against the isolated evil minority'. The former can be observed in the CCP's discourse on America, Britain and other Western countries. The latter helped the CCP to isolate its enemies, like the KMT during the Chinese Civil War and the landed class during the land reform movement in the early years of the PRC.

* * *

Finally, let me answer the two questions posed at the beginning of this chapter. What was the correlation between remembrance of the Fifteen-Year War and Sino–Japanese relations? The CCP's war remembrance activities, which were centred on its Japanese militarist-bashing campaigns, positively correlated with the Sino–Japanese inter-governmental relationship. However, as the war was consistently discussed by the CCP leaders, by Chinese people and by Japanese people – regardless of the bilateral relationship – speaking generally, China's relationship with Japan and remembering the war did not necessarily correlate. Nevertheless, in accordance with the second layer of the slogan, that kind Japanese people should not be blamed for the misdeeds of evil Japanese militarists, remembering the war was not contradictory to the CCP's pursuit of friendship with Japan. This layer was introduced to the Japanese so they would not hesitate to embrace the PRC even though there was a history of war between the two nations which still lingered in the minds of their people. This layer was also instilled in the minds of Chinese people so that their resentment would not harm China's relationship with the majority of kind Japanese people. Furthermore, the slogan could also be considered as acting as the CCP regime's code of conduct when it dealt with the legacy of the Fifteen-Year War with its friendly Japanese counterparts, as well as with the Chinese masses, and it reflected the CCP regime's stance on remembrance of the Fifteen-Year War.

What was the CCP's position on how to remember the Fifteen-Year War in the context of its diplomatic conduct towards Japan? According to Zhou's toast, quoted in the third section, the regime considered the present friendship with Japan to be more important than the militarists' past misdeeds. Nevertheless, both Chinese and Japanese 'should firmly bear the experience and the lesson in mind': the Chinese side would praise as well as forgive the 'friendly' Japanese people who repented, but criticise past and present Japanese militarists who did not show sincere repentance.[132] More specifically, the CCP's stance was that the condition for Sino–Japanese friendship was remembering the war past – even the darkest parts of it – rather than forgetting about it. In addition, many factors caused the CCP regime to *have to* and to *want to* choose this stance – most of which were actually factors in the domestic sphere. How the remembrance of the war was dealt with in the domestic context will be discussed in the next chapters.

Notes

1 See, articles in *Xinhua Ribao* (*Xinhua Daily*), a Nanjing-based newspaper published around these dates.

2 See, Nanjing Municipal Archives (NMA)-6002-2-255: 'Jiedai "Zhong Ri qingnian youhao dalianhuan" Riben qingnian daibiaotuan jihua caoan' [Draft of
receiving Japanese delegation for the 'Sino–Japanese Youth Friendship Get-
together' 接待 '中日青年友好大联欢' 日本青年代表团计划草案], 27 June 1965.

3 For Japanese accounts of this event, see, Endo Kyoon, 'Bukkyou kouryuu tsuuji,
nicchu yuukouni jinryoku' [Devotes himself to Sino–Japanese friendship,
through Buddhism], *Watashi to Chuugoku*, 2009: www.jcfa-net.gr.jp/watashi/
2009/090815.html, date accessed, 16 March 2014 遠藤教温, 仏教交流通じ 日中
友好に尽力, 私と中国, 2009; *Asahi Shinbun*, e.g. 'Pekin Nitsuku Nicchu Seinen
Youkouno 270 jin' [Sino–Japanese Youth Friendship's 270 people arrive at Beij-
ing], 24 August 1965.

4 'NMA-6002-2-255: 'Guanyu "Zhong Ri qingnian youhao dalianhuan" xiang-
qunzhong jinxing xuanchuan jiaoyu deyijian' [Advice of educating the masses
about Sino–Japanese Youth Friendship Get-together 关于 '中日青年友好大联欢'
向群众进行宣传教育的意见], 21 August 1965.

5 A conference for preparing the forthcoming reception work was held from 23
August to the 25th. The complaints from the citizens were passed by them in this
conference. NMA-6002-2-255: 'Zhong Ri qingnian youhao dalianhuan qingkuang
jianbao diwuqi' [Bulletin for the Sino–Japanese Youth Friendship Get-together,
issue 5 中日青年友好大联欢情况简报 第五期], 25 August 1965.

6 This story was recorded differently by different people. This part is based on
NMA-6002-1-25: 'Guanyu Zhong Ri qingnian youhaodalianhuan zai Nanjin-
ghuodong dezongjiebaogao' [Report about the activities of Sino–Japanese Youth
Friendship Get-together in Nanjing 关于中日青年友好大联欢(继续) 在南京活动
的总结报告]. Other records see, 'NMA-6002-2-256: 'Laochuangong jiexian
fenming' [Old boatman has clear ideological boundary 老船工界限分明], 18
December 1965; and Guan Zhihao, 'Kawaranu yonjuunen noyoujyou' [Friend-
ship that has lasted for 40 years], *Jinminchuugoku*, 2005: www.peoplechina.com.
cn/maindoc/html/teji/200508/teji-5.htm, date accessed, 16 March 2014 関志豪,变
わらぬ四十年の友情, 人民中国, 2005.

7 Translated by the author. How *The Red Lantern* reflected Chinese people's
hatred of wartime Japan is also discussed by H. R. Christopher, 'Japan in the
politics of Chinese leadership legitimacy: recent developments in historical
perspective', *Japan Forum*, 20 (2008), 245–266.

8 NMA-6002-2-256: 'Riqingxie ting Nanjing datusha jieshaode fanying' [The
reaction of Japanese Association of Youths after hearing the introduction on
Nanjing Massacre 日青协听南京大屠杀介绍的反映], 16 December 1965.

9 NMA-6002-2-255: 'Zhong Ri qingnian youhao dalianhuan jianbao dishiqiqi'
[Bulletin for the Sino–Japanese Youth Get-together, issue 17 中日青年友好大联
欢情况简报 第十七期], 8 September 1965.

10 NMA-6002-2-257: 'Riben Diguozhuyi zai Nanjing datusha dezuixing' [Japanese
imperialists' crime of massacre in Nanjing 日本帝国主义在南京大屠杀的罪行],
December 1965.

11 NMA-6002-2-225: 'Zhong Ri qingnian youhao dalianhuan jianbao diershijiuqi'
[Bulletin for the Sino–Japanese Youth Get-together, issue 29 中日青年友好大联
欢情况简报第二十九期], 12 September 1965.

12 'NMA-6002-2-256: 'Waibin dui Riben diguozhuyi zai Nangjing datusha zuixing
baogao, fanying qianglie' [Foreign guests reacted strongly after hearing the
report about the Nanjing Massacre 外宾对日本帝国主义在南京大屠杀罪行报告
反映强烈], 16 December 1965.

13 This paragraph is based on file NMA-6002-1-25.

14 NMA-6002-1-25, p. 6.

15 *Asahi Shinbun*, 'Homusho fukyoka no houshin' [The Ministry of Justice's line of
No Permission 法務省不許可の方針], 8 September 1966.

16   *Xinhua Ribao*, 'Renmin zhanzheng shengli wansui: jinian Zhongguo renmin kang Ri zhanzheng shengli ershi zhounian' [Long live the victory of People's War: commemorate the 20th anniversary of Chinese people's victory in War of Resistance against Japan 人民战争胜利万岁: 纪念中国人民抗日战争胜利二十周年], 3 September 1965.

17   The leadership of the CCP, the importance of Maoist theory and the importance of the People's Liberation Army as well as the farmers were always emphasised. The message, that since we won the war against Japanese imperialists we must be able to win over the American imperialists, the Soviet revisionists and their running dogs, was also always expressed.

18   *Xinhua Ribao*, 'Zhongyang renmin guangbo diantai bosong youxiu jiemu jinian weida kang Ri zhanzheng shengli ershi zhou nian' [Central people's radio station broadcasts outstanding programs to commemorate the 20th anniversary of winning the great Anti-Japanese War 中央人民广播电台播送优秀节目 纪念伟大抗日战争胜利二十周年], 19 August 1965; 'Youdiangbu faxing kang Ri zhanzheng shengli ershi zhounian jinian youpiao' [Ministry of post and telegraph issued commemorative stamps for the 20th anniversary of the victory of Anti-Japanese War 邮电部发行抗日战争胜利二十周年纪念邮票], 4 September 1965.

19   See, for examples, *Xinhua Ribao*, 'Shouzhan Pingxingguan' [First battle in Pingxing Pass 首战平型关], 11 August 1965; 'Minbing dabai dileizhen' [Militia soldiers lay a mine 民兵大摆地雷阵], 16 August 1965;'Yexi yangmingbao moubu sanying xunli' [The army used to make a night assault on Yangmingbao, 夜袭阳明堡部队某部三营巡礼], 1 September 1965. For examples of books, see a list of newly published books by Jiangsu People's Publisher in 1965: *Huaiyin bashier lieshi* [Eighty-two martyrs in Huaiyin 淮阴八十二烈士], *Kang Ri zhanzheng gequxuan* [Collection of War of Resistance against Japan themed songs 抗日战争歌曲选], *Yehuo chunfeng dougucheng* [Struggles in an ancient city 野火春风斗古城].

20   *Xinhua Ribao*, 'Yanmenguan fuji' [Ambush in Yanmen Pass 雁门关伏击], 13 August 1965.

21   See, *Xinhua Ribao*, 'Jinian Kangri shengli ershi zhounian sheying meishu zhanlan zai shoudu kaimu' [Exhibition of the art to commemorate the 20th anniversary of the victory of the great Anti-Japanese War inaugurates in Beijing 纪念抗日战争胜利二十周年摄影美术展览在首都开幕], 23 August 1965.

22   In *Xinhua Ribao*, 'Nanjing budui moubude buduishi zhanlan' [Exhibition of a Nanjing unit's army history 南京部队某部的部队史展览], 25 August 1965. For another example, see, *Xinhua Ribao*, 'Nanjing budui moubu juban buduishi zhanlan jinxing chuantong jiaoyu' [A Nanjing unit organised a army history exhibition to educate about tradition 南京部队某部举办部队史展览进行传统教育], 25 August 1965.

23   *Xinhua Ribao*, 'Jinian weida kang Ri zhanzheng shengli ershizhounian zhanlanhui zuokaimu' [Exhibition to commemorate the 20th anniversary of the victory of the great Anti-Japanese War inaugurated yesterday 纪念伟大抗日战争胜利二十周年展览会昨开幕], 30 August 1965.

24   *Xinhua Ribao*, 'Guanggao' [Advertisement 广告], 13 August 1965; 'Jinian kang Ri zhanzheng shengli ershi zhounian wenhuabu deng danwei juban gezhong wenyihuodong' [Ministry of Culture will organise various artistic activities to commemorate the 20th anniversary of the victory of the Anti-Japanese War 纪念抗日战争胜利二十周年 文化部等单位将举办各种文艺活动], 15 August 1965.

25   *Xinhua Ribao*, 'Nanjing gejie qingnian shenghui huanying Riben qingnian pengyou' [Youths in Nanjing welcome Japanese youth friends by grand meetings 南京各界青年盛会欢迎日本青年朋友], 9 September 1965. Advertisements about artistic activities to commemorate the 20th anniversary of the great victory of

Anti-Japanese War, like the concert of Anti-Japanese War themed songs, carried in *Xinhua Ribao*, 9 September 1965.

26 *Xinhua Ribao*, 'Nanjing guanzhong yongyue guankan 'Renmin zhanzheng shengli wansui'' [Nanjing audiences swarmed to watch *Long Live the Victory of People's War* 南京观众踊跃观看‘人民战争胜利万岁'], 10 September 1965.

27 Chinese terms like 'Japanese devil' and *Rikou* (日寇 Japanese bandit) often hurt Japanese people's feelings, see, for example, Tori Tami, *Han Nichide Iki Nobiru Chuugoku Kou Takumin no sensou* (Soushisha, 2004) 鳥居民,「反日」で生きのびる中国 江沢民の戦争 (草思社, 2004).

28 *Junguo zhuyi* was also applied to other nations, such as the Soviet Union.

29 See, for examples, *Renmin Ribao*, 'Jiangzei goujie Meidi Rikou dagan zousi shengyi zhumei jingji qinhua' [Chiang Kai Shek the thief colludes with American imperialist and Japanese bandit, doing smuggling business excessively and helping the America invade China by economic means 蒋贼勾结美帝日寇 大干走私生意助美经济侵华], 30 September 1947; 'Jiangzhengfu wushi kangzhan cantong meimei qinri jingtongguo huifu duiri maoyi fujiang quanbu gongye zhuquan maigei meiguo ta baba' [The Chiang Kai Shek government ignores the pain of the Anti-Japanese War and colludes with America and Japan, selling the industrial sovereignty to its American dad again through resuming trade with Japan 蒋政府无视抗战惨痛媚美亲日竟通过恢复对日贸易复将全部工业主权卖给他美国爸爸], 4 August 1947.

30 *Renmin Ribao*, 'Riben 'peichang wuzi' kaishi yunhua sidajiazu hanran dutun jujue fenpeigei kangzhan zhong shou sunshide minying gongchang' [Japanese reparations have started to be transferred to China, the four big families outrageously take everything along and refuse to distribute them to the private factories which suffered during the war, 日本'赔偿物资'开始运华四大家族悍然独吞拒绝分配给抗战中受损失的民营工厂], 22 February 1947; 'Rikou tusha renmin banfa jiangzei hanran jiayi yunyong' [Chiang Kai Shek the thief outrageously adopts the way which was used by the Japanese bandits to kill Chinese people 日寇屠杀人民办法蒋贼悍然加以运用], 9 September 1947; 'Xuyi neizhan bugu yiqie! Guomindang yong gaoguan houlu shouliu Rikou tusha tongbao' [Malicious and venturesome conduct in the Civil War! KMT bribes Japanese bandits with government posts and money to kill its fellow countrymen 蓄意内战不顾一切!国民党用高官厚禄收留日寇屠杀同胞], 22 September 1946.

31 *Renmin ribao*, 'Zhongsu maoyi tiaoyue dada bangzhule Zhongguo kangzhan dangshi Meiguo quejiji zi Ri qin Hua' [China–USSR trade treaty helped Chinese Anti-Japanese War enormously; the US, however, assisted Japan to invade China 中苏贸易条约大大帮助了中国抗战 当时美国却积极资日侵华], 26 June 1948.

32 *Renmin Ribao*, 'Yuandong guoji fating shangde guaiju' [The strange drama in IMTFE 远东国际法庭上的怪剧], 2 August 1946; 'Heze liangwanyuren jihui kongsu deheji zhanfan zuixing: jiefangjun baohu shoufa waiqiao, dandui peihe Rikou cansha renmin de zhanfa jueyuyi yingde zhicai' [The Chinese People's Liberation Army protects foreigners, but will punish the war criminals who co-operated with Japanese bandits to harm Chinese people 荷泽两万余人集会控诉德荷籍战犯罪行:解放军保护守法外侨 但对配合日寇残害人民的战犯决予以应得制裁], 4 August 1946.

33 Accounts about China's good relations with another socialist friend – North Korea – during the war also started appearing during this period. See, for example, *Renmin Ribao*, 'Zhong Chao renmin zai Dongbei kang Ri zhanzheng zhongde guojizhuyi tuanji' [The internationalist solidarity between Chinese and Korean people in northeast China during the Anti-Japanese War 中朝人民在东北抗日战争中的国际主义团结], 11 November 1950.

34 Zhonghua renmin gongheguo waijiaobu and Zhongyang wenxian yanjiushi, *Mao Zedong waijiao wenxuan* [Selected diplomatic works of Mao Zedong]

(Zhongyang wenxian chubanshe, 1994), p. 122 中华人民共和国外交部 中共中央文献研究室 (1994). 毛泽东外交文选, 中央文献出版社.

35   See, for example, 'Zhou Enlai waizhang guanyu Meiguo jiqi pucong guojia qianding Jiujinshan dui Ri heyue de shengming (18 September 1951)' [Foreign Minister Zhou Enlai's statement that the US as well as its satellite countries signed the San Francisco Treaty 周恩来外长关于美国及其仆从国家签订旧金山对日合约的声明]; 'Zhang Hanfu fuwaizhang guanyu Riben Jitian zhengfu xiang Meiguo zhengfu baozheng yu Guomindang fandong canyu jituan dijie heyue de shengming (23 January 1952)' [Vice Foreign Minister Zhang Hanfu's statement about Japanese Yoshida government's promise to American government to sign a peace treaty with the remaining KMT reactionary group 章汉夫副外长关于日本吉田政府向美国政府保证与国民党反动残余集团缔结和约的声明]', in Shijiezhishi chubanshe (ed.), *Ribenwenti wenjian huibian* (1) [Compilation of documents of Japanese issue] (Beijing: Shijiezhishi chubanshe, 1955) 世界知识出版社, 日本问题文件汇编 (1), (世界知识出版社, 1955).

36   Officials' speeches of denouncement and nationwide victims' accusations started being reported in March 1950 in *Renmin Ribao*. These reports gradually stopped in December that year. See, for example, *Renmin Ribao*, 'Feng Wenbin, Liao Chengzhi Xie Bangding fabiao tanhua tongchi Meidi baobi Rikou zuixing yaoqiu yancheng nvesha huafu xiong fan' [Feng Wenbin, Liao Chengzhi and Xie Bangding gave speeches, rebuking scathingly the American imperialists' crime of shielding Japanese bandits and demanding they punish the criminals who killed the Chinese captives 冯文彬廖承志谢邦定发表谈话痛斥美帝包庇日寇罪行], 16 April 1950; 'Rehe Shanxi Gansu dengdi renmin kangyi Maimo shifang zhanfan Chongguang Kui' [People in places like Rehe, Shanxi and Gansu protest against the release of Shigemitsu Mamoru by MacArthur the demon 热河山西甘肃等地人民抗议麦魔释放战犯重光葵], 29 November 1950.

37   *Xinhua Ribao*, 'Lifu waizhang daibiao zhongyang zhengzhong shengming' [Vice Foreign Minister Li made a solemn statement on the behaviour of the central government 李副外长代表中央郑重声明], 9 February 1950.

38   *Renmin Ribao*, 'Weishengbu yaojizhuanjia zuotan zhengshi xijun zhanfan zai Hua zuixing bing jielou Guomindang wei Rikou yanshide wuchixingwei' [Ministry of Health held a discussion of experts, proved the atrocities of Japanese biological warfare criminals and revealed the KMT's shameless behaviour of covering up for the Japanese bandits 卫生部邀集专家座谈证实细菌战犯在华罪行并揭露国民党为日寇掩饰的无耻行为], 11 Feb 1950; 'Qinshen shouhaide Ningbo shimin zhengshi Rikou cengsanbu dujun' [The victim residences of Ningbo proved the Japanese bandits' emitting of toxic bacteria 亲身受害的宁波市民证实日寇曾散布毒菌, 21 February 1950.

39   See, for example, *Renmin Ribao*, 'Cengzao Rikou xijun duhaide Haerbin Changchun Ningbo dengdi renmin kangyi qinchao meijun goujie Riben zhanfan jinxing xijun zhanzheng' [The people in places like Harbin, Changchun and Ningbo who suffered the Japanese biological warfare, protest against the American troops which are invading the Korea colluding with the Japanese war criminals to conduct biological warfare 曾遭日寇细菌毒害的哈尔滨长春宁波等地人民抗议侵朝美军勾结日本战犯进行细菌战争], 1 March 1952. *Xinhua Ribao*, 'Weishengju wenjiaoju deng juban aiguo weisheng fangyi zhanlanhui' [Patriotic hygiene epidemic prevention exhibition is organised by Public Health Bureau, Cultural and Education Bureau, and so forth 卫生局文教局等举办爱国卫生防疫展览会], 4 April 1952.

40   According to interview with Sun at his home in Nanjing, 22 June 2012.

41   'Guanyu zhanzheng zuifande jianju he chengfa 6 September 1951' [As regards informing against and punishing war criminals 关于战争罪犯的检举和惩罚] in *Riben wenti wenjian huibian* (1955).

42 See, for example, *Renmin Ribao*, 'Janyi chuban Rikou baoxing zhaopian zhuanji' [Suggest publication of a photo album revealing Japanese bandits' atrocities 建议 出版日寇暴行照片专集], 25 February 1951; 'Wurenqu' he "wurenquan" – huiyi Rikou dexuexing baoxing' ['No Man district' and 'No Man circle'– recollect the Japanese bandits' bloody atrocity. '无人区'和'无人圈' – 回忆日寇的血腥暴行], 28 Feb 1951.

43 'NMA-6001-1-11: 'Benshi gongren kang Mei yuan Chao yundong degaikuang yudangqiangongzuo dejigewenti' [The general situation of the mobilisation movement of our city's workers for the Korean war and several problems of the current task 本市工人抗美援朝运动的概况与当前工作的几个问题], 26 February 1951.

44 *Xinhua Ribao*, 'Gongshanglian changweihui jueding fenqu kongsu Rikou baoxing fandui Meidi wuzhuang Riben dongyuan gongshangjie funv canjia sanba youxing' [Standing committee of the association of the industrialists and businessmen decided to accuse Japanese bandits' atrocities in each district, protest against American imperialist's rearmament of Japan and encourage women in the two sectors to participate in the demonstration on 8 March 工商联常委会决 定分区控诉日寇暴行 反对美帝武装日本 动员工商界妇女参加三八游行], 25 February 1951.

45 See, for example, *Renmin Ribao*, 'Zaixuanchuan fandui Meiguo wuzhuang Ribenshi, yingyindao renmin choushi Meidiguozhuyi' [When propagandising 'against America's rearmament of Japan', the people should be guided to hate American imperialism 在宣传反对美国武装日本时 应引导人民仇视美帝国主 义], 22 April 1951.

46 To get a better sense of the Chinese perspective, this chapter's discussion about Sino–Japanese relations is largely based on mainland Chinese scholars' research, e.g. Liu Jianping, *Zhanhou Zhong Ri guanxi 'buzhengchang' lishide guocheng yujiegou* [Sino–Japanese relations after World War II: abnormal historical process and construction] (Beijing: Shehui Kexue Wenxian chubanshe, 2010) 刘建 平, 战后中日关系'不正常'历史的过程与结构 (社会科学文献出版社, 2010); Zhang Lili, *Xin Zhongguo yu Riben guanxishi (1949–2010)* [History of relations between new China and Japan] (Shanghai: Shanghai Renmin chubanshe, 2011) 张历历, 新中国与日本关系史 (1949–2010) (上海人民出版社, 2011). Chinese official documents and Japanese newspaper reports were also used, such as *Yomiuri Shinbun*, 'Chuugoku "Gensoku no fudou" no kiseki' [Track of 'China's unwavering principles' 中国「原則の不動」の軌跡], 25 September 1972.

47 Shijiezhishi chubanshe, *Shijie zhishi cidian* [World knowledge dictionary] (Beijing: Shijiezhishi chubanshe, 1950) 世界知识出版社, 世界知识辞典 (世界知识出 版社, 1950).

48 *Xinhua Ribao*, 'Duzhe laixin: xiangqi Riben qiangdao zai Nanjing de datusha wojianjue yonghu heping huiyide jueyi' [I support the resolution of the peace conference when I recall the Nanjing Massacre 读者来信:想起日本强盗在南京 的大屠杀 我坚决拥护和平会议的决议], 16 October 1952; 'Duzhe laixin' [Reader's letter 读者来信], 19 October 1952.

49 Liu, *Zhanhou Zhong Ri guanxi*.

50 'Zhonghua renmin gongheguo he suweiai shehuizhuyi gongheguo lianmeng guanyu dui Riben guanxide lianhe xuanyan' [Joint statement of the PRC and the USSR about their relationship with Japan 中华人民共和国政府和苏维埃社会主 义共和国联盟关于对日本关系的联合宣言], 12 October 1954, in *Riben wenti wenjian huibian (1955)*.

51 Liu, *Zhanhou Zhong Ri guanxi*.

52 'Lun Riben he Zhongguo huifu zhengchang guanxi' [Talk about Japan and China normalising their relationship 论日本和中国恢复正常关系], 30 December 1954, in *Riben wenti wenjian huibian*(1955).

53 'Zhou Enlai zongli tong Riben jizhe tan Zhong Ri guanxi' [Prime Minister Zhou Enlai talks about Sino–Japanese relationship with Japanese reporters 周恩来总理同日本记者谈中日关系], 25 July 1957, in Shijie zhishi chubanshe (ed.), *Riben wenti wenjian huibian(2)* [compilation of documents of Japanese issue] (Beijing: Shijiezhishi chubanshe, 1958) 世界知识出版社, 日本问题文件汇编(2) (世界知识出版社, 1958).

54 For more on this incident, see Zhao Quangsheng, *Interpreting Chinese foreign policy: the micro-macro linkage approach* (Oxford: Oxford University Press, 1996), p. 123; Zhang, *Xin Zhong yu Riben;* 'Zhongguo renmin waijiao xueyuan huizhang Zhang Xiruo, Riben shehuidang fanghua daibiaotuan tuanzhang Qianzhao daocilang gongtong shengming' [Present of Chinese people's diplomacy society Zhang Xiruo and chief of Japanese socialist delegation Asanuma make a joint statment 中国人民外交学会会长张奚若 日本社会党访华代表团团长浅沼稻次郎共同声明], 17 March 1959, in Shijiezhishi chubanshe(ed.), *Riben wenti wenjian huibian (3)* [compilation of documents of Japanese issue] (Beijing: Shijiezhish chubanshe, 1961) 世界知识出版社, 日本问题文件汇编(3) (世界知识出版社, 1961).

55 *Nanjing Ribao,* 'Liao Chengzhi tongzhi zai shoudu gejie zhiyuan Riben renmin zhengyi douzheng dahui shang de jianghua' [Comrade Liao Chengzhi's speech in the assembly in Beijing 廖承志同志在首都各界支援日本人民正义斗争大会上的讲话], 10 May 1960.

56 See, *Nanjing Ribao,* 'Quanguo yiyou jin jiubaiwanren jihui shiwei zhiyuan Riben renmin zhengyi douzheng' [Around 9 million people participated in the assembly and demonstration nationwide to support Japanese people's justice struggle 全国已有近九百万人集会示威支援日本人民正义斗争], 15 May 1960.

57 'NMA-5003-3-788: 'Zhiyuan Ri benrenmin fandui Mei Ri junshi tongmeng tiaoyue dahui jihuacaoan' [Draft plan for the assembly of supporting Japanese people's protest against Japan–US security treaty 支援日本人民反对日美军事同盟条约大会计划草案], 9 May 1960.

58 *Nanjing Ribao,* 'Nanjing sishi duowanren juxing dashiwei zhichi Riben renmin fan Mei aiguo douzheng' [Around 400,000 Nanjing citizens launched a demonstration to support Japanese people's patriotic struggle against the US 南京四十多万人举行大示威 支持日本人民反美爱国斗争], 14 May 1960.

59 NMA-5003-3-788.

60 *Nanjing Ribao,* 'Zijinshan xiade housheng' [Roar at the foot of Purple Mountain 紫金山下的吼声], 14 May 1960.

61 Still, there were a few articles reporting South Korean's criticism of resurgent Japanese militarism, see, for example, *Renmin Ribao,* 'Chaoxian minzhu falvjiaxiehui lishu Riben diguozhuyi qin Chao zuixing' [Korean association of democratic law experts lists Japanese imperialists' crime of invading Korea 朝鲜民主法律家协会历数日本帝国主义侵朝罪行], 26 March 1964; 'Dongbei xianhouyou wushiduowanren dao Fangjiafen pindiao 'wanrenken' daonian Riben diguozhuyi qinzhanshiqi sinan kuanggong' [500,000 people in Northeast China went to Fangjia Cemetery to visit the 'mass grave' and mourn for the miners who died during the period of Japanese imperialist occupation 东北先后有五十多万人到方家坟凭吊'万人坑' 悼念日本帝国主义侵占时期死难矿工], 8 April 1964.

62 *Xinhua Ribao,* 'Tiqian shifang Riben zhanfan Guhai Zhongzhi' [Release of Japanese war criminal Furumi Tadayuki ahead of schedule 提前释放日本战犯古海忠之], 14 February 1963; 'Wotiqian shifang wuming Riben zhanfan' [We release five Japanese war criminals ahead of schedule 我提前释放五名日本战犯], 4 September 1963; 'Zhanfan fuxing qijian shoule fandui qinlve zhanzheng weihu hepingde jiaoyu, chanhuile zijide zuixing zuigaorenmin fayuan caiding tiqian shifang zuihou san ming Riben zhanfan' [War criminals received education of protesting against invasion and safeguarding peace and repented their crimes; the

supreme court of the PRC decided to release the last three Japanese war criminals ahead of schedule 战犯服刑期间受了反对侵略战争维护和平的教育 忏悔了自己的罪行最高人民法院裁定提前释放最后三名日本战犯], 7 March 1964.

63 Examples of such bombs include the Mitsuya Plan (which was a secret battle plan made by Japan, South Korea and the US in June 1963, and was exposed by Japanese left-wingers on February 10, 1965. The plan's imaginary enemies were China and North Korea) and the second Yoshida Letter to Taiwan (which would damage the Liao-Takasaki trade), see, S. Hongyan, 'Impact of the second Yoshida Letter on LT trade', *Journal of Changchun University,* 19 (2009).

64 For examples of evidence reported in previous two phases, see, *Renmin Ribao,* 'Zhanqian Riben zuidade junguozhuyi zuzhi "zaixiang junrenhui" kaishi huodong' [The biggest wartime Japanese militarism organisation 'association of solders who are not on active duty' starts limbering up again 战前日本最大的军国主义组织 '日本在乡军人会'开始活动), 14 August 1952;'Anzhengfu jiajin fuhuo junguozhuyi jieli liyong jiaoyu he xuanchuan guan shu duliu' [Kishi government hurry up to revise militarism, and is desperate to use education and propaganda to instill poisonous ideas 岸政府加紧复活军国主义 竭力利用教育和宣传灌输毒素], 27 December 1959; 'Riben junguo zhuyi fenzi jingwei Dongtiao deng jianjinianbei' [Japanese militarists go so far as to build memorials for people like Tojo Hideki 日本军国主义分子竟为东条等建纪念碑], 19 August 1960.

65 For examples of articles, see, *Renmin Ribao,* 'Buzhun Riben junguozhuyi jieshi huanhun' [Reviving Japanese militarism in a new guise is forbidden 不准日本军国主义借尸还魂], 7 July 1971. For an example of a special column, see a series of articles published in *Renmin Ribao* on 29 January 1971:'Riben fandongpai liyong xinnian dasifangdu' [Japanese reactionaries used the new year to spread poisonous ideas 日本反动派利用新年大肆放毒]; 'Zhanlan bingqi guchui kuozhang qinlve' [Display weapons to advocate expansion and invasion 展览兵器鼓吹扩张侵略]; 'Jisishengui weiqinlvejun zhaohun' [Hold rite to call back the soul of the dead militarists 祭祀神鬼为侵略军招魂] and 'Guangbo junge xuanyang duwu jinshen' [Broadcast military songs to preach warlike spirit 广播军歌宣扬黩武精神].

66 *Xin Nanjing Ribao,* 'Riben junguo zhuyi quanmian fuhuode zuizheng' [Evidence of that Japanese militarism is reviving overall 日本军国主义全面复活的罪证], 19 August 1970.

67 See, for example, *Renmin Ribao,* 'Riben fandongpai zhengwei xiangwai qinlve dazao fangeminyulun zaijiajin kuojun beizhan tongshi liyong chubanwu, dianyinghegequ dasixuanyang junguozhuyi' [Japanese reactionaries whip up public opinion by using publications, films and songs to advocate militarism, at the same time accelerate arms expansion to prepare the war 日本反动派正为向外侵略大造反革命舆论在加紧扩军备战同时,利用出版物,电影和歌曲等大肆宣扬军国主义], 29 August 1970; 'Jiechuan zuoteng zhengfu souluo paohuide pianju – ping Riben fandongyingpian A, Haijun' [Disclose Sato administration's fraud of search for cannon fodder – review Japanese reactionary film Aa,kaigun 揭穿佐藤政府搜罗炮灰的骗局 – 评日本反动影片 '啊 海军'], 20 July 1971; The book is: Qi Pingzhi and Tao Diwen, *Jisui Mei Ri fandongpai demimeng* [Strike at the delusive dream of American and Japanese reactionaries] (Beijing: Renmin chubanshe, 1971)齐平芝, 陶第文, 击碎美日反动派的迷梦 (人民出版社, 1971).

68 *Renmin Ribao,* 'Zuoteng zhengfu jingzai Riben touxiang ershizhounian dasi xuanchuan junguozhuyi shandong fuchou zhuyi' [Sato government stirred up revanchism on the 20th anniversary of the end of the war 佐藤政府竟在日本投降二十周年大肆宣传军国主义煽动复仇主义], 20 August 1965; 'Zuoteng fandong zhengfu liyong 'jiyuanjie' shandong junguozhuyi kuangre' [Sato reactionary government used 'kigensetsu' to stir up militarist fanaticism 佐藤反动政

府利用'纪元节'煽动军国主义狂热], 1 March 1971. *Kigensetsu* 紀元節 was Empire Day in Japan and was abolished during American Occupation period. It was revised as the National Foundation Day in 1966 as a national holiday.

69 E.g. *Renmin Ribao*, 'Zuoteng meihua tianhuang cuangai lishi wei junguozhuyi zhaohun qianfangbaiji liyong jiaokeshu xiang Riben qingshaonian guanshu junguozhuyi dejiaoyu' [Sato beautifies Japanese emperor, revises history, calls back the souls of the dead militarists, and uses textbook to instil militarism in Japanese youths and children 佐藤美化天皇篡改历史为军国主义招魂千方百计利用教科书向日本青少年灌输军国主义的教育], 28 June 1969; 'Zuoteng zhengfu tuixing junguozhuyi jiaoyu pizhun chuban dierci shijie dazhanshi de xiaoxue jiaokeshu, bing jieli xiugai xianxing xiaoxue jiaokeshu' [Sato administration promote militarism education: authorise publication of the wartime primary school textbook and revise current primary school textbook 佐藤政府推行军国主义教育批准出版第二次世界大战时的小学教科书,并竭力修改现行小学教科书], 23 June 1970.

70 E.g. *Renmin Ribao*, 'Riben fandongpai wei erbaiwan "zhanwangzhe" zhaohun' [Japanese reactionaries call back the souls of 2 million war dead 日本反动派为二百万'战亡者'招魂], 14 January 1971; 'Riben fandongpai jinggei qiming jiaji zhanfan kai "zhuidaohui"' [Japanese reactionaries hold mourning ceremony for seven Japanese Class A war criminals 日本反动派竟给七名甲级战犯开'追悼会'], 11 June 1971.

71 E.g. *Renmin Ribao*, 'Riben fandongpai litu huifu "tianhuangzhi"' [Japanese reactionaries attempted to restore the Emperor 日本反动派力图恢复'天皇制'], 1 June 1971; 'Sandao youjifu yinhun busan' [Yukio Mishima's soul is still haunting 三岛由纪夫阴魂不散], 20 February 1971.

72 *Renmin Ribao*, 'Latiemoer shuo Meizhengfu suozuowei tong sanshiniandai Riben yiyang Meiguo zoushangle Riben junguozhuyi huimiede laolu' [Owen Lattimore said America government's current behaviour is similar to Japan's behaviour during the 1930s, America is walking along the Japanese militarists' old road of destruction 拉铁摩尔说美政府所作所为同三十年代日本一样美国走上了日本军国主义毁灭的老路], 14 April 1965; 'Faxisi zhouxin youxiang jiumeng chongwen Xidezongli tong Ribenshouxiang mitan' [Fascism axis countries want to revive an old dream, prime ministers of West Germany and Japan have a secret discussion 法西斯轴心又想旧梦重温西德总理同日本首相密谈], 25 May 1969; 'Ruguoshuiganyu bazhanzheng qiangjiazai Zhongguo renmin shenshang women jiuxiang xiaomie Riben diguozhuyi yiyang xiaomieta' [Whoever dares inflict a war upon the Chinese people, we will destroy as we destroyed the Japanese imperialists 如果谁敢于把战争强加在中国人民身上 我们就像消灭日本帝国主义一样消灭它], 22 September 1958.

73 E.g. *Renmin Ribao*, 'Ribendiguozhuyi cengjing zheyang qinlve Chaoxian' [Japanese imperialists invaded Korea like this 日本帝国主义曾经这样侵吞朝鲜], 23 June 1965; 'Riben diguozhuyi cengjing zenyang qinlve Jianpuzhai' [How Japanese imperialists invaded Cambodia 日本帝国主义曾经怎样侵略柬埔寨], 6 January 1966.

74 E.g. *Renmin Ribao*, 'Riben zhongxuesheng fandui Junguozhuyi jiaoyu' [Japanese middle school students oppose militarism education 日本中学生反对军国主义教育], 28 March 1969; 'Riben gedi qunzhong jihuishiwei xianshile Riben renmin de xinjuexing he fandui fuhuojunguozhuyi de jianqiang juexin' [Grassroots demonstrations were organised all over Japan, which showed Japanese people's new arousal and their determination against militarism resurgence 日本各地群众集会示威显示了日本人民的新觉醒和反对复活军国主义的坚强决心], 21 February 1972.

75 E.g. *Renmin Ribao*, 'Fandui Mei Ri fandongpai hanranxuanbu "zidongyanchang" Ri Mei "anquan tiaoyue" Riben yibai liushiwanren juxing daguimo jihui

shiwei' [Protesting against American and Japanese reactionarys' declaration to renew automatically the Japan–US security treaty, 1.6 million Japanese hold large-scale assemblies and demonstrations 反对美日反动派悍然宣布'自动延长'日美'安全条约' 日本一百六十万人举行大规模集会示威], 25 June 1970; Anonymous, 'Down with revived Japanese militarism', *China reconstructs*, 1970.

76 *Renmin Ribao*, 'Riben gejie qunzhong zai Dongjing juxing jihui juebuyunxu sanshisannianqian Riben junguozhuyi zhi zaode Lugouqiao shibian Chongyan' [Japanese masses hold an assembly in Tokyo, insisting that the Marco Polo Bridge Incident of 33 years ago is not allowed to happen again 日本各界群众在东京举行集会决不允许三十三年前日本军国主义制造的芦沟桥事变重演], 8 July 1970; 'Fandui junguozhuyi buxu "jiuyiba shibian" chongyan Dongjing xuesheng he shimin jihui shiwei' [Oppose militarism, September 18 Incident must not be allowed to happen again, students and residences hold assembly and demonstration in Tokyo 反对军国主义 不许'九一八事变'重演东京学生和市民集会示威], 20 September 1971.

77 An editorial titled in 'Dadao fuhuode Riben junguozhuyi -jinian Zhongguo renmin kang Ri zhanzheng shengli ershiwu zhounian' [Down with the resurgent Japanese militarism: commemorate the 25th anniversary of Chinese people's victory in the Anti-Japanese War 打倒复活的日本军国主义 - 纪念中国人民抗日战争胜利二十五周年], was carried in the front page as the lead story of *Renmin Ribao*, the PLA newspaper, and other local newspapers, like *Xin Nanjing Bao*, on 3 September 1970.

78 Mao and Zhou's public speeches about Japan decreased after the Sino–Japanese normalisation in 1972. In the early stage of the Deng Xiaoping administration, Deng paid great attention to Japan's economic miracle; although he mentioned PLA's success during the Anti-Japanese War in his speeches, which nevertheless were targeted at Chinese domestic audiences, see, Deng Xiaoping, *Dengxiaoping wenxuan* [Selected works of Deng Xiaoping] vol. 2 (Beijing: Renmin chubanshe, 1994) 邓小平, 邓小平文选 第二卷, (人民出版社, 1994).

79 E.g. when asked in May 1974 'are you believing the peace view advocated by the Japanese?' Mao answered that 'we believe it now, but in the future it's difficult to judge'. Mao Zedong waijiao wenxuan, pp. 606 in *Mao Zedong waijiao wenxuan* (1994).

80 *Xinhua Ribao*, 'Riben yixiaocuo fanhua shili youzai chundong' [A handful of Japanese anti-PRC forces carried out disruptive activities again 日本一小撮反华势力又在蠢动], 2 February 1974.

81 *Renmin Ribao*, 'Ri Zhong youxie fabiao shengming qianglie fandui fandongde "Jingguoshenshe faan"' [Japan–China friendship association made a statement to strongly protest against the reactionary Yasukuni Shrine Bill 日中友协发表声明强烈反对反动的'靖国神社法案'], 26 April 1974; 'Riben zhongyuan qiangxing tongguo fandong de "Jingguoshenshe fa an"' [Japanese House of Representatives coercively passed the Bill of Yasukuni Shrine 日本众院强行通过反动的'靖国神社法案'], 27 May 1974.

82 Zhonghua renmin gongheguo waijiaobu and Zhonggong zhongyang wenxian yanjiushi, *Zhou Enlai waijiao wenxuan* [selected diplomatic works of Zhou Enlai] (Zhongyangwenxian chubanshe, 1990), p. 44. 中华人民共和国外交部 中共中央文献研究室, 周恩来外交文选 (中央文献出版社, 1990). This statement used a friendly tone towards kind and peace-loving Japanese people as always.

83 *Zhou Enlai Waijiao Wenxuan* (1990), p. 40.

84 I checked the talks of Mao and Zhou, which were included in *Mao Zedong Waijiao Wenxuan (1994)* and *Zhou Enlai Waijiao Wenxuan (1990)*. I found four entries all together. Three of them were given in 1954 and 1955.

85 Pages 87–88 in *Zhou Enlai Waijiao Wenxuan (1990)*.

86   See memoir of Li Fushan, the chief prosecutor of Shenyang military tribunal, Li Fushan, 'Wocanyu zhenxun Riben zhanfan shimo' [The story of how I participated in investigating and interrogating Japanese war crimals], *Dangshi bolan*, 2008: http://dangshi.people.com.cn/GB/85039/12826451.html, date accessed, 16 March 2014 李甫山, 我参与侦讯日本战犯始末, 党史博览, 2008.

87   Anonymous, 'Human Leniency', *China Pictorial*, 1956.

88   See memoir of a reporter covering the Taiyuan Military Tribunal: Ma Ming, 'Taiyuan shenpan Riben zhanfan baodaode huiyi' [Memoir about reporting on the Taiyuan military tribunal], *Xinwen caibian*, 1966, 43–44 马明, 太原审判日本战犯报道的回忆, 新闻采编, 1966, 43–44.

89   See, for example, *Renmin Ribao*, 'Beishifangde Riben zhanzheng fanzuifenzi zai Tianjin kang Ri lieshijinianguan lingtang qian chanhui' [The released Japanese war criminals show repentance in the memorial for the martyrs of Anti-Japanese War, Tianjin 被释放的日本战争犯罪分子在天津抗日烈士纪念馆烈士灵堂前悔罪], 24 June 1956; 'Beishifangde Riben zhanzheng fanzui fenzi huiguohou xielai ganxiexin' [The released Japanese war criminals send thanksgiving letter after returning home 被释放的日本战争犯罪分子回国后写来感谢信], 1 August 1956.

90   Kosuge, *Sengo wakai*, p. 178.

91   For this translation of Zhou's toast, see, Anonymous, 'Premier Chou's toast', *China Reconstructs*, 1972, p. 8.

92   See Mao's talk of 11 December 1954, in *Mao Zedong Waijiao Wenxuan,* pp. 192 and 194.

93   *Yomiuri Shinbun*, 'Senso Shazai, Socchoku'; Wu Xuewen, *Ribenwai jiaoguiji* [The trajectory of Japanese diplomacy] (Beijing: Shishichubanshe, 1990) 吴学文, 日本外交轨迹 (时事出版社, 1990). For Zhou's speech, see: Zhang, *Xinzhongguo yu Riben*, p. 121. Chinese leaders did not avoid the war memorial dates when they planed meetings with Japanese visitors, see, for example, *Renmin Ribao*, 'Liao Chengzhi jiejian Riben keren' [Liao Chengzhi meets Japanese guests 廖承志接见日本客人], 15 August 1964; 'Wang Kuang yanqing Riben chuban yinshua daibiaotuan' [Wang Kuang holds banquet for the Japanese publication and print delegation 王匡宴请日本出版印刷代表团], 7 July 1977; 'Zhu Muzhi yanqing Riben gongtong tongxunshe bianji juzhang' [Zhu Muzhi at banquet with the head of the editing bureau of Japan Kyodo News 朱穆之宴请日本共同通讯社编辑局长], 3 September 1975.

94   A similar episode, see: 'Zhongguo renmin gongheguo waijiaobu fayanren guanyu Riben zhengfu tichu suowei chetui liuzai woguodalude Ribenren wenti shengming' [Chinese MFA spokesperson's statement about Japanese government's request of repatriating Japanese nationals remaining in mainland China 中华人民共和国外交部发言人关于日本政府提出所谓撤退留在我国大陆的日本人问题的声明], in *Riben wenti wenjian huibian (1958)*, p. 8.

95   Zhang Xiangshan, 'Zhong Ri fujiao tanpanhuigu' [Review the negotiations on Sino–Japanese normalisation] *Riben xuekan*, 1998, p. 37: http://xuewen.cnki.net/CJFD-REED801.001.html, date accessed, 16 March 2014 张香山, 中日复交谈判回顾, 日本学刊, 1998.

96   For Prime Minister Tanaka's toast in Japanese, see, Ikei Masaru, *Nihon gaikoushi gaisetsu* [An outline of Japanese diplomatic history] (Tokyo: Keiou gijyukudaigaku shuppankai, 2002) 池井優, 日本外交史概説 (慶応義塾大学出版会, 2002).

97   See the memoirs of the cadres who were in the dinner party, as in Ji Pengfei, 'Yinshui buwangjuejinren' [Don't forget the well-diggers when you drink from this well] in An jianshe (ed.), *Zhou enlai zuihoudesuiyue* [Last days of Zhou Enlai] (Beijing: Zhongyangwenxian chubanshe, 1995, p. 289) 姬鹏飞, 饮水不忘掘井人, 安建设(ed.) 周恩来最后的岁月(北京, 中央文献出版社, 1995). Also see, NHK Shuzaihan, *Shuu Onlai no ketsudan* [Zhou Enlai's determination] (Tokyo:

Nihon Housou Kyokai, 1993), p. 149 NHK 取材班,周恩来の決断 (日本放送協会, 1993).

98 Zhang, 'Zhong Ri fujiao tanpan'.

99 See, 'Joint Communique of the Government of Japan and the Government of the People's Republic of China'.

100 'Lun Zhong Riguanxi (30 October 1953)' [About the Sino–Japanese relationship 论中日关系] in *Riben wenti wenjian huiban (1955)*.

101 'Zhou Enlai jiejian Riben qianshouxiang Shiqiao Zhansan (9 October 1963)' [Zhou Enlai receives Japanese former prime minister Ishibashi Tanzan 周恩来接见日本前首相石桥湛三] in *Zhou Enlai waijiao wenxuan (1990)*, p. 340.

102 Sun Pinghua, *Zhong Ri youhao suixiangu* [Memoirs of Sino–Japanese friendship] (Shenyang: Liaoningrenmin chubanshe, 2009), p. 8 孙平化, 中日友好随想录 (辽宁人民出版社, 2009); Wu Xuewen, *Fengyuyinqing wosuo jinglide Zhong Ri guanxi* [Sino–Japanese relationship I experienced] (Beijing: Shijiezhishi chubanshe, 2002) 吴学文, 风雨阴晴 我所经历的中日关系 (世界知识出版社, 2002).

103 Page 415 in *Zhou Enlai Waijiao Wenxuan (1990)*. An incident involving a Japanese flag that was damaged due to rain was reported in Japanese media, e.g. *Asahi Shinbun,* 'Pekinno Nihon Shouhin Mihonichi' [Beijing's Japanese trade fair 北京の日本商品見本市], 8 October 1956.

104 Cai Chengxi, 'Hongdong Beijingde diyici Riben shangpin zhanlanhui' [The first sensational Japanese merchandise exhibition in Beijing], *Zonghen*, 2002, 38–41 蔡成喜, 轰动北京的第一次日本商品展览会, 纵横, 2002, 28–41.

105 Senjin Zhuangnei, 'Renmin shizenyang duidai taiyangqide', in Baigenzilang (ed.) and Fang Guizhi (trans.), *Zhanhou Ri Zhong maoyishi* (Liaoning Renmin chubanshe, 1988), 52–55 森井庄内 人们是怎样对待太阳旗的, 白根滋郎 and 方桂芝 [译], 战后日中贸易史 (辽宁人民出版社, 1988)

106 Cai Chengxi, 'Hongdong Beijingde Diyici Riben', and Sun Pinghua, *Zhong Ri youhao suixianglu*, p. 36.

107 Liu, *Zhanhou Zhong Ri guanxi*; Gao Fanfu 高凡夫, 'Bunengyong ganqing daiti zhengce – Zhong Ri fujiaoqian Zhongguo zhengfu duiminzhongde shuifu jiaoyu' [Chinese government persuades and educates Chinese people before Sino–Japanese normalisation 不能用感情代替政策 – 中日复交前中国政府对民众的说服教育]. www.iccs.cn/contents/610/13339_3.html, 31 October 2012, date accessed, 16 March 2014.

108 For instance, Zhou met a Japanese delegation on 27 June 1956, which had come to China to discuss the issue of repatriating Japanese POWs. He said China had to sentence forty-five war criminals who had committed serious crimes, since 'we cannot face our people if we don't do this', see: Zhonggong zhongyang wenxian yanjiushi, *Zhou enlai nianpu (1949–1976)* [Chronicle of Zhou Enlai's life] (Beijing: Zhongyangwenxian chubanshe, 2007) 中共中央文献研究室, 周恩来年谱 (1949–1976) (中央文献出版社, 2007), p. 593.

109 Wang Junyan, *Zhong Ri guanxi juejingren: ji sishiwuwei Zhong Ri youhaode xianqu* [Well-diggers of Sino–Japanese relationship: forty-five forerunners of Sino–Japanese friendship] (Beijing: Shijiezhishi chubanshe, 2010), p. 66 王俊彦, 中日关系掘井人:记45位中日友好的先驱 (世界知识出版社, 2010).

110 Zhang, *Xin Zhongguo yu Riben waijiao*, p. 28.

111 Anonymous, 'Sanshinian,youyide jianzheng – Hangzhou Qifu youhao sanshi zhounian' [30 years, witness of frierndship – Hangzhou and Gifu establish friendship for 30 years 30年,友谊的见证 – 杭州岐阜缔结友好30周年]. http://z.hangzhou.com.cn/09yhszfh/content/2009-10/14/content_2825432.htm, 14 October 2009, date accessed, 8 March 2014.

112 Japan brought around 1,000 Chinese captives and farmers to the town of Hanaoka in northern Japan as forced labour. These forced labourers rose up in

June 1945, and in the crackdown around half of them were killed by the Japanese.

113   *Xinhua Ribao,* 'Dongjing Huaqiao minbao jielu Riben fandongpai touxiangqianxi cengsha woguo shibing gongren' [Tokyo Huaqiao Minbao revealed that Japanese reactionaries killed Chinese soldiers and works before its surrender 东京华侨民报揭露 日本反动派投降前夕曾残杀我国士兵工人], 14 April 1950; 'Wobei qiuzai Riben zuo kugong' [I was taken prisoner as forced labour 我被囚在日本做苦工], 18 April 1950.

114   'Zhongyang renminzhengfu jiuyouguan Riben zai Zhongguo de Riben qiaominde gexiangwenti daxinhua jizhewen (1 December 1952)' [Chinese government answered questions from journalists of Xinhua news agency about Japanese nationals in China 中央人民政府有关方面就在中国的日本侨民的各项问题答新华记者问] in *Riben Wenti Wenjian Huibian (1955)*; Zhang, *Xin Zhongguo yu Riben.*

115   *Xinhua Ribao,* 'Riben gongchandang fabiao shengming chize Jitianzhengfu guyi zurao huaqiao huiguo yinmou' [Japanese Communist Party makes a statement, accuses Yoshida government of hindering Chinese nationals from returning to China 日本共产党发表声明 斥责吉田政府故意阻挠华侨回国的阴谋], 10 June 1953; 'Ziliao: Huagang canan' [Information: Hanaoka Massacre 资料:花冈惨案], 30 June 1953.

116   *Renmin Ribao,* 'Riben junguo zhuyizhede taotian zuixing – "Huagang canan"' [The atrocity of Japanese military – 'Hanaoka Massacre' 日本军国主义者的滔天罪行 – 花冈惨案], 8 July 1953; 'Woguo xishengzai Ribende kang Ri lieshi yigu yunhui zuguo' [The remains of martyrs sacrificed in Japan had been carried back to the motherland], 8 July 1953 我国牺牲在日本的抗日烈士遗骨运回祖国 ; 'Gejie daibiao liangqian duorenzai Tianjin longzhong juxing zhuidao woguo xisheng zai Ribende kang Ri lieshi' [Around 2,000 representatives from various field held a memorial ceremony for the martyrs sacrificed in Japan 各界代表两千多人在天津隆重举行大会追悼我国牺牲在日本的抗日烈士], 9 July 1953.

117   *Renmin Ribao,* 'Riben liangyouhao tuanti zuzhi Huagang canan diaocha gejierenshi fennu kongsu Riben diguozhuyi de canbao zuixing' [Two Japanese friendly groups investigate Hanaoka Massacre, people from various fields accuse Japanese imperialists of atrocities 日本两友好团体组织花冈惨案调查各界人士愤怒控诉日本帝国主义的残暴罪行], 12 November 1970.

118   *Renmin Ribao,* 'Riben 'Huagang wuyu' banhua yuanmuban shierfude' [The original Japanese woodblock of 'Hanaoka Story' is found again 日本《花冈物语》版画原木版失而复得], 20 February 1981; Anonymous, 'Jinrui no yisan,mokuchou rensaku hanga "Hanaoka monogatari"' [Human beings' legacy, woodblock produced in collaboration, 'Hanaoka story'. 人類の遺産 木彫連作版画「花冈ものがたり]. www.inori-ha.com/tuiki1_10.htm, date unknown, date accessed, 9 March 2014.

119   Note: since the rally occurred during the Great Leap Forward period, the report that about 400,000 citizens showed up to the rally on 13 May 1960 might be an exaggeration.

120   Niu argues the PRC's diplomacy was directly evolved from the CCP's diplomatic conduct during the 'revolutionary years' before October 1949. Niu Jun, *Zhonghua renmin gongheguo duiwai guanxi shigailun (1949–2000)* [An introduction to PRC's international relations] (Beijing: Beijingdaxue chubanshe, 2010) 牛军, 中华人民共和国对外关系史概论(1949–2000) (北京大学出版社, 2010).

121   This part is largely based on Liu, *Zhanhou Zhong Ri guanxi*'s excellent analysis about the CCP's idea of 'Japanese people', how the Chinese people's image of the Japanese was shaped by their experience of fighting with Japan since the first Sino–Japanese War, and the continuity of history.

122   Liu, *Zhanhou Zhong Ri guanxi*, p. 49.

123 'Zai Yanan fanqinlve dahuishang deyanshuo' [Speech to the anti-invasion assembly in Yanan 在延安反侵略大会上的演说], 21 January 1938, in *Mao Zedong Waijiao wenxuan*; Liu, *Zhanhou Zhong Ri guanxi*, pp. 36–49.

124 Liu, *Zhanhou Zhong Ri guanxi*.

125 See, Mao Zedong's conversation with Japanese delegates: 'Zhong Ri guanxi heshijie dazhan wenti' (15 October 1955)' [Sino–Japanese relations and the issues about world war 中日关系和世界大战问题] and 'Riben renmin douzhengde yingxiang shishenyuande (24 Jan 1955)' [The impact of Japanese people's struggle is profound 日本人民斗争的影响是深远的], in *Mao Zedong waijiao wenxuan*.

126 'Meidiguozhuyi shi Zhong Ri liang guo renminde gongtongde diren (21 June 1960)' [American imperialism is the common enemy of Chinese and Japanese people 美帝国主义是中日两国人民的共同敌人], in *Mao Zedong waijiao*, p. 438.

127 'Zhong Ri guanxi heshijie dazhan wenti', p. 226.

128 Huang Tzu-chin, 'Chiang Kai-shek in East Asia: the origins of the policy of magnanimity toward Japan after World War II', *Journal of the Institute of Modern History*, Academia Sinica, 45 (2004), 143–194 黃自進 抗戰結束前後蔣介石對日態度 「以德報怨」真相的探討 中央研究院近代史研究所集刊, 45 (2004), 143–194.

129 Kosuge, *Sengo wakai*.

130 Prasenjit Duara, 'Nationalism in East Asia', *History Compass*, 4 (2006), 407–427.

131 James Mark, 'Socialism goes global: the shaping of a new transnational culture in Hungary, 1956–75', research seminar talk, University of Bristol, 1 October 2013.

132 Anonymous, 'Premier Chou's toast', p. 8.

3 The necessity of commemorating the war

Honouring the martyrs

Honouring a KMT pilot killed in action

The CCP regime issued hundreds of thousands of 'Glorious Certificates to the Sacrificed Revolutionary Military Personnel's Dependents' (*Gemin xisheng junren jiashu guangrong jinianzheng* 革命牺牲军人家属光荣纪念证). For the martyrs' bereaved families, these certificates were not only spiritual consolations but also functional documents with which one could claim benefits from the state. According to a certificate counterfoil preserved in the Nanjing municipal archives, in 1952 a certificate was issued to the family of a former KMT airman who died at the very young age of 21, in an air battle during the War of Resistance against Japanese aggression. This case is of particular interest and relevance for this chapter and I will tell the story from the very beginning.[1]

In 1915, Ba Shijie 巴士杰, who grew up in a landowning family in old Manchuria (Bao county, Jilin Province), graduated from a prestigious university in Nanjing. Two years later, a baby son was born to Shijie and was given the name Qingzheng 清正, meaning 'pure and upright'. Qingzheng received primary as well as secondary education in Manchuria up until the time of the September 18th Incident in 1931. The whole Ba family had to flee for safety and gradually resettled in Beijing. Shijie became a businessman and Qingzheng entered the private Zhixing Middle School.[2] In June 1933, Qingzheng was admitted to the Military Academy of the Republic of China (ROC) and joined the KMT with the cadets in the same year.[3] In 1934, Qingzheng was recommended for admission to the ROC's Air Force Academy. After graduating in October 1936, he joined the ROC Air Force in the 22nd Squadron, 4th Group, as a second lieutenant. Qingzheng soon got the chance to prove that he was as competent on the battlefield as he was in school.

On 13 August 1937, the Battle of Shanghai began – probably the largest and bloodiest battle of the entire War of Resistance. The next day, the Japanese Air Force started to bombard the airports in Nanjing and other big cities. At 2 o'clock that afternoon, the 4th Group of the ROC Air Force, to which Qingzheng belonged, started to return fire in the sky above Jian Bridge 笕桥, Hangzhou. The group suffered zero casualties and shot down six

Japanese aircraft, an achievement which was glorified by the ROC government and portrayed as the 'Great Victory of August 14th Air Battle'. Furthermore, in 1940 the ROC government declared August 14th the ROC Air Force Festival, in commemoration of this victory.[4] Qingzheng contributed to this military success by shooting down one Japanese aircraft. As the war between China and Japan went on, his personal 'military success' accumulated. He shot down a Japanese aircraft above the Huangpu River in Shanghai and another above Nanjing, on 2 September and 6 September 1937, respectively.

However, Qingzheng's young life was ended just five months later. Japan launched an air strike at noon on 18 February 1938, which preceded the Battle of Wuhan, another major engagement fought between the ROC army and the Japanese army.[5] The awaiting Chinese Air Force and Soviet Volunteer Group repelled the Japanese attack with all their strength.[6] In a fierce battle, twelve Japanese aircraft were shot down. The Wuhan citizens were 'elated in spirits and rapt with excitement' and went to the sites where Japanese aircraft had crashed.[7] Some of them even waded into the water to collect the fragments of these aircraft as mementoes of the battle. Nevertheless, the Chinese side also lost seven aircraft. The legendary commander of the 4th Group, Li Guidan 李桂丹, and four other pilots were killed in this battle. Qingzheng was one of the casualties.

A mourning ceremony for the fallen airmen was hosted by Chiang Kai-Shek on 20 February in Hankou's Chamber of Commerce. The next day, a large-scale mass ceremony was held in Wuhan to celebrate this victory and to grieve for the Air Force martyrs. Some senior KMT officials, such as Kong Xiangxi and Feng Yuxiang, participated in the ceremony. Furthermore, representatives of the CCP's Eight Army, such as Wang Ming and Zhou Enlai, also participated. Around 20,000 citizens took part in the funeral procession after the ceremony.[8] Ba Qingzheng, as a participant of the sacred martyrdom of the ROC Air Force, has been glorified since then. The ROC government awarded him a Medal of One Star, and retroactively conferred on him the status of lieutenant.[9] Although compared to other legendary Air Force martyrs such as Captain Li Guidan, Qingzheng is far less well known, there are places where the deeds of this ordinary pilot are commemorated. For example, after the end of the war, Qingzheng, together with other fallen airmen, was re-buried in the Air Force Martyrs' Cemetery in Nanjing.[10] Visitors can read his name and brief biography at the cemetery. His deeds are also recorded by certain veterans' organisations (mainly in Taiwan) and alumni associations of the schools/academies he attended.

Ba Qingzheng's life ended when he was 21 years old; however, the lives of his family members had to continue. When Qingzheng's belongings were being sorted, an unsent letter to his friend was found, dated 16 February (two days before his death). It revealed that, as a soldier fighting on the front line, the only thing Qingzheng was concerned about was not his own life and death, but his family's well-being:

Life inevitably dies away, just a matter of time; sacrifice is inevitable in the war, also just a matter of time. I entered the military academy at 16 years old, it has been six years up until now, every morning and night, I practise combat skills and the aim is to kill the enemy; this time [the mission on 18 February] is a good chance, even if I die I will feel no regret. However, as the only son of my family, I am worried that there will be no one to take care of my parents. Nevertheless, people without blood ties can be siblings as well. I admire you as my brother and never thought of you as an outsider. If I had an accident in the future, could you please take care of them, in consideration of our friendship?[11]

The Ba family was probably also in Wuhan when Qingzheng was killed in action, since they had started another epic journey to flee to safety as more and more Chinese territory fell into Japanese hands. They resettled in Wuhan in November 1937 (they had settled in other cities before Wuhan, including Shanghai and Hangzhou). It is unknown how sad or proud the Ba family felt when they learned the news that their only son had sacrificed his life on the battlefield. It is also unclear whether or not Qingzheng's friend took care of Qingzheng's family as requested. The ROC government issued a Certificate of Consolation for the Dead 恤亡给与令 and started to provide material support to the Ba family from 1940 onwards. Although the KMT's material support (seven decalitres of rice per month) was very slender, after losing their only son, it was the only stable income the Ba family had in the tumultuous years during and after the War of the Resistance. After Wuhan had fallen, the whole family fled to Kunming, where Ba Shijie worked as a manager in a friend's book-printing house. However, Kunming was bombed in 1941 and Shijie had to make money by running a small store.

In August 1946, the Ba family resettled in Nanjing and in 1947 Shijie was offered a job in the Division of Population of the Ministry of the Interior of the KMT. The KMT's material support ceased in January 1949 when the KMT regime approached its demise on mainland China.

After the Communists entered Nanjing, Ba Shijie helped them with the takeover, but was soon ousted. Shijie resumed running a small store to earn a living. In June 1950, Shijie was around 57 years old, his wife was around 59 and they had a 12-year-old grandson who attended a school in Nanjing. This vulnerable and bereaved family was reliant on the income from the store so Shijie decided to petition the CCP government in Nanjing for monetary support. In the letter, he explained the amount of the material support he used to get from the KMT regime. He then wrote: 'the People's Government is looking after the livelihood of the martyrs' dependents extremely well ... I hope the government can empathise with us, and commiserate the bereaved old parents and orphan of the martyr, and give relief to us every month'. To justify his request Shijie also wrote in detail about the 'meritorious service and accomplishment' of his son, and how he 'gloriously sacrificed himself for the country' in the skies over Wuhan during the initial stage of the War of

Resistance.[12] Nevertheless, Shijie's first petition was unsuccessful. The explanation given by the Nanjing Municipal Bureau of Civil Affairs (NMBCA) was that there was no standard policy and procedure for dealing with Ba's situation at the time.

One year later, in November 1951, Shijie made another attempt, this time with more preparation – for instance, he enclosed relevant certificates (for example, Qingzheng's diploma and the KMT regime's Certificate of Consolation for the Dead).[13] This time he was more successful, mainly thanks to two newly promulgated rules. The PRC's Ministry of Internal Affairs (PRCMIA) made it clear that soldiers of the KMT killed in action against the Japanese should be given the title of Revolutionary Martyr, as stated in an announcement titled 'Several Explanations about the Revolutionary Martyrs', published in the 'Readers' questions' column in *Renmin Ribao* on 15 October 1950:

> From 1937 to 1945, the soldiers of the Eighth Army, the New Fourth Army as well as other people's anti-Japanese armies, who sacrificed by participating in the War of Resistance against Japanese aggression, and the soldiers of the KMT (including the Air Force) who were indeed killed in actions against the Japanese [can be called Revolutionary Martyrs].[14]

On 15 November 1951, the Ministry of Civil Affairs of the East China Military Government Committee (ECMGC, which the majority of Jiangsu Province was administered by) issued an internal document stipulating detailed requirements and procedures as to how to deal with the dependents of KMT anti-Japanese martyrs:

> If it was provable that an ex-KMT soldier indeed sacrificed for the War of Resistance and had not shown any reactionary behaviour in his life, after being generally acknowledged by the masses and approved by the provincial-level (or above) government, a Certificate to the Revolutionary Martyrs' Dependents can be issued to [the soldiers' dependents].[15]

Following the guidance and instructions provided in these two documents, the NMBCA started an investigation into Ba Qingzheng's case. They made a preliminary judgement that Ba Qingzheng had indeed been sacrificed in action against the Japanese and that he died too young to have shown reactionary behaviour based on the documents submitted by his father. Furthermore, the bureau also sent a cadre to the Ba family, who came to the same judgement that what Shijie claimed was true. The cadre did not interview Ba's neighbours about the issue, but was told by the Ba family that Qingzheng's deed was well known in the neighbourhood.[16] The NMBCA then made a decision that a 'Glorious Certificate to the Revolutionary Martyrs' Dependents' should be issued to the Ba family and they submitted a report for approval by the higher authorities on 7 December 1951.[17] The report was directed to the Nanjing Municipal Political and Law Committee (NMPLC) 南京市政法委会, who informed the NMBCA by phone that unless the neighbourhood of the Ba family had been properly consulted, they could not approve the case.[18]

The NMBCA therefore invited the Ba family's neighbours, some of the martyrs' dependents and other relevant people to attend a meeting to discuss Qingzheng's case on 26 December 1951. All of the meeting participants agreed that Qingzheng had sacrificed his life for the War of Resistance: nevertheless, they were concerned about two issues. The first issue related to the personal history of Shijie, which was raised by a representative from the Public Security Bureau in Daguang Street (where the Ba family was dwelling). It was revealed that before the war, Shijie worked as the president of a business association in Shanghai and participated in some reactionary organisations. Shijie denied the revelation and the participants decided to investigate this issue further after the meeting. The second issue related to Qingzheng's identity as a KMT member. One participant, who was a fellow townsman and good friend of Qingzheng, told others very affirmatively that Qingzheng did not do anything harmful to the people. Other participants also thought Qingzheng had not carried out any actions that were deemed harmful to the Chinese people, as he was only 21 when he perished. Still, they were sceptical, and thought that Qingzheng may have harboured thoughts that were deemed harmful to the Chinese people, and that although Qingzheng had sacrificed himself during the war, his ultimate purpose was to protect Chiang Kai-Shek's empire as a member of the KMT's Air Force. Finally, the participants agreed that because he perished when the Chinese were united under the National United Front of Resisting Japan, and he made a contribution to the country, he should be given the title of Martyr and his family should be taken care of by the neighbourhood – nevertheless, they should not be treated preferably as a martyr's family.

Fortunately for Shijie, the cadres in the NMBCA did not make a decision based solely on the opinions of the meeting participants. In the report for the NMPLC on 8 January 1952, they stated their opinion and the solution that Qingzheng should be given the title of Martyr and the Ba family should be treated preferably as a martyr's family, in accordance with the purpose of the National United Front and relevant policies. The NMPLC favoured the bureau's solution and soon approved it.[19] On 16 January 1952, Shijie finally received a confirmation letter from the NMBCA that his request had been approved.

* * *

By retroactively awarding the title of Martyr to Ba Qingzheng and taking care of his family, the PRC government showed one rationale for the state-sponsored Fifteen-Year-War remembrance activities: there were moral and pragmatic considerations to be taken into account that meant the state had to commemorate the war for the sake of the fighters who had sacrificed their lives. It was not convenient for the CCP regime to remember the Fifteen-Year War, as the KMT force played an important role in the conflict. However, the war had to be remembered, and the KMT's contribution to the war had to be acknowledged to some extent by the PRC. The political significance of soldiers who were killed in the war and their bereaved families was one of the reasons for this: morally, honouring martyrs was necessary as any attempt to ignore or discredit the sacred martyrdom risked inviting popular discontent; pragmatically, honouring martyrs is also necessary for any state that is currently participating in a conflict, or has recently emerged from one.[20] For the CCP regime, which had recently emerged from two major conflicts (the Fifteen-Year War and the Chinese Civil War), and had been affected by the reality or possibility of wars during the Cold War era (e.g. the Korean War and an envisioned third world war), dealing with martyrs properly was an even more pressing matter compared to other countries which enjoyed peaceful environments during the same period.

In contemporary China, honouring martyrdom in the Fifteen-Year War (and martyrdom in general) involved two different yet interacting activities: honouring (*baoyang* 褒扬) the martyrs, and giving preferential treatment, consolation and compensation to the bereaved families (*youdai fuxu* 优待抚恤). The *baoxu* (an abbreviation of *baoyang* and *youdaifuxu*) activities carried out for the Fifteen-Year-War martyrs also simultaneously helped people remember the Fifteen-Year War. Although there were different methods of honouring the martyrs by the state, and these honours varied in scale – as humble as a martyr's certificate and as rare as a state funeral in a grand martyrs' cemetery park – the aim was to make people remember their sacrifice. Inevitably, generalisations – like the idea that they sacrificed their lives to save the country from the invading Japanese – and detailed information – like the particular battles in which they fell – had to be lodged in people's minds as well. The action of giving mental and material support to the martyrs' families also contributed to the remembrance of the war. First, one of the aims of this action was to enhance the social status of the martyrs' dependents. Feeling symbolically superior, the bereaved families would talk about the martyrs' experiences in their communities or in public assemblies. Second, their status as Martyrs' Dependents would bring some material benefits. Thus, for people who claimed the title of Martyrs' Dependents and the cadres who adjudicated on those claims, the deeds of the martyrs had to be made as public as possible.[21]

What the Ba family case shows in its entirety is these two interlocking necessities: of honouring the Fifteen-Year-War martyrs, and therefore of remembering the Fifteen-Year War for both the KMT and CCP regimes. Regardless of the hurdles faced by the KMT during and after the turmoil of the war, Qingzheng had to be mourned and his bereaved family had to be supported properly by the KMT regime. Furthermore, regardless of the political inconvenience, the CCP regime was also obliged to give similar treatment to the Ba family after 1949. At the same time, the battle in which Qingzheng died was remembered through the official mourning for him and through his family's efforts to secure compensation from the state. The remainder of this chapter will explore these two necessities and their interlocking nature by exploring the panorama of honouring the Fifteen-Year-War martyrs (of both the KMT and the CCP) in mainland China. The second section discusses the prehistory of the PRC's *baoxu* activities for the Fifteen-Year-War martyrs (1931–1945), and the third section explores the activities during the first seventeen-year period of the PRC (1949–1966).[22] *Baoxu* activities during the Cultural Revolution period and thereafter will be briefly dealt with in the final section. The whole of Jiangsu Province will be used as a case study.

Prehistory of the PRC's *baoxu* activities for the Fifteen-Year-War martyrs

The PRC's *baoxu* activities for the Fifteen-Year-War martyrs were a continuation of the pre-1949 practices. In Republican China, the *baoxu* activities were normally carried out soon after the soldier was killed in action by different factions in their controlled areas (e.g. the KMT-controlled southwest China and the various CCP-controlled bases).[23] So, when they took over from the KMT regime in 1949, the CCP inherited many commemorative facilities in regard to the KMT's Fifteen-Year-War martyrs, as well as a large number of the families of these martyrs who requested symbolic as well as material support. Moreover, one can observe that in the PRC, there were many legacies of the CCP regimes' *baoxu* practices in various bases of the party during and after the War of Resistance. Thus, to understand the PRC's practice of honouring the Fifteen-Year-War martyrs, it is necessary to know how these martyrs were treated during the period between 1931 and 1949 in both the KMT- and the CCP-controlled areas.

Generally, the systems of the KMT and the CCP's *baoxu* activities were indistinguishable. At the centre of the two parties' *baoxu* systems during this period were the relevant organs of administration and a series of laws and regulations which had developed along with the inception of the KMT and CCP armies. According to these laws and regulations, the martyrs themselves were praised and were the subject of propaganda by the KMT and CCP regimes. The methods normally involved holding memorial ceremonies on memorial days (as well as on normal days), writing the martyrs' biographies and constructing martyrs' memorials throughout the country during and after the Fifteen-Year War. Martyrs' memorials, such as the martyrs' tombs/cemetery parks, commemorative *ta* (塔 pagoda or monument), pavilions and halls, were always at the centre of the practices honouring martyrs. This was not only because the scale of these memorials required greater commitment from the government, in terms of manpower, materials and other administrative support, but also because the memorial ceremonies took place at, and the martyrs' biographies were always preserved in, the martyrs' memorials. Also, according to these laws and regulations, the martyrs' families were given certain kinds of material support. In addition, the bereaved families could also receive symbolic support: for example, being awarded martyr certificates and being honoured at various festivals.[24]

But despite the general similarities, there were some distinctions and differences in the details of the KMT's and the CCP's *baoxu* activities. The following section will discuss this history in the KMT and the CCP-controlled areas prior to the establishment of the PRC.

The KMT government's practices

Between the September 18th Incident in 1931 and the Marco Polo Bridge Incident in 1937, soldiers killed in action against the Japanese army were well commemorated by the KMT government. For example, soldiers killed in the Shanghai Incident (18 January 1932) were enshrined in the Grand Cemetery for National Revolution Army Soldiers Killed in Action (Guomin geminjun zhenwang jiangshi gongmu 国民革命军阵亡将士公墓), which was located on the site of the former Lingu Temple, on the southeastern side of the Purple Mountain, Nanjing.[25] Constructed between 1929 and 1933, the main buildings of the cemetery, arranged along the south–north axis, were a main gate, an archway, a mourning hall, three graves, a memorial hall (where the martyrs' mementoes were displayed and exhibitions were held), and a monument. Two monuments to the soldiers of the 5th Corps and 19th Corps of the National Revolution Army killed in the Shanghai Incident were erected in front of the three cemeteries. Seventy-eight soldiers from the two corps who died in Suzhou were also properly buried in the same area and two cenotaphs were built for them.[26] Also, the airmen who died in the same incident were enshrined in the Air Force Martyrs' Cemetery (Hangkong lieshi gongmu 航空烈士公墓), which is where Ba Qingzheng is buried.[27] As the conflict with the Japanese army heightened, more and more military personnel were killed and enshrined in these three cemeteries and elsewhere. The KMT government also adopted some measures for taking care of the martyrs' families. For example, on 16 October 1934 it promulgated a 'Regulation for Giving Soldiers Consolation and Compensation in Peace and War Time 陆军平战时抚恤暂行条例', which stipulated that the families of soldiers killed in the war could receive a one-off compensation and annual allowance of an amount concomitant with the soldiers' military rank.[28]

After full-scale war between China and Japan broke out in 1937, the outlook of the area which was under the administration of what is now Jiangsu Province had changed completely. The Japanese puppet regime gradually seized control of Nanjing as well as the main traffic arteries, cities and big towns in Jiangsu. The KMT had to retreat to a few counties on the edge of the province. The CCP's forces also started to penetrate the area – a development that will be discussed in greater detail later.[29] Despite the constant military retreats and financial hardships due to the war, to inspire the morale of its soldiers and to steady the rearward area under its control, the KMT government gave even more weight to *baoxu* activities.[30] Many memorials to soldiers killed in action were destroyed by the Japanese army in the areas it occupied, such as the Air Force Martyrs' Cemetery. Nevertheless, more martyrs' memorials were constructed throughout the KMT-controlled areas. For example, a martyrs' shrine was built in Hunan Province in 1941 to commemorate the soldiers killed in the Ninth war theatre. In terms of the martyrs' families, the KMT regime set up a special committee directly under the Military Committee to deal with activities related to their consolation and compensation.[31]

In the immediate post-war phase, *baoxu* activities were among the top priorities of the KMT government, as reflected in its leaders' speeches and in practice.[32] After returning to its capital Nanjing, it made several moves to commemorate the soldiers killed in the War of Resistance. On 5 May 1946, it held a 'Ceremony for Celebrating the Nationalist Government's Return to the Capital and Commemorating the Government's Foundation' in Purple Mountain. During the ceremony a three-minute silence was observed for soldiers and ordinary people killed in the War of Resistance.[33] Moreover, the old martyrs' cemeteries in Nanjing were revived and played a major role in the commemorative activities for soldiers killed in the War of Resistance. Many martyrs' remains buried throughout the country were re-interred in these cemeteries and state funerals were held for them. For instance, the coffins of Chinese and foreign Air Force martyrs buried in places like Hangzhou, Shanghai and Wuhan after 1937 were re-buried in the Air Force Martyrs' Cemetery between 1946 and 1948.[34] The KMT government held a public mourning ceremony for the fallen airmen in late March 1946. Furthermore, it stipulated that a spring rite (March 29) and autumn rite (September 3) would be held every year for these martyrs.[35] The Cemetery of the National Revolutionary Army in the former Linggu Temple was the location of these rites.[36]

Moreover, many new commemorative projects for the martyrs were planned by local KMT governments and some of these plans were realised.[37] For example, many soldiers from Guangdong Province participated in the Battle of Shanghai. Some of them were wounded and transferred to a hospital in Nanjing. Around fifty were killed when the Japanese bombed Nanjing before the Nanjing Massacre, and around twenty more were killed during the massacre itself. A grave was built for these unfortunate soldiers outside the walled city of Nanjing. After the war, the Army of Guangdong Province started to make regular visits to the grave and built a monument for the grave, with the inscription 'Grave of Anti-Japanese Martyrs' (Kangri lieshi zhimu 抗日烈士之墓) carved on it.[38] Also, the Juhuatai Nine Diplomatic Anti-Japanese Martyrs' Cemetery was built in the south part of Nanjing after the war. Nine diplomatic personnel serving in the Philippines were killed separately in Japanese-occupied Manila in 1942 and 1945. Their remains were airlifted to Nanjing in 1947. Some residents in Juhuatai donated their land for the graves of these nine martyrs. On 3 September, a public funeral and mourning ceremony was held for them and Juhuatai changed its name to 'the Martyrs' Park'.[39] However, most of the plans were only partially realised due to the outbreak of the Civil War.[40] For example, on 28 January 1947 the central KMT government approved the plan to rebuild Hengyang 衡阳 – a city in Hunan Province that was almost completely destroyed during the Battle of Hengyang between 22 June and 8 August 1944, as a 'commemorative city of the War of Resistance'. However, the project was suspended in the second half of 1948.

In terms of martyrs' families, the newly promulgated 'Regulation of Praising the Martyrs of the Resistance to the Japanese 褒扬抗战忠烈条例 (1946)' stipulated that all soldiers and civilians who had died in, or were disabled because of, the war would be consoled and compensated. The families of the soldiers killed in action against the Japanese received symbolic as well as material benefits from the society, including being accorded a special degree of respect.[41] For example, the orphans of martyrs could enter school for free and any unfair treatment received by the martyrs' families gained significant and sympathetic media attention.[42]

The CCP's practices

During the War of Resistance the CCP established several anti-Japanese base areas, which covered most rural areas in Jiangsu Province. On the outskirts of Japanese puppet government-controlled Nanjing alone, by August 1945 there were eight county-level regimes of the CCP.[43] Thus, there were many legacies of the CCP's practice of honouring soldiers killed in action against Japan throughout Jiangsu (aside from the city of Nanjing). After the Marco Polo Bridge Incident, in August 1937 the CCP Central Committee published the Ten Principles of 'Resisting Japan and Saving the County 抗日救国十大纲领' and advocated that the treatment of military personnel should be improved. The governing body of the CCP base in each location developed various *baoxu* policies in accordance with this declaration. For example, the Shanxi-Chahar-Hebei Base Area promulgated several regulations to honour soldiers killed in action and to console and compensate their families.[44] In practice, the CCP's methods of honouring martyrs during the War of Resistance were similar to those used in previous period, but with significant improvements.[45]

Before 1937, the CCP had three major ways of honouring martyrs (mainly those killed in action against the KMT force): collecting and publicising information about the martyrs' deeds and deaths (e.g. the name, time and location of the battle in which they died); building martyrs' memorials; and displaying martyrs' mementoes, as well as medals awarded to the martyrs who did not have any family, in revolutionary museums.[46] After 1937, these ways of honouring martyrs were also applied by the CCP to honour soldiers killed in action against the Japanese. Nonetheless, with the CCP growing in strength during the War of Resistance, the party was able to build larger-scale martyrs' memorials in its expanded areas of control. For instance, three relatively extensive cemeteries were built on the north side of Hongze Lake alone, which today is encompassed by Suqian city, Jiangsu. These were part of the CCP's Henan-Anhui and Jiangsu Base Area. The latter was established mainly by units of the New Fourth Army led by Peng Xuefeng 彭雪枫 between 1938 and 1939.[47]

In the winter of 1942 the Japanese army started a large-scale military campaign on the north side of Hongze Lake. The 26th Regiment, Ninth Brigade, Fourth Division of the New Fourth Army engaged in a fierce battle with the Japanese army in Zhujiagang 朱家岗 (in what is now Sihong county, Suqian). The CCP claimed that around 300 Japanese and 100 Chinese soldiers were killed in the battle. In August 1943, with the encouragement and support of the residents in the area, the Zhujiagang Cemetery Park was built. Peng Xuefeng, army commander of the Fourth Division at the time, took charge of the construction. The cemetery was surrounded by a 2.5-metre wall decorated with paintings and featuring an archway. Inside the cemetery, apart from the main memorials, were two parterres and a wood. Caretakers were appointed to take care of the park.[48] In the same year another martyrs' cemetery – Aiyuan 爱园 – was built northeast of Zhujiagang (Siyang county, Suqian). The local cadres believed that this cemetery not only honoured the revolutionary martyrs, but also 'inspired the people's patriotism, encouraged them to participate in the struggles of resisting the Japanese' and contributed to victory in the war'.[49]

In September 1944, Peng Xuefeng himself was killed in action. Most of the CCP's official accounts described the death of Peng in a vague way, as follows: in the spring of 1944 the Japanese army started a large-scale invasion that moved towards Henan Province. To save people from terrible hardship and suffering, Peng led his army into Henan. Unfortunately, in September, Peng was shot in Xiayi, Henan. Other sources have pointed out, however, that Peng died in action not against the Japanese army, but against the KMT's 'unregenerate army (*wangujun* 顽固军)'.

Regardless of the lack of precision about his death, Peng was treated as an anti-Japanese martyr and his remains were buried in the Huaibei Anti-Japanese Martyrs' Cemetery (also in Sihong county). Apart from Peng Xuefeng's tomb, the cemetery contained commemorative buildings for other New Fourth Army soldiers killed in battle resisting Japanese in the north area of the Huai River (Huaibei).[50] In the Civil War period, in addition to Aiyuan cemetery, two other cemeteries on the north side of the Hongze Lake were destroyed by the KMT army, in the autumn of 1946.

Many other martyrs' memorials built by the CCP in Jiangsu Province during the War of Resistance were also despoiled by the KMT forces in this period, such as the Mount of Resisting Japan cemetery, the Eighty-Two Martyrs' Cemetery Park (Huaiyin city, 1943), the Lupu Martyrs' Commemorative monument (Yancheng city, 1943) and Xinyi Martyrs' monument (Xuzhou city, 1944).[51] To illustrate the history of martyrs' memorials in other parts of Jiangsu Province, the Mount of Resisting Japan cemetery park will be described as an example. Since the Mount Ma'an area had been taken by the CCP, becoming its base in 1939, many soldiers had fallen in battles against Japan. In 1941 construction started on a martyrs' cemetery in Ma'an

Mount (Ganyu county, Lianyungang city), the name for which later changed to Kangrishan (抗日山 meaning Mount of Resisting Japan). By 1944, when the cemetery was completed, 138 martyrs' graves (with around 5 to 12 bodies in each grave) had been dug. Some famous anti-Japanese martyrs were buried there, among whom was General Fu Zhuting 符竹庭 (to commemorate his sacrifice in 1943, Ganyu county even changed its name to Zhuting county), and a Pole who came to China to assist in its fight against the Japanese. The cemetery was regularly visited on memorial days and festivals during the War of Resistance. For instance, Zhu De came on the fifth anniversary of the Marco Polo Bridge Incident and wrote an essay in which he mourned the martyrs buried there. The essay was inscribed on a commemorative monument within the cemetery. In 1947, after the KMT seized the area, its soldiers attacked the statues of Fu Zhuting, as well as other martyrs' statues, with mortars and machine guns. The whole cemetery was destroyed.[52]

In terms of taking care of martyrs' families, before the War of Resistance material compensation would be accorded to the bereaved families of the Red Army soldiers who were killed in action. The amount each family received was normally decided by special committees.[53] After the War broke out, the level of compensation was increased several times. Also, the policies relating to the martyrs' families became more detailed. For example, some places gave a very explicit definition of the term 'soldiers resisting the Japanese', and some places made distinctions between different types of martyrs' families, such as martyrs' families with assets who could maintain a good standard of living and martyrs' families without assets who were unable to maintain even a basic living standard. Furthermore, an increasing number of practical methods of giving assistance to martyrs' families were popularised. For instance, the practice of helping martyrs' families to cultivate crops was carried out in the CCP bases.[54] Also, the CCP's organs of civil affairs in some bases regularly checked the level of performance on consoling and compensating martyrs' families. The CCP's regime in the Shanxi-Gansu and Ningxia Base even set up special committees for this job.[55] In the phase between the last stage of the War of Resistance and the Civil War, the CCP made increased efforts to take care of the families of anti-Japanese martyrs.[56] Different activities were carried out, including the distribution of land and school places for martyrs' orphans. Some symbolic activities were also carried out to enhance the status of the martyrs' families, such as awarding families a 'glorious tablet'.[57]

During this period, many families of the anti-Japanese martyrs were given these forms of material and symbolic compensation. For example, a young man called Zhang Yilang joined the New Fourth Army and served as the head of a militia organisation in Hengshan county, Nanjing, in 1943. On the night of 21 December 1944 he was captured by Japanese soldiers while organising a mass assembly in a nearby county. He was then stabbed to death. To publicise his deeds and to console his dependents a mourning service was held for him. More importantly, his bereaved family members were given material support by the local CCP regime. However, after the New Fourth Army retreated to the north following the Double Tenth Agreement with the KMT on 10 October 1945, Zhang's family was insulted by 'reactionaries' (it is unclear who these so-called 'reactionaries' were).[58] Although the evidence is sparse, it is likely that the unfortunate experience of Zhang's family might reflect the experience of other CCP martyrs' families during the Civil War.

* * *

Both the KMT and the CCP's practices of honouring the Fifteen-Year-War martyrs were seriously disrupted by the Civil War. After the CCP replaced the KMT as the new ruling party of China in 1949 – almost four years after the Fifteen-Year War had ended – the question arose as to what the Communist regime would do with respect to these martyrs. Would the CCP regime tarnish the reputations of KMT soldiers killed in the Fifteen-Year War? Would the regime value its martyrs who died in the Civil War more than its soldiers who were killed in the War of Resistance? Answers to these questions are to be found in the next section, which will discuss the *baoxu* activities carried out for the Fifteen-Year-War martyrs during the early PRC era.

The first seventeen-year period of the PRC

When the PRC was established, it inherited a great deal of the practices in respect of honouring the Fifteen-Year-War martyrs, such as recording and circulating martyrs' deeds in written or spoken form, holding memorial ceremonies, and supporting the bereaved families of those killed during the pre-1949 period. Moreover, it also immediately started to set up its new nationwide system (i.e. relevant government organs and rules) to guide the *baoxu* activities for Fifteen-Year-War martyrs, which to some extent was also a legacy of the pre-1949 period in terms of the personnel of the organs and the methods of honouring martyrs stipulated by the rules. This section will discuss how the PRC dealt with the pre-1949 legacy and how it carried out the *baoxu* activities for Fifteen-Year-War martyrs according to the guidance of its new *baoxu* system.

Before it became the only party to rule over China, the CCP did not have a nationwide *baoxu* system. The establishment of a nationwide and top-down network of *baoxu* organs was swiftly carried out soon after it seized power. The PRC's Ministry of Internal Affairs was established on 1 November 1949. This was in charge of an extremely wide range of activities, including the *baoxu* activities. On a local level, for instance, the PLA took over the ROC's Nanjing Municipal Bureau of Civil Affairs after it took Nanjing on 23 April 1949. The CCP'S Nanjing Municipal People's Government formed its own Bureau of Civil Affairs towards the end of May, and several lower-level civil affairs organs in the wards and on the outskirts of Nanjing in June 1949. In January 1953, Jiangsu Provincial Department of Civil Affairs (JPDCA) came

Figure 3.1 The KMT and the CCP's Fifteen-Year War Martyrs' memorials in Jiangsu
  Province mentioned in this section

Notes: 1. Mount of Resisting Japan Cemetery Park; 2. Xinyi Martyrs' Monument; 3.
Peng Xuefeng's Grave, Zhujiagang Martyrs' Cemetery Park, Aiyuan Cemetery Park; 4.
82 Martyrs' Cemetery Park; 5. Lupu Martyrs' Monument; 6. The KMT's cemetery in
Suzhou for the soldiers of the Fifth Corps and 19th Corps; 7.Grave of Anti-Japanese Martyrs, Air Force Martyrs' Cemetery, Cemetery of National Revolution Army, Juhuatai Nine
Diplomatic Martyrs' Cemetery, Commemorative monument and cemetery for the soldiers
of the 87th Division (Note: The commemorative monument and cemetery was built in a
hill northeast to Yuhuatai for the soldiers of the KMT's 87th Devision killed in the
Shanghai Incident, see, NMA-5012-1-141: the project chart of building main roads
for the construction of the Yuhuatai. However, it was destroyed by the Japanese
imperial army in the war, see, Yu Feng 于峰, 'Yuhuatai kangzhan jinianta yiji chencang jumin xiaoqu' [The ruins of the monument commemorating the War of Resistance is hiding in a resistance area 雨花台抗战纪念塔遗迹深藏居民小区]. http://news.
163.com12/0707/00/85P711N400014AED.html, 7 Jul 2012, date access, 9 Mar 2014.)
Source: the map of Jiangsu province is downloaded from: www.china-tour.cn/Jiangsu/
Jiangsu-Location-Map.htm, date unknown, date accessed, 8 Mar 2014. The dots are
added by the author.

into existence and settled in the provincial capital Nanjing, soon after Jiangsu Province was established in December 1952.[59] As regards the rules, the importance and necessity of the *baoxu* activities were stipulated in the PRC's major laws and the details of how to honour martyrs were illustrated in a series of regulations and documents introduced during the first seventeen-year period. Five regulations announced by the Ministry of Internal Affairs (MIA) on 11 December 1950 perhaps amount to the 'constitution' of the PRC's *baoxu* activities and were used until 1979.[60] The local civil affairs organs also promulgated a large number of relevant documents according to the MIA's guidance. In this way, a serviceable *baoxu* system was gradually established throughout mainland China.

Among the five 'constitutional' regulations, the 'Provisional Regulation of Praising, Consoling and Compensating the Sacrifice and Death caused by Disease of Revolutionary Soldiers (hereafter the Regulation for Dead Soldiers)' and the 'Provisional Regulation of Treating Preferably the Families of Revolutionary Martyrs and Soldiers (hereafter the 'Regulation for Military Families)' were directly related to practices of honouring martyrs.[61] Many other rules were also closely related to these practices. Although there seemed to be no separate rule for soldiers killed in action against Japanese, it was explicitly stated several times by different levels of civil affairs organs that these soldiers should be called martyrs. For instance, the MIA's announcement on 15 October 1950 stipulated that soldiers who had died in various conflicts since the 1911 Xinhai Revolution, including during resistance against Japanese aggression between 1931 and 1937, and in the War of Resistance, were to be called martyrs.[62] A regulation of Wuxi city, Jiangsu, which stipulated who could be buried in martyrs' cemeteries, also suggested that soldiers who died in the Fifteen-Year War ('war of defending the nation' in the original text) deserved the title of Martyr from the PRC.[63] Similarly, in practice, anti-Japanese soldiers killed in action were normally honoured together with martyrs of other conflicts as 'revolutionary martyrs'. Nevertheless, in places where the experience of resisting the Japanese was distinctive, the Fifteen-Year-War martyrs were honoured exclusively. With respect to the families of soldiers killed in the Fifteen-Year War, they also enjoyed symbolic and material benefits from the PRC as one of many categories of martyrs' families. Nevertheless, in practical terms, the families of Fifteen-Year War soldiers could receive greater material compensation than their Civil War counterparts – the amount of which was partially decided by the service length of the martyrs. The main body of this section will explore more stories of the PRC's practices of honouring the Fifteen-Year-War martyrs and taking care of their families.

Honouring Fifteen-Year-War martyrs

The methods of honouring martyrs in the PRC era generally stipulated in the 'Regulation for Dead Soldiers' were not very original when one compares them to those of pre-1949 China. Also, these methods were centred around the martyrs' memorials (see my earlier argument concerning the ways of honouring martyrs in pre-1949 China). Consequently, this part of the chapter will focus on discussing the practices of building martyrs' memorials in order to visualise the whole practice of honouring martyrs in the PRC.

The practice of building martyrs' memorials particularly flourished in the first three years of the PRC, as the country placed a great emphasis on *baoxu* activities in this period.[64] 'To pay respects and tributes to the martyrs', the centre (by which I mean the PRC and the CCP's central authorities) instructed that, 'each place should build commemorative monuments, pavilions, graves and cemeteries for the martyrs'.[65] Most of the martyrs' memorials built during this period were for martyrs in general: for example, the Yuhuatai Memorial was built for the revolutionary martyrs killed by 'the KMT reactionaries and Japanese imperialists' in Nanjing in the previous twenty years. Even small counties where funds were lacking tried hard to build something: for instance, in 1952 Lianshui county built a humble monument for the soldiers who had died in the area during the War of Resistance and the Civil War.[66] In addition, the CCP's pre-1949 memorials for soldiers killed in action against the Japanese were well preserved and continued to be used as sacred places dedicated to martyrs. Several pre-1949 anti-Japanese martyrs' memorials which had been destroyed by the KMT army were restored as well. For instance, the cemetery where Peng Xuefeng was buried was restored after the Huaibei area was seized by the PLA in 1949, and the Mount of Resisting Japan was repaired in 1952.

In terms of the KMT's memorials to the Fifteen-Year-War martyrs, according to certain official gazetteers these were preserved quite well by the CCP government until the Cultural Revolution period.[67] This is surprising, as destroying the martyrs' memorials of opponents was something of a 'convention' in Republican China, as elsewhere in the world. However, as far as can be seen, there is no convincing source to invalidate this official claim. On the contrary, a document of the Nanjing Municipal Bureau of Culture (NMBC) may back up the official claim indirectly. This document states that at the beginning of the Cultural Revolution, 'the majority of the revolutionary masses are very furious about what remains of the KMT and request unanimously that these remains be destroyed'. The NMBC approved the request and stated, 'The KMT's remains, such as graves and cenotaphs, should be smashed resolutely'. Several of the KMT's anti-Japanese martyrs' commemorative buildings were included in the list of buildings that should be radically 'transformed'.[68] Moreover, considering the PLA's military discipline (of which the CCP was proud) and the CCP's united front policy towards the so-called democratic parties, the CCP's soldiers and cadres were unlikely to destroy KMT martyrs' memorials at random. Even the grave of Dai Li (head of the KMT's Military Intelligence Service – an 'infamous' figure for the CCP) in Purple Mount survived until 1964 – not to mention the memorials of the KMT's Fifteen-Year-War martyrs, who had fought against Japanese under the banner of national salvation.[69]

Nevertheless, these memorials were not part of the PRC's *baoxu* activities, as there is hardly any mention of them in the documents of the PRC's civil affairs organs and instead they are only occasionally dealt with by the NMBC as 'revolutionary relics'.[70] The names of some of these memorials were also changed: for example, the Cemetery of the National Revolution Army was changed to Linggu Park. Furthermore, some commemorative buildings for the CCP members who died in conflicts with the KMT were also built near or in the grounds of these memorials by the PRC government. For instance, the grave of Deng Yanda, who was killed by the KMT regime in November 1931, was dug inside Linggu Park in 1957.

After the first three years of recovery, the CCP entered the Socialist Transformation period. The majority of activities carried out in the country were required to serve the industrialisation-oriented socialist policies. Against this background, the centre started to discourage the construction of martyrs' memorials (which were not considered to be 'productive construction') and the budget given to maintaining completed martyrs' memorials was also very tight. In 1952, Prime Minister Zhou Enlai instructed that the construction of all kinds of martyrs' memorials should be halted. The very next year, the budget for building martyrs' memorials in Jiangsu Province was suspended.[71] After this initial instruction the centre also sent out several similar instructions during the first seventeen-year period.

For instance, in 1954 the centre instructed again that, apart from construction of the Monument to the People's Heroes in Beijing, any other construction of martyrs' memorials was not allowed, as the country's resources should be spent on the development of national defence and heavy industry.[72] Nevertheless, regardless of the repeated instructions from the centre, not only did many expensive maintenance or extension projects continue to be carried out, but also new constructions of martyrs' memorials began throughout China. By 1963, the PRC had built 5,834 martyrs' memorials throughout the country, and most of the places where there had been influential incidents or battles had already seen the building of some kind of martyrs' memorial. Thus, the MIA promulgated a document in December 1963 restating its discouraging stance towards these kinds of projects. This time the MIA did not try to ban the construction of martyrs' memorials completely, as it had done in the early 1950s. Rather, it ordained a strict condition that only under certain circumstances (such as being approved by the provincial-level People's Committee and following the principle of diligence and frugality) were new martyrs' memorials allowed to be built. In November 1964 the centre changed its condition so that new martyrs' memorials could only be built after being approved by the centre, which was effective until at least the early stages of the Cultural Revolution.[73] This irrational situation, I argue, should be attributed to the irresoluteness of the senior leaders and the enthusiasm of the lower-level cadres and the masses.

The centre actually valued the martyrs' memorials per se as precious political assets, in spite of its reluctance to spend money on them. The importance of visiting martyrs' memorials regularly was emphasised by the central government. Every year, around festivals like Tomb-Sweeping Day (or Qingming Festival on 5 April), various mass activities took place in front of the martyrs' memorials, the majority of which were organised from the top down.[74] The value the centre placed on martyrs' memorials was also evident on certain special occasions. For instance in 1959, the 10th anniversary of the PRC, the MIA planned to compile a photo album of martyrs' memorials to 'further propagandise the heroic deeds of martyrs and educate the masses'. The ministry requested photos of the memorials, and of the cadres and masses visiting them, from the JPDCA. The latter then requested contributions from the cities and counties under its jurisdiction. Several anti-Japanese martyrs' memorials were specially chosen by the JPDCA, like the cemetery park where Peng Xuefeng was buried, the Eighty-Two Martyrs' Cemetery Park, the Mount of Resisting Japan and the Mao Mount Wood of Resisting Japan and Marching Eastwards (Zhenjiang city).[75] Thus, it was difficult for the centre to ban the construction or expensive maintenance of martyrs' memorials completely, considering how much it valued these memorials.

Furthermore, when the centre realised that a new martyrs' memorial had to be built, it would sometimes break its own rules. For example, the MIA ordered Nanjing to construct a grave for the three CCP commanders who died in the Wannan Incident (or the New Fourth Army Incident of 1941) on 24 October 1953. Both the Nanjing Municipal and Jiangsu Provincial governments took this order very seriously. After inspection visits, it was decided that the remains of these three martyrs would be buried in the Juhuatai area. The provincial government also appropriated funds to buy land from local residents for the burial site. The graves were completed in 1955.[76]

Another reason for the top-down irresoluteness was that the centre had no alternative but to take care of the martyrs' memorials, otherwise discontent among the people would be invited. Thus, it kept a regular check on them, in terms of their distribution, condition, maintenance, visitor numbers, so forth. These kinds of inspections normally took place around Tomb-Sweeping Day every year, or sometimes at other times.[77] The documents guiding such inspections always stipulated that if a repair or re-burial was necessary, it should be carried out properly.[78] Specifically, the cadres and masses were actually encouraged to take care of martyrs' memorials, but on a small-scale and at low cost. As a result, the JPDCA approved a large number of relatively inexpensive projects.

In periods when the MIA placed special importance on the inspection of memorials, the provincial-level (or lower) organs of civil affairs tended to make exceptions for large-scale projects. For example, before Tomb-Sweeping Day in 1955 the MIA instructed that a thorough inspection of the martyrs' memorials was to be carried out nationwide. In response to this, Jiangsu Provincial government decided that the construction and maintenance of the martyrs' memorials would be a focus of its activities in 1955 and informed each location in the province about this decision in an announcement issued on 31 March 1955. Consequently, many previously rejected or postponed applications from local governments were approved and more new applications made in 1955 were accepted by the JPDCA.[79] This 'spring' of the martyrs' memorials in Jiangsu lasted until 1957, when the JPDCA again started to reject or postpone applications, using the excuse that the budget was tight and that the province had suffered from natural disasters.[80] Similarly, another nationwide thorough inspection was initiated by the MIA in 1958. The JPDCA appropriated special funds for several famous martyrs' memorials, which were rejected in 1957, although the JPDCA had issued an announcement on 9 April declining the constant applications relating to martyrs' memorials from the local authorities.[81] Surprisingly, all three memorials that were entitled to this funding were for the Lupu Martyrs' Commemorative monument, the Eighty-Two Martyrs' Cemetery and the Mount of Resisting Japan, all dedicated to anti-Japanese martyrs.[82]

Moreover, some clauses in the centre's guidlines created loopholes for extensive and expensive projects. For example, a document guiding the inspection in 1958 stipulated that if the land on which a martyrs' grave stood had to be used for the purposes of other constructions, the grave should be properly rebuilt in another place. The Yuntai Mount (Jiangnin county, Nanjing) Martyrs' Memorial was a typical beneficiary of this clause. Around eighty New Fourth Army soldiers killed in a battle with the Japanese on 26 February 1939 were buried in the Yuntai Mount area. In 1956, local residents petitioned the county's government to build a cemetery for these soldiers, but were not successful. In 1964, a sulphur mine was to be constructed in Yuntai Mount, and the buried remains of the soldiers were in danger. Thus, although the centre had been intensifying its control over the construction of new martyrs' memorials since 1963, the JPDCA still approved the construction.[83]

Although it was the senior-level authorities that made exceptions for unforseen projects, it was the grassroots cadres who made applications to them from the bottom up. When the policy was favourable their applications were easily accepted, as mentioned previously. However, when the policy was not optimistic, they continued to push the senior-level authorities and most of the time, got them to compromise to some extent. Nevertheless, most of the time these grassroots cadres themselves were actually pressured by smaller communities, groups or people in the area governed by them.

The martyrs' families were one constituency among the local people who made applications to the centre for a memorial. It was common for the family of a soldier killed in action to make the effort to find the burial place of the soldier.[84] After having found the location, a family would sometimes request the local or basic-level authorities to transport the soldier's remains to their birthplace, while others would request that proper memorials for the soldier(s) be built (or maintained, if a memorial had been built already). For example, the wife of a CCP martyr who died in 1937 found a commemorative monument for her husband in Luodian, Baoshan county. She was very upset by the poor condition of this monument and in 1953 she asked the local authority to carry out maintenance work. Although the policy of the centre was unfavourable at the time, her request was approved by the JPDCA after some twists and turns.[85] Also, the family of Liao Haitao, who was an army commissar in the New Fourth Army who died in late 1940 in the Tangma Battle in Liyang county, wanted to re-bury him in Yuhuatai in Nanjing, or, alternatively, in his birthplace. Liao's family first voiced their wish in 1962, asking the organ of civil affairs in the county to negotiate the matter with the higher-level authorities.[86]

The martyrs' comrades-in-arms were another constituency among the local people who made applications to the centre. For example, Yuan Zhongxian 袁仲贤 was the political commissar of the Eighth Army's Zhuxian Anti-Japanese Guerrilla Army (named after a famous anti-Japanese martyr, Fan Zhuxian) during the War of Resistance. The editor of his army newspaper, Zhu Lianghua, died in 1939. For various reasons, Yuan could not bury Zhu's remains on his own and he greatly regretted this. In 1955, Yuan came back to Beijing to report in person on the performance of his official duties as China's ambassador to India. Although his schedule was tight, he made a special trip to Nanjing as he had been informed that Zhu was buried there. He paid tribute at Zhu's grave and wrote an epitaph for Zhu (Figure 3.2). A cenotaph with the epitaph was erected by the local authority.[87] Also, until early 1960, Zhujiagang Martyrs' Cemetery (Sihong county) had not been repaired since the time when it was destroyed in the Civil War. Luo Yinghuai, who was the regimental commander of the soldiers buried in the cemetery, had written to the relevant organs and sent his subordinate staff to Sihong county several times to request repairs be made to the cemetery. In 1963, the JPDCA gave 5,000 RMB to the county to rebuild part of the cemetery, despite the increasing discouragement from the centre and the economic difficulties faced by the country.[88]

Apart from making an application to higher authorities on behalf of a particular martyr's family or comrade in arms, the local authorities also made applications on behalf of 'the people' or 'the masses'. The following are examples of applications submitted to the JSPCA:

> Although [Peng Xuefeng's grave] has been repaired on a small scale in recent years, [the standard of the repaired grave] cannot fulfil the people's wish ... to accommodate the people's request ...
>
> The masses in the area appealed in unison that the [Mount of Resisting Japan] should be repaired immediately.
>
> The masses were very discontented [about the unrepaired martyrs' monument in Lupu], and wrote to the county one after the other to request the reconstruction of the martyrs' monument.
>
> [The Xinyi Martyrs' Monument in Xinyi county] still has not been repaired ... in recent years, the masses and people's representatives from everywhere have consistently appealed and requested to ... build a stele to praise the martyrs' deeds, and the troops in the area also suggested it several times.

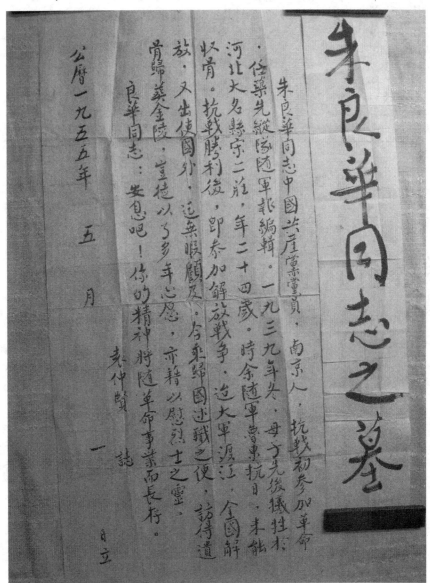

Figure 3.2 Epitaph for Zhu Lianghua
Source: NMA-5012-2-293.

All the people of the county [Rudong county] ... experienced the serious test of the War of Resistance and the War of Liberation [the Civil War] ... only a martyrs' monument could satisfy people's requirements. According to the requirement of the county's 83,000 people ... our unit [of Civil Affairs] decided to ... carry out maintenance for the monument and built two martyrs' halls.[89]

Sometimes these kinds of applications, at the request of the local 'masses', were over-enthusiastic. For example, during the Great Leap Forward period, Wu county planned to build a martyrs' cemetery for New Fourth Army personnel who had died in the War of Resistance and the Civil War. The residents of five nearby towns under the jurisdiction of the county also donated the building materials and offered voluntary labour for the planned project. Wu county claimed in its letter to the JSPCA of 10 April 1958 that the people's 'enthusiasm was very high and the construction project had to be carried out'. Without any reply from the JSPCA, Wu county wrote another letter to the JSPCA again in June:

The martyrs' dependents have also prepared for the re-burials and have recently come to the county to urge [the construction to begin] one by one. We think that although we should concentrate spending and energy to support agricultural production, the Big Leap Forward, we cannot abandon the martyrs' commemorative buildings which have a profound influence ... so, we write to you again to ask for 5,000 RMB to fulfil the sincere wishes of the people.

Although Wu county's enthusiasm and efforts to get funds from the JSPCA were impressive, they were ignoring a very important document issued by the JSPCA on 9 April informing all locations in Jiangsu Province that no funds would be appropriated for martyrs' memorials. So, just as one would expect, in its reply to Wu county in July, the JSPCA cited that document and rejected its request for funds. Nevertheless, the JSPCA was willing to allow the county to carry out the construction of the planned martyrs' memorials if it could raise funds by itself.[90]

In conclusion, due to the pragmatic value of the martyrs for the PRC's senior leaders and the respect accorded the martyrs by the people (i.e. the masses, as well as cadres and senior leaders acting outside of their official capacities), many projects relating to constructing, maintaining and extending martyrs' memorials were consistently carried out. If a plan relating to a martyrs' memorial was supported by the leaders and the people, it was most likely to be realised. For instance, in the late 1950s a group of martyrs' cemeteries were constructed in Wangjiangji 望江矶. Following this, a province-wide project to find unidentified martyrs' graves, learn about the deeds of the graves' occupants, and re-bury them in a dispersed way in Jiangsu Province in Wangjiangji was carried out. The realisation of this project was attributed to several leaders of Jiangsu Provincial Government who initially envisaged this construction and re-burial project in 1953, the troops stationed in Nanjing who canvassed for the project in 1955, local Nanjing residents who expressed their discontent about the poor conditions of the martyrs' graves dispersed throughout the city (some of their grave sites were even combined with garbage dumps and manure pits), and people throughout Jiangsu Province who were extremely co-operative in the province-wide project.[91]

Martyrs' dependents

While the martyrs were praised by the PRC in various ways, their dependents were also entitled to a variety of benefits from the state and society, which were generally stipulated in the 1950 'Regulation for Military Dependents'.[92] In the first seventeen-year period of the PRC, when the country was not very affluent, these benefits were very precious. It was not rare for people to try to falsely claim the title of Martyr's Dependent.[93] Thus, the MIA decided on a procedure to discriminate between false and real claims on a preliminary basis. By definition, 'all the revolutionary soldiers who [were] sacrificed due to participation in wars or in official business (such as choosing to die rather than giving in after being captured, and being assassinated by an operative) are called Martyrs and their families are called Martyrs' Dependents'.[94]

Nevertheless, the Ministry further added that only the families of those dead soldiers who had already obtained the title of Martyr could obtain the title of Martyr's Dependents. The standard procedure was for a 'Certificate of the Sacrifice of the Revolutionary Soldiers 革命军人牺牲证明书' to be issued by the dead soldier's army unit and sent to the people's government of the soldier's birthplace, which would issue a 'Certificate of the Revolutionary Martyrs' Dependents' to the dead soldier's family. Nevertheless, many families of soldiers killed in action failed to obtain the title of Martyr's Dependents because the soldier's status as a martyr could not be proved in the first place, due to the turbulence of the war and the sheer length of China's revolution (1911–1949). After 1949, most families of soldiers killed in the Fifteen-Year War were faced with this situation.

Fortunately, the PRC's relevant organs had also developed some rules for helping this category of dependents. The 1950 regulations actually had a special clause for the dependents of soldiers whose sacrifice had occurred a long time ago, who could not get certificates from the soldiers' army units. It stipulated that if these dependents could provide any kind of proof of a soldier's sacrifice and obtain approval from the county-level (or above) government, they should be treated as martyrs' dependents.[95] The local authorities were also concerned about this issue. For example, in November 1950, the General Office of the ECMGC advised the civil affairs organ of the ECMGC that if there was no evidence for a martyr who died before the surrender of the Japanese, the county-level (or above) governments were responsible for initiating investigations and making decisions; the staff in the army also had a responsibility to give evidence. After the 1950 regulations were promulgated, these suggestions were formally approved by the civil affairs organ, which issued an announcement that was in accordance with the suggestions. The announcement further added that the investigation should especially be carried out in newly liberated areas, but that it should not be too precipitate, in order to avoid disturbing families emotionally.[96] Thanks to these rules, a large number of families of soldiers who died in the Fifteen-Year War were approved as Martyrs' Dependents, after evidence regarding the soldiers' sacrifices was unearthed by the families themselves, by local cadres and by 'the concerned' between 1949 and 1951.

After a provincial conference of the civil affairs organ was held in 1956 there was a new wave of activity relating to resolving the cases of martyrs' families who had already registered with the relevant organs but had yet to receive compensation, and handling claims from bereaved military families that had not yet been investigated.[97] A document to guide this activity explicitly stipulated what counted as 'evidence from the concerned': all soldiers for whom testimony was obtained from one of the following people could be recognised as a martyr: comrades-in-arms, the commanders of the dead soldier, the fellows who stayed in the same hospital with the dead soldier, the doctors and caring staff in the hospital who took care of the dead soldier, and the general public in the place where the soldier died. During this wave, the civil affairs staff took the initiative to obtain testimonies by contacting the relevant witnesses and carrying out investigations in the localities where the soldiers had sacrificed their lives. As a result, more people whose family members died in the Fifteen-Year War obtain the title of Martyrs' Dependents.[98]

Quite apart from the two waves I have noted, the practice of handling claims from bereaved military families occurred consistently throughout the seventeen-year period. Two major problems emerged with this kind of practice, and it was through the process of handling them that the deeds of soldiers killed in the Fifteen-Year War were publicised by their families and the 'necessary' nature of honouring martyrs could be manifested.

The first problem was how to deal with the KMT soldiers who were killed in action against the Japanese. As mentioned previously in the discussion of Ba Qingzheng's case, both the central and local government had promulgated documents which indicated that the KMT soldiers killed in action against Japan – whose deeds had been approved by the masses and the government in the area – could be called martyrs.[99] Another document promulgated by the MIA also suggested that the PRC's stance towards KMT soldiers who participated in the Fifteen-Year War would be accommodating:

> Since the 'September 18th [incident]', the KMT army's commanding officers and soldiers who indeed became disabled caused by injuries when fighting with Japan, have evidence that [he/she] had already broke off from the Chiang robber's army, have not committed anti-people crimes and have been generally acknowledged by the masses locally, can be

treated as revolutionary disabled personnel ... [they] can be compensated according to the 'Revolutionary Disabled Military Personnel Preferential Treatment and Compensation Regulation'.[100]

The Ba family was a beneficiary of this accommodating stance of the PRC. Many similar cases can be found in Jiangsu. For example, Xu Yihe was a major staff officer of the KMT's 35th Corps, a follower of Fu Zuoyi 傅作义 who crossed over to the CCP in the last stage of the Civil War.[101] During the War of Resistance, Xu died in Fenhe, Shanxi Province, at the age of 46. Around 1956, Xu's son started to request that the NMBCA award his father the title of martyr. Fu Zuoyi also wrote a letter in support of the request of Xu's son. To find out whether Xu had done anything harmful to the people, the cadres of the NMBCA did not organise any mass meeting as they did in the Ba family's case. Instead, they turned for help to the head of another bureau in Nanjing, who was a close relative of Xu.[102]

This suggests that in 1956 the procedure for awarding the title of Martyr to the KMT's anti-Japanese soldiers was much simpler than the procedure in the earlier years of the PRC. After having gathered enough evidence, the cadres decided that Xu should be called a martyr. Nevertheless, the cadre thought Xu's family should not be given any material compensation as it had already obtained compensation from the KMT government and it had no financial difficulties. The cadre stated his opinions in a report to the higher authorities, which was finally approved by the JSPCA on 2 June 1956. Nevertheless, the JSPCA added that if Xu's family had any financial difficulties, a certain amount of relief should be given to them.[103]

Xu's case was slightly different to Qingzheng's case – the former was much more senior than the latter in terms of military ranking and age. This is very interesting, considering the main reason that the masses thought Qingzheng did not do anything harmful to the people was that he died at a very young age. If, for the CCP regime, Qingzheng's image was that of an innocent young man who went astray but ultimately redeemed himself by his own death for the nation, then Xu's image was of a sophisticated political alien whose death could have been for the nation or could have been to maintain the KMT regime. That both Qingzheng and Yihe were awarded the title of Martyr by the CCP regime indirectly implied the high status of anti-Japanese martyrs in the PRC. Similar cases could be found in other parts of the PRC as well. For example, the family of a KMT navy marine who was killed in a battle in Guangdong in 1938 was allocated some land in the Land Reform Movement thanks to a Martyr's Certificate issued by the KMT regime.[104] General Zhang Zizhong and two other high-ranking KMT military officers who were killed in the Fifteen-Year War were recognised retroactively as martyrs by the CCP in 1952. Their Martyrs' Certificates were issued in person by Chairman Mao. There were also three roads named after them in Beijing.[105]

The second problem was related to the evidence given by those whose family members had died in the War of Resistance. Many requests to be considered as martyrs' dependents were rejected due to insufficient evidence. For example, soon after the PLA entered Nanjing in April 1949, Zhang Yilang's mother often tried to re-register with the local authority as a martyr's dependent. All of her attempts failed due to a lack of evidence. Then, she went to a local farmers' association and managed to obtain a reference signed by five representatives of the association. In spite of the letter, she was rejected again. She was told that another letter from the dead soldier's former superior was necessary. Zhang's mother then wrote a very emotional letter to Zhang's former superior, who happened to be the vice head of the NMBCA at the time. In July, a letter from this former superior arrived at the local government, and finally Zhang's mother got everything she needed in order to claim her title.[106]

Also, investigations were made into evidence that seemed suspicious to the civil affairs cadres at any point (when the request was still being considered or after a decision about the request had been made). If the suspicious evidence was perceived as being false, the request would be rejected or the title would be revoked immediately. For example, a resident in Haimen county claimed that his son was killed after being captured by the Japanese in 1943; however, according to the investigation conducted by the staff of the county's Civil Affairs office, the claim was groundless and therefore the resident's application was rejected.[107]

Nevertheless, there were some cases where a soldier's title of Martyr which had been revoked previously was reinstated after new evidence became available. For example, in 1950 three martyrs' families were deprived of their titles by the government of the Ninth Ward of Nanjing, due to their perceived falsification. However, one year later it was realised that although one of these families – the family of Tang Liuliu – did not have evidence to prove Tang's sacrifice, there was no evidence to suggest their falsification either, according to further investigation by Civil Affairs staff. Moreover, the residents of Tang's village, and the former superior of Tang who made a special trip to the Civil Affairs office of the Ninth district in March 1951, had testified about Tang's sacrifice in Gaoyou, Jiangsu, on the evening of 13 August 1945 when the Japanese attacked. On top of this, to steer a cautious course, the Ninth Ward had also required a reference from the workplace of the former superior of Tang, according to instructions from the high authorities. In response, the staff of the workplace also made an investigation into Tang's deeds and provided more detailed information about him, such as that Tang joined the CCP army in July and was praised verbally by the commander of his regiment; he died in the battle of Gaoyou and his body could not be found. After all this bureaucracy, Tang's title of Martyr was reinstated in April 1951.[108]

In cases like this, in order to defend the glory of their beloved ones and to secure the material benefits during very difficult years, the families of both the KMT and the CCP's Fifteen-Year-War martyrs tried to negotiate with the officials and various people concerned. Most of their efforts paid off, thanks to the CCP's glorification of the Fifteen-Year-War martyrs, and especially its accommodating attitude to the KMT's anti-Japanese martyrs. However, after 1958, the CCP regime became increasingly reluctant to pay support money to non-CCP fighters killed in actions against Japan. This was reflected in a document issued by the MIA on 4 February 1958 in response to a Shanxi Provincial Department of Civil Affairs' enquiry about the KMT's anti-Japanese martyrs. This document stated unambiguously that the KMT soldiers who were killed in the Fifteen-Year War were martyrs. However, it went on to state that these soldiers did not need and should not be given further material compensation by the PRC.[109]

Similarly, in 1965 a resident of Xuyi county requested the local authority to award the title of Martyr to his younger brother Tao Youcai, who was killed in action against the Japanese army in 1937 as a member of a local militia. However, the militia existed from 1937 to 1938 when the KMT still controlled the area and their primary aim was to maintain local security. Some members of the militia started to fight against the Japanese only after the latter occupied the area and carried out the 'three-alls' policy, which angered them. Xuyi county's Civil Affairs office was not sure about this situation and asked for instruction from the higher authorities. On 2 July 1965, the JPDCA gave their opinion that although Tao sacrificed his life resisting the Japanese, the leadership of his militia was not the CCP, so the claim should be rejected.[110]

* * *

According to the PRC's *baoxu* regulations, its practice of preserving pre-1949 anti-Japanese martyrs' memorials, as well as constructing new ones, and dealing with the martyrs' dependents, meant both KMT and CCP soldiers killed in the Fifteen-Year War were honoured enthusiastically in the PRC, at least before the leftist mood became tense in the late 1950s. Although their construction continued until 1966 (and thereafter), it was noticeable that after 1957 the climate against personality cults had spread to the field of martyrs' memorials.[111] For instance, in 1958 Suqian county planned to build a grave for General Zhu Rui. However, it was worried about this contradicting the 'climate' and thought about changing the grave's name to 'Anti-Japanese Martyr's Grave'.[112] The 1963 document issued by the MIA also stipulated that martyrs' biographies should not be inscribed on their graves. In 1964, the centre instructed that unless approved by the central government, no memorial to commemorate an individual could be built. Also, in the eyes of several leftist movements, such as the Anti-Rightist Movement (1957–1959) and the Socialist Education Movement (1963–1966), many martyrs or martyrs' families were perceived as belonging to one of four elements – landlords, rich farmers, anti-revolutionaries or evil elements – and their titles of Martyrs or Martyrs' Dependents were taken away as a result. Nevertheless, the worst was still to come.

The Cultural Revolution and thereafter

After the Cultural Revolution broke out in August 1966, apart from the fact that they adopted some characteristics of the Cultural Revolution period, the guidelines of the top-down *baoxu* activities were similar to those of the previous period.[113] Nevertheless, the *baoxu* system built up during the first seventeen-year period was paralysed. The MIA was discharged in 1968, and its activities were taken over by the Ministry of Finance and Public Security. The local organs of civil affairs in Jiangsu Province were closed several times due to the disturbances caused by the common practice of 'stopping working and making revolution' during the Cultural Revoution, and due to shortages of staff. Also, more martyrs and martyrs' dependents were deprived of their titles.

The martyrs' memorials suffered similarly during the Cultural Revolution. Many memorials were destroyed as their owner's title of Martyr was rescinded. Also, riots were prevalent during the period, and many martyrs' memorials were implicated. The Yuhuatai Memorial had to be closed between 1967 and 1971, to protect its buildings and exhibitions. Also, Yingshan Martyrs' Cemetery Park, which was another memorial built in Sihong county for eighty-three martyrs killed in the War of Resistance in 1966, was soon despoiled by the 'rebel' faction.[114] Furthermore, numerous anti-Japanese martyrs' memorials of the KMT were destroyed in the campaign to destroy the 'Four Olds'.[115] In Nanjing, all buildings in the Air Force Cemetery were destroyed apart from its archway and the entirety of the Juhuatai Diplomats' Cemetery was destroyed. However, most memorials in the Cemetery of the National Revolutionary Army in the Linggu Park suffered only some cosmetic damage, mainly because these memorials were actually built upon the buildings of the former Linggu Temple, which were strictly protected by the Nanjing government. For instance, the cemetery's mourning hall was built on the remains of Wuliang Hall. While the symbols associated with the KMT, such as emblems and leaders' inscriptions, were dug out and the names of the KMT martyrs inscribed in the hall were covered with paint, the hall itself survived quite well.[116] Furthermore, many martyrs' memorials of the CCP also suffered in the campaign to destroy the Four Olds, due to the feudalistic elements they contained.[117]

Many Fifteen-Year-War martyrs' memorials were involved in this disaster, but none of them were destroyed because of the martyrs' deeds in resisting the Japanese. On the contrary, there seemed to be a bottom-up fever for the anti-Japanese martyrs during this chaotic period of destruction. Many applications to construct or expand martyrs' memorials were submitted to the JPDCA in the initial stage of the Cultural Revolution and the majority of these were for anti-Japanese martyrs. For instance, in 1966, Muyang county applied to extend the grave of Zhu Qitao, who 'actively participated in the struggle for national liberation during the War of Resistance'. In 1967, Liuhe county applied to extend its cemetery for 'the anti-Japanese fighters who drained the last drop of their blood to attack the Japanese fascist bandits'.[118] Also, some of these applications were obviously promoted by the aggressive masses. For instance, enraged by Gaoyu county's rejection of their application to build a martyrs' memorial in the area, the rebels wrote an extremely rude letter exhorting the officials to 'stretch their dog's ears to hear the angry voice of the revolutionary masses' and to threaten that they 'give strict instruction to build a martyrs' stele and cemetery in Linze town, otherwise we will take necessary revolutionary action'.[119]

After the Cultural Revolution, the grievances of certain martyrs' dependents were gradually redressed. Many destroyed memorials were also slowly restored; and the *baoxu* activities, for which no specialised institution had responsibility during the Cultural Revolution period, were taken over by the newly established Ministry of Civil Affairs (1978). In June 1979 the CCP regime started to rehabilitate the KMT's anti-Japanese martyrs. However, in 1980 the central government promulgated a new 'Regulation of Praising the Revolutionary Martyrs 革命烈士褒扬条例' which suggested that only the 'people' and PLA personnel could be called martyrs. The explanations issued in September made it clear that KMT soldiers killed in the War of Resistance could no longer be subject to the procedure for being recognised as martyrs. Nevertheless, the centre soon realised the shortcomings of this policy vis-à-vis the KMT's anti-Japanese soldiers and stipulated in an internally circulated document in 1983 that if dependents of these soldiers took initiatives that were supported by reliable evidence, KMT soldiers could be recognised as martyrs.[120]

* * *

This chapter has shown that the Chinese governments honoured the Fifteen-Year-War martyrs very earnestly, which in turn promoted remembrance of the Fifteen-Year War in China. Honouring Fifteen-Year-War martyrs was not an optional but a necessary practice for the KMT and CCP regimes before 1982. This necessity was reflected in the continuity of *baoxu* activities – no matter how the regime changed in China – between 1931 and 1982. Furthermore, there was a popular pressure from ordinary people and lower-level cadres to commemorate their war dead. We can see this, for example, in the fact that the centre tried to order restraint in this regard but it was unable to stop a ground-level movement to build memorials. The state's tendency to compromise over the issue when confronted by non-state forces or lower-level administrators, and the vacillation in, as well as several reverses of, official policy concerning martyrs' memorial projects also indicated the necessity of honouring the Fifteen-Year-War martyrs.

Moreover, the fact that the KMT played a vital role in the Fifteen-Year War had very little negative influence on the PRC's *baoxu* activities for that war's martyrs, and the CCP regime even honoured several KMT martyrs. Two factors account for this. First, the CCP's relevant regulations suggested that only a KMT soldier killed in the Fifteen-Year War who 'had not engaged in any reactionary behaviour in his life' could be awarded the status of Martyr. As a result, KMT martyrs who were recognised by the CCP regime were restricted to those who were 'proven' to be unconnected to the KMT. Moreover, with its general propaganda that the KMT was 'reactionary' and impotent in the Fifteen-Year War, the CCP regime did not need to worry that honouring several 'good' KMT martyrs would damage its authority. Second, the CCP used every possible opportunity to publicise its own sacrifices during that war. For instance, there were many cases in which CCP soldiers killed by Chinese soldiers of the Japanese puppet regime or the KMT were publicised as 'anti-Japanese martyrs'. (Unless stated specifically, as in the case of Peng Xue-feng's death, it was claimed of all the CCP's anti-Japanese martyrs mentioned in this chapter that they had been killed in conflicts with the Japanese Imperial Army.)

Furthermore, once recognised by the PRC, there was no big difference between the state's treatment of KMT martyrs and their CCP counterparts. The PRC's honouring of both the CCP and KMT martyrs of the Fifteen-Year War was obstructed by the objective conditions of the PRC. The biggest obstruction was not grand considerations like Sino–Japanese relations or party loyalty (apart from the atypical Cultural Revolution period), but was more pragmatic: financial constraints. The CCP regime was not stingy in regard to giving KMT soldiers the title of Martyr. However, it was very reluctant to give them material support. Similarly, the main reason why the centre discouraged projects related to CCP martyrs' memorials was either because there was 'no money' or due to 'the extravagance and waste of some projects that spent too much money'. Moreover, because the local authorities and other organs co-ordinating the projects were preoccupied with economic construction (as opposed to symbolic construction), they struggled to carry on with and devote themselves to martyrs' memorial projects.[121]

Another obstruction was poor implementation of the centre's policy on martyrs in the day-to-day scenario. For instance, the centre promulgated several measures to improve the status and welfare of martyrs' families. However, as Diamant and Hung have pointed out, there were many reports that PLA martyrs' families were mistreated in their local communities, and the centre was seriously concerned by this problem. The overall political atmosphere can also be considered as a further hindrance. During the Cultural Revolution, for example, many KMT martyrs were attacked because of their political affiliation. Nevertheless, the circumstances of their CCP counterparts were not much better.

Apart from 'necessity', 'usefulness' was another rationale for the state's honouring of the Fifteen-Year-War martyrs, as well as for the state-sponsored Fifteen-Year-War remembrance activities.[122] The next chapter will discuss the usefulness of commemorating the Fifteen-Year War for the CCP regime. Several themes that were briefly mentioned here will also be dealt with in the next chapter in greater detail, such as how the regime created a CCP-centric national remembrance of the Fifteen-Year War, and the local dimension of this national war remembrance.

Notes

1 Unless cited separately, this entire section is based on NMA-5012-2-174: '1952 nian lieshi zhengming jifuxude cailiao' [Documents about martyrs' evidence and

consolation/compensation to their bereaved families 1952 年烈士证明及抚恤的材料]. I also used other available sources (mainly from internet) to confirm the correctness of these archival recordings, as many of them were based on Ba Shijie, as well as other people's memories.

2 NMA-5012-2-174, Qingzheng studied in Peking's private Zhixing middle school 志行中学, however, only information about private Zhicheng middle school 志成中学 can be found.

3 Qingzheng's information can also be found in the 'Huangpu junxiao dishiqi tongxuelu (dishiqi)' [List of students' names of Huangpu Military Academy (10th session) 黄埔军校第十期同学录].

4 Xu Rongsheng and Lin Chengxi, *Guomindang kongjun kangzhan shilu* [Record of the KMT Air Force's War of Resistance 国民党空军抗战实录] (Zhongguo dangan chubanshe, 1994), p. 445. 'Jianqiao yinglie zhuan' [Heroes of the eastern skies 笕桥英烈传], a film describing this air battle, was released on 7 July 1977 in Taiwan.

5 Unless cited separately, this paragraph is based on Li Mengwen and Jin Shuang, *Wuhan huizhan: Baowei Dawuhan* [The battle of Wuhan: defend the great Wuhan] (Beijing: Tuanjie chubanshe, 2005) 李梦文, 金爽, 武汉会战: 保卫大武汉 (团结出版社, 2005).

6 Volunteer Soviet Air Forces came to support the ROC between 1937 and 1941, based on the Sino–Soviet Non-Aggression Pact signed on 21 August 1937.

7 Li and Jin, *Wuhan huizhan*.

8 Li and Jin, *Wuhan huizhan*.

9 Anonymous, 'Ba Qingzheng 巴清正'. http://lov.vac.gov.tw/Protection/Content. aspx?i=151&c=5&e=&p=8, date unknown, date accessed, 9 March 2014. The KMT's Medal of Stars 星序奖章 was awarded to pilots who shot down successively enemy aircraft. The number of the stars represents the number of the aircraft shot down successively by the pilot. According to this source, Qingzheng was awarded the Medal of One Star, which means he only shot down one Japanese aircraft. This is contradictory to what Ba's father Shiji claimed in his letter to Nanjing officials.

10 Nanjing difangzhi bianzuan weiyuanhui, *Nanjing Minzheng Zhi* [Gazetteer of Nanjing civil affairs] (Shen Zhen: Haitian chubanshe, 1994) 南京地方志编纂委员会, 南京民政志 (海天出版社, 1994).

11 Anonymous, 'Ba Qingzheng'.

12 NMA-5012-2-174, Ba Shijie's letter to Nanjing Municipal People's Government on 26 June 1950. Previous descriptions of Ba Qingzheng's deed are largely based on Ba Shijie's letters.

13 NMA-5012-2-174, Shijie's letter to the NMBCA on 20 November 1951.

14 NMA- 5012-2-174, the NMBCA's report to the Nanjing Municipal Communist Party's Committee, of 7 December 1951. *Renmin Ribao*, 'Guanyu geming lieshi dejieshi' [Explanations of the term 'Revolutionary Martyr' 关于革命烈士的解释], 15 October 1950.

15 The NMBCA's report, 7 December 1951.

16 According to a handwritten note stuck to Ba's letter of 20 November 1951.

17 The NMBCA's report, 7 December 1951.

18 NMA-5012-2-174, the NMBCA to the NMPLC, 8 January 1952.

19 NMA-5012-2-174, The NMPLC to the NMBCA, 14 January 1952.

20 Several items of literature deal with Fifteen-Year-War veterans and their families, who were another significant group for whose sake the Fifteen-Year War had to be remembered. For issues about Chinese veterans and their families, see, G. White, 'The politics of demobilised soldiers from liberation to cultural revolution', *The China Quarterly*, 82 (1980), 181–213; N. J. Diamant, *Embattled glory: veterans, military families, and the politics of patriotism in China (1949–2007)* (Lanham, MD: Rowman & Littlefield, 2010). Diamant, 'Conspicuous silence'.

21 Similarly, in order to claim compensation, some Nanjing citizens also acted as agents of the Nanjing Massacre memory during the Wang Jingwei administration and during the post-1949 period. Interview, Liu, Liu's office at the Nanjing Massacre Memorial, 11 June 2012.

22 A few scholars have discussed PRC's *baoxu* system, see, for example, C.-t. Hung, 'The cult of the Red Martyr: politics of commemoration in China', *Journal of Contemporary History*, 43 (2008), 279–304; N. J. Diamant, 'Between martyrdom and mischief: the political and social predicament of CCP war widows and veterans, 1949–66', in D. Lary and S. Mackinnon (eds), *Scars of war: the impact of warfare on modern China* (Vancouver: UBC Press, 2001), 162–189.

23 Due to the political divisions in Republican China, the commemoration of martyrs was strongly regionalised, see, Henrietta Harrison, 'Martyrs and militarism in early republican China', *Twentieth Century China*, 23 (1998), 41–70.

24 *Gazetteer of Nanjing Civil Affairs*; Anonymous, *Jiangsusheng difangzhi* [Gazetteer of Jiangsu Province 江苏省地方志]. www.jssdfz.com/, date unknown, date accessed, 9 March 2014; Shen Yang, 'Guomin zhengfu kangzhan shiqi junshi youfu pingxi' [Review concerning the KMT's manoeuvring to give preferable treatment and compensation to military personnel during the War of Resistance period], *Kang Ri zhanzheng yanjiu,* 2008. 沈阳, 国民政府抗战时期军事优抚评析, 抗日战争研究, 2008.

25 See, *Gazetteer of Nanjing Civil Affairs*.

26 Fan Ning and Chen Jianzhong 樊宁 程建中, 'Guomin gemingjun dishijiulu jun, diwujun wuming yingxiong jinianbei' [Monument to the unknown heroes of the 5th Corps and 19th Corps, National Revolutionary Army 国民革命军第十九路军、第五军无名英雄纪念碑]. www.hoplite.cn/templates/gjzlc0020.html, date unknown, date accessed, 9 March 2014.

27 The main campus of the cemetery, which was completed in August 1932 and located in Purple Mount as well, included an archway, a stele pavilion, a mourning hall, a monument and many individual tombs, *Gazetteer of Nanjing Civil Affairs*.

28 *Gazetteer of Nanjing Civil Affairs*, p. 99.

29 Nanjing difangzhi bianzuan weiyuanhui, *Nanjing jianzhi zhi* [Gazetteer of Nanjing's Administrative Development] (Shenzhen: Haitian chubanshe, 1994), p. 244 南京市地方志编纂委员会, 南京建置志 (海天出版社, 1994).

30 See, Li Xiang, 'Kangzhan shiqi guomin zhengfu qianghua junren fuxu zhidu yuanyin zhifenxi' [Analysis of the reasons why the KMT government strengthened its policy of compensating military personnel during the War of Resistance period], *Junshi lishi*, 1 (2008), 18–21 李翔, 抗战时期国民政府强化军人抚恤制度原因之分析, 军事历史 2008, 18–21; Li Xiang (2008), 'Kangzhan shiqi guominzhengfu lujun fuxu jigou chutan' [Exploration of the KMT's method of consoling and compensating the army during the War of Resistance period], *Kang Ri zhanzheng yanjiu*, 2008, 82–109 李翔, 抗战时期国民政府陆军抚恤机构初探, 抗日战争研究 1 (2008), 82–109; Lan Xuehua, 'Kangzhan shiqi guomin zhengfu de junren youfu anzhi zhidu pingshu' [Review of the KMT's policy of giving preferable treatment and compensation to military personnel], *Changchun shifanxueyuan xuebao* 28 (2009), 63–68 兰雪花, 抗战时期国民政府的军人优抚安置制度评述, 长春师范学院学报 28 (2009), 63–68.

31 *Gazetteer of Nanjing Civil Affairs, Gazetteer of Jiangsu Province*, Shen, 'Guomin zhengfu kangzhanshiqi junshi youfu'.

32 Chiang Kai-Shek, 'Jiang Jieshi shengliri yanshuo quanwen (3 September 1945)' [Chiang Kai-Shek's speech on the victory day], in Hunan Zhijiang xianzhi bangongshi (ed.), *Kangzhan shengli shouxiang* [Receive surrender after winning the War of Resistance] (Zhijiang: Internal circulated materials, 2002) 湖南芷江县志办公室, 蒋介石胜利日演说全文 抗战胜利受降 (内部资料, 2002).

33 *Gazetteer of Nanjing Civil Affairs*, p. 101.

34 A public funeral was held for the Air Force martyrs in April 1946, see, *Zhongyang Ribao*, 'Kongjun xunzhi jiangshi gongmu gongzang dianli' [Ceremony of public funeral in the Air Force Martyrs' Cemetery 空軍殉職將士公墓公葬典禮], 4 April 1946; *Gazetteer of Nanjing Civil Affairs.*

35 The spring rite and autumn rite continued to be held in post-1949 Taiwan as well, i.e. National Archives Administration in Taiwan 0041/129.2.8 /01/03/020, 'Kangzhan zhenwang jiangshi chunqiu erji' [Spring and autumn rites for the military personnel killed in the War of Resistance 抗戰陣亡將士春秋二祭], 24 March 1952; NAA-0069/0800/10/1/019: 'Gejie chunji kangzhan zhengwang jiangshi deng' [People from all walks of life attended the spring rites for the military personnel killed in the War of Resistance 各界春祭抗戰陣亡將士等], 8 August 1980.

36 See, *Gazetteer of Jiangsu Province; Zhongyang Ribao*, 'Linggusi qiuji xianlie' [Autumn rite for the martyrs in Linggu Temper 靈谷寺秋祭先烈], 3 September 1948; 'Zhongshu juxing chunji dianli' [The centre held the spring rite 中樞舉行春祭典禮], 30 March 1949.

37 *Zhongyang Ribao*, 'Nixingjian kangzhan jiniantang' [Plan to build memorial to victory in the War of Resistance 擬興建抗戰紀念堂], 29 May 1946; 'Kunlunguan zhanyi zhenwang jiangshi jinianta' [Monument to the military personnel killed in the Kunlunguan battle 昆崙關戰役陣亡將士, 紀念塔], 27 July 1947; 'Tengchong zhanyi jinianbei' [Monument of the Tengchong battle 騰衡戰役紀念碑], 19 February 1948.

38 This cenotaph was rebuit in July 2000, see, *Zhongguo Qingnianbao*, 'Guangdongshanzhuang kang Ri yuejunmu jinru Nanjing datusha yanjiu shiye' [The grave of anti-Japanese martyrs from Guangdong Province in Guangdong Manor was considered by Nanjing Massacre Research 广东山庄抗日粤军墓进入南京大屠杀视野]. http://news.qq.com/a/20090812/000640.htm, 12 August 2009, date accessed, 9 March 2014.

39 'Juhuatai waijiao jiu lieshimu 菊花台外交九烈士墓'; 'Zhonglie gongyuan 忠烈公园', *Gazetteer of Nanjing Civil Affairs.*

40 Such as, *Zhongyang Ribao*, 'Jianshe Hengyang wei kangzhan jiniancheng' [Develop Hengyang as a memorial city to the War of Resistance 建設衡陽為抗戰紀念城], 5 December 1946; Yang An, 'Fuqin Yang Xiaolu degushi: "Hengyang kangzhan jiniancheng" jianshe shimo' [My father Yang Xiaolu's story: the whole story of developing the 'Hengyang War of Resistance Memorial City'], *Wenshi cankao*,2010: www.people.com.cn/GB/198221/198819/198849/12412595. html, date accessed, 14 March 2014 杨安, 父亲杨晓麓的故事"衡阳抗战纪念城"建设始末, 文史参考, 2010; A similar thing happened for Zhijiang, see: 'Zhijiang shouxiang jiniancheng jianshe jilve' [Story of developing Zhijiang as the city that received the surrender 芷江受降城建設紀略] in *Kangzhan shengli shouxiang (2002)*, 203–208.

41 *Zhongyang Ribao*, 'Shimin kejiansong shiji chengqing jiangxu' [Residents can send deeds and apply for award and aid 市民可檢送事蹟呈請獎卹], 3 August 1946; 'Duikangzhan yougongxian gongren shehuibu tebanfa jiangzhang' [Ministry of Social Affairs issued medals to workers who contributed to the War of Resistance 對抗戰有貢獻工人社會部特頒發獎章], 14 August 1946.

42 *Zhongyang Ribao*: 'Kangzhan zhengwang jiangshi zidimianfei ruxue' [Children of the military personnel killed in the War of Resistance can have free education 抗戰陣亡將士, 子弟免費入學], 18 April 1947; 'Daochu pengbi fuyi shangxin, ququ xujin buneng huomin, kangzhan yishu qinsu kuzhong' [Families of people killed in the War of Resistance complain 到處碰壁俯仰傷心, 區區卹金不能活命, 抗戰遺屬傾訴苦衷], 18 May 1947; 'Weiwen kangzhan jiangshi yizu, mingri zhuhu fenfa wukuan' [Comfort the families of the military personal killed in the

War of Resistance: money and materials are distributed to them, family by family 慰問抗戰將士遺族, 明日逐戶分發物款], 6 July 1947.

43 *Gazetteer of Nanjing's Administrative Development*, p. 244. The base areas were: Middle China Base 华中抗日根据地, Northern Jiangsu Base 苏北抗日根据地, Middle Jiangsu Base 苏中抗日根据地, Jiangsu, Zhejiang and Anhui Base 苏浙皖.

44 Luo Pingfei, 'Jianguoqian Zhongguo gongchandang junren fuxu youdai jituiyi anzhi zhengce yanjiu' [A study of the CPC's Policy on pensions, favoured treatment and demobilisation placement for servicemen before the founding of New China], *Zhonggong dangshi yanjiu*, 2005. 罗平飞, 建国前中国共产党军人抚恤优待及退役安置政策研究, 中共党史研究, 6 (2005).

45 For the CCP's laws and regulations on *baoxu* manoeuvres in its earlier stage, see, Luo, 'the CPC's policy on pensions'.

46 Zhou Shiyu and Li Bengong, *Youfu baozhang* [Consolation, compensation and indemnification] (Zhongguo shehui chubanshe, 1996), pp. 7–8 周士禹, 李本公, 优抚保障 (中国社会出版社, 1996).

47 豫皖苏抗日根据地, Jiangsu Provincial Archives (JPA)-4007-3-249: Sihong County's correspondence to the Jiangsu Provincial Department of Civil Affairs (JPDCA), 12 April 1955.

48 JPA-4007-2-587: Sihong county's Bureau of Civil Affairs' report about rebuilding Zhujiagang Martyrs' Cemetery, 2 April 1963.

49 JPA-4007-3-656: Siyang county's correspondence to the JPDCA, 12 November 1959.

50 JPA-4007-3-249: Sihong county's correspondence to the JPDCA, 12 April 1955; Hu Changfang, 'Yong sheng ming baohu Peng Xuefeng yigude Liyaba' [Li the mute who sacrificed his life to protect the remains of Peng Xuefeng], *Dangshi wenhui*, 9 (2012), 62–63 胡昌方, 用生命保护彭雪枫遗骨的李哑巴, 党史文汇, 2012, 62–63.

51 JPA-4007-3-656: Funing County CCP Committee's announcement about the foundation of the 'Committee for the construction of the Lupu Martyrs' commemorative monument', 1959; 4007-3-582: Xinyi county's correspondence to the JPDCA, 21 February 1958; 4007-3-734: the budget for expending the Huaiying city's Eighty-Two Martyrs' Cemetery, 13 March 1960.

52 JPA-4007-3-249: Ganyu county's correspondence the JPDCA about the plan of repairing the Mount of Resisting Japan.

53 Zhou and Li, *Youfu baozhang*.

54 Luo, 'The CCP's policy on pensions'.

55 Zhou and Li, *Youfu baozhang*.

56 Luo, 'The CCP's policy on pensions'.

57 Zhao Cuisheng and Pan Hong, 'Junren shehui baozhang zhidu tanwei' [Explore the policy of military personnel's social indemnification], *Wujing Xueyuan xuebao*, 6 (2001), 69–73. 赵翠生, 潘红, 军人社会保障制度探微, 武警学院学报, 2001, 69–73.

58 NMA-5012-2-40: Ms Zhang's application to Piaoshui county.

59 *Gazetteer of Nanjing Civil Affairs, Gazetteer of Nanjing's Administrative Development.*

60 E.g. 'The Common Program of the Chinese People's Political Consultative Conference 中国人民政治协商会议共同纲领 (1949)', 'Constitution of the People's Republic of China 中华人民共和国宪法 (1954)', 'Military Service Law of the People's Republic of China 中华人民共和国兵役法 (1955)'. Xie Miao, 'Zhongguo gongchandang de fuxu zhengce yanjiu' [Research on the CCP's policy of consolation and compensation], 1949–1966 (Shandong shifan daxue, Master's dissertation, 2010) 谢苗, 中国共产党的抚恤政策研究 (1949–1966) (山东师范大学, 硕士论文, 2010).

61 'Gemin junren xisheng, binggu baoxu zanxing tiaoli 革命军人牺牲 病故褒恤暂行条例' and 'Gemin lieshi jiashu gemin junren jiashu youdai zanxing tiaoli 革命烈士家属革命军人家属优待暂行条列'.

62 The conflicts are: the 1911 Xinhai Revolution, the Eastern Expedition and Northern Expedition (1924–1927), the Land Revolution War (1927–1937), the battles against Japan (1931–1937), the War of Resistance (1937–1945), and the War of Liberation (1945–1949). Also, the announcement stipulated that the individuals killed by imperialists and reactionaries since the 1919 May Fourth Movement be called Martyrs.

63 JPA-4007-3-248: Wuxi Municipal Bureau of Civil Affairs announcement, 1954.

64 Hung, 'The cult of the Red Martyr', mentioned this in his paper as well.

65 The 'Regulation for Dead Soldiers'.

66 NMA-5012-1-141: reports about martyrs' memorials under construction, October 1950–October 1951; JPA-4007-1-107, Wuxi city's martyrs' grave, 1961; JPA-4007-3-582: Lianshui county's report on building a martyrs' cemetery, pavilion, park and display hall, 3 March 1958.

67 See, *Gazetteer of Nanjing Civil Affairs, Gazetteer of Jiangsu Province*.

68 NMA-5063-2-215: opinions about protecting the relics during the Cultural Revolution, 1966; surprisingly, a stele pavilion of the Japanese imperial army also survived and ordered to be removed during the Cultural Revolution, according to this document.

69 Shen Zui, *Shen Zui huiyi zuopin quanji* [Collection of Shen Zui's recollective articles] (Beijing: Jiuzhou tushu chubanshe, 1998) 沈醉, 沈醉回忆作品全集 (九洲图书出版社, 1998); Funingke 福宁客, 'Mao Zedong weihe pishi xiufu Dailimu' [Why Mao Zedong ordered the repair of Dai Li's grave 毛泽东为何批示修复戴笠墓]. http://fn01.i.sohu.com/blog/view/258182837.htm, 21 March 2013, date accessed, 9 March 2014. According to these articles, the grave had been destroyed in 1951 and repaired afterwards.

70 NMA-5063-2-215.

71 JPA-4007-3-32: the JPDCA's correspondence to President Tan and Vice President Ke, October 1953.

72 JPA-4007-3-141: Jiangsu Provincial People's Government's correspondence to Yangzhou Municipal People's Government, 10 May 1954.

73 Guowuyuan pizhuan neiwubu, 'Guanyu lieshijinian jianzhuwu xiujian he guanli gongzuo de baogao' [MIA's report forwarded by the State Council about repair, construction and management of martyrs' memorials 国务院批转内务部关于烈士纪念建筑物修建荷管理工作的报告 国秘字863号], 20 December 1963; Zhonggong zhongyang, Guowuyuan, 'Guanyu jinhou xiujian jianzhuwu dengyouguan wentide tongzhi' [Central Committee of the CCP and State Council's announcement on issues of constructing and maintainning memorials 中共中央, 国务院关于今后修建纪念建筑物等有关问题的通知], 18 November 1964; JPA-4007-2-729: PLA, Jiangsu provincial Military Control Committee's reply about developing Wangjie Martyrs' Cemetery, 20 July 1967.

74 E.G. NMA-5012-3-275: the MIA's announcement about visiting the martyrs' graves on Tomb-sweeping Day, 2 March 1955; 5012-3-575: Nanjing Municipal People's Committee's announcement about carrying out activities to commemorate revolutionary martyrs for Tomb-sweeping Day, 25 March 1961.

75 JPA-4007-3-550: the JPDCA's announcement, 28 March 1959.

76 NMA-5012-2-293: about building the graves for Xiang Ying and other two martyrs, 12 November 1953–12 November 1955.

77 E.g. JPA-4007-2-71: a statistical table indicating the distribution of martyrs' memorials in Jiangsu Province, 25 November 1954; MIA's announcement about inspecting and registering martyrs' graves, 18 March 1958; JPA-4007-1-107: the

MIA's letter to the JPDCA to ask about the situation of the martyrs' memorials in Jiangsu, 6 May 1961.

78 The constitutional document of this kind was the MIA's 'Guanyu jianchadengji lieshi fenmu detongzhi' [Announcement about inspecting and registering the martyrs' graves 关于检查 登记烈士坟墓的通知], 29 April 1954.

79 NMA-5012-3-275: the MIA's announcement about visiting the martyrs' graves on Tomb-sweeping Day, 2 March 1955; 5012-3-275: Jiangsu Provincial People's Committee's announcement, 31 March 1955.

80 NMA-5012-2-529: the JPDCA's letter about deterring the construction of martyrs' memorials, 6 July 1957.

81 JPA-4007-3-582: the JPDCA's announcement, 9 April 1958. It said there was no budget for repairing or constructing martyrs' memorials this year and if any locality needed to do so, would it please raise the funds locally.

82 MIA's announcement about inspecting and registering martyrs' graves, 18 March 1958; JPA-4007-3-582: the joint announcement of the Jiangsu Provincial Department of Finance and the JPDCA, 17 April 1958.

83 Still, the JPDCA only gave 2,500 RMB to the construction, while 7,443 RMB was requested. JPA-4007-3-937: Jiangning county's report to ask for approval of the construction of the Yuntaishan Martyrs' Cemetery, 29 April 1964; Correspondence to the JPDCA, 14 July 1964; the JPDCA's reply, 15 July 1964.

84 E.g. many letters from families of the soldiers killed in action, which request local government to find the burial sites of the soldiers and re-bury them, can be found in NMA-5012-2-709 (1950–1952) and NMA-5012-2-210 (16 December 1951–25 December 1952).

85 JPA-4007-3-32: Baoshan county's correspondence to the JPDCA, 30 March 1953; the JPDCA's reply, 10 April 1953.

86 NMA-5012-2-529: Liyang county's correspondence to the Zhenjiang Zhuanshu's ('The name of a government office at a specific level', dictionary) Civil Affairs unit, 25 April 1956. JPA-4007-3-871: Zhenjiang Zhuanshu's Civil Affairs unit's correspondence to the JPDCA, 12 September 1962.

87 Yuan died during his term in office as the PRC's vice-minister of foreign affairs in 1956 and was buried in the Babaoshan Revolutionary Cemetery. NMA-5012-2-293: Epigraph for Zhu Lianghu martyr.

88 JPA-4007-2-587: Luo Yinghuai's letter to the Provincial People's Committee, 27 December 1962; Sihong county's report, 2 April 1963; the JPDCA's reply, 16 December 1963.

89 JPA-4007-3-249, 12 Arp 1955; JPA-4007-3-582, 24 May 1958; JPA-4007-3-582, 16 April 1958; JPA-4007-3-582 21 February 1958; JPA-4007-3-871, 12 December 1962.

90 JPA-4007-3-582: Wu county's report, 10 April 1958; Wu county's second report, 3 June 1958; the JPDCA's reply, 29 July 1958.

91 NMA-5012-2-364 (20 April 1954–18 December 1956) and NMA-5012-2-529: the JPDCA's announcement about re-burying the bodies of martyrs, 16 February 1958.

92 See, 'Regulation for military dependents'.

93 Diament, 'Between martyrdom and mischief'.

94 Clause 3 in ' Regulation for deceased soldiers'.

95 Clause 3, clause 6 in 'Regulation for deceased soldiers'; clause 5 in 'Regulation for military families'.

96 NMA-5012-3-40: the civil affairs organ of the ECMGC, 9 January 1951.

97 NMA-5012-2-363: the JPDCA's announcement about the management of retro-active consolation and compensation for the martyrs, 22 May 1956; the JPDCA's reply to several inquires about the management of retroactive consolation and compensation for the martyrs, 8 October 1956.

98   See documents in NMA-5012-2-332 (6 January 1950–21 November 1956), NMA-5012-2-384 (16 January 1957–4 December 1957), NMA-5012-2-418 (3 November 1958–18 November 1959).

99   Diamant also noticed, based on archives dated to the 1950s and 1960s, that former KMT officers could receive the same amount of state aid as PLA veterans, Diamant, 'Between martyrdom and mischief', p. 168.

100   MIA, 'Neiyouzi di 69 hao wenjian' [The 69th document, Neiyouzi 内优字第69号 文件], 29 April 1951.

101   NMA-5012-2-332 (6 January 1950–21 November 1956).

102   NMA-5012-2-332: the NMBCA to the head of the Nanjing Municipal Bureau of Public Health Xu Tongqing, 26 March 1956.

103   NMA-5012-2-332: the Jiangsu Provincial People's Committee's reply, 2 June 1956.

104   Interview, Yu, Nanjing Municipal Archives, 19 June 2012.

105   The names were changed during the Cultural Revolution. Chen Xubin 谌旭彬, 'Guojun kang Ri lieshi daiyu bianqian' [The changes of the treatment of the KMT's anti-Japanese martyrs 国军抗日烈士待遇变迁]. http://view.news.qq.com/ zt2013/gjkrls/index.htm, 12 April 2013, date accessed 9 March 2014. For an article about the evolution of commemorating Zhang Zizhong, see, A. Waldron, 'China's new remembering of World War II: the case of Zhang Zizhong', *Modern Asian Studies,* 30 (1996), 945–978.

106   NMA-5012-2-40, Ms Zhang's letter.

107   See, JPA-4007-3-1187, Haimen county's correspondence to the JPDCA, 14 September 1965; the JPDCA's reply, 28 September 1965.

108   NMA-5012-2-40: the 9th Ward People's Government's letter, 13 March 1951; the note of Nanjing Municipal Senate, the letter of the Political Department of the Logistics Cadres' Academy, East China Military Region Field Army, 4 April 1951.

109   Minzhenbu fagui bangongshi, *Zhonghua renmin gongheguo minzheng gongzuo wenjian huibian (1949–1999)* [Compilation of the documents of the PRC's Civil Affairs] (Beijing: Zhongguo fazhi chubanshe, 2001) 民政部法规办公室, 中华人 民共和国民政工作文件汇编 (中国法制出版社, 2001).

110   JPA-4007-3-1187: Xuyi county's Civil Affairs Bureau's letter of 2 July 1965, the JPDCA's reply of 8 July 1965.

111   E.g. JPA-4007-2-729: Pei county's correspondence to the JPDCA, 12 April 1966.

112   JPA-4007-3-582: Suqian county's correspondence to the JPDCA, 12 January 1958.

113   JPA-4007-3-1275: the JPDCA's announcement about strengthening the management of revolutionary martyrs' memorials, 29 August 1966. NMA-5003-3-681: 'Guanyu qingmingjie kaizhan jinian geminglieshi huodong de tongzhi' [Announcement about organising activities of commemorating revolutionary martyrs 关于清 明节开展纪念革命烈士活动的通知], 23 March 1967.

114   Sihong xian renmin zhengfu 泗洪县龙集镇人民政府, 'Yingshan Lieshi lingyuan jianjie' [Brief introduction to the Yingshan Martyrs' Cemetery Park 应山烈士陵 园情况简介]. www.longji.gov.cn/whly/yslsly/130.aspx, 15 June 2012, date accessed, 9 March 2014.

115   Things which were considered to be feudalism, capitalism, revisionism and foreign were the common targets to be destroyed during the campaign. Many foreigners' cemeteries, like the one located in southeast Beijing, were destroyed during the campaign, The National Archives (UK)-FO-676/554: Foreigners' cemetery South East of Peking, 10 June 1970; H. L. Davies, Esq., 6 July 1970.

116   NMA-5063-2-215.

117   For example, the stone-carved lions and paintings with feudalistic elements in a stele pavilion of a martyrs' cemetery were removed, JPA-4007-3-1275: Wuxi city's correspondence to the JPDCA, 5 September 1966. Also, many 'feudalistic'

sculptures on a martyrs' commemorative archway in Rudong county were destroyed, such as the sculptures of two dragons and the Eight Immortals, JPA-4007-3-1275: Rudong county's correspondence to the JPDCA, 1 September 1966.

118 JPA-4007-2-729: Muyang county's report, 11 December 1966; Liuhe county's document, 1967.

119 JPA-4007-2-729: an attachment of a Gaoyu county's letter, 24 February 1967. For other examples, see, JPA-4007-2-729: Funing county's report asking for funds to build martyrs' memorials, 12 March 1967.

120 PRC's State Council, 'Guanyudui Xinhaigemin, Beifazhanzheng, Kang Ri zhanzheng zhong xishengde guomindang ren heqita aiguorenshi zhuirenwei geminlieshi wentide tongzhi' [Announcement about issues related to the recognition of the KMT members and other patriotic individuals who were sacrificed during the Xinhai Revolution, the Northern Expedition and the War of Resistance, as martyrs 关于对辛亥革命、北伐战争、抗日战争中牺牲的国民党人和其他爱国人士追认为革命烈士问题的通知], 1983. Nevertheless, it stipulated that no one-off consolation money would be given to them.

121 See, JPA-4007-3-582: Yancheng county's People's Committee to the JPDCA, 17 September 1958.

122 See, Diamant, 'Between martyrdom and mischief', p. 164.

4 Remembrance of the war

Using the past to serve the present

National anthem

Arise, ye who refuse to be slaves!
Let us mount our flesh and blood towards our new Great Wall!
The Chinese nation faces its greatest peril,
The thundering roar of our people will be heard!
Arise! Arise! Arise!
We are many, but our hearts beat as one!
Selflessly braving the enemy's gunfire, march on!
Selflessly braving the enemy's gunfire, march on!
March on! March on! On![1]

These are the lyrics from the song 'March of the Volunteers 义勇军进行曲', written by the playwright Tian Han 田汉, with music composed by the celebrated musician Nie Er 聂耳. The song was written for the film *Sons and Daughters in a Time of Storm* 风云儿女, first released on 24 May 1935, in Shanghai's Jincheng Theatre. The film tells the story of an intellectual who decides to devote himself to resisting the Japanese invasion after the Manchurian Incident. Since then, 'March of the Volunteers' has become widely known in China It was sung by patriotic students during the December 9th Movement in 1935; by the Kuomingtang soldiers in Burma; and by Chinese people overseas whose emotions were triggered by the war in their motherland.[2] During the Fifteen-Year War this was a tragic-heroic fighting song that was known to all Chinese people, regardless of age, gender, party loyalty and social status. What is more, the song was promoted by China's sympathisers and featured in many international events.[3]

Four years after the end of the war, this Fifteen-Year-War themed song resounded again in Tiananmen, following Mao Zedong's announcement that 'today, the People's Republic of China Central People's Government has been established', and was accompanied by the raising of the PRC's national 'Five-star Red Flag'. This song, born during the peril of the Fifteen-Year War, was played in the founding ceremony of the PRC as a provisional national anthem.

The decision to use 'March of the Volunteers' as the national anthem was almost uncontested. On 10 July 1949 the preparatory meeting of the new

Chinese People's Political Consultative Conference (CPPCC) issued a notice via major newspapers to call for suggestions for the design of the national flag and emblem, as well as the lyrics and melody for the national anthem.[4] Before the deadline on 20 August, numerous suggestions for the national anthem were submitted; however, the sixth section of the preparatory meeting – which was in charge of deciding on these national symbols – found none of them to be satisfactory. On 25 September, Mao Zedong and Zhou Enlai met relevant experts in the Fengze Garden, Zhongnanhai, to discuss the issue. As the person in charge of the sixth unit, Ma Xulun declared, 'our government will be established soon; it is impossible to create a national anthem in such a short period of time based on the current situation. Can we use "March of the Volunteers" as the provisional national anthem?'[5] His suggestion was welcomed by other participants, including Guo Moruo, who said, 'not only Chinese people but also foreign people can sing the song'. However, some of the participants, including Tian Han himself, thought lines like 'The Chinese nation faces its greatest peril' were out of date and should be revised. Meanwhile some participants, like Liang Sicheng, argued that the song 'is a product of history; I contend that we should not change either its melody or lyrics to preserve its integrity'. Zhou Enlai also insisted that it was better to use the original lyrics so that 'emotion can be triggered. If we change the lyrics, you won't feel that kind of emotion anymore when you sing it.' In the end, Mao gave the final verdict and decided to use the song as it was.[6]

The decision was formally passed in the first CPPCC on 27 September 1949. As indicated by the discussion in the Fengze Garden, 'March of the Volunteers' was chosen as the provisional national anthem not only because of its popularity, but also because it embodied the tragic-heroic history of China's war of resistance against Japan and the Chinese people's spirit of fighting against invaders. The Chinese government shared its view in *Renmin Ribao*, through the 'Answering readers' questions' column:

> Why use 'March of the Volunteers' as PRC's provisional national anthem? Why not revise some lines of the lyrics, which cannot represent the current situation anymore? [Because] it has been the most popular song in the past years of the Chinese people's revolutionary fighting, it has got a historical meaning. [Keeping the lyrics can] arouse people's memories of the difficulty as well as their suffering during the process of creating our motherland, and can inspire people's patriotic enthusiasm for resisting imperialist invasion, to carry out the revolution till its victory.[7]

The lyrics of 'March of the Volunteers' were sung as the PRC's provisional national anthem for seventeen years, until 1966. The reason why the lyrics were then banned was not because China's relationship with Japan had improved, nor because the Chinese thought the tragic-heroic past as well as the spirit of fighting were not necessary anymore, but rather because of

China's own political problems. At the beginning of the Cultural Revolution, Tian Han was charged as a traitor and with crimes such as representing 'black-line art' – thus, his works were accused of being 'poisonous weeds' and were criticised and banned.[8] Throughout the Cultural Revolution period, the song was only played without the lyrics, or was replaced by other songs like 'The East Is Red'. According to some memoirs, there were also calls for new lyrics to be written for the song and many lyrics with strong Cultural Revolution features were written during the period. However, these forms of the song did not achieve long-term or nationwide popularity.[9] After the overthrow of the 'Gang of Four', Chinese leaders felt the urge to bring order to the chaotic situation with respect to the national anthem – one of the most important national symbols. Their solution was to commission a new Chinese national anthem nationwide, since Tian Han had not yet been exonerated. A special unit for this task was formed by the Ministry of Culture.

There were two schemes for creating a new national anthem: composing new lyrics to fit the original melody or composing both new lyrics and a new melody. From October to December 1977, military and government sections at all levels chose 318 submissions to pass on to the special unit. There were also many submissions directly from the Chinese public. The special unit invited amateur as well as professional musicians and writers to review the submissions. After the first round of screening, the special unit organised many forums, in places like factories, farms and barracks, to hear the opinions of the masses and experts on the selected entries. The majority of those consulted preferred the first plan of keeping the original melody, because:

> The original melody had been used throughout the 'Anti-Japanese War', the War of Liberation [the Chinese Civil War from 1945 to 1949] and the period of Socialist Revolution and Construction, [and] the masses feel a deep connection with it. It has inspired our revolutionary morale and is still has a strong vitality … [also], the original melody has a large influence domestically and internationally; wherever one goes, if they only hear the melody, people would feel this is the great embodiment of the PRC and it would engender a lofty pride for the nation.[10]

Consequently, on 5 March 1978, new lyrics to the original melody of 'March of the Volunteers' were passed in the first session of the fifth National People's Congress (NPC). 'March of the Volunteers', born in the smoke of the Fifteen-Year War, continued, in this modified form, as the embodiment of the PRC. Nevertheless, many people were still not happy with this. Despite being heavily promoted, the new lyrics were not welcomed. Even the representatives of the NPC who approved them could not sing them.[11] It was widely complained that, despite being very 'revolutionary', they were not right: their content was empty and monotonous. So, after 1 March 1979, when Tian Han was formally exonerated, motions to re-adopt his lyrics for 'March of the Volunteers' for the national anthem were frequently tabled.[12]

Chen Dengke 陈登科, the first to advance such a motion, recalled that he held a dissenting view regarding the new lyrics when they were first passed in 1978, as he felt a deep connection with the original ones. He said:

> The people of our generation, in the period [of the Fifteen-Year War], were singing this song while marching towards a hail of bullets, marching towards the battle of resisting the Japanese and saving our country. At that time, whenever this song was sang, I would think of the peril of the Chinese nation, and the situation of the rivers and mountains of my country being tramped, and that the people were devastated; so I could not help the enthusiasm of committing myself to offer my hot-blood and life for my country and people.[13]

However, since Tian Han was still considered a 'traitor' at that time, Chen made no formal motion. Once Tian Han's status had been redressed, Chen immediately submitted a proposal to the second session of the fifth NPC held in June 1979. Although his motion was ignored at the time, he insisted on tabling a similar motion at every session, until it was eventually passed in the fifth session of the fifth NPC on 3 December 1982. 'March of the Volunteers' was written into the PRC's Constitution as the national anthem by the second session of the tenth NPC on 14 March 2004.

* * *

Karen Cerulo suggests that national anthems, as one national symbol, 'provide the strongest, clearest statement of national identity'. Kyridis and his collaborators, who worked on an ambitious project of comparing national anthems worldwide, has further pointed out that national anthems are chosen by national leaders, and due to their importance those leaders will want to choose national anthems that are most appropriate, effective and appealing to the national population. In the PRC's case, the CCP leaders chose a national anthem whose content, meaning and emotions were provided by the Fifteen-Year War.[14]

Why did the CCP give the Fifteen-Year-War memory such a central place? Following the logic of Kyridis et al.'s findings, they did so because the Fifteen-Year-War memory remained 'most appropriate, effective and appealing' to the Chinese population. Following the reasons given by the supporters of 'March of the Volunteers', memory of the war could automatically trigger emotions of dedication, loyalty and patriotism. In short, because remembrance of the the Fifteen-Year War was useful, it was promoted by the CCP regime to such a central position. Now that the Fifteen-Year War was an unavoidable and epic part of China's past, as I argued in Chapter 3, the CCP regime wanted to adapt this past to serve the present. Furthermore, there were many facets to the war memory: which ones were especially useful to the CCP, and thus promoted by it? Regarding the 'March of the Volunteers', which conveys the message that although the nation had faced great peril it had nevertheless fought back and risen again under the guidance of the CCP, it was the CCP-centric and tragic-heroic aspect of that message and that memory that was cherished by China's leaders.

This chapter first explores these two questions in greater detail against the wider historical background before 1982, and through an analysis of a wide range of state-sponsored realms of Fifteen-Year-War remembrance. The second section introduces three such realms: Fifteen-Year-War memorial days, school history textbooks and national history museums. The third section examines how Fifteen-Year-War remembrance was employed by the CCP regime to nurture popular support for its changing domestic as well as foreign policies, and explores the corresponding adjustments in the regime's narrative of the war brought about by policy changes. This section then moves on to discuss the relatively long-term usefulness of Fifteen-Year-War remembrance in the PRC's nation-building practice – war remembrance was used to create a new socialist national identity and to justify the legitimacy of the CCP. One version of Fifteen-Year-War memories, which was consistent and mostly intact before 1982, was promoted by the CCP regime for this long-term purpose: the regime preferred to remember the war as a heroic and tragic war that had been led by the CCP.

By various means, the CCP regime promoted its version of the war as the 'national' memory of the Fifteen-Year War. Was this national memory embraced throughout China? Did different regions remember the war differently, as different areas had different experiences during the war? In its fourth section, the remainder of this chapter examines the complicated picture of local war remembrance through the case study of Nanjing. It finds that local communities enjoyed 'autonomy' in remembering the war, as long as their remembrance was not contradictory to the national one.

The chapter concludes that Fifteen-Year-War remembrance was a valuable asset for the CCP regime before 1982, and because of this the regime promoted war remembrance on its own initiative in the PRC before 1982. The conclusion also emphasises that the CCP did not reject a victimhood narrative with respect to the Fifteen-Year War – quite the opposite: both the central and local governments used the miserable facets of the war to serve both their short- and long-term aims.

State-sponsored realms of memory

Before 1982 the Fifteen-Year War was commemorated by the CCP regime mainly on five key dates, namely: July 7 (commemorating the Marco Polo Bridge Incident), August 15 and September 3 (both commemorating V-J Day), September 18 (commemorating the Manchurian Incident) and December 9 (commemorating the December 9th Movement to Resist Japan and Save the Nation).[15] The Fifteen-Year War was also taught in the PRC's schools and national museums as an important part of contemporary Chinese history. This section introduces these realms of memory, to set the scene for the rest of the chapter.

Research into the presentation of the Fifteen-Year War in these realms, which have not yet been systematically studied, can also fill in some gaps in the literature. In terms of the five key memorial days, some researchers have tended to look at the history of one single memorial day, rather than the whole system of memorial days. Second, scholarly study linking the pre- and post-1949 commemoration of these days is lacking. Third, the existing literature normally only associates these days with the Sino–Japanese relationship and overlooks their other functions for the CCP regime.[16] As regards the narrative of the Fifteen-Year War in school history textbooks and history museums before 1982, most existing literature suggests this narrative was CCP-centric and stressed the victorious nature of the Chinese forces.[17] Furthermore, these discussions in the literature are not based on a sufficient amount of sources. Although a few scholars have mentioned these two realms' presentation of the Japanese atrocities, they have not got to the bottom of the matter.[18]

War memorial days

The official commemoration of the five Fifteen-Year-War memorial dates was relatively consistent from 1949 to 1982. Throughout this period, at least one of these dates was commemorated every year, with some exceptions. Commemoration was through memoirs, special exhibitions, films, concerts and posters, among other forms, in a similar way as described in Chapter 2 for the 20th anniversary commemoration in 1965. In addition, during the December 9th celebrations, participants or witnesses were normally invited to give talks, and street dramas, which were popular during the December 9th Movement, were performed, such as *Lay Down Your Whip* 放下你的鞭子. Nevertheless, commemoration of these days had taken place since the wartime. The party leaders simply chose to continue this pre-1949 practice, capitalising on its usefulness in mobilising the masses, which was proved during the wartime period, for their present aims in the PRC. Next, I will briefly introduce the commemorative history of these five memorial dates.

Five days after the Manchuria Incident, the KMT regime decided to fly all flags at half-mast and to stop entertainment nationwide to mourn the loss of Shenyang on 23 September 1931.[19] Commemoration of the Marco Polo Bridge Incident began in 1938, and July 7 was designated as the 'the war of resistance and nation-building day' (*kangzhan jianguo jinianri* 抗战建国纪念日).[20] During the war, these two dates were regularly commemorated nationwide, by everyone from the leaders of the KMT government (e.g. Chiang Kai-Shek, who wrote a series of commemorative articles for these two days) to the soldiers, as well as residents in remote areas of China (for example, the residents and the soldiers stationed in Zhaoqing 肇庆 organised an assembly to commemorate the second anniversary of the July 7 Incident, and they built a monument in the local school).[21]

During the Civil War period, August 15 and September 3 became a part of the Fifteen-Year-War commemorative system. However, for both the KMT

.and the CCP, other enemies replaced Japan as targets for criticism. For example, Chiang Kai-Shek published an article on 7 July 1947 which claimed that suppressing the 'Communist bandits' (*gongfei* 共匪) was an unfinished mission of the War of Resistance. The ultimate aim of the article was to advocate that all Chinese people should unite to get rid of the Communist Party.[22] The KMT regime also warned that the Soviet Union planned to instigate a second September 18th Incident and was a big threat to China.[23] For the CCP, the extra messages contained in their commemorative activities were 'anti-KMT and anti-America', which was exactly the opposite of the KMT's.[24] For the KMT regime, moreover, reclaiming Taiwan as a result of the war was a great achievement. In 1946, October 25 was proclaimed to be Taiwan's Retrocession Day 台湾光复节. During the Civil War, this day was commemorated annually as a platform for displaying this great achievement and as an occasion to mobilise the newly returned Taiwanese.[25]

On the other hand, after the Manchuria Incident, Japan gradually gained control over northern China. Against this catastrophic background, a demonstration movement was initiated by a group of patriotic students in Beijing on 9 December 1935.[26] Their main aim was to call for an immediate end to the Civil War and for a national armed resistance against Japan. Following the December 9th demonstration, another organised demonstration was carried out by citizens from the outskirts of Beijing on December 16.[27] These demonstrations in Beijing soon sparked similar actions throughout China. From 3 January 1936, students in Beijing started their 'south crusade' – they went southwards to mobilise resistance among the workers and peasants. Scholars sometimes include these follow-up actions as part of the December 9th Movement.[28]

Since its inception, this movement has been commemorated annually. In terms of the CCP's commemoration, during the early war years it praised the youthful patriotism displayed by the movement but always tried to rally patriotism for resisting the external enemy under the government (led by the KMT), for the sake of a united front. Since around 1944, when the defeat of Japan was predictable, the party line started to change.[29] First, the CCP started to portray this movement as an anti-Japanese and anti-traitorous-KMT movement under its own direct leadership.[30] Second, the external enemy also changed, as indicated by a December 9 commemorative meeting organised in Yanan on 5 December 1946. Speakers accused the KMT government, together with the US, of subjecting the Chinese people to ill treatment. The CCP's propaganda minister Lu Dingyi said that the KMT–US business agreement signed on 14 November was a contract by which Chiang Kai-Shek had sold out the Chinese people, and was more serious than the twenty-one demands made by Imperial Japan to the Republic of China in 1915. This meeting of around 1,000 participants ended with the singing of two songs, including 'March of the Volunteers'.[31]

After the foundation of the PRC in 1949, these five days continued to be commemorated. The Government Administration Council of the Central

People's Government promulgated 'Measures on taking a holiday for national festivals and memorial days' on 23 December 1949. According to this document, July 7, August 15 and September 18 were recognised officially as national memorial days as early as the inception of the PRC. The status of these three days as the only nationwide war memorial days (until now the Fifteen-Year War has been the only war to be officially commemorated according to the Measures and its revised versions) have stayed intact since then, with the exception that the central government replaced August 15 with September 3 as V-J Day in 1951.[32] December 9 was also consistently commemorated in Beijing and elsewhere (except during the Cultural Revolution). July 7, August 15, September 3 and September 18 – I will call them humiliation and victory dates – were often linked with the Sino–Japanese relationship by the CCP regime as well as foreign observers, while December 9 was mainly used by the CCP for domestic purposes.

There was a regular pattern in the Chinese government's commemoration of these five days: the government intended only to commemorate every first, fifth, or tenth anniversary of them, as shown in Table 4.1. For example, 1967 was the 30th anniversary of the July 7th Incident. The incident was commemorated at the high tide of the Cultural Revolution. There was no mention of other days in the same year. This was particularly 'abnormal', considering that the Chinese government had seriously protested over incidents that happened on September 8 and 9, when Chinese staff in a Chinese institution (the Liao Chengzhi Office) in Tokyo had taken part in violent conflicts with Japanese right-wingers and police. On September 18 that year, articles expressing 'Chinese people's anger' were published in *Renmin Ribao*, but there seemed to be no mention of the September 18th Incident.[33]

Nevertheless, there were exceptions to this pattern. Four such exceptions that are of most relevance to this chapter will be analysed in greater detail later: these dates were commemorated in an exceptional way when a special event or campaign took place; the frequency of commemorating August 15 and September 3 was exceptionally high between 1946 and 1962; commemoration of the four humiliation and victory dates was unusually rare after 1972; and December 9, one of the CCP's favourite memorial days, totally disappeared between 1966 and 1979.

History textbooks and museums

Throughout the period between 1949 and 1982, exhibitions related to the Fifteen-Year War in museums were basically 'supplementary reading matter' related to the relevant parts of the textbooks. The textbooks set the basic tone, while the museums provided more detail, sometimes in a more flexible manner. I will next summarise the pre-1982 presentation of the Fifteen-Year War in these two realms of memory.

The People's Publishing House (*Renmin chubanshe*, which was administered by the PRC's Ministry of Education) published the first PRC-produced

Table 4.1 Commemorating five dates related to the Fifteen-Year War in *Renmin Ribao*

	July 7	August 15	September 3	September 18	December 9
1946	Y	Y	Y	Y	Y
1947	Y	Y		Y	
1948	Y	Y		Y	
1949	Y	Y			
1950	Y	Y	Y	Y	Y
1951	Y	Y	Y	Y	Y
1952	Y	NKY	Y		Y
1953	JY	NKY	Y		Y
1954		NKY	Y		
1955		NKY	Y		Y
1956		NKY			Y
1957	Y	NKY	Y		Y
1958					Y
1959		JY	Y		Y
1960		NKY/JY	Y		Y
1961		NKY	Y	Y	Y
1962	Y	NKY			Y
1963					Y
1964					
1965	NKY	Y	Y		Y
1966					
1967	Y				
1968					
1969					
1970	JY	NKY/JY	Y		
1971				Y	
1972					
1973					
1974					
1975			Y		
1976					
1977					
1978					
1979					Y

	July 7	*August 15*	*September 3*	*September 18*	*December 9*
1980					Y
1981		Y			Y
1982		NKY/JY	Y	Y	Y

Source: Author.

Key: Y = There were commemorative articles/activities on the date. Also, if a date was comme-morated by both Chinese and foreigners, only Y will appear. NKY = There were Chinese rep-rints/reports about North Korea's commemorative articles/activities; or China sent congratulatory messages to North Korea. JY = There were Chinese reports about Japan's commemorative activities.

textbooks in 1955. All subsequent textbooks were based on the 1955 edition, with minor changes, until the 1990s, when a completely new series was pub-lished.[34] I have surveyed a selection of history textbooks used in the PRC's primary and secondary schools, covering the first seventeen-year period after the PRC's foundation, the Cultural Revolution period and the post-Cultural Revolution period.[35] The Fifteen-Year War was usually divided into two parts in these textbooks: the war-related events that occurred between 18 Septem-ber 1931 and 7 July 1937, which were incorporated into the 'Second Civil Revolution War period', and the events between 7 July 1937 and 2 September 1945, which were included in the 'War of Resistance against Japan period'.[36]

These textbooks normally start with a section providing their readers with background knowledge of the events of the first period and presents the fol-lowing narrative: For a long time Japan had the ambition of turning China into a colony and this ambition was further stimulated by the Great Depres-sion. The KMT was impotent when faced with this external threat; further-more, it concentrated its troops to fight against the CCP, which gave Japan an opportunity to attack. Following this, the Manchurian Incident and the Japanese invasion of Shanghai on 18 January 1932 are described. These text-books always emphasise that despite the fact that Chiang Kai-Shek issued an order of non-resistance, the Chinese people's own resistance (which was either spontaneous or led by the CCP) was never halted. The Volunteer Armies, the Northeast Anti-Japanese United Army, the guerrillas led by Kim Il Sung, and even the patriotic soldiers of the KMT's 19th army (who withstood the invading Japanese army in Shanghai in 1932) are frequently praised. The North China Crisis and the December 9th Movement are then introduced. The latter is normally evaluated as being the stimulus for a new high tide of resisting the Japanese, as a national united front of resistance against Japan was formed after the movement. The narrative for this period usually finishes with a description of the Xi'an Incident and how Chiang Kai-Shek was forced to take action against the Japanese invasion.

The 'War of Resistance period' is sub-divided in these textbooks into the initial phase of the war, which was fought under the national united front, and the deadlock period, which was characterised by the split between the

CCP and the KMT. These textbooks normally start their account of this period with the Marco Polo Bridge Incident, when the Japanese army started the all-out war with China on the pretext that one Japanese soldier was missing. Table 4.2 is directly translated from a reference book for high school history teachers. Most textbooks I surveyed followed this narrative.[37]

In terms of the national history museums, the Museum of the Chinese Revolution (hereafter the Revolution Museum) and the Military Museum of the Chinese People's Revolution (hereafter the Military Museum) were chosen as case studies. As shown in Table 4.3, the Revolution Museum's forerunner was the Central Preparatory Office for the Museum of the Revolution.[38] After it was established in 1950, the Preparatory Office immediately started to recruit revolutionary period pieces and organised artists to make paintings reflecting the Chinese Revolution. The Preparatory Office intensified its recruiting work after a decision to construct a new building for the Revolution Museum was made in 1958.[39]

On the other hand, the Preparatory Office started organising exhibitions soon after its inception, such as the exhibition to commemorate the 30th anniversary of the CCP and the exhibition of the massacres committed by America and the KMT's operatives.[40] The former (which was modified, becoming an exhibition of the Party's history in 1955) was the basic exhibition of the Preparatory Office. Relevant officials gradually started to consider expanding the exhibition by adding the periods of the Old Democratic Revolution, the New Democratic Revolution and the Socialist Revolution.[41] This idea was reported to the central government and approved by Deng Xiaoping in 1957.[42] In 1958, the Exhibition of Chinese Revolution History was formalised. After several further revisions, it was finally opened to the public on 1 July 1961 as the basic exhibition of the Museum of Chinese Revolution, which was also formally inaugurated on the same day (the Preparatory Office was moved to the new venue in 1959, and was renamed in 1960). Construction of the Military Museum was also completed in 1959, to mark the 10th anniversary of the PRC. The museum, as well as its basic exhibition, was formally inaugurated on 1 August 1960.[43]

The pieces relating to the Fifteen-Year War were included in both the basic exhibition and the several temporary exhibitions of these two museums. For instance, items related to the war were part of the Exhibition of Chinese Revolutionary History. Similar to the textbooks surveyed above, events following the Marco Polo Bridge Incident were presented in the War of Resistance against Japan section, and those that took place before this incident were presented in the Second Civil Revolution War section. The exhibition suggested that there were four major elements that contributed to victory in the Fifteen-Year War: the development of the CCP, the armed struggle guided by the CCP's strategy of the 'people's war', the united front and international assistance (especially assistance from the USSR).[44] In the Military Museum, items related to the Fifteen-Year War were displayed in several halls, such as the 'Hall of the War of Resistance against Japan', which had been popular

Table 4.2 Text book's table narrating the 'War of Resistance period'

	Japanese bandits' invasion	Unilateral resistance led by the KMT	Multilateral resistance led by the CCP
Strategic defence phase, July 1937–October 1938	Blitzkrieg strategy aimed at conquering China within a short period.	First retreat in disorder, from Beijing, Tianjin, Shanghai to Wuhan.	Battle of the Pingxing Pass: Resistance goes deep into the Japanese occupied areas, carries out guerrilla warfare and establishes anti-Japanese bases.
Strategic deadlock phase, 1938–1945 / Initial stage of deadlock, October 1938–1940	Strategy of politically luring China into surrender, assisted by military attack.	Wang Jinwei surrenders publicly, Chiang Kai-Shek becomes more vacillating, adopts policy of replacing the War of Resistance with civil war.	The Eighth Army and New Fourth Army became the main force of the War of Resistance; launch of the Hundred Regiments Offensive that strikes terror into the enemy's hearts.
Middle stage of deadlock, 1941–1942	Policies of 'searching the country and eliminating anti-Japanese forces', mopping up, and the 'three alls'.	The second anti-CCP high tide – Wannan Incident.	The situation in the Japanese occupied area becomes unprecedentedly difficult; the soldiers and people of the liberation army fight bravely.
Later stage of deadlock, 1943–1945	Preparations to put up a last ditch struggle in mainland China and rescue the isolated forces in Southeast Asia; launch of a battle to open up the continental traffic line.	Second big retreat in disorder, from Henan, Hunan, in Guangxi Province to Dushan in Guizhou Province.	Through the Yan'n large-scale production campaign and Yan'an Rectification Movement, the situation in liberated areas improves; a counterattack is launched in part.
Strategic counterattack phase, August 1945: Japanese bandits surrender	Japanese bandits surrender unconditionally.	Scheme to scramble for the fruits of victory of People's War.	Troops march to counterattack and liberate 197 cities.

Source: Gaozhong Jiaoxue Cankaoshu, 1960, p. 82.

Table 4.3 A brief history of the Museum of Chinese Revolution before 1982

Year, 19-	50	51	52	53	54	55	56	57	58	59	60	61	62	63	64	65	66	67	68	69	70	71	72	73	74	75	76	77	78	79	80	81	82
Jurisdictional agency	Ministry of Culture										Beijing Cultural Bureau				Ministry of Culture																		
Name/location	Preparatory Office of the National Revolution Museum										National Museum of Chinese Revolution				National Museum of Chinese Revolution and History																		
Permanent exhibition							Exhibition of the Party's history								Exhibition of Chinese revolution history																Exhibition of the CCP's history (democratic revolution period)		
Events	• The Preparatory Office was established in March 1950. • Announcement of soliciting revolutionary period pieces was issued in 1950.						Exhibition commemorating 30th anniversary of the founding of the CCP		The CCP Central Committee meeting in August 1958 decided to construct a building to host both the National Revolution and History museums.			• The project was completed in August 1959. • The two museums were opened to the public in October 1959.							The museum was renamed the National Museum of Chinese Revolution in August 1960.					The museum and its permanent collection was opened formally on 1 July 1961.				The National Museum of Chinese History and the National Museum of Chinese Revolution merged in September 1968.					

Source: This table is based on 'Centennial of the National Museum of China', the official website of the National Museum of China, and Zhongguo gemingbo wuguan, Zhongguo gemingbo wuguancang pinxuan [Selections from the collection of the Museum of Chinese Revolution] (Beijing: Wenwuchubanshe, 2003) 中国革命博物馆, 中国革命博物馆藏品选 (文物出版社, 2003).

with the museum's visitors since its inception.[45] The periodisation of the Hall of the War of Resistance was the same as that of the War of Resistance against Japan section. Nevertheless, the former focused mainly on the martial aspects of the war.

In terms of the temporary exhibitions, the most famous one related to the Fifteen-Year War before 1982 was probably the Revolution Museum's Exhibition to Commemorate the 20th Anniversary of the Victory of the Great Anti-Japanese War, in 1965. This special exhibition had four parts. Part 1 told visitors about various 'criminal activities' conducted by the Axis powers, via items such as the notorious Tanaka Memorial and photos of the Japanese invasion of the three provinces in Northeast China. Part 2 displayed items that suggested how the CCP had led the Chinese people to fight against Japan during the war. Part 3 was about the Civil War and Part 4 dealt with the American 'crimes' of occupying Taiwan and re-arming Japan and West Germany.

* * *

The five Fifteen-Year-War memorial dates were used very flexibly by party propagandists. This flexibility makes these war memorial dates suitable as a case study for exploring how the CCP's propagandists exploited Fifteen-Year-War remembrance on a short-term basis prior to 1982. On the other hand, the national anthem, history textbooks and national history museums are also very essential symbols of a nation, and thus the regime has had to choose very carefully what to present through these realms of memory. Furthermore, because school textbooks and national museums (besides temporary exhibitions) cannot be exploited by the authorities as flexibly as the memorial days, the content related to the war presented through these realms has been more stable. These two features – stability and careful selection – make textbooks and museums better candidates for exploring the long-term usefulness of war remembrance and those parts of the narrative of the war that have remained intact. At the same time, both war memorial days and textbooks, as well as museums, can be used to examine how the CCP leaders have exploited memories of the war in the diplomatic field, as well as in their struggles for power. Nevertheless, the above categorisation was not absolute.

The narrative that changed and the narrative that remained intact

Before 1982 a few adjustments were made over time to the narrative of the Fifteen-Year War presented on war memorial days, in textbooks and by museums. Behind these adjustments lay the changing usefulness of Fifteen-Year-War remembrance for the CCP regime. Nonetheless, thanks to the relatively long-term utility of war remembrance, there were some aspects of the narrative of the Fifteen-Year War that stayed intact in these realms of memory between 1949 and 1982. These intact aspects reflect the CCP regime's preferences in terms of Fifteen-Year-War remembrance. This section discusses, in turn, the adjustments made to the narrative, as well as what remained intact.

Adjustments

The CCP regime utilised Fifteen-Year-War remembrance to facilitate its short-term propaganda in many ways. The series of Japanese militarist-bashing campaigns I introduced in Chapter 2 are examples of this. Here, I will use the party's commemoration of the five war memorial dates to illustrate this point. When special occasions and mass campaigns occurred around the dates of the five war memorial days, these days were likely to be commemorated in an exceptional way, in terms of the frequency and scale of commemoration. As the CCP regime's short-term propaganda varied from time to time, various 'extra messages' were attached to the commemorations on the five war memorial days.

For example, in 1949, just before the foundation of the PRC, July 7 was commemorated in a spectacular way as part of the July 1– July 7 commemorative week in Beijing, Shanghai and other liberated places. The commemoration was unavoidably a ceremonial display of the CCP's triumph and a mobilisation for the foundation of the PRC, as well as for further battles with KMT troops. In Beijing, at 8 p.m. on July 7, 200,000 people, including Mao Zedong and other party leaders, participated in an assembly in Tiananmen, to commemorate the 12th anniversary of the Marco Polo Bridge Incident and to celebrate the establishment of the preparatory meeting of the new CPPCC. Portraits of Mao Zedong and Zhu De were hung on the Tiananmen gate tower, and between the portraits there was a 'huge red star, radiating and eye-dazzling'[46]. The assembly started with singing of the 'March of the Volunteers' and forty-nine (seven sets of seven) gun salutes. All participants then stood up and paid silent tribute to the martyrs who had died in the War of Resistance. Peng Zhen, the would-be mayor of Beijing, started his opening speech by stating: 'there were thunders of guns just now; twelve years ago there were roars of guns in Beijing as well; that time it was the roaring guns of the Japanese imperialist invasion, but today it is the thunder of people celebrating the victory of the People's liberation war ...'[47] In Shanghai, the scale of commemoration was even greater. The central activities included a 'commemorating July 7 and celebrating liberation' demonstration, which involved around 1 million citizens, the PLA's infantry divisions and eleven special corps. It also included a dress parade reviewed by Chen Yi and other party leaders, which took place from 4 p.m. onwards on July 6. [48]

During the Korean War, especially in 1950 and 1951, the five dates (especially the four humiliation and victory dates) were commemorated in an unusually intensive way. The extra message attached to these commemorations was a protest against the American invasion of Korea and its intervention in Japan. The commemorations were also used to stimulate Chinese people's confidence in the war and to mobilise their patriotism in regard to constructing the newborn PRC.[49] For the December 9 commemoration, in addition to the above messages, a more practical one was attached: that, like the December 9th generation, 'patriotic youths now should integrate with workers, peasants and soldiers, and in particular, should devote themselves to the national defence'.[50]

In 1951, a nationwide campaign of 'thought reform' – using proletarian ideology to criticise non-proletarian ideology – was carried out. Consequently, the December 9th movement was commemorated from a new perspective. Commemorative articles suggested that:

> in the beginning of the movement, the youths with proletarian ideology and non-proletarian ideology had different approaches as to how to defeat Japanese invaders and their running dogs. Without the leadership of the CCP and the Maoist theory, dangerous non-proletarian ideology almost destroyed the movement; from this we should learn the lesson that if we did not transform the petty bourgeois ideology, we would be eroded by it.[51]

In 1955, the agricultural co-operative movement approached its climax, and Mao Zedong enthusiastically urged intellectuals to go down to the countryside. Not surprisingly, from 1955 onwards the party propagandists started to emphasise the 'south crusade' aspect of the December 9th movement and called for the youth to integrate with workers and peasants and go to the countryside. Unlike the message during the Korean War, the importance of integrating the youth with soldiers was less emphasised during the mid-1950s.[52] In response to the call, university students developed a new way of commemorating December 9 – by participating in various agricultural activities in the nearby countryside. For example, postgraduates in Beijing Petroleum College helped an agricultural co-operative team pick 1,000 kilos of cotton in a single day.[53] This call was continued and became a main message that was attached to the December 9 commemorative activities in the following years.[54] Other messages reflecting current affairs, like 'carrying forward the spirit of the December 9th Movement, preparing for defeating the invasion of the US' in 1965, were sometimes attached as well.[55] During the post-Cultural Revolution period, young people's crisis of belief, which was a hot topic at the time, was addressed in the commemoration of December 9.[56]

Apart from for the purposes of short-term propaganda, Fifteen-Year-War remembrance was also employed by the CCP regime to mobilise the Chinese to support its position in the international community. In line with the PRC's altered relations with its socialist 'friends' and capitalist 'enemies', content related to the Fifteen-Year War on the memorial days, in textbooks and in museums was also modified.

For instance, the frequency of commemorating August 15 and September 3 was exceptionally high between 1946 and 1962. A possible explanation for this is that a very important function both days was to facilitate the consolidation of the PRC–USSR and the PRC–North Korea alliance. As early as the first anniversary of September 3, CCP leaders had started to associate the Chinese V-J day with the assistance provided to China by the Soviet Red Army, led by Stalin. After that time, almost every year on August 15 and September 3, the CCP's propaganda organ carried articles reporting how Chinese people, particularly those in the northeastern provinces, were grateful to Stalin, as well as reporting their activities of paying tribute to the Soviet martyrs who had died on Chinese battlefields. After Mao Zedong decided on China's 'leaning one side' policy of allying with the Soviet Union in 1949, the Soviet assistance was portrayed as 'decisive' – the Soviet invasion of Manchuria played a vital role in defeating Japan, and thus the USSR helped the Chinese people win the war.[57]

In terms of North Korea, since 15 August 1950 it had joined the Soviet Union as another friend the Chinese people should thank on the two memorial days.[58] From 1952, August 15 became a day for celebrating Korea's liberation from Japan's colonialism (while September 3 was reserved for the USSR). Commemorative activities also took place in North Korea: memoirs or commemorative articles by North Korean writers, and congratulatory messages from CCP officials would be shown in Chinese media. For the Chinese people, this was a chance to learn about the Japanese atrocities and to celebrate the defeat of Japan by witnessing the suffering and glory of another brother country.[59]

Gradually, however, as the PRC–USSR and PRC–North Korea alliances became increasingly unstable, the nuances and frequency of the August 15 and September 3 commemorations changed.[60] The Sino–Soviet relationship reached a low point in 1958.[61] Accordingly, no commemorative activity on September 3 was reported in *Renmin Ribao* in that year. That annversary was resumed the following year, but the USSR's decisive role in defeating Japan was less emphasised. In 1961, the bravery in the battlefields of Northeast China of Soviet martyrs was only briefly mentioned.[62] After that, the annual or biennial commemoration of September 3 as a showcase for the Sino–Soviet friendship ended.

Four years later, in 1965, the 20th anniversary of V-J day was commemorated on a grand scale, as I have described in Chapter 2. Almost all the commemorative articles and activities tried to attribute the victory of the war to the brave Chinese people and the significance of the leadership of the CCP and Maoist theory was emphasised.[63] Other messages, like protesting against the American revival of Japanese militarism, were attached to the commemoration that year. However, there was no mention of the Soviet Union. After 1965, the commemoration of September 3 became a five-yearly event, mainly as an occasion to celebrate the people's power and the Party's brilliance. This coincided with a so-called indigenisation process in respect of Chinese national identity after the Sino–Soviet split.[64] Although not as swiftly as the commemoration of September 3, the textbooks and museums, which had initially praised the USSR's decisive contribution to defeating Japan, also gradually downgraded that contribution.[65]

August 15, as an occasion for praising the China–North Korea friendship, also seems to have been embroiled in the Sino–Soviet conflict. It was not commemorated in 1958, 1963 (in this year, the ideological conflict between Mao's China and Khrushchev's Soviet Union turned white-hot and the Chinese domestic media heavily criticised the latter, even on September 3) or 1964.[66] After 1965, the nearly annual report related to North Korean commemoration also became a five-yearly occurrence.

Furthermore, Sino–Japanese relations also had some impact on the pattern of commemorating the four humiliation and victory days. However, this impact only became significant after the two countries normalised their relations in 1972. After 1972, following the five-yearly pattern, the CCP regime commemorated September 3 in 1975. However, July 7 and August 15, which were previously commemorated every five years, did not receive any attention in *Renmin Ribao*. After 1978, when the Treaty of Sino–Japanese Friendship was signed, as some scholars have argued, the four commemorative dates were either ignored or they became occasions for praising Sino–Japanese friendship. Nevertheless, although there was no official 'commemoration of the September 18th Incident', relevant activities were organised and articles were published around these dates. For example, a chorus of veterans of the New Fourth Army performed in Beijing on 17 September 1979.[67] In 1981, the Chinese V-J Day was explicitly commemorated again on a small-scale and most of these war memorial days were fully resumed after the 1982 Textbook Incident.[68]

Finally, the alleged American and British scheme to encourage Japan to invade China in order to preserve their interests in the country and to make money through the arms trade was a subject that taught in PRC schools in the 1950s and 1960s. This 'scheme' was seldom mentioned after the improvement in China's relations with Western countries in the 1970s.

Fifteen-Year-War remembrance was also used in the political struggles of the factions within the CCP regime. For example, the left-wing literature movement and the literature during the War of Resistance period were initially substantially discussed in history textbooks. These two areas were omitted from the textbooks published during the Great Leap Forward. Discussion of the left-wing literature movement reappeared during the Cultural Revolution but the movement was criticised and textbooks were used to attack the individuals who were involved in that movement.[69] Similarly, the Battle of Pingxing Pass, which was led by Lin Biao (a CCP statesman and a general in the PLA, who died after an unsuccessful coup in 1971), disappeared from the textbooks after his fall. Although he was introduced again after the Cultural Revolution, Lin's name was no longer associated with the Battle of Pingxing Pass in these textbooks. The two museums were also disturbed by the turbulence of the Cultural Revolution: some people who had been praised in the museums were defamed and the displays relating to them were banned as a result. For example, items relating to Peng Xuefeng (a famous commander of the New Fourth Army who died during the war) were removed from both museums.[70] Nonetheless, after the Cultural Revolution, many people were rehabilitated, and consequently some items that had been banned from the national museums were once again on display. For example, items relating to Peng Xuefeng reappeared in the new basic exhibition – the exhibition of the CCP's history (during the Democratic Revolution period) – in the Revolution Museum.[71]

Similarly, December 9, one of the CCP's favourite memorial days, totally disappeared between 1966 and 1979. What happened? An article reporting resumed commemorative activities in 1979 provides a clue: 'Lin Biao and the "gang of four" did their utmost to vilify the December 9th movement; many organisers and participants of this movement were oppressed cruelly'.[72] Although very brief, this line is actually informative enough to imply what had happened: many cadres who were directly involved in the movement, like Liu Shaoqi and Peng Zhen, were overthrown at the beginning of the Cultural Revolution and, similarly to the fate of the lyrics of 'March of the Volunteers', the movement became taboo during that period. As those involved with the movement were subsequently exonerated, its regular commemoration was resumed.

In short, the alterations made by the CCP regime described above were related to the additional propaganda messages associated with commemorative days and exhibitions, and to the evaluation of individuals and third-party countries. The basic narrative of the war itself (see Table 4.2) remained almost intact during the period, as did the evaluation of the Japanese invasion. For instance, offensive language directed at Japan continued to be used substantially in textbooks, even those published after Sino–Japanese normalisation. In a textbook published in 1973, the word 'Japanese bandits' appears five times in five sentences. Furthermore, on 7 July 1980 a Sino–Japanese relations scholar published an article in *Renmin Ribao* which devoted a lot of discussion to the argument that 'there is no long-term hatred between nations, but still the history should be objectively written down', which reflects the CCP government's stance at the time.[73] I next discuss these intact parts of the basic narrative of the war in greater detail and explore which facets of the Fifteen-Year War were specifically favoured by the CCP regime.

The CCP-centric narrative and its tragic-heroic tone

Fifteen-Year-War remembrance was promoted by the CCP regime for certain long-term and fundamental purposes. Consequently, the narrative regarding the aspects of the war remembrance that were related to these purposes was consistent and stable.

First and foremost, the KMT's role in the war was denounced in the CCP regime's basic narrative of the Fifteen-Year War, as shown in the surveyed textbooks and museums. For instance, when discussing the events of the War of Resistance period, the textbooks claim that although in the initial phase the CCP and the KMT were united in resisting the Japanese, the former's fighting and strategy was actually independent from and superior to the latter's. Thus, from the beginning of the war, the KMT's forces were defeated in quick succession, while the CCP thrived by developing guerrilla forces in the Japanese-occupied areas, and won several battles. After talking about the deadlock phase, the focus of the textbooks' narrative turns to how the CCP became the leader of China's resistance against Japan and its 'running dogs' (various puppet governments and the KMT regime) by beating back Japan's attacks on the CCP bases; as well as the KMT's anti-CCP campaigns; and supporting the democratic movements in the KMT-occupied areas.

Moreover, although Sino–Soviet relations declined drastically in the 1960s, the CCP did not totally invalidate its previous discourse in this regard. The regime still encouraged Chinese people to be grateful for the assistance from the Soviet people, led by Stalin, during the war, although the 'revisionist Soviet Union' had become an 'insatiably avaricious' Socialist Imperialist – another example of the CCP's philosophy of dichotomy.[74] Similarly, although the CCP had fallen out with many of its communist friends during this period, the Canadian doctor Norman Bethune, a beloved communist friend of the CCP who died during his service in China, was consistently applauded.[75]

Furthermore, despite the improvement of the PRC's relations with the capitalist camp, the wartime actions of Westerners were still denounced to some extent. For example, middle school textbooks printed in 1980 (the PRC normalised its relationship with the USA on 1 January 1979) still contain criticisms. For example: 'with the help of American imperialist support, the diehards of the KMT ... stole the fruit of victory of the People's war'.[76]

Why did the CCP continuously favour a version of the Fifteen-Year-War memory that denounced the KMT as well as the Western 'villains', and emphasised the Soviet assistance? I argue that it did so because these aspects were useful for the regime in relation to fostering a new CCP-centric socialist identity, and in relation to justifying the Party's leadership of the PRC. Globally, the CCP regime was also keen to foster an international socialist identity. Tales of the CCP's wartime cooperation with its socialist friends were useful as a means by which to demonstrate an international socialist solidarity.[77]

Domestically, as Wang has argued, the CCP made class distinction the foundation of political identity. The period between 1931 and 1945 was also interpreted by the regime, based on its class struggle theory, as being a period of war against the Chinese people's class enemies, who consisted not only of Japanese imperialists but also Western imperialists and the KMT, as the representative of bureaucratic capitalists and landlords. The Fifteen-Year War was portrayed by the regime as one of many CCP-led class struggles which brought about the final socialist victory in 1949. For instance, the main theme that the Revolution Museum's basic exhibition tried to convey was that only after the establishment of the CCP did the Chinese Revolution take on an entirely new outlook. It was the CCP and Mao Zedong who led the Chinese people: they experienced a twenty-eight-year struggle but finally defeated imperialism, feudalism and bureaucratic capitalism to build the new China.

The period pieces related to the Fifteen-Year War were organised so as to be in line with this main theme.[78]

The presentation of the Fifteen-Year War in the surveyed textbooks and museums generally adopted a victorious tone. The majority of items that stayed intact in the Revolution and Military Museums were those that reflected the bravery of the CCP's army, the militia soldiers and ordinary Chinese people who supported the CCP.[79] For example, some letters and a pistol used by Zuo Quan (a famous Eighth Army commander who was killed in action by the Japanese in 1942), have been on display in the Revolution Museum and the Military Museum since 1952 and 1959, respectively.[80] A Five-star Medal was awarded to Song Xueyi, one of the famous 'Five Warriors of Langya Mountain', who threw himself off a cliff on Langya mountain after expending the last of his strength fighting the Japanese soldiers but who survived miraculously. Song donated the medal to the Revolution Museum in 1959. It was displayed in the Revolution Museum's 1965 exhibition and it continues to be displayed today. A boat which was used to ambush Japanese boats by some of the CCP-affiliated militia soldiers in Baiyangdian, Tianjin, was turned over to the Revolution Museum in 1959; it has been displayed on various occasions and continues to be on show today.[81]

Captured equipment and small items belonging to Japanese soldiers, like weapons and a Japanese flag with *buunchokyu* (武運長久 'continued luck in the fortunes of war') written on it, were also permanent fixtures in the two museums. For example, Okamura Yasuji submitted his sword as a token of giving up his arms in the ceremony marking the surrender of Japanese forces in the Chinese theatre of the war. The sword was found by the PLA in the Office of the President in Nanjing and displayed in the PLA's own weapons display hall. The sword was then turned over to the Military Museum in 1959 and has stayed there ever since.[82]

However, despite the overall heroic tone, Japanese atrocities were also mentioned to varying degrees in almost all of the surveyed textbooks and museums, and the narrative directly related to war atrocities stayed almost intact between 1949 and 1982.[83] In the textbooks, detailed descriptions of the Japanese army's atrocities are normally included in three places. The first of these is after the account of the Manchurian Incident: the textbooks explain how the Japanese had cruelly ruled Northeast China in order to foreshadow the main narrative of how the Northeastern people did not surrender and how they started to resist under the leadership of the CCP:

> After having occupied Northeast China, the Japanese imperialists began their cruel colonial rule over the Northeastern people. Both the central government of the fake 'Manchukuo' and its local administrations were controlled by the Japanese invaders. There was a kind of tithing system – if one person broke the law, ten households related to that person would be punished – this was in practice widely. The Japanese imperialists carried out slave education in order to suppress the Northeastern people's

patriotism. They also encouraged people to plant and smoke opium, which destroyed the Northeastern people's health. The Japanese army's atrocities, such as arson, killing, looting and rape, were countless. The Japanese imperialists monopolised the economic lifeline in the Northeast. They controlled the mines, factories, transportation and so forth, forced Northeastern people to work like slaves, and grabbed the land as well as properties of the Northeastern people as they wished ... but the North-eastern people did not surrender ... they established the 'anti-Japanese' guerrillas ... in 1935 the 'anti-Japanese' guerrillas in various places were re-organised as the Northeast Anti-Japanese United Army [which was under the leadership of the CCP's Manchuria branch].[84]

The second place where Japanese atrocities are discussed is after the account of the Marco Polo Bridge Incident, where, in order to criticise the KMT's one-sided resistance, it is described how the Japanese army brutally occupied Chinese cities. The Nanjing Massacre is singled out in a 1960 high school textbook and its successive editions.[85] An accompanying reference book for teachers (in Shanghai) includes more detail about this history, which indicates that there might be differences in the teachings about Japanese atrocities received by students according to the region, the teacher and other aspects.[86] During and after the Cultural Revolution, the Nanjing Massacre was still described in textbooks and there seems to have been a tendency to describe it more graphically:

The Japanese army carried out an insane massacre after occupying Nanjing. Some peaceful citizens in Nanjing were used as targets for practising shooting, and some of them were used as objects for competing bayonet [skills]; some of them had gasoline thrown on them and were burned to death, some of them were buried alive and the hearts and livers of some of them were cut out. Within one month, the number of people killed was more than 300,000 and more than one-third of the houses had been burned. During that period, in the city of Nanjing, there were skeletons everywhere, rubble was heaped up and a sinister wind blew sadly: the whole city became a hell on earth.[87]

The third location where Japanese atrocities are recounted is where the textbooks narrate the difficult situation faced by the CCP base areas in the Japanese-occupied zone. How the Japanese created a miserable world where 'there was no village that was not in mourning and where the noise of grief could be heard everywhere' through brutal methods such as 'burning all, killing all and looting all (the 'three-alls' policy) is normally be described to demonstrate how admirable the soldiers and people of the liberation army were to have fought back bravely and to have overcome the difficulties.[88]

Items relating to Japanese atrocities, such as how the Japanese army carried out the 'three-alls' policy in its occupied area, were also exhibited in the two museums.[89] For example, a map of the 'no-man's' district of Xinglong county in Hebei Province, designed by the Japanese army, was turned over to the Hebei Provincial Museum in 1959. Since then, this map has been exhibited in the Revolution Museum, and it remains there now.[90] Also, a photo of Panjiayu village in Hebei Province, where around 1,000 residents were killed by the Japanese soldiers, was displayed in the pre-1982 Revolution Museum. The swords and hand grenades of the 'Pangjiayu revenge delegation' – comprised of the survivors of the Pangjiayu massacre as well as villagers from the adjacent area – were exhibited in the Military Museum.[91] Moreover, a skull recovered from a 'pit of 10,000 corpses' (万人坑 *wanrenken*), or mass grave, in Shandong Province, was exhibited in the Military Museum. This might be the museum's most sensational memento of the Japanese invasion of China. After seeing this skull, a cadre, originally from Shangdong Province, found himself compelled to describe the miserable experience of when his sister and ten members of her family were killed by the Japanese.[92]

Why did the regime favour both the tragic and heroic aspects of the war before 1982? I argue that whilst the heroic aspect was used to boost the morale of Chinese people in the PRC and to provide grounds for the CCP's claim to legitimacy, the tragic aspect (although minor) was also necessary, in order to provide a contrast.[93]

In summary, this section has found that the CCP-centric stance, triumphalism and victimhood were the three essences of the CCP regime's version of the Fifteen-Year War. Without the tragic aspect of the war, its heroic aspect and the greatness of the CCP's leadership could not be demonstrated. What is more, patriotic emotion was aroused when Chinese people remembered the war as both tragic and heroic – their motherland was almost destroyed by an invader but finally achieved self-salvation after their unbowed resistance. By foregrounding the CCP leadership during the war, the regime could turn these patriotic feelings for the Chinese nation into a patriotism for the PRC state, as well as the CCP government.

* * *

The regime did not greatly change its version of the Fifteen-Year-War memory between 1949 and 1982. The alterations made by the regime were related to the evaluation of the KMT, the USA, the USSR or to individuals. As a short-term propaganda aim, the regime exploited the memory of the war by emphasising, exaggerating or distorting a particular aspect of it which could best serve that aim. Nevertheless, the Party did not try to re-interpret the war as a whole or invent something from scratch in the interests of its short-term propaganda. The basic narrative of the war itself, the evaluation of the Japanese invasion, as well as the CCP-centric narrative, stayed intact during the period. In particular, this section has found that the heroic aspect of Fifteen-Year-War remembrance as well as its tragic aspect was continuously employed by the CCP regime to assist in its nation-building practices before 1982. By various means, a specific version of the Fifteen-Year

War – manifested by a set of CCP-centric and tragic-heroic events – was promoted by the CCP regime throughout China.

Was this CCP version of Fifteen-Year-War remembrance embraced throughout China? What was the relationship between local and national memories? The central–local dichotomy in terms of war remembrance will be discussed in the next part of this chapter.

Local war remembrance

On 14 June 1971 two Japanese journalists arrived in Beijing with different agendas, after having undertaken a complicated journey that had begun in Tokyo three days earlier.[94] One of them was Honda Katsuichi, who wanted to study the Japanese Imperial Army's atrocities in China during the war from a Chinese perspective. One of the motives for this mission was his desire to understand the historical and psychological reasons why the Chinese were so cautious about the developments in Japan at the time, with respect to a possible resurgence of Japanese militarism.[95] Thus, his journey followed the route of Japan's invasion of China, from the cities in old Manchuria, to Marco Polo Bridge, Shanghai, Nanjing and finally Panjiayu. Honda later published a book based on this trip, which has been frequently referred to for its detailed descriptions of Japanese atrocities. However, the most fascinating thing conveyed by this book, from the perspective of the theme of the present book, is how profound and diverse Chinese people's memories of the Japanese army's atrocities were in the early 1970s. The 'voices' Honda attentively listened to during the trip were from the local cadres who normally gave a general introduction to the atrocities committed by the Japanese army in the areas under their jurisdiction, and from victims who conveyed tearful testimonies on the subject. Some meetings with the victims were arranged by local cadres, but some of the victims made a special trip to meet Honda of their own accord to offer their stories. It is also striking how well the Chinese preserved and exhibited these memories of victimhood. Honda carefully photographed the monuments, memorials or 'remnants', which would have been indiscernible had they not been pointed out by the witnesses. Three places he mentioned especially caught my attention.

The first place was Liutiaohu, where the September 18th Incident took place. The Japanese army had built a memorial tower on this spot where the first Japanese bombardment landed. After Japan was defeated in 1945, the local residents attacked the tower. By the time Honda visited, the tower had fallen sideways and there was a board with the words 'the ironclad proof of Japanese militarists' invasion of China' written on it, along with other introductory text, erected beside it.

The second place was a mass grave in Dashiqiao, Liaoning Province, where the Japanese South Manchuria Mining Industry Company 南満州株式会社 had started to develop a magnesite mine in 1918.[96] According to Honda's interviewees, many Chinese workers died of exhaustion or were killed by

Japanese staff, and their bodies dumped into pits nearby (sometimes Chinese people were tied up and put into the pits whilst still alive). By the end of the war, three mass graves were formed nearby. When Honda visited, one of these graves was open to visitors. Honda described his shock as follows:

> I had not visited the scene of the Nazi's Auschwitz killing factory. So it was the first time in my life to see such a horrible scene like *wanrenken*. The shock, when I went through the entrance with 'don't forget the bitterness of class' written on its front, left a wound in my mind which could not disappear for a lifetime. It was a hill of heaps of skeletons. [From] the section of the hill, [you can see] the stratums formed by the skeletons. This was called *wanrenken* and was a human dumping ground.[97]

The third place was 'the village of the three-alls policy' – Panjiayu – which I have introduced previously. When Honda visited Panjiayu, the memory of that tragedy was still vivid for the villagers, and the whole village was set up so that visitors could learn about the 'Japanese army's heinous crimes'. There were four mounds where 1,230 victims from the village were buried: even a tree with new branches, which had been burned by Japanese troops, had been carefully preserved by the villagers. In addition, several commemorative buildings had been constructed, such as a memorial tower, a temple with memorial tablets for the victims enshrined within it, and an exhibition hall which narrated the beginning and subsequent development of this tragedy and displayed a few photos taken by the Eighth Army of the immediate aftermath of the massacre.

The Fifteen-Year-War remembrance in these three places was similar in a way – all of them were victimhood-oriented. Most scholars think that victimhood in memories of the war was discouraged during the Maoist period. I argue that memories of victimhood were encouraged as a minor yet important part of China's national war memory during this period. Still, that the memory of victimhood was prevalent in these local places to such a substantial extent was unusual, even within the context of my argument. That the memory of victimhood of these three places was somehow incorporated into national memory during 1949–1982 may explain this strangeness. The September 18th Incident was commemorated regularly nationwide. Mass graves were common throughout China. In addition, mass graves were exhibited in the national museums, included in the Chinese textbooks, and talked about during various top-down campaigns.[98] The Three-Alls policy was related in school history textbooks and items related to the Panjiayu massacre were also exhibited in the history museums. Nevertheless, I think the whole situation of how the war was remembered locally can explain why the memory of victimhood was prevalent in these local places to such a substantial extent and more profoundly. So, before further discussing this unusual phenomenon, I will use Nanjing, which Honda also visited during his trip, as an example by which to explore the situation of local war remembrance.[99]

Fifteen-Year-War remembrance in Nanjing

The most famous memorial in Nanjing is Yuhuatai 雨花台, which was used as an execution ground during the Republican period. The decision to build memorial facilities there for people to cherish the memory of the martyrs who were killed 'during the 22 years when Nanjing was ruled by the KMT gang of bandits and Japanese imperialists', was made during Nanjing's second People's Representatives Conference.[100] Many stories of 'anti-Japanese' fighters were collected and exhibited at the Yuhuatai memorial. There were stories of fighters who devoted themselves to either armed struggle or movements to resist Japan and save the nation (抗日救亡运动), but who were killed by the KMT regime before the war between China and Japan entered its fullest phase on 7 July 1937. Luo Dengxian 罗登贤, a Communist leader who established the 14th unit of the Northeast Anti-Japanese United Army, after the September 18th Incident, was an example of the former, and a group of patriots who tried to expand the Jiangsu Provincial anti-Japanese organisations and actions nationwide were an example of the latter.[101] The deeds of Communists (e.g. soldiers, intelligence agents and propaganda agents) and CCP-led anti-Japanese guerrillas who were killed by the Japanese during the Fifteen-Year War were also included in the memorial.[102] There were also stories of 'anti-Japanese' heroes who fought the Japanese under the leadership of both the KMT and CCP, and who were killed by the Nationalist regime during the Civil War. However, according to the available sources, the KMT servicemen whose deeds were included in Yuhuatai, crossed over to the CCP during the Civil War.[103] The Nanjing Massacre was also mentioned in the Yuhuatai memorial.[104]

The narrative of the Fifteen-Year War presented in Yuhuatai was CCP-centric and tragic-heroic – perfectly in line with the national memory of the war. In addition to Yuhuatai, similar memories were propagated through Nanjing's museums, newspapers and so forth. For example, Nanjing Municipal Committee for the Preservation of Antiquities organised an Exhibition of the 'Birth of the New China' in 1950. The narrative style of this exhibition about the Fifteen-Year War was similar to that of the two national museums I have discussed previously. The items were displayed in such a way as to make audiences, even those who were not sure who led the Anti-Japanese War, 'realise' that 'Chinese people had gained victory through difficult battles under the leadership of the CCP'.[105] Memories about particular elements of the CCP's leadership were also promoted. For example, stories of the Yan'an style of education during the Anti-Japanese War and the PLA's famous 'Hard-Bone Sixth Company', which was established during the war, could always be heard in Nanjing. Regional history about the tragically heroic fighting of the New Fourth Army and the guerrilla force led by the CCP in the bases surrounding Nanjing was also promoted.[106]

Nevertheless, what the Nanjing citizens could identify with most in terms of memories of the Fifteen-Year War was not the kind of tragic-heroic fighting narrative promoted by the CCP that I mention above. This was because such fighting only happened in the rural areas surrounding Nanjing and not in Nanjing itself. As the capital city of Jiangsu Province, Nanjing was the hub for various memories of the Fifteen-Year War in the province. This did not affect the fact that the kinds of memories that thrived in Nanjing locally were memories of the events that took place in the city during the war – the Nanjing Massacre and successive suffering during the War of Resistance. Also, whenever the local government tried to mobilise Nanjing residents by triggering their memories of the war for various campaigns, or to educate them into patriotism and a revolutionary tradition, what was mostly emphasised was not the kind of memory I introduced above. The memory of the Fifteen-Year War that was most exploited by the Nanjing officials was the memory of the Nanjing Massacre – which had been most deeply imprinted in Nanjing residents' minds.

The memory of victimhood emerged immediately after the Nanjing Massacre. Individual atrocities that were carried out during the massacre had a long-term and enormous impact on the survivors, not only because of the traumatic experience of the atrocities per se, but also as a result of the after-effects of these experiences – the post-traumatic emotional, physical and financial difficulties suffered by the survivors.[107] For instance, some survivors were only children when their parents were killed during the massacre. What did these survivors go through when sustaining themselves during the war and growing up on their own? They may have had a decent childhood before the tragedy, and suddenly their fate was changed completely by the atrocities. How could they forget these events? Also, it is unlikely that they would have received a good education due to their poor financial conditions, and thus their adult lives would be difficult too. Consequently, their own children would also not have a good upbringing and probably would not enjoy a good education. Thus it is not unusual to find that the next generation of these survivors also attributes the difficulties in their lives to those atrocities.[108] In short, it is very unlikely that the survivors and their families would ever forget these atrocities; due to their devastating impact, the memories of these events would always remain with them.

Active remembrance of the massacre was also carried out soon after it happened. Even during the occupation period, mourning for the victims was observed, although normally in a very veiled way. The victims' families would consecrate them at home, sweep their tombs (if they had tombs), and burn joss sticks and 'paper money' (as an offering to the dead), in accordance with Chinese traditions in respect of families mourning the dead.[109] Furthermore, the atrocities that occurred in Nanjing were recorded during and shortly after the massacre. Those who recorded them were both foreign and Chinese staff undertaking humanitarian work in Nanjing, KMT soldiers and a few Nanjing residents (many residents who remained in Nanjing were poor and illiterate, so they were unable to produce many records of the atrocities themselves), among others.[110]

What is more, the Nanjing Massacre also became a part of local legend in Nanjing. The memory of the massacre was integrated into Nanjing citizens' everyday lives. The survivors and the older generation always mentioned the events of the massacre on everyday occasions. Some place names in the area also record that unfortunate history. For instance, there is a lane called Qijiawan (七家湾 seven-family bend). According to the locals, this name was given because all residents here were killed by the Japanese, apart from seven households. In brief, to quote an interviewee's comment, all Nanjingnese people had heard about the Nanjing Massacre 'in the dribs and drabs of their life' (i.e. knowledge of the massacre was simply a part of their lives).[111]

In this way, the Nanjing Massacre was remembered by survivors and local residents consistently during the Japanese occupation, the Civil War and the turbulent period between 1949 and 1982. However, most of the time remembrance was carried out in a very quiet way. Sometimes it was even suppressed (during the Japanese occupation). However, remembrance was occasionally stimulated by the local governments, for various aims. Whenever there was such an occasion, the locals expressed their emotions – sometimes to an extreme extent.

The commemoration activities carried out by local officials started as early as the Occupation period. The victims were mourned by the puppet government in Nanjing as well, although in a veiled way. For instance, a stele was built near the Lingu Park in Nanjing in 1939. The name of the stele was 'No-owner and lonely-ghost stele (*wuzhu guhun bei* 无主孤魂碑)'.[112] Serious commemoration of the Nanjing Massacre was begun by the KMT government in the Civil War period. First, the KMT's Nanjing trial of Japanese war criminals (and the IMTFE) not only provided a fuller picture of the events that took place in Nanjing between 1937 and 1938 for the first time, but also created a greater degree of popular feeling around the objective history of the war. The verdict of the Nanjing trial offered a basis for official Chinese statements that more than 300,000 people had been killed in the massacre. What is more, the public, sensational and resounding way in which Nanjing prepared and conducted the trial, as well as the manner in which it executed the criminals, instilled the objective criminal facts revealed by the trial with a high degree of emotion. Ever since, the figure of 300,000, as well as its attached victimhood, has been an essential factor whenever the city of Nanjing has talked about its past – or when its citizens have related their family stories.[113] The media also gave a lot of attention to the Nanjing Massacre: for example, for many years special issues on the massacre appeared around December 13 and survivors' memories were published from time to time.[114] It was decided that December 13 would be the '*Jingshi zhonglie jinianri* (memorial day for the capital's martyrs 京市忠烈纪念日)'.[115] There were official proposals to build memorial facilities for the massacre; however, none of these were realised due to the Civil War.[116]

After Nanjing came under the control of the CCP in the spring of 1949, commemoration of the Nanjing Massacre was taken over by the local CCP

cadres. Their first official intervention was during the grand July 7th commemoration in 1949. Apart from showcasing the triumph of the Communists, a
side-aim of that year's commemoration was to criticise the release of Okamura
Yasuji and other Japanese war criminals by the US and Chiang Kai-Shek.[117]
Nanjing citizens were encouraged to give testimonies during organised group
discussions and on other occasions. Some of the testimonies were published in
the media, with messages like 'Japanese imperialism inflicted such intense and
deep-seated hatred on Chinese people, and American imperialists treated
them with such leniency, it was absolutely impossible for Chinese people to
tolerate.'[118] Since then, memories of the Nanjing Massacre have continued to
be used during various war memorial day commemorations (Figure 4.1).

Also, during the mass campaigns aimed at the US and the right-wing
Japanese government in the early 1950s and 1960s, as discussed in Chapter 2,
the memory of the Nanjing Massacre was exploited by the local government.
For example, at a mass meeting in 1960, almost all the speakers mentioned the
massacre in their speeches.[119] The response to the government's promotion of
the memory was very strong among local citizens. Numerous testimonies
appeared in newspapers in the form of special columns and readers' letters.[120]
In addition, there were many forms of commemoration around December
13th or on other occasions: for instance, mourning ceremonies, exhibitions
and fasting.[121] As well as visits to the memorial in Xiaguan Electricity Factory during the period there were also initiatives by Nanjing citizens to
donate money to build new memorials to the victims.[122] The memory of the
massacre was also used for domestic propaganda purposes. For example, it was
used to carry out 'class education' in the 1960s, and in the campaign of criticising Lin Biao's 'Self-Restraint and Return to the Rites' (*keji fuli* 克己礼)
doctrines in 1974.[123] Sensational material describing the cruelty of the Japanese Imperial Army was included in an exhibition for the 30th anniversary of
the liberation of Nanjing in 1979.[124]

Consequently, there developed in Nanjing locally a deep sense of victimhood, as a result of a 'joint enterprise' among citizens and the local governments
spanning various periods since the time of the massacre. During the PRC era,
this victim mentality was very apparent. Sometimes the presentation of the
Nanjing Massacre was criticised (even by residents of Nanjing itself) for being
overly tragic. In response, the local officials tried to label the massacre a tragic-
heroic event, emphasising how Chinese people did not surrender even to the
most brutal enemy, and they tried to promote individual testimonies which supported this perspective.[125] Nevertheless, a feeling of victimhood actually existed deep in the minds of local officials and was sometimes manifested by them.
For example, the local cadres always compared Nanjing with other cities that
suffered a great deal during the war. Among their usual comparisons was
Hiroshima, as reflected in a poem published in Nanjing's party organ:

Japanese people are keeping firmly in mind,
The mushroom-shaped shadow in the sky of the island country;

Figure 4.1 Pictures presented as 'Photos of the Nanjing Massacre' in a newspaper
The captions to these four pictures read: 'This group of Japanese military officers are
conducting a killing competition; there is a second lieutenant Noda who killed one
thousand people 这一帮日本军官，正在进行杀人比赛，有野田少尉者连杀一千人';
'Thirteen years ago, Chiang Kai-Shek withdrew from Nanjing in panic, Japanese
imperialists entered Nanjing and started a crazy massacre in which more than 200,000
people were killed 十三年前蒋介石仓惶退出南京⊠日本帝国主义入城疯狂大屠杀，死
难者达二十万人以上'; 'Our siblings suffered from the insult and ravage of the infamous enemies 我们的姊妹，遭受无耻敌人的侮辱与蹂躏'; 'Japanese bandits killed
around 1,000 people every day, lasting for two months. They felt that it was too exhausting
to execute by shooting or slashing and thus buried Chinese people alive 日寇每日屠杀
千余人，连续两月，他们觉得枪决与刀砍太费力气，于是把中国人民生生活埋.'
Source: Xinhua Ribao, 7 July 1950.

Who committed this monstrous crime?
Listen, the Hiroshima lady has been groaning until now
Nanjing people will never forget the deeply grieved scene:
Blood flowed and has become a river in the foot of Mufu Mountain
The scythe of the devils killed numerous lives.[126]

Not only the sense of victimhood, but also the details of the Nanjing
Massacre itself were well remembered before 1982, both privately and officially. That is why after the Textbook Incident there were so many spontaneous protests by Nanjing citizens and a large-scale exhibition and
documentary films were swiftly created.[127] After the official campaign finished

in late August 1982, activities to publicise the massacre were still prevalent in Nanjing, and many citizens wrote to the local authorities requesting that a memorial to it be constructed. They managed to obtain approval from the centre and opened the Nanjing Massacre Memorial Hall in 1985.[128]

Through this case study of Nanjing's local war remembrance, we can consider the relationship between local war remembrance and its relationship with national war remembrance between 1949 and 1982.

First, the national memory of the Fifteen-Year War penetrated local people's attitudes. War-related memorial days, like July 7, were celebrated locally in Nanjing. The activity of compiling, publishing and distributing school textbooks was controlled centrally in the PRC (except in a few periods, e.g. during the Cultural Revolution).[129] Furthermore, exhibitions in the national history museums were reported in Nanjing's local media.

Second, although there was a version of national war memory, remembrance of the war differed from place to place. When asked 'What Japanese atrocities did you know about before 1982?', none of my interviewees singled out the Nanjing Massacre, except those who had grown up or worked in Nanjing before 1982. Apart from the well known ones, like the 'Three-Alls' policy, the atrocities singled out by them were those committed in their hometown or nearby. Personally, I had never before heard of most of these atrocities. For example, the interviewee born in Yangzhou, Jiangsu Province, singled out the Wanfu Bridge Massacre in Yangzhou of 14 December 1937, and the interviewee born in Langzhong, Sichuan Province singled out the Langzhong Air Raid of July 1941.[130] This suggests that the memory of the Fifteen-Year War was highly regionalised prior to 1982.

Third, the local/regional and national remembrance had a mutual reliance. The national memory, to a large extent, was a selection of local war memories. For instance, the Nanjing Massacre was mentioned in school history textbooks. One method used by the Preparatory Office of the Museum of Chinese Revolution to obtain period pieces was public solicitation. Items turned over or donated by regional government departments and ordinary citizens made up the major part of the museum's collection. The office also sent their staff to so-called 'old revolutionary areas' to directly collect period pieces, or to organise exhibitions to encourage local residents to hand in period pieces.[131] Furthermore, although most regional memories of the war were held only by locals, a few were well incorporated into the national war memory and were thus widely known, like Liutiaohu's Manchuria Incident, Shanghai's January 28th Incident and Marco Polo Bridge Town's July 7th Incident.[132]

Finally, locals had to adopt what was the essence of the national memory of the Fifteen-Year War: the CCP's solitary leadership of the war effort, and its tragic but ultimately victorious tone. As long they did not contradict the essence of the national memory (e.g. were not pro-KMT or pro-US), local people were free to remember their particular war experiences without suppression or discouragement from above. It was that memory that was identified with most strongly by locals that thrived locally. When a local authority wanted to exploit the memory of the Fifteen-Year War, it was inclined to employ the most thriving local memory, for both short-term mobilisation (e.g. in the July 7th celebration) and long-term usefulness (e.g. in education efforts relating to the revolutionary tradition and to class). Thus, memories of victimhood could be openly expressed by local people, even substantially, as long as the that victimhood was useful and could be associated with something heroic.

Let us return to the inquiry made at the beginning of this section: why was the sense of victimhood evident to such an extent in the three places visited by Honda? The fundamental reasons are as follows: first, their experiences during the war were tragic; second, all the stories told in these three places were given some kind of victorious ending – Liutiaohu residents knocked down the memorial tower, the workers near mass graves became their own owners and the survivors of the Panjiayu Massacre successfully gained their vengeance; and third, the CCP was portrayed as the obvious or invisible leader who led the people to their final victory.

* * *

This chapter has suggested that remembrance of the Fifteen-Year War was very profitable for the CCP regime and thus was employed by it for various diplomatic as well as domestic purposes. Moreover, by employing the war remembrance, the regime actually promoted that remembrance among the Chinese people. For instance, regardless of the extra-attachments of the five memorial days, these days were, first and foremost, occasions on which to commemorate the events of the Fifteen-Year War. The December 9th Movement commemoration was always commemorated as a youthful and patriotic activity, which played a vital role in rousing the Chinese to resist the Japanese invasion. The actions of the December 9th Movement, which were described again and again during the Movement's commemoration days, involved shouting slogans like 'Down with Japanese imperialism', singing national salvation songs, performing salvation dramas and distributing leaflets or directly speaking to townsfolk and farmers to explain the importance of a united resistance against Japan. Similarly, when commemorating September 18th, the humiliation and devastation of life under the occupation of the Japanese army was always described. By regularly reproducing the events of the Fifteen-Year War, the memory of that war was consolidated among Chinese people.

Furthermore, to foster a new socialist identity and to support its claims to legitimacy, the CCP regime even promoted a stable version of the Fifteen-Year-War memory nationwide. This national war memory, characterised by its CCP-centric narrative and tragic-heroic tone, was well embraced by local people. Nevertheless, as long as it adopted the essence of the national war memory, it was the local memory that was identified with most.

Finally, the CCP regime did not reject the victimhood narrative of the Fifteen-Year War. On the contrary, both the central as well as local governments used the miserable facets of the war to serve their short-term as well as fundamental aims. Days associated with national humiliation – July 7 and September 18 – were continuously commemorated. The atrocities committed by the Imperial Japanese Army were presented in PRC school history textbooks and museums without hesitation. The tragic tales about mass graves and the 'Three-Alls' policy in the village of Panjiyu were both central and local CCP elements. As part of the top-down mass campaigns, the Nanjing Massacre was substantially employed by the Nanjing local government. The importance and presence of the sense of victimhood in Fifteen-Year-War remembrance in the PRC will be further analysed in the next chapter, which examines the realms of the war remembrance constructed by unofficial agents.

Notes

1 Chinese Government's Official Web Portal, 'National Anthem'. http://english. gov.cn/2005-08/16/content_23523.htm, 2012, date accessed, 6 March 2014.

2 See, Wu Beiguang 吴北光, 'Jiducangsang guogede dansheng ji beihou xianwei renzhi de gushi' [Inside story behind the birth of the national anthem 几度沧桑 国歌的诞生及背后鲜为人知的故事]. www.gov.cn/test/2006-02/27/content_211883. htm, 27 February 2006, date accessed, 6 March 2014. 'March of the Volunteers' was the official martial song of the Kuomingtang's 200th Division, which fought the Japanese army in Burma in 1942, see, Fang June 方军, 'Ba Dai Anlan jiangjun beihuiguode erbaishi baisui laobing' [One-hundred-year-old veteran who on his back carried General Dai Anlan back to China 把戴安澜将军背回国的二百师百岁老兵]. http://news.ifeng.com/history/special/zhongguoyua nzhengjun/200903/0305_5741_1046780.shtml, 5 March 2009, date accessed, 6 March 2014.

3 This song was sung around the world by the black American singer and actor Paul Robeson, and recorded as 'Chee Lai', *Renmin Ribao*, 'Huainian Baoluo Luoboxun Jianada jinian Meiguo heiren gechangjia de huodong' [Think of Paul Robeson, Canada's activity of commemorating the black American singer 怀念保罗·罗伯逊加拿大纪念美国黑人歌唱家的活动], 28 January 1981. It was featured in Frank Capra's wartime propaganda film *The Battle of China* and at a international conference held in Prague in February 1949.

4 Central Archives (CA): 'Zhengqiu guoqi guohui tuanji guogecipu qishi' [Announcement of calling for contributions to the pattern of the national flag and emblem, as well as the lyrics and melodies of the national anthem 征求国旗国徽图案及国歌词谱启示], 10 July 1949. The photos of the CA documents I used in this chapter are included in Zhonggong zhongyang wenxianyanjiushi, *Mao Zedong zhuan* [Biography of Mao Zedong] (Beijing: Zhongyang wenxian chubanshe, 2003) 中共中央文献研究室, 毛泽东传 (1949–1976) (中央文献出版社, 2003).

5 Ma Xulun 马叙伦 was a leader of the China Association for Promoting Democracy and was the president of several 'Anti-Japanese' organisations after the Manchuria Incident, such as the Intellectual Circles' Association of National Salvation (北平文化界救国会).

6 In CA: 'Mao Zedong, Zhou Enlai zhaojide guoqi guohui guoge jinian guodu xieshangzuotanhui jilu' [Record of the meeting called by Mao Zedong and Zhou Enlai to talk over national flag, emblem and anthem, as well as the calendar era and the location of capital 毛泽东 周恩来召集的国旗 国徽 国歌 纪年 国都协商座谈会记录], 25 September 1949.

7 *Renmin Ribao*, 'Xinhuashe xinxiang guanyu guoqi guoge henianhao' [Letter box of Xinhua News Agency about national flag, national anthem and calendar era 新华社信箱 关于国旗国歌和年号], 15 November 1949.

8 A 'crime' attributed to Tian Han was that he promoted a literature of capitulation when China was facing the Japanese invasion during the 1930s. See two articles published in *Xinhua Ribao* on December 7, 1966: 'Ba xijujiede zushiye fandangfenzi Tian Han doukua doudao douchou' [Overthrow Tian Han, the founder of the theatrical circles and a anti-party element 把戏剧界的祖师爷反党分子田汉斗倒斗垮斗臭] and 'Lu xun nuchi pantu Tian Han' [Lu Xun fulminated against the traitor Tian Han 鲁迅怒斥叛徒田汉]. Also, see, *Xinhua Ribao*, 'Zhongguo heluxiaofu hesuowei "sanshiniandai" wenyi' [Chinese Khrushchev and the so-called '1930s literature and art' 中国赫鲁晓夫和所谓'三十年代文艺'], 17 September 1967.

9 The remainder of this section is mainly based on *Renmin Ribao*, 'Jixu gemingde zhange Zhonghuarenmingongheguo guoge zhengjixiaozu' [Continue the fighting song of revolution, PRC's unit of soliciting the national anthem 继续革命的战歌中华人民共和国国歌征集小组], 9 March 1978. Secondary literature was used as well, see, Lei Shenghong, 'Guogegeci congfeizhi qudai daohuifu de quzhelicheng' [The vicissitudes of the lyrics of national anthem from being banned, replaced and recovered], *Dangshi bolan*, 2008 雷声宏, 国歌歌词从废止, 取代到恢复的曲折历程, 党史博览, 2008; Shi Zhen, 'Wengehou gaihuan guogegeci shimo' [the whole story about the changes to the lyrics of the national anthem after the Cultural Revolution], *Wuhan wenshiziliao*, 10 (2004), 38 史真, "文革"后改换国歌歌词始末, 武汉文史资料 10 (2004), 38; Xubin Chen 谌旭彬, 'Guogegeci chenfu' [Ups and downs of lyrics of national anthem 国歌歌词沉浮]. http://news.qq.com/zt2011/ghgcd013/, date unknown, date accessed, 16 March 2014.

10 *Renmin Ribao*, 'Jixu gemingde zhange zhonghua renmin gongheguo guoge zhengjixiaozu'.

11 Lu Zhicheng, 'Chen Dengke de liangjian yian' [Two motions of Chen Dengke], *Jianghuai wenshi*, 5 (2006), 127–131 陆志成, 陈登科的两件议案, 江淮文史, 5 (2006), 127–131. Chen once asked more than 100 representatives of NPC one by one, and the majority of them could not sing.

12 *Renmin Ribao* published an article on 1 March 1979 claiming that there was no so-called black list of art.

13 In Lu, 'Chen Dengke de liangjian yian'.

14 K. A. Cerulo, 'Symbols and the world system: national anthems and flags', *Sociological Forum*, 8 (1993); A. Kyridis, A. Mavrikou, C. Zagkos, P. Golia, I. Vamvakidou and N. Fotopoulos, 'Nationalism through state-constructed symbols: the case of national anthems', *International Journal of Interdisciplinary Social Science*, 4 (2009), 244.

15 Other memorial dates were often associated with the Fifteen-Year War before 1982 as well, for example, July 1 (the foundation day of the CCP) and August 1 (Army Day). See, for example, *Xinhua Ribao*, 'Zhongguo renmin zenyang zhanshengle Riben faxisi qinlvezhe jinian Zhongguo gongchandang dansheng 30 zhourian' [How the Chinese people defeated the Japanese fascist invaders – commemorate the 30th anniversary of the CCP 中国人民怎样战胜了日本法西斯侵略者- 纪念中国共产党诞生30周年], 30 June 1951; *Xinhua Ribao*, 'Qinzhu jiefangjun jianjun 30 zhounian da Riben guizi dediyizhang' [Commemorating the 30th anniversary of the PLA, the first battle of fighting with Japanese devils 庆祝解放军建军30周年 打日本鬼子的第一仗], 26 July 1957.

16 E.g. the only work which links pre-1949 and post-1949 China I have encountered is Israel's study on the commemoration of the December 9th Movement in pre-Cultural Revolution China: J. Israel, 'The December 9th Movement: a case study

in Chinese communist historiography', *The China Quarterly*, 23 (1965), 140–169; J. Israel, 'The December 9th Movement', *The China Quarterly*, 27 (1966), 166–167.

17 For studies on how the Fifteen-Year War was presented in the PRC's pre-1982 textbooks, see, Zhang Shaozhe, Kang Xianshu and Huang Xiaochun, 'Chuugoku' [China], in Tetsu Nakamura (ed.), *Higashi Ajia no rekishi kyoukasyou wa dou kakareteiruka* [How the history textbooks have been written in East Asia] (Tokyo: Nihon hyouronsya, 2004) 張紹哲, 康賢淑, 黄孝春, 中国, 中村哲, 東アジアの歴史教科書はどう書かれているか (日本評論社, 2004); Yinan He's works.

18 As regards the museums, according to Kawamura, China started to unearth, preserve anti-Japanese remains and build memorials after the 1982 Textbook Incident, Kawamura Kazuyuki, 'Chuugoku no heiwa kinenkan' [Chinese peace memorials] in *Seikaino heiwa hakubutsukan* [Peace museums in the world] (Tokyo: Nihon zusho sentai, 1995) 川村一之, 中国の平和記念館, 世界の平和博物館 (日本図書センター, 1995). Nevertheless, before 1982, there were exhibitions and memorials devoted to the Fifteen-Year War, see, Rana Mitter, 'Behind the scenes at the museum: nationalism, history and memory in the Beijing War of Resistance Museum, 1987–1997', *The China Quarterly*, 161 (2000); Kirk A. Denton, 'Horror and atrocity: memory of Japanese imperialism', in Ching Kwan Lee and Guobin Yang (eds), *Re-envisioning the Chinese Revolution* (Palo Alto CA: Stanford University Press, 2007), 245–286.

19 Since then, September 18th had been commemorated annually by the KMT government until 1941 (excepting 1935 and 1936) when it started to be commemorated with the Marco Polo Bridge Incident. Xubin Chen 谌旭彬, 'Fansi bashinian "jiuyiba" jinianshi' [Reflect on the eighty-year commemorative history of 'September 18th' 反思八十年'九一八'纪念史]. http://view.news.qq.com/zt2012/jyb/index.htm, 18 September 2012, date accessed 10 March 2014.

20 Many official commemorative articles of the KMT regime were included in Zhongguo guomindang zhongyangzhixing weiyuanhui xuanchuanbu, *Qiqijinian zongcai wengao huibian* [Compilation of the president's statements for commemorating July 7] (Zhongguo guomindang zhixingweiyuanhui xuanchuanbu, 1942) 中国国民党中央执行委员会宣传部, 七七纪念总裁文告汇编 (中国国民党中央执行委员会宣传部, 1942). Many other commemorative activities were reported in KMT's party organ *Zhongyang Ribao* as well, see, for example, 'Qiqi jinian choubeichu zuokai diyicihuiyi' [The preparatory office of July 7 commemoration had its first meeting yesterday, 七七'紀念籌備處昨開第一次會議], 30 June 1938; 'Zhongxuanbu zhuban kangzhan jinian huazhan' [Ministry of propaganda is organising an art exhibition to commemorate the War of Resistance 中宣部主辦, 抗戰紀念畫展], 5 July 1943; 'Zhongshu zuochen zhankaijinian kangzhanjianguo qizhounian' [The central administration had a meeting yesterday to commemorate the 7th anniversary of the War of Resistance and Nation-Building Day 中樞昨晨開會紀念, 抗戰建國七周年], 8 July 1944.

21 'Gaodongbei tongbao shu (18 September 1938)' [A message to the Northeastern compatriots], in Qin Xiaoyi (ed.), *Xian zongtong Jianggong sixiangyanlun zongji* [Compilation of Chiang Kai-Shek's thoughts and speeches] (Unpublished source, 1982) 告东北同胞书, 秦孝仪, 先总统蒋公思想言论总集 (未出版资料, 1982); Zhonggong zhaoqing shiwei dangshi yanjiushi 中共肇庆市委党史研究室, 'Qiqijianguo jinianbei' [July 7 cenotaph of the war of resistance and nation-building 七七抗战建国纪念碑]. http://ds.zhaoqing.gov.cn/xqds/sh/201204/t20120409_153391.html, 9 April 2012, date accessed, 10 March 2014.

22 See, 'Kangzhanjianguo shizhounian jinian gaoquanguojunmin tongbaoshu (7 July 1947)' [10th anniversary of July 7, message to compatriots of soldiers and people 抗戰建國十週年紀念告全國軍民同胞書] in Qin (ed.), *Jianggong sixiang*, p. 172.

23   The KMT's criticism of the USSR, e.g. *Shishi Gongbao* 时事公报, 'Sulianqinlve weixie zhongguo juxinzaocheng xinjiuyiba' [Soviet invasion threatens China, harbours evil intentions of making a new September 18 苏联侵略威胁中国 居心造成新九一八], 28 August 1947.

24   E.g. articles in *Renmin Ribao*: 'Meiguo fandongpai fuchirikou weijinian jiuyiba erzuo' [American reactionary gives support to Japanese bandits, write to commemorate September 18 美国反动派扶持日寇为纪念"九一八"而作], 21 September 1946; 'Xiangmaiguozei Jiang Jieshi taohuanxuezhai jinian jiuyiba shiliuzhounian' [Demand repayment of a bloody debt from Chiang Kai-Shek the traitor, commemorating the 16th anniversary of September 18 向卖国贼蒋介石讨还血债纪念"九一八"十六周年], 20 September 1947.

25   See, 'Taiwansheng guangfu yizhounian jinian gaoquansheng tongbaoshu (25 October 1946)' [Commemorating the first anniversary of reclaiming Taiwan, message to the compatriots of Taiwan province 臺灣省光復一週年紀念告全省同胞書] in Qin (ed.), *Jianggong sixiang*.

26   See, E. Snow, 'December 9th Movement', *China Quarterly*, 26 (1966), 171–176.

27   See, Anonymous, 'The students aroused the nation', *China Reconstructs*, 1965: 12. There is a debate about the actual casualty; Israel, 'The December 9th Movement'.

28   See, Tang Baolin, 'Liu Shaoqi yu yierjiuyundong dezhuanzhe' [Liu Shaoqi and the turning point of the December 9th Movement], *Jindaishi yanjiu*, 3 (1988), 195–211 唐宝林, 刘少奇与一二九运动的转折, 近代史研究, 3 (1988), 195–211.

29   Israel, 'The December 9th Movement'.

30   According to a commemorative speech given by Liu Shaoqi in 1944 – the main party cadre who was involved in the movement, *Renmin Ribao*, 'Liushaoqi yijiusisinian zai yanan jinian "yierjiu" yundong dahuishangde jianghua zhaiyao' [Excerpt of Liu Shaoqi's speech in 1944 at the Yanan youths' meeting of commemorating December 9th movement 一九四四年在延安青年 纪念"一二九"运动大会上的讲话摘要], 9 December 1950.

31   *Renmin Ribao*, 'Lu Dingyi tongzhisai yierjiu yieryi jinianhuishang yanjiang' [Lu Dingyi give a speech in the commemorative meeting for December 9 and December 1 陆定一同志在"一二九""一二一"纪念会上演讲], 10 December 1946; 'Fanduineizhan fanduimaiguo yananjuxing yierjiu yieryi jiniandahui' [Anti-Civil War, anti-quisling, Yan'an organise a commemorative meeting to commemorate December 9 and December 1 反对内战反对卖国延安举行"一二九""一二一"纪念大会], 10 December 1946, 12.

32   The Measures (Quanguo nianjieji jinianri fangjiabanfa 全国年节及纪念日放假办法) were revised twice after that on 18 September 1999 and on 14 December 2007. According to 'Zhongyang renminzhengfu zhengwuyuan tonggao (13 August 1951)' [Announcement of the Government Administration Council of the Central People's Government 中央人民政府政务院通告], the Chinese government had realised that Japan surrendered after it signed the surrender treaty on 3 September 1945, so the government decided that the V-J Day should be changed to September 3.

33   See, *Renmin Ribao*, 'Liao Chengzhi banshichu zhudongjing lianluoshiwusuodeng yanzheng bochi zuotengzhengfu dewuchijiaobian Ribenzhengfu zongrong baotu ouda wozhu Riben renyuan zuizenantao' [The Tokyo branch of Liao Chengzhi Office refutes the shameless sophistry of the Sato government; the Japanese government connives with the rioters to beat up our staff residing in Japan, it cannot escape the responsibility for this offence 廖承志办事处驻东京联络事务所等严正驳斥佐藤政府的无耻狡辩   日本政府纵容暴徒殴打我驻日人员罪责难逃], 17 September 1967; 'Wozhu Ri renyuan zunzhaoweida lingxiu maozhuxi dejiaodao, buweiqiangbao, yingyongzhandou' [Our staff residing in Japan, obeying the

guidance of Chairman Mao, are not afraid of the violence and fight bravely 我驻日人员遵照伟大领袖毛主席的教导, 不畏强暴, 英勇战斗], 18 September 1967.

34　Zhang et al., 'Chuugoku'; for research on the PRC's school textbooks system, see, Fang Chengzhi, 'Jianguo chuqi zhongxiaoxue jiaokeshu de bianage' [The transformation of the primary and secondary school textbook in the early period after the founding of New China], *Journal of Educational Science of Hunan Normal University*, 6 (2007), 13–28 方成智, 建国初期中小学教科书的变革, 湖南师范大学教育科学学报, 6 (2007), 13–28; Shi Ou and Li Xin, 'Xin Zhongguo 60 nian zhongxiaoxue jiaocai jianshe zhi tanxi' [The research in the development of Chinese and secondary textbooks over sixty years], *Journal of Educational Science of Hunan Normal University*, 8 (2009), 5–10. 石鸥, 李新, 新中国60年中小学教材建设之探析, 湖南师范大学教育科学学报 8 (2009), 5–10.

35　A seventeen-year period: Ma Jingwu and Li Gengxu, *Gaoji xiaoxue keben lishi disice* [Senior primary school textbook, history, volume 4] (Renminjiaoyu chubanshe, 1957) 马精武 李赓序, 高级小学课本 历史 第四册 (人民教育出版社出版, 1957); Beijingshi jiaoyuju zhongxiaoxue jiaocai bianshenchu, *Beijingshi gaojixiaoxue shiyongkeben Lishi xiace* [Beijing municipal senior primary school trial textbook, history, volume 2] (Beijing chubanshe, 1961) 北京市教育局中小学教材编审处, 北京市高级小学试用课本 历史 下册 北京出版社出版, 1961.

Yao Yongbin and Su Shoutong, *Chujizhongxue Zhongguo Lishi disice* [Junior high school textbook, Chinese history, volume 4] (Renmin jiaoyu chubanshe, 1956) 姚涌彬 苏寿桐, 初级中学课本 中国历史 第四册 (人民教育出版社, 1956); also, its 7th edition published in 1963; Renminjiaoyu chubanshe, *chujizhong xuekeben Zhongguo Lishi disice jiaoxue cankaoshu* [Junior high school textbook, Chinese history, volume 4, teaching reference book] (Renminjiaoyu chubanshe, 1959), 人民教育出版社, 初级中学课本 中国历史 第四册 教学参考书 (人民教育出版社, 1959).

Renming jiaoyu chubanshe, *Gaoji zhongxue keben shijie jindai xiandaishi xiace* [Senior high school textbook, world modern and contemporary history, volume 2] (Renmin jiaoyu chubanshe, 1958) 人民教育出版社, 高级中学课本 世界近代现代史 下册 人民教育出版社, 1958); Renminjiaoyu chubanshe, *Gaoji zhongxue keben Zhongguo xiandaishi* [Senior high school textbook, Chinese contemporary history] (Renmin jiaoyu chubanshe, 1960) 人民教育出版社, 高级中学课本 中国现代史 (人民教育出版社, 1960); Also, the second print of its third edition published in 1964

Shanghai jiaoyu chubanshe, *Gaozhong Zhongguo xiandaishi jiaoxue cangaoshu xiace* [Senior high school Chinese contemporary history teaching reference book, volume 2] (Shanghai jiaoyu chubanshe, 1960) 上海教育出版社, 高中中国现代史教学参考书 下册 (上海教育出版社, 1960第一版).

Cultural Revolution period: Beijingshi jiaoyuju jiaocai bianxiezu, *Beijingshi zhongxue shiyong keben lishi disance shangce* [Beijing municipal high school trial textbook, history volume 3, issue 1] (Renmin jiaoyu chubanshe, 1973) 北京市教育局教材编写组, 北京市中学试用课本 历史第三册 (上册), 人民教育出版社, 1973; Liaoningsheng zhongxiao xue jiaocai bianxiezu, *Liaoning sheng zhongxue shiyong keben Zhongguo lishi xiandaibufen* [Liaoning Provincial High School trial textbook, Chinese history, contemporary part] (Liaoning renmin chubanshe, 1977) 辽宁省中小学教材编写组, 辽宁省中学试用课本 中国历史 现代部分 (辽宁人民出版社, 1977).

Post-Cultural Revolution period: Zhongxiaoxue tongyongjiaocai lishi bianxiezu, *Quanrizhi shinianzhi xuexiao chuzhongkeben disice* [Full-time, ten-year schooling Junior high school textbook, Chinese history, volume 4] (Renmin jiaoyu chubanshe, 1980, 1979 first print) 中小学通用教材历史编写组, 全日制十年制学校初中课本 中国历史 第四册, (人民教育出版社出版, 1980, 1979第一版); Zhongxiaoxue tongyong jiaocai lishi bianxiezu, *Quanrizhi shinianzhi xuexiao chuzhong Zhongguo lishi disice jiaoxue cankaoshu* [Full-time, ten-year schooling junior high school Chinese history, volume 4, teaching reference book] (Renmin jiaoyu chubanshe, 1980, 1979 first print) 中小学通用教材历史编写组, 全日制十年制学校 初中中国历史 第四册 教学参考书人民教育出版社出版, 1980, 1979第一版.

36 The 'second Civil Revolution War period' was called the 'Land Revolution War period' during the Cultural Revolution.

37 It seems that the idea of 'strategic deadlock phase' had not been adopted by school textbooks published in 1950s. Also, a few textbooks, published after 1960, simply taught the historical facts without a strict periodisation, *Beijingshi zhongxue shiyong keben lishi disance shangce (1973)*.

38 For details about the history of the Revolution Museum, see the official website of the National Museum of China: http://en.chnmuseum.cn/tabid/497/Default. aspx, date accessed, 6 March 2014. The Revolution Museum was under the control of the PRC's Ministry of Culture, while the Military Museum was under the control of the PLA.

39 *Renmin Ribao*, 'Xiangrenmin qunzhong jinxing aiguozhuyi he gemingchuantong jiaoyu, gemingbowuguan lishibowuguan jiancheng' [Educate people on patriotism and revolution tradition, the revolution museum and history museum is completed 向人民群众进行爱国主义和革命传统教育革命博物馆 历史博物馆建成], 20 September 1959. PRC's Ministry of Culture, 'Weizhiyuan Zhongguo geming bowuguan, Zhongguo lishi bowuguan, gugong bowuguan zhengji wenwuziliao' [Recruit period pieces for Chinese Museum of Revolution, Chinese Museum of History and Museum of the Forbidden City 中华人民共和国文化部为支援中国革命博物馆 中国历史博物馆 故宫博物院征集文物资料], 10 November 1958.

40 National Museum of China's exhibition 'Centennial of National Museum of China', visited on 24 September 2012; Yang Fang, 'Guojiabowuguan qiaoran bianhua: cong gemingmiankong dao shechipin zhanshi' [Quiet change of National Museum of China: from the face of revolution to the exhibition of luxury goods], *Zhongguo guojia bowuguan meizhou kuaixun*, 25 (2011), 4–8 杨芳, 国家博物馆悄然变化:从革命面孔到奢侈品展示, 中国国家博物馆 每周快讯, 25 (2011), 4–8.

41 The three periods are: 1840–1919, 1919–1949, post-1949, and based on Maoist theory.

42 CA: 'Deng Xiaoping guanyu mingque Zhongguo gemingbowuguan fangzhen deyijian pishi' [Deng Xiaoping's opinion on the guiding principle of the Chinese Museum of Revolution 邓小平关于明确中国革命博物馆方针的意见批示], 18 October 1957. A photocopy of this document is displayed in the exhibition of the 'Centennial of the National Museum of China'.

43 The official website of the military museum: www.jb.mil.cn/gk/jbjj/index.shtml

44 See, *Xinhua Ribao*, 'Zhongguo geming lishi bowuguan jieshao' [Introduction of Chinese Revolution Museum and History Museum 中国革命历史博物馆介绍], 30 June 1961.

45 The display in the War of Resistance Hall was a part of the museum's basic exhibition as well, which was previewed internally since October 1959. See, *Nanjing Ribao*, 'Gemingjunshi bowuguan longzhong kaiguan' [The Military Museum is opened solemnly 革命军事博物馆隆重开馆], 2 August 1960; 'Jinsanshi wanren canguanle junshi bowuguan' [Nearly 300, 000 people have visited the Military Museum 近三十万人参观了军事博物馆], 18 August 1960.

46 *Renmin Ribao*, 'Ping liangwanren maoyujihui jinian qiqi shierzhounian' [200, 000 people assemble in the rain to commemorate the 12th anniversary of July 7 in Beiping 平两万人冒雨集会纪念七七十二周年], 9 July 1949.

47 *Renmin Ribao*, 'Ping liangwanren maoyujihui jinian qiqi shierzhounian', 9 July 1949.

48 *Renmin Ribao*, 'Shanghai jinian qiqi qingzhu jiefang dayouxing jixiang' [Record of the big demonstration to commemorate July 7 and celebrate the liberation of Shanghai 上海纪念"七七"庆祝解放大游行纪详], 10 July 1949.

49 *Renmin Ribao*: 'Fanduijintian yuandong deqinlvezhe – Meidiguozhuyi, jinian jiuyiba shijiuzhounian' [Protest against the invader in the Far East today – American imperialism, commemorate the 19th anniversary of September 19 反对今天远东的侵略者 – 美国帝国主义 纪念"九一八"十九周年], 19 September 1950; 'Yingjiaqiang xuanchuan meiguoqinhua zuixing hewoguo renmin kang Ri de gongji' [We should enhance the propaganda against American crimes and the achievement of our people's resistance against Japan 应加强宣传美国侵华罪行和我国人民抗日的功绩], 3 September 1951; 'Qingzhu qiyi jinian qiqi, xinjian bolichang kaishi shengchan jingsai' [Celebrate July 1 and commemorate July 7; Xinjian glass factory starts production competition 庆祝"七一"纪念"七七" 新建玻璃厂开始生产竞赛], 2 July 1950; 'Yierjiu yundong shiwuzhounian' [Fifteen years of the December 9th Movement "一二·九"运动十五周年], 9 December 1950.

50 E.g. *Renmin Ribao*: 'Heguangdade gongnongbing xiangjiehe' [Intergrate with the workers, farmers and soldiers 和广大的工农兵相结合], 9 December 1950; 'Shoudu xuesheng jinian yierjiu, juexinjicheng geming chuantong, canjiaguofang jianshe, shenrukaizhan kangmeiyuanchao yundon' [To commemorate December 9, students in the capital decide to carry on the revolution tradition, participate in developing the national defence and carry out the movement of 'anti-the US and assisting North Korea 首都学生纪念"一二九" 决心继承革命传统 参加国防建设 深入开展抗美援朝运动], 10 December, 12.

51 *Renmin Ribao*, 'Jinxing sixianggaizao yundong yaoxiqu yierjiu dejiaoxun' [To carry out the campaign of thought reform, we need to learn lessons of December 9 进行思想改造运动要吸取"一二、九"的教训], 9 December 1951.

52 *Renmin Rbao*, 'Yao Yilin yierjiu delishi jingyan' [Yao Yilin, the historical experience of December 9 姚依林 "一二·九"的历史经验], 9 December 1955.

53 *Renmin Ribao*, 'Yierjiu yundong ershizhounian he yieryi yundong shizhounian, shoudu gaodengxuexiao kaizhan gezhong jinian huoodng' [For the 20th anniversary of the December 9th Movement and 10th anniversary of the December 1 Movement, university students in capital took part in various commemorative activities "一二·九"运动二十周年和"一二·一"运动十周年 首都高等学校展开各种纪念活动], 9 December 1955.

54 See, for example, *Renmin Ribao*: 'Yugongnong xiangjiehe Beijingdengdi xuesheng yishiji xingdong jinian yierjiu' [Joining with workers and farmers, students in Beijing and other places commemorate December 9 by their actions 与工农相结合北京等地学生以实际行动纪念一二·九], 9 December 1957; 'Tonggongnong jiehe shi zhishi qingnian delishidaolu jinian yierjiuyundong sanshizhounian' [Integrating with workers and farmers is the historical path of intellectual youth – commemorate the 30th anniversary of the December 9th movement 同工农结合是知识青年的历史道路 – 纪念一二·九运动三十周年], 9 December 1965.

55 See, for example, *Renmin Ribao*, 'Fayang yierjiu yundong degemin jingshen weidabai meidiqinlve zuohaoyiqie zhunbei shoudujuban yerjiuyundong sanshizhounian jinianzhanlan' [Carrying forward the spirit of the December 9th Movement, preparing for defeating the invasion of the US, the capital organises a commemorative exhibition for the 30th anniversary of the December 9th movement 发扬一二·九运动的革命精神 为打败美帝侵略做好一切准备首都举办一二·九运动三十周年纪念展览], 10 December 1965.

56 *Renmin Ribao*: 'Zhijing xiangei yierjiu yundong deqianbei' [Show respect to the older generation of the December 9th movement 致敬献给"一二·九"运动的前辈], 9 December 1980.

57 See, for example, 'Shao Lizi tankang Ri shiqi zhongsuguanxi sulian chu-
bingdongbei jueding rikoutouxiang' [Shao Lizi talks about Sino–Soviet relations
during the Anti-Japanese War, and says that the Soviet Union's dispatching of
troops to the Northeast clinched Japan's surrender 邵力子谈抗日时期中苏关系
苏联出兵东北决定日寇投降], 16 August 1949; 'Sujuncanzhan shi Riben shibaide
zhuyaoyuanyin' [The Soviet entry into the war was the main reason for Japan's
defeat 苏军参战是日本失败的主要原因], 15 August 1950; 'Sulian jikui Riben
diguozhuyi delishiyiyi' [Historical significance of the Soviet Union's defeat of
Japanese imperialists 苏联击溃日本帝国主义的历史意义], 3 September 1955.

58 E.g. *Renmin Ribao*, 'Zhong Chao renmin zai Dongbei kang Ri zhanzhengz-
hongde guojizhuyi tuanjie' [The internationalist solidarity between Chinese and
Korean people in northeast China during the Anti-Japanese War 中朝人民在东
北抗日战争中的国际主义团结], 11 November 1950.

59 E.g. *Renmin Ribao*, 'Jinian bayiwu' [Commemorating August 15 纪念"八·一
五"], 15 August 1955. This article was written by a North Korean writer 李箕永.

60 Hasegawa singled out 1956 as a turning point in Sino–Soviet relations (Nikita
Khruschev gave a speech against Stalin's cult of personality in 1956) and in
Sino–North Korean relations (the PRC's joint intervention with the USSR in
North Korea in 1956). See, T. Hasegawa (ed.), *Cold war in East Asia* (Washing-
ton, DC: Woodrow Wilson Center Press, 2011).

61 Shen Zhihua, 'Zhong Su zai 1958 niande guanxi weihe jiangdao bingdian' [Why
Sino–Soviet relations fell below freezing point in 1958], *Wenshitiandi*, 2013:
www.faobserver.com/Newsinfo.aspx?id=9270, date accessed, 16 March 2014 沈
志华, 中苏在1958年的关系为何降到冰点, 文史天地 2013:7.

62 *Renmin Ribao*, 'Jinian kangzhan shengli liushi zhounian, Shenyang dengdijiedian
sujunlieshi' [To commemorate the 16th anniversary of victory in the War of
Resistance, Shenyang and other places hold a memorial ceremony for the Soviet
martyrs 纪念抗战胜利十六周年沈阳等地祭奠苏军烈士], 5 September 1961.

63 See, for example, *Renmin Ribao*, 'Zhongguo renmin kang Ri zhanzheng deweidashengli [The great victory of the Chinese people's Anti-Japanese War], 15
August 1965, 'Bingmin shishenglizhiben' [Soldiers and people were the foundation of the victory 兵民是胜利之本], 17 August 1965; 'Mao Zedong sixiang
deweidashengli' [The great victory of Mao Zedong thought 毛泽东思想的伟大胜
利], 2 September 1965; 'Renmin zhanzheng shengli wansui [Long live the victory
of the people's war 人民战争胜利万岁], 3 September 1965.

64 See, L. Dittmer and S. S. Kim (eds), *China's quest for national identity* (Syracuse,
NY: Cornell University Press, 1993), p. 269.

65 For textbooks, see, *Beijingshi zhongxue lishi (1973)*, pp. 55–56, and *Beijingshi
zhongxue lishi (1973)*, pp. 55–56. For museums, e.g. *Renmin Ribao*: 'Jinian kangrizhanzheng shengli ershizhounian junshibowuguan kangri zhanzhengguan
jijiang chongxinkaifang' [To commemorate the 20th anniversary of victory in the
Anti-Japanese War, the 'Anti-Japanese War Hall' will be reopened 纪念抗日战争
胜利二十周年军事博物馆抗日战争馆即将重新开放], 16 August 1965; 'Zai kang
Ri zhanzhengguan shou gemingjiaoyu' [Receive revolution education in the
'Anti-Japanese Hall' 在抗日战争馆受革命教育], 27 August 1965.

66 Many articles with the theme, 'Qingkan Sulian baokan shizenyang feibang he
gongji Zhongguo de' [Please read how Soviet newspapers and magazines slander
and attack China 请看苏联报刊是怎样诽谤和攻击中国的], were published on 3
September 1963 in *Renmin Ribao*.

67 *Renmin Ribao*: 'Xinsijun laozhanshi geyongdui zaijingyanchu' [Chorus of veterans of New Fourth Army performed in Beijing 新四军老战士歌咏队在京演出],
17 September 1979.

68 *Renmin Ribao*: 'Kangri zhanzheng' [Anti-Japanese War 抗日战争], 3 July 1981;
'Mao Zedong tongzhi zai kang Ri zhanzheng chuqi guanyu jianchiduli zizhude

youjizhanzheng de wugediangbao' [Mao Zedong's five telegrams insisting on guerrilla warfare at the beginning of the Anti-Japanese War 毛泽东同志在抗日战争初期关于坚持独立自主的游击战争的五个电报], 7 July 1981; 'Weijinian kang Ri zhanzheng sanshi liuzhounian Zhangbeixian xiang Su Meng lianjun jinianta jingxian huaquan' [To commemorate the 36th anniversary of the Anti-Japanese War, Zhangbei county laid flowers at the Soviet–Mongolian United Army martyrs' memorial towers 为纪念抗日战争三十六周年张北县向苏蒙联军烈士纪念塔敬献花圈], 4 September 1981.

69 For example, two chapters in *Chuji zhongxue Zhongguo lishi (1956)* were used to discuss the left-wing literature movement and the literature during the War of Resistance period, respectively. However, the two chapters disappeared from this textbook's 1963 edition. The left-wing literature movement and its supporters, like Wang Ming, Liu Shaoqi and Tian Han, were heavily criticised in a school textbook published in 1973, see, *Beijingshi zhongxue Lishi (1973)*.

70 Lei Yi, 'Qu Qiubai yuanan bushiyu sirenbang depohai' [Qu Qiubai's case of injustice did not start from the persecution of the 'Gang of Four'], Wenshi cankao, 2010. http://news.ifeng.com/history/zhongguoxiandaishi/detail_2012_09/ 10/17483072_0.shtml, 10 September 2012, date accessed, 16 March 2014 雷颐, 瞿秋白冤案不始于四人帮的迫害, 文史参考, 2010:10; *Xinhua Ribao,* 'Wang Zhang Jiang Yao sirenbang pohuai Zhongguo renmin gemming junshi bowuguan chenliexuanchuan gongzuo de zuixing' [Gang of Four's crime of sabotaging the Revolution Museum and Military Museum's exhibition and propaganda work 王张江姚四人帮破坏中国人民革命军事 博物馆陈列宣传工作的罪行], 23 January 1977.

71 *Renmin Ribao*, 'Zhongguo gongchandang lishi chenlie (minzhu gemingshiqi)' [Exhibition of the CCP's history (Democratic Revolution period) 中国共产党历史陈列 (民主革命时期)], 6 July 1981.

72 *Renmin Ribao*, 'Beijing gaoxiao shisheng juxing wenyiwanhui jinian yierjiu yundong sishisi zhounian' [Students and teachers in Beijing's universities organised parties to commemorate the 44th anniversary of the December 9th Movement 北京高校师生举行文艺晚会纪念一二九运动四十四周年], 10 December 1979.

73 *Renmin Ribao*, 'Wang Yunsheng xiansheng hetade liushinianlai Zhongguo yu Riben' [Mr Wang Yunsheng and his book *China and Japan during the past sixty years* 王芸生先生和他的《六十年来中国与日本》], 7 July 1980.

74 *Renmin Ribao*, 'Jinian kangrizhanzheng shengli sanshizhounian' [Commemorating the 30th anniversary of victory in the Anti-Japanese War 纪念抗日战争胜利三十周年], 3 September 1975; 'Jinian kangrizhanzheng shengli sanshouzhounian, Liaoning, Jilin, Heilongjiang, Hubei dengdi xiang Sujunlieshi lingmu, jinianbei he jinianta xianhuaquan, Hebeisheng Zhangbeixian geweihui xiang sumenglianjun lieshijinianta xianhuaquan' [Commemorating the 30th anniversary of victory in the Anti-Japanese War, Liaoning, Jilin, Heilongjiang, Hubei and other places brought flowers to the Soviet martyrs' tombs, cenotaphs and memorial towers; Zhangbei county in Heibei province offered flowers to the Soviet–Mongolian United Army martyrs' memorial towers 纪念抗日战争胜利三十周年辽宁、吉林、黑龙江、湖北等地向苏军烈士陵墓、纪念碑和纪念塔献花圈河北省张北县革委会向苏蒙联军烈士纪念塔献花圈], 4 September 1975.

75 E.g. *Xinhua Ribao*, Zhongguo geming lishi bowuguan jieshao. Also, several memorials were built to commemorate Bethune, see, *Xinhua Ribao*: 'Shijiazhuang junmin jisao baiqiuen tongzhimu' [Soldiers and people in Shijiazhuang commemorate Bethune at his grave 石家庄军民祭扫白求恩同志墓], 12 November 1964; 'Baiqiuen jinianguan kaimu' [Bethune memorial inaugurated 白求恩纪念馆开幕], 1 September 1976.

76 *Quanrizhi shinianzhi xuexiao chuzhongkeben disice (1980)*, pp. 81–82.

77   See, Dittmer and Kim (eds) (1993), *China's quest for national identity*, p. 269. Wang also suggested that Mao put great emphasis on 'internationalism', Wang, *Never forget national humiliation*.

78   This paragraph is based on various sources cited previously.

79   Two sources used for this part were: two books edited by the Revolution Museum and Military Museum, which describes some items from their collections: Zhongguo geming bowuguan, *Zhongguo geming bowuguan cangpinxuan*; Zhongguo renmin junshi bowuguan, *Zhongguo junshi bowuguan wenwujianshang* [Appreciate the period pieces of the Chinese Museum of the Military] (Shanghai: Shanghai renmin chubanshe, 2006) 中国人民军事博物馆, 中国军事博物馆文物鉴赏 (上海人民出版社, 2006). Also, a few pre-1982 newspaper reports, which described the exhibitions in the two museums. If an item was mentioned by the pre-1982 reports and the two books, I speculate that it has been displayed/possessed by the museums since they were turned over.

80   According to *Gemin bowuguan (2003)*, p. 156 and *Junshi bowuguan (2006)*, p. 152, the items were turned over to the Revolution Museum and Military Museum in 1952 and 1959 respectively. The items relating to Zuo Quan were also displayed in the new basic exhibition of the Revolution Museum in the post-Cultural Revolution period, see, *Renmin Ribao*, 'Zhongguo gongchandang lishi chenlie (minzhu gemingshiqi)'.

81   Both the medal and the boat were mentioned in, *Xinhua Ribao*, 'Jinian weida kang Ri zhanzheng shengli ershi zhou nian zhanlan xunli'. The medal is described in *Gemin bowuguan*, 180. The boat is described in *Gemin bowuguan*, 173.

82   E.g. *Xinhua Ribao*, 'Jinian weida kang Ri zhanzheng shengli ershizhounian zhanlan xunli'; *Renmin Ribao*, 'Jinian kangrizhanzheng shengli ershizhounian junshibowuguan kangri zhanzhengguan jijiang chongxinkaifang'; *Junshi bowuguan,* p. 182.

83   Even in the two primary school textbooks I surveyed, the Imperial Japanese Army's atrocities were described. E.g. 'The Japanese army brutally massacred many Chinese people, and humiliated Chinese women. Whenever the Japanese army went, it would burn down the villages and loot all the assets there'. *Xiaoxue lishi (1957)*, pp. 28–29.

84   *Gaojizhongxue Zhongguo xiandaishi (1960)*, p. 54–55.

85   A misconception that the Nanjing Massacre was an academic forbidden zone and not taught in the PRC's schools has been popular among some amateur historians and even postgraduate students, see, for exmaple, Anonymous, 'Nanjing datusha cengshi yanjiu jinqu beizhongguo chedi yiwang 35 nian' [The Nanjing Massacre used to be the academic forbidden zone, and had been forgotten in China completedly for 35 years 南京大屠杀曾是研究禁区 被中国彻底遗忘35年]. www.hottx.net/history/lsmw/201012/73592.html, 13 December 2010, date accessed, 10 March 2014.

86   The Nanjing Massacre and the figure of 300, 000 was mentioned in *Gaojizhongxue Zhongguo xiandaishi (1960)*, p. 57 and in the same place in its third edition published in 1964.The reference book, which was based on other history books edited/written by some mainstream Chinese historians at the time, further pointed out that cruelty was a feature of the Imperial Japanese Army and the Nanjing Massacre was only a typical example, see, *Gaozhong jiaoxue cankaoshu (1960)*.

87   *Chuzhong Zhongguo lishi (1979)*, p. 51.

88   *Chujizhongxue Zhongguo lishi (1956)*, p. 87.

89   According to a memoir of a Japanese technician who visited China three times between 1965 and 1966, although there were items reflecting Japanese atrocities in the Revolution Museum and Military Museum, the atrocities exhibited in the two museums were not as disturbing as these displayed in the National Cultural Palace, see, Anonymous, 'Watashi to Chuugoku' [Me and China 私と中国]. http://

homepage3.nifty.com/harakicindexotolith/dexchugoku.html#ryokou, 26 March 2006, date accessed, 10 March 2014.

90   *Xinhua Ribao*, 'Jinian weida kangri zhanzheng shengli ershizhounian zhanlan xunli'; *Geming bowuguan*, 184.

91   *Xinhua Ribao,*'Jinian weida kangri zhanzheng shengli ershizhounian zhanlan xunli'; *Junshi bowuguan*, 147–148.

92   See, *Renmin Ribao*, 'Zaikangri zhanzhengguan shou gemingjiaoyu'; *Xinhua Ribao*, 'Wanrenken debeiju qineng chong yan' [How could the tragedy of wanrenken be performed again 万人坑的悲剧岂能重演], 14 July 1974.

93   'Victory' was the key word of the CCP's legitimacy claims, Wang, 'Never forget national humiliation', p. 88.

94   This section is based on, Honda Katsuichi, *Chuugoku No Tabi* [Travels in China] (Tokyo: Asahi Shinbunsha, 1981) 本多勝一, 中国の旅 (朝日新聞社, 1981). This is the pocket edition of the original book which was published in 1972. Another journalist was Hurukawa Mantaro 古川万太郎, who wanted to see China's situation during the Cultural Revolution and had a separate journey from Honda from Beijing; he published a book based on this trip: *The country of Nihao* [ニイハオの国 Niihao no kuni].

95   Honda, *Chugoku no Tabi*, pp. 10–12.

96   Honda, *Chugoku no Tabi*, p. 153.

97   Honda, *Chugoku no Tabi*, p. 147.

98   Wanrenken was a kind of common 'legacy' left by imperial Japan throughout China, see, for exampl ee, Interview, Duan, Nanjing Massacre Memorial Hall, 13 May 2012; Zhengxie Anhui wenshi ziliao yanjiu gongzuozu, *Anhui wenshi ziliao xuanji* [Selection of materials about Anhui's history] (Hefei: Anhui renmin chubanshe, 1964) (政协安徽文史资料研究工作组, 安徽文史资料选辑, 安徽人民出版社, 1964); 'Chouman wanrenkeng' [Mass grave filled up with hatred] in Beijingshi Jiaoyuju Zhongxiaoxue Jiaocai Bianxiezu (ed.), *Beijingshi Zhongxue Keben Yuwen Diqice* [Beijing Municipal School textbook, Chinese, volume 7] (Beijing: Beijing Renmin Chubanshe, 1972) 仇满万人坑, 北京市教育局中小学教材编写组, 北京市中学课本 语文 第七册 (北京人民出版社出版, 1972). As regards the campaign, see, *Xinhua Ribao*, 'Zhanyou' [Comrade in arms 战友], 14 July 1974, which is a poem written by a miner after a 'meeting of criticizing' Lin Biao and Confucius, during which the *wanrenkeng* was mentioned.

99   In Nanjing, Honda mainly listened to testimonies from the victims and visited some scenes, which were not specially preserved, under the testifiers' guidance. Also, some graphic photos, preserved by the Nanjing Municipal Authority, were shown to Honda.

100   NMA-5012-1-141 'Nanjingshi xingjian renmin lieshiling jihua gaishuo' [Plan for building a martyrs' cemetery in Nanjing 南京市兴建人民革命烈士陵计划概说], 1950–1951. There were six sessions of Nanjing's second People's Representatives Conference (Renmin Daibiao Huiyi 人民代表会议) organised between October 1950 and September 1953, see, Nanjing difangzhi bianzuan weiyuanhui bangongshi, *Nanjing Jianzhi* [Brief history of Nanjing] (Nanjing: Jiangsu guji chubanshe, 1986) 南京市地方志编纂委员会办公室, 南京简志 (江苏古籍出版社出版, 1986).

101   Luo then moved to Shanghai to organise an Anti-Japanese strike among workers in a Japanese-run-cotton mill, and was killed in Yuhuatai in 1933, see, NMA-5012-1-141 'Nanjing Xunnanlieshi shilve jieshao' [Introduction of the brief biographies of martyrs who died in Nanjing 南京殉难烈士史略介绍]. Around 100 representatives from several anti-Japanese organisations in Shanghai and Jiangsu province had a meeting on 17 July 1932 to prepare a national conference for patriotic organisations throughout China scheduled for 1 August. Eighty-eight people were arrested by the KMT regime when it learned of this conference,

among them thirty-three people were executed on 1 October, NMA-9080-2-75, 'Fandong tongzhi shiqi (1927–1949) zainanjing xunnan lieshi dashijiyao' [Chronicle of events about the martyrs who died in Nanjing during the reactionary ruling period 反动统治时期 (1927–1949年)在南京殉难烈士大事纪要], April 1960.

102 The CCP-led anti-Japanese guerrillas surrounding Nanjing were mainly Renmin kang Ri ziweidui 人民抗日自卫队 or Minkang 民抗. NMA-5012-1-14, 'Zai Nanjing xisheng lieshi chubudiaocha mingce' [The name list of martyrs who died in Nanjing, after a initial investigation 在南京牺牲烈士 初步调查名册] and NMA- 9080-2-75, 'Fandong tongzhi shiqi'.

103 NMA-9080-2-75, 'Fandong tongzhi shiqi'.

104 Page 21 in NMA-9008 'Yuhuatai geming lieshi jinianguan chenlie fangan' [A plan for the exhibition of the Yuhuatai memorial 雨花台革命烈士纪念馆陈列方案], 20 January 1970.

105 See, *Xinhua Ribao*, 'Dazhongxuexiao Zhengzhi Lishi jiaoshi zuotan xinzhong-guodansheng shiliao zhanlan yizhirenwen shiyibu shengdong de gemingshi' [Politics and history teachers of universities as well as middle schools discuss the exhibition on the Birth of the New China in 1950; all of them think this is a lively history of the revolution 大中学校政治历史教师 座谈"新中国诞生"史料展览 一致认为是一部生动的革命史], 14 October 1950; 'Kanzhanlan shoujiaoyu gongchan zhuyijiaoyu zhanlanhui' [visit the exhibition and receive education: the Exhibition of Communist Education 看展览受教育 《共产主义教育展览会》], 6 January 1961.

106 E.g. *Xinhua Ribao*, 'Kangda xiaoshi zai Nanjing zhanchu' [The history of the Chinese People's Anti-Japanese Military and Politics University was exhibited in Nanjing 抗大校史在南京展出], 25 October 1966; *Nanjing Ribao*, 'Xiangyingu-tou liulian xuexi zhanlan mingri zaijunshi bowuguan zhengshizhanchu nanjing-budui zhengzhibu juban xiang yingutou liulian xuexi zhanlan zaining tongshi zhanchu' [The Exhibition of Learning from the Hard-bone Sixth Company will be formally displayed in the military museum tomorrow, at the same time, the Exhibition of Learning from the Hard-bone Sixth company organised by the Nanjing army will be displayed in Nanjing 向硬骨头六连学习展览》明日在军事博物馆正式展出 南京部队政治部举办《向硬骨头六连学习展览》在宁同时展出], 31 July 1977; *Nanjing Ribao*, 'Xinsijun zhengtu shuhuazhan' [Exhibition of calligraphy and paintings about the New Fourth Army's long journey 新四军征途书画展], 7 January 1981.

 E.g. *Xinhua ribao*, 'Nanjing xiangtu lishi zhanlanguan' [The exhibition hall of Nanjing local history 南京乡土历史展览馆], 20 July 1958; 'Kangrizhanzheng shiqi Jiangsu gegeming genjudi baodao xuanji' [The selection of the reports about the resistance against Japan in the bases in Jiangsu Provinces during the Anti-Japanese War period 抗日战争时期江苏各革命根据地抗日斗争报道选辑], 24 August 1965.

107 The Nanjing Massacre survivors' psychological problems caused by the traumatic memory, see Xu Shuhong, 'Kongjuyu jiyi – Nanjing datusha xingcunzhe dexinlu licheng' [Fear and memory – the psychological process of the Nanjing Massacre survivors] in Wang Jin and Xu Lei (ed.), *Chuangshangde lishi Nanjing datusha yuzhanshi Zhongguo shehui* (Nanjing: Nanjing shifandaxue chubanshe, 2005), 63–102 许书宏, 恐惧与记忆 – 南京大屠杀幸存者的心路历程, 王瑾, 徐蕾 创伤的历史 – 南京大屠杀与战时中国社会 (南京师范大学出版社, 2005), 63–102.

108 According to Interview, Liu.

109 See, Interview, Zhang, Zhang's office in Nanjing, 21 June 2012.

110 Zhang Lianhong, 'Nanjing datusha xingcunzhe deriji yuhuiyi' [The dairies and remembrance of the Nanjing Massacre survivors], *Kangri zhanzheng yanjiu*, 2005 张连红, 南京大屠杀幸存者的日记与回忆, 抗日战争研究, 2005; Liu Yanjun,

'Nanjing datushade lishijiyi' [The historical memory of the Nanjing Massacare], *Kangri zhanzheng yanjiu,*2009, 5–22 刘燕军, 南京大屠杀的历史记忆, 抗日战争研究, 2009, 5–22.

111 Interview, Zhang and Luo (husband born in 1957 and wife born in 1958, Nanjing), Nanjing Municipal Library, 30 June 2012; Interview, Zhu (born in Nanjing in 1957), Gulou Park, 12 May 2012; Interview, Lv (born in Langzhong in 1941, moved to Nanjing in 1961), Gulou Park, 12 May 2012.

112 The information about this stele can be seen in the archives and newspaper during the Republican era, see, *Zhongyang Ribao*, 'Nanjing datushaxuede jinian, shoudufangmian juxing yishi wei ninan junmin zhiai' [Blood commemoration of the Nanjing Massacre: the capital organises ceremony to mourn the soldiers and civilians who were killed 南京大屠杀血的纪念, 首都方面举行仪式为罹难军民致哀], 13 December 1945; Interview, Sun.

113 See, Sun Zhaiwei, 'Lun Guo Gong liangdang dui Nanjing datusha degongshi' [A survey of common recognitions of the Nanjing Massacre between the KMT and the CCP], *Republican Archives*, 2 (2005) 105–109 孙宅巍, 论国共两党对南京大屠杀的共识, 民国档案, 2 (2005), 105–109; Liu Yanjun, 'Guominzhengfu dui Nanjingdatusha deshenpan shideyouguan nanjingbaoxing deshehuijiyi deyishengcheng' [The KMT government's trial of the Nanjing Massacre give birth to the social memory about the Nanjing Massacre], *Nanjing datushashi yanjiu*, 2002, 117–120 刘燕军, 国民政府对南京大屠杀案的审判使得有关南京暴行的社会记忆得以生成, 南京大屠杀史研究, 2002, 117–120.

114 See articles published in *Zhongyang Ribao* on 13 December 1945, and Tao Xiufu, 'Rikou huojing shimoji' [Record of how Japanese bandits brought calamity to the capital] (Nanjing: Nanjing wenxian, date unknown) 陶秀夫, 日寇祸京始末记, 南京文献.

115 Wang Yi and Xu Yishi, *Guoyu cidian disice* [A Chinese dictionary, volume 4] (Beijing: Shangwu yinshuguan, 1948) 汪怡, 徐一士等编, 国语辞典 第4册 (商务印书馆, 1948).

116 Liu, 'Guominzhengfu dui Nanjingdatusha deshenpan'.

117 *Xinhua Ribao*, 'Jinian qiqi qingzhu jiefang dahuishang liushizhang duiquanshi tongbao jiangci' [Divisional commander Liu's speech in the assembly for commemorating July 7 and celebrating liberation 纪念七七庆祝解放大会上刘师长对全市同胞讲词], 8 July 1949.

118 See, for example, *Xinhua Ribao*: 'Yuhuatai jumin kongsu Rikou xuechou Junda tongxue fenchi Meidi fu Rizuixing' [Residents in Yuhuatai district accuse Japanese bandits of the blood hatred, students in military college denounce American imperialists' hatred 雨花台区居民控诉日寇血仇 .军大同学愤斥美帝扶日罪行], 5 July 1949; 'Jinian qiqi tongyi Nanjing datusha shimin yizhi fanmei kang Ri' [Commemorate July 7th, recall the Nanjing Massacre 纪念七七痛忆南京大屠杀], 7 July 1949.

119 NMA-5003-3-788: 'Zhiyuan Ribenrenmin fandui Ri Mei junshi tongmeng tiaoyuedahuijihua (caoan)' [Plan of assembly of assisting Japanese people to protest against Japan–US treaty (draft) 支援日本人民反对日美军事同盟条约大会计划 草案], 9 May 1960.

120 For example, *Xinhua Ribao*: 'Nanjing Rikou datsuha Meidi yimian banshourongsuo yimian song nvrenqu weilao' [Japanese bandits conducted massacre in Nanjing, the American imperialists set up a refugee camp, at the same time sent women to express regards 南京日寇大屠杀 美帝一面办收容所 一面送女人去慰劳], 26 December 1950; 'Bunengzai rang Ribengui laiciwo shibadao' [I cannot let Japanese devils come and slap me eighteen times again 不能再让日本鬼来刺我十八刀], 22 February 1951. *Nanjing Ribao*, 'Riben qinlvezhe "Nanjing datusha" dexuexing zuixing' [Japanese invaders' cruel crime of 'the Nanjing Massacre' 日本侵略者 "南京大屠杀"的血腥罪行], 1 May 1960.

121 E.g. *Xinhua Ribao*: 'Jieshi yican jinian sinan tongbao' [Skip one meal to commemorate the fallen compatriots 节食一餐纪念死难同胞], 7 March 1951;
'Zhuidao sawan sinan tongbao jiniandahui jinri juxin' [Mourning the 300,000
fallen compatriots commemorating meeting is organised today 追悼卅万死难同
胞 纪念大会今日举行], 11 March 1951; 'Fan Mei fu Ri tupian zhanlan' [picture
exhibition against American assistance to Japan 反美扶日图片展览], 6 March
1951; The photos about the Nanjing Massacre together with the Japanese army's
invasion of Shanghai and atrocities in Wuxi, were also exhibited for the 20th
anniversary of the V-J day, *Xinhua Ribao*, 'Jinian weida kang Ri zhanzheng
shengli ershizhounian zhanlanhui zuokaimu'.

122 See, for example, *Xinhua Ribao*, 'Yuanjieshi wei xunnan tongbao juanjian
jinianbei' [Fasting in order to donate towards constructing a monument for the
fallen compatriots 愿节食为殉难同胞捐建纪念碑], 1 March 1951; 'Xiaguan dian
chang sinan gongren jinianbei tupian' [Picture of the Xiaguan electricity plant's
monument to the fallen workers 下关电厂死难工人纪念碑图片], 14 May 1960.
The text of the monument was changed many times according to the political
climate, see studies by Liu Yanjun and Su Zhaiwei.

123 See, for example, *Xinhua Ribao*, 'Nanjing jieji jiaoyu zhanlanhui zhengshi zhanchu jielu sandadiren de taotian zuixing xuanyang reminde douzheng
chengjiu' [Nanjing class education exhibition has been officially launched, reveals
the crimes conducted by the three kinds of enemies 南京阶级教育展览会正式展
出 揭露三大敌人的滔天罪行], 10 August 1963; 'Lianxi dangnian Rikou zhizao
"Wanfuqiao xuean" de lishi henpi Lin Biao [Use the history of 'Wanfuqiao
Massacre' conducted by Japanese bandits to criticize Lin Biao 联系当年日寇制
造 "万福桥血案" 的历史 狠批林彪], 30 May 1974.

124 *Nanjing Ribao*, 'Kan "jiefang Nanjing zhanlan"' [Visit the 'Exhibition of the
liberation of Nanjing' 看 "解放南京展览"], 20 April 1979.

125 *Xinhua Ribao*, 'Zai Nanjing datushazhong beihaide aiguorenmin yongchuibuxiu'
[Long live the memory of patriotic people killed in the Nanjing Massacre 在南京
大屠杀中 被害的爱国人民永垂不朽], 26 February 1951; 'Yige buqude gunian'
[An unyielding girl 一个不屈的姑娘], 1 March 1951; 'Yingyong buqude muqin'
[Brave and unyielding mother 英勇不屈的母亲], 8 March 1951. *Nanjing Ribao*,
'Riben qinlvezhe "Nanjing datusha" dexuexing zuixing' (1 May 1960) first
described the Japanese atrocities in detail, then suggested America's crimes
during the Nanjing Massacre, and finished by talking about how the patriotic
KMT servicemen tried to bravely resist the Japanese even after Chiang Kai-Shek
ordered the army to retreated from Nanjing on December 12; as well as the
deeds of Nanjing citizens' unconquerable spirit.

126 See, *Nanjing Ribao*, Kong Zhong 孔中, 'Lishi buxu chongyan' [History cannot
be repeated 历史不许重演], 14 May 1960; NMA-5003-3-788: 'Nanjingshi gejie
renmin zhiyuan Riben renmin fandui Ri Meijunshi tongmen tiaoyue dahui zhi
Riben Guangdaoshi Anbaogaiding zuzhifeiqi Guangdao xianmin gongdou huiyi
de zhichidian' [Telegram from Nanjing to Hiroshima 南京市各界人民支援日本
人民反对日美军事同盟条约大会致日本广岛市 "安保改订阻止废弃广岛县民共
斗会议" 的支持电 (草稿)], 13 May 1960.

127 For Nanjing citizens' protests, see articles carried in the local newspaper during
this period. According to 'Chronicle of events in Nanjing' (published on the
official website of the NMA), from 12 August 1982 and 25 September, Nanjing
Museum and the Chinese Second Historical Archives organised 'Qinhua Rijun
zai Nanjing datushsa zuizheng shiliao zhanlan' [Exhibition of historical documents about the crimes of the Nanjing Massacre conducted by the Japanese
army invading China' 侵华日军在南京大屠杀罪证史料展览]. Around 1,568,000
people attended the exhibition.

128 Interview, Sun; Interview, Zhang; Interview, Liu.

129   Zhang Shaozhe et al., 'Chuugoku', Fang Chengzhi, 'Jianguo chuqi zhong-xiaoxue jiaokeshu de biange'; Shi Ou and Li Xin, 'Xin Zhongguo 60 nian zhongxiaoxue jiaocai'.

130   Interview, Sun; Interview, Lv.

131   NMA-5003-3-409: 'Zhongyang geming bowuguan choubeichu zhi Nanjingshi fangdichan gongsi disi banshichu fuzetongzhi' [The Central Preparatory Office for the Museum of Revolution to the staff of Nanjing Municipal Land Company 中央革命博物馆筹备处 至 南京市房地产公司第四办事处负责同志], 11 August 1955; PRC's Ministry of Culture, 'Weizhiyuan Zhongguo geming bowuguan (10 November 1958)', and *Geming bowuguan (2003)*.

132   *Renmin Ribao*, 'Lugouqiaozhen renmin jinian qiqi' [People of Marco Polo Bridge Town commemorate July 7 芦沟桥镇人民纪念"七七"], 10 July 1950; 'Shanghaigejie jihui jinian yierba sanshizhounian yanchi Meidi fuhuo Riben junguozhuyi Jiang Guangnai, Cai Tingkai deng zhuishu songhu kangzhan deyiyi' [Shanghai commemorates the 30th anniversary of the first Shanghai Incident 上海各界集会纪念"一·二八"三十周年严斥美帝复活日本军国主义蒋光鼐、蔡廷锴等追述淞沪抗战的意义], 28 January 1962.

5 Beyond the state

Non-official agents of the Fifteen-Year-War memory

Three unofficial agents

In 1960, at the height of the Great Chinese Famine (1958–1961) and the tail end of the Great Leap Forward campaign (1958–1960) three efforts were made to bring something new to the mainland Chinese memory of the Fifteen-Year War, by a scholar, by a group of farmers and workers, and by a writer.

That year, Gao Xingzu 高兴祖, who was teaching in the History Department at Nanjing University (Nanda), started a research project on the Nanjing Massacre. In 1960 the final year students in the History Department of Nanda were divided into several groups for their graduation fieldwork. The research topic and location of each group was different: for example, one group went to Jintan to study the New Fourth Army's activities and another group was brought by their tutor to investigate the history of textile manufacture in Suzhou. Gao was also allocated a group consisting of seven students whom he led to research the Japanese Imperial Army's atrocities in Nanjing.[1] Four other teachers in the department were also included in Gao's research team.[2] The team interviewed several survivors of the massacre and collected primary sources in archives, such as the Nanjing Municipal Archives and the Nanjing Intermediate Court Archives.[3] They also searched a number of wartime and post-war newspapers for relevant information.[4] The testimonies I introduced in the previous chapters, which were published in the PRC's newspapers in late 1949 and the 1950s, were used substantially by this team. In addition, a wide range of published sources were employed.[5] The research continued to be carried out after the participating students left the university. In 1962, after two years of hard work and around the 25th anniversary of the Nanjing Massacre, this project yielded fruitful results, culminating in a manuscript entitled *The Japanese Imperialists' Massacre in Nanjing* 日本帝国主义在南京的大屠杀 (Figure 5.1).[6] In 1963, Jiangsu People's Publisher planned to publish the manuscript and even produced a proof copy. However, the plan stalled.

Despite not being published, the whole research project was not in vain.[7] Although most participants gradually readjusted their research directions, some of them remained interested in the topic of the Nanjing Massacre. They

内部刊物
注意保存

日本帝国主义
在南京的大屠杀

南京大学历史系编著

Figure 5.1 The Japanese Imperialists' Massacre in Nanjing (1979 edition)
Source: Xinhua Ribao, 7 July 1950. Photograph taken by the author.

collected more materials, and presented as well as discussed their results with audiences during Nanda's anniversary celebrations in 1963 and 1978. Many elite members of various trades and professions must have attended these two celebrations at this prestigious university. After the talks, it was likely that the influence of these elite attendees would help the presented information to reach a wider audience. Also, it was possible that some Nanda alumni in the auditorium had experienced the massacre and would relate their own experiences when talking about the presentation to other people. Thus, although the presentations in 1963 and 1978 were exclusive, their impact might be profound. In addition, these scholars also presented their research elsewhere beyond Nanda, and provided other organisations with the unpublished manuscript. These kinds of efforts to circulate the memory of the Nanjing Massacre were always 'supported ebulliently'.[8] Moreover, on several occasions these scholars were also invited by foreign affairs departments to introduce their research to Japanese delegates or historians. The presentation and photo display organised for the Japanese youth delegates in 1965 was among these kinds of 'achievements'.

On the other hand, in 1960 a group of less elite Nanjing citizens also took on the role of public storytellers of the wartime Japanese atrocities.[9] Having been instructed by the Nanjing Municipal Communist Party Committee, the Nanjing Municipal Federation of Trade Unions organised for some typical individuals (i.e. individuals deemed to be representative) who had miserable experiences in old China to establish a 'Speech Corps of Farmers and Workers 工农群众讲演团'. They were supposed to talk about their sad stories after the leaders gave reports in mass meetings, in order to back up the latter's reports with some real-life accounts. Most of the speeches tried to convey a particular message: the imperialists, bureaucratic capitalists (on this occasion, the KMT) and feudalists (the landlords) imposed great miseries upon the Chinese people before 1949 – the CCP liberated Chinese people from 'these three big mountains 三座大山' and brought them happiness in the new China. Often the speeches contained recollections about the sufferings under imperial Japan, which were related together with other miseries or on their own.

The experiences of being abused by imperial Japan recalled by these typical individuals were 'all-embracing'. For instance, those who told of their experiences held a wide range of occupations. Zhu Xing, who was born to a farming family in Dafeng county, Yancheng city, recalled a day when Japanese soldiers came to his village to carry out a mopping-up action. Many villagers were killed and houses were burned down. Zhu lost his mother in this event – she was raped and then killed by the soldiers. Wang Guogui told of his experience as a worker in a Japanese-controlled factory. At the beginning of his speech, Wang described the street in front of the factory as a living hell: covered in horse excrement, rubble, bodies, screaming voices and so on. To prevent workers from bringing in bombs or removing the factory assets out, the Japanese staff were very careful in allowing the workers to enter and leave the factory. According to Wang, this process was humiliating and frightening: the workers would be checked thoroughly, from their lunch boxes to their underwear; they would be showered with a chemical mixture regardless of the season; if a worker was considered to be insolent, he would be slapped on the face; and anyone accused of stealing the factory's assets would be tortured to death. Wang also complained about the low salaries workers received and various methods by which these scant earnings were squeezed. Zha Laiguang related an incident that took place when he was a sock-seller in occupied Nanjing: a group of Japanese soldiers took his socks without paying and ordered a dog to bite him. After the instance, Zha became a cart-driver, but his 'bad luck' did not end there. He was tortured and thrown into prison after being accused of stealing the bag of a Japanese female customer, and he was slashed with bayonet five times by another Japanese customer who wanted him to pull the cart more quickly.

Moreover, although most of the recollections were expressed in a very subjective and sometimes exaggerated style, the emotions conveyed by the speeches were manifold. Some speeches called for a kind of revenge on the Japanese. For instance, Zhu Xing recollected that, when seeing the mopped-up village left by the Japanese soldiers, an old man cried out 'When can this huge debt of blood be requited?' and other people also sobbed and sighed with the thought 'Revenge! wreak vengeance!'. According to Zhu, even the frogs in the river chimed in with the villagers, and it seemed like these creatures also cried 'Blood, hatred!' and wanted people to remember this debt of blood forever.[10] Furthermore, both recollections of victimhood and of victorious were related by these typical individuals. For instance, Bai Fengxiang, a survivor of the massacre, told audiences how he hid in a boat with his family after Nanjing was captured. He also recollected how his mother, big sister and little brother were killed by the Japanese soldiers. Also, Shen Xiuling recalled how one of her fellow villagers cunningly killed a Japanese soldier who tried to catch a chicken belonging to the village. However, most stories were of only passive resistance, like sabotage in the factories and escaping from Japanese barracks. For instance, Liang Gengsheng was forced to do military service for the Japanese when he was 19 years old. He recalled the horrible treatment received by his fellow Chinese soldiers and told of how many of these soldiers were sent to their grave by the Japanese commanders. He then told the audiences about his own exciting and successful escape.

If the Nanjing Municipal Federation of Trade Unions' initiative was intended to set the main theme – attacking 'the three big mountains' – and then to elaborate on the theme of the Japanese atrocities, the intention of the writer Yang Mo's 杨沫 practice was just the opposite. In 1960, Yang Mo republished her bestseller *Song of Youth* (*Qingchun Zhige* 青春之歌), after a substantial revision.[11] Still referred to as a War of Resistance-themed novel, after the revision this novel's theme actually became a hybrid – apart from telling of the heroine's involvement in activities of national salvation, it also included the heroine's struggles against the landowners and the KMT operatives.

Around ten years earlier, Yang Mo had left her work due to poor health. Furthermore, she was upset that she had not been put in any important position after returning to Beijing in 1949, although she had a long revolutionary history (she became a CCP member in late 1936 and joined the local resistance against the Japanese in Hebei Province as a CCP propaganda cadre after the July 7th Incident). She thought she would soon die and was in despair. In this desperate situation, an idea came to her: why not 'use all my strength to finish a long literary piece, just like draining all the oil from an oil lamp?'[12] Soon after, she embarked on drafting a novel, which tells of how a rich-born girl was influenced by the Communist ideology after the Manchuria Incident and started to devote herself to resisting the Japanese invasion. This novel was actually semi-autobiographical, taking place against the background of the Fifteen-Year War. Many stories in the novel were based on Yang's real experiences, e.g. the life-changing Chinese New Year's Eve get-together. The heroine joined a group of Northeastern students, during which they wept for the loss of their homeland and sang resistance songs together. The heroine was deeply moved by their patriotism and Communist-inspired spiritual outlook. In April 1955 the final draft of the novel was completed.[13]

At this time an author who merely expressed their own nostalgia in their works would be labelled as 'individualist'.[14] Also, during the early years of the PRC having main characters who were intellectuals was discouraged. Thus, some scholars argued that Yang had engaged in self-censorship when she wrote the story: she tried to combine her own desire for self-expression with a political rhetoric – an intellectual could find an escape only if they followed the CCP and only the CCP could save China from the foreign invasion.[15] Thus, many plots reflecting the struggles between the 'rightful saviours' of the CCP and the 'evil capitulators' of the KMT regime in Beijing and Nanjing, which were not based on the experiences of Yang herself, were written into the 1955 draft.

Nevertheless, this 'self-censored' draft was still considered to be politically problematic by a censor, who criticised the heroine's 'petty bourgeoisie' consciousness and the fact that the novel did not expose enough leftist opportunism. As Yang was reluctant to take on the censor's criticisms, her first attempt to publish the piece failed.[16] In 1956, another publisher (the Writers' Publisher) noticed Yang's manuscript, and decided to publish it regardless of its 'political problems'. For a number of reasons, such as a nationwide shortage of paper and the Anti-rightist Campaign, *Song of Youth* was not sold in bookstores throughout the country until January 1958, after which it soon became a bestseller and was adapted as a film in 1959 as a 'gift' for the 10th anniversary of the foundation of the PRC.

However, the book's run of success was interrupted by a worker's criticism of it which was published in *China Youth* magazine in 1959.[17] The worker's article started a nationwide debate about the book. The *Journal of Literature and Art* and *China Youth* ran special columns in which they published the opinions of the public on the issue. The book's opponents were mainly unhappy about Yang's motives for writing this novel, the book's 'petty bourgeois' mood, the lack of description of the integration between intellectuals and farmers/workers, and the problem that the heroine stopped developing and did not play a role after joining the CCP.[18] Although many prominent writers, the CCP leaders and most readers testified to the righteousness of the book, Yang decided to revise *Song of Youth* according to the criticisms made by its opponents and she republished it in 1960.

In the new edition, the 'petty bourgeoisie' mood was substantially erased, chapters about the heroine's fight against the rural landowners were added, and the part dealing with the heroine's struggles with the KMT's 'stooges' to lead the December 9th Movement as a party member was enriched. On the surface, it seems that the new edition also responded to the criticism that Yang's motivation was to fulfil her own petty bourgeois need for self-expression: *Song of Youth* was no longer merely a novel that artistically recorded Yang's own past, it became a textbook-like piece about how an intellectual from the old China became a firm Communist through the baptism of the struggles against the Japanese and all of the country's other enemies. In this way, under various internal and external influences, Yang gradually turned *Song of Youth* from a nostalgic piece on life during the war, into a Fifteen-Year-War themed piece with strong PRC characteristics. Together, the original and the revised *Song of Youth* remained a national favourite during the Seventeen-Year Period (1949–1966).

* * *

After 1949, practices like those described above were carried out every year by people like Yang Mo, Gao Xingzu and Nanjing's farmers and workers. They directly or indirectly used their own wartime experiences to mould or add something to the Chinese memory of the Fifteen-Year War, acting as 'agents' of that memory. They differed from those people who set the agenda for war memorial day celebrations, and who compiled the sections related to the Fifteen-Year War in school history textbooks and national history museums. The latter's practice of manipulating the war memory was directly controlled by the state apparatus. Although artists', scholars' and grassroots actors' efforts of relating the wartime experience were always constrained by the CCP regime through various means, as discussed in the introduction above, they were individuals – physically and mentally independent of the regime. Thus, when they mediated the memory of the war between themselves and the public, they were motivated and affected by other things apart from the CCP regime. Thus they can be considered as non-official agents of the Fifteen-Year War memory (although in a Communist totalitarian context, calling them semi-non-official agents might be more accurate).

This chapter examines non-official agents' efforts to make the Chinese people remember the Fifteen-Year War prior to 1982. Artists who produced Fifteen-Year-War themed films, novels, songs and so forth, scholars who educated people about the events during the war, and grassroots individuals who purposefully talked publicly about their wartime experiences, will be dealt with as examples of various kinds of non-official agent. For convenience, artists and scholars will be termed 'elite' non-official agents, to distinguish them from grassroots individuals. Further aspects related to Gao

Xingzu, the Speech Corps and Yang Mo, which were not spelt out in the introduction, will be revealed in the main body of the chapter. The myths related to the KMT and the victimhood narrative are kept in mind. However, the main mission of the chapter is to explore what influenced non-official agents' efforts to mediate Fifteen-Year-War remembrance. The second section looks at the influence of the CCP regime. The third section goes beyond the regime and explores other influential factors. This chapter argues that when relating the Fifteen-Year War, the non-official agents were influenced by various factors apart from the state.

Artists, scholars and individuals as CCP-infused storytellers

All three efforts – of Yang Mo, the Nanda scholars and the Nanjing farmers, as well as workers – to bring the wartime past back to the public were somewhat influenced by the CCP regime. Why was it that the sufferings imposed by imperial Japan were revealed on such a scale by Nanda researchers and Nanjing's farmers, as well as workers, despite the dreadful situation of the Great Chinese Famine, during which a positive narrative was arguably necessary for the national morale? Why was the publication plan of the Nanda project not fulfilled, while the 'problematic' book by Yang Mo was accepted for publication? Why did Yang insist on revising *Song of Youth*, when most people at the time thought a revision was unnecessary? The CCP regime's influence is central to answering these questions. It was this top-down influence that paved the way for these unofficial agents, at the same time as it handicapped them. This section of the chapter will discuss the kind of influence exerted by the CCP regime, mainly from three perspectives: the regime's attitudes, direct initiatives, and indirect impact.

Attitudes and prevalence

First and foremost, the CCP regime's attitude towards Fifteen-Year-War related arts, research and public recollection has to be taken into consideration. Was the CCP regime supportive of Fifteen-Year-War themed arts and academic research between 1949 and 1982? The answer should be positive. This was because, to begin with, according to my empirical research presented in previous chapters, the regime was required to, and wanted to, let the war memory spread in the PRC during this period. More importantly, the existence of a large number of artistic and scholarly works on the subject of the Fifteen-Year War and the spread of these works during the period was the most convincing evidence of the CCP regime's supportive stance. Considering the CCP's sophisticated ability to control intellectuals, if the party was not supportive of a certain type of artistic work or research, it would not be allowed to see the light.[19]

In terms of the Fifteen-Year-War themed arts that appeared between 1949 and 1982, some of these were produced before the establishment of the PRC and continued to be appreciated after 1949. For instance, the film *The Spring*

River Flows East (一江春水向东流 1947), which told the story of how a family was broken due to the chaos caused by the War of Resistance, was shown in cinemas several times after the Communist takeover.[20] Also, songs created during the war, such as 'The Yellow River Cantata' (黄河大合唱 1939), were widely sung by the Chinese masses and often performed on stage in the PRC era. The anniversary of the death of Communist musician Xian Xinghai 冼星海 (1905–1945), the composer of this and many other resistance songs, was commemorated regularly between 1949 and 1982 as well.[21]

A diverse collection of Fifteen-Year-War themed arts was also created during the PRC era, such as the popular novel *Railway Guerrillas* (铁道游击队 1954) which was written by Liu Zhixia 刘知侠 and based on real wartime events. This novel portrays a group of anti-Japanese guerrillas and their resistance activities along the Linzao railway line after the Battle of Xuzhou and the consequent fall of Shangdong Province. During the 'cultural desert' of the Cultural Revolution, many themes were not encouraged or allowed to be touched on in artistic works; however, mention of the Fifteen-Year War was still permitted. For instance, in 1966 the Nanjing Municipal Bureau of Culture started to control the renting of comic books in the city. The Bureau designed a special list of comic books adapted from films, and suggested that these be circulated in the rental market. Several Fifteen-Year-War themed comic books were included in the list.[22] In addition, several model operas produced during the Cultural Revolution were related to the Fifteen-Year War (e.g. three of the so-called 'eight model operas': *The Red Lantern, Shajiabang* and *Shajiabang Symphonies*; as well as other less known ones, such as *Fighting on the Plains*). The impact of Fifteen-Year-War themed arts on the Chinese people's lives during the period was profound, as they were circulated to almost every corner of Maoist China, and were adapted into various artistic forms by the state's propaganda tools.[23]

Several academic projects on the Fifteen-Year War were also carried out during the period.[24] For instance, just after the end of the Cultural Revolution, the History Department of Shanghai Normal University collected a very comprehensive range of materials related to the War of Resistance, and published them (without footnotes or comments) as a three-volume book series.[25] Generally, three kinds of materials generated during the wartime were included in these volumes: official documents, articles written under the names of individuals, and newspaper reports.[26] Furthermore, scholarly articles, leaders' speeches and memoirs, which were published in various newspapers, books and journals in the PRC era, were also a part of the series.[27] The series also included several articles revealing the atrocities perpetrated by the Japanese Imperial Army, such as a fifteen-page piece entitled 'Recall the Japanese Bandits' Nanjing Massacre' (追记日寇南京大屠杀).[28] The grassroots practice of publicly relating wartime stories was also commonplace between 1949 and 1982.

Fifteen-Year-War themed works did not merely exist in the PRC – they were also widely circulated. The state apparatus was behind most of this distribution. For instance, many wartime resistance songs were carefully

collected and published. In around 1954, a PLA editorial team started collecting songs created during the Fifteen-Year War and they published a four-
volume songbook series entitled *Selection of Songs of the War of Resistance*
(抗战歌曲选) in 1957 to commemorate the 20th anniversary of the Marco
Polo Bridge Incident and the 30th anniversary of the foundation of the PLA.
Around 2,000 songs were gathered from the areas controlled by both the CCP
and the KMT during the war. Nine hundred and ninety-seven songs were
published in the series, including both famous and lesser known songs (e.g.
those that were only popular among the Northeast Anti-Japanese United
Army before 1937).[29] The practice of collecting wartime songs was also
widely carried out locally; many that were popular in Jiangsu Province were
included in songbooks published between 1949 and 1982, such as the *Jiangsu
Folksong Reference Book* (江苏民歌参考资料, 1958).[30] Similarly, the lyrics of
some anti-Japanese songs from Northeastern China were collected and published in a *Selection of Northeastern People's Anti-Japanese Songs* (东北人民
抗日歌谣选, 1959), with the cooperation of publishers in Liaoning, Jilin and
Heilongjiang Province.[31]

Likewise, the inclusion of Fifteen-Year-War themed literary works in the
PRC's school Chinese textbooks helped them greatly to reach a wider audience. For instance, a story called 'On the Plain' (平原上), which talked about
how the people and the Eighth Army united to resist the Japanese, with
detailed a description of the Japanese Imperial Army's misdeeds, was included in a secondary school Chinese textbook in 1950.[32] Sun Li's famous Fifteen-
Year-War themed novel *Baiyangdian* (白洋淀) was included in another school
textbook published in 1955.[33]

Several state-organised activities also promoted Fifteen-Year-War themed
works. For instance, in 1958, Nanjing Municipal Education Bureau and other
departments launched an 'I Love Reading Books' activity to encourage students to read books about revolutionary stories, deeds of worthy people and
science. Many Fifteen-Year-War themed books were included in the list of
'recommended books', such as a book about a female anti-Japanese hero,
Zhao Yiman 赵一曼, and a book about a young miner who joined the anti-
Japanese guerrillas after his father, mother and several colleagues in the mine
were killed by the Japanese.[34] Activities of encouraging the masses to sing
revolutionary songs were regularly organised, and Fifteen-Year-War themed
songs were often sung on these occasions.[35] For instance, in 1962, to prepare
a mass campaign of singing revolutionary songs in Nanjing, twenty songs
were selected by the relevant arm of the Nanjing Municipal government to be
popularised among citizens by amateur singers, school music teachers and so
forth. Some Fifteen-Year-War themed songs, like 'Sing About the Cowhand
Erxiao (歌唱二小放牛郎)' were included in this list. This song, with its
mournful melody and lyrics, tells the story of the little martyr Erxiao, who led
lost Japanese soldiers into a Chinese ambush in 1942 and was consequently
killed by the Japanese soldiers (he 'was raised with the tip of the rifle and
thrown down to a big rock to his death').[36]

In short, the prevalence of Fifteen-Year-War themed arts, research and grassroots testimonies (which I will discuss further later) suggests that the CCP regime supported these things. In addition, the CCP initiated various events and campaigns which contributed to the creation of various unofficial Fifteen-Year-War memories. These state-initiated practices that were executed by unofficial agents were inevitably influenced by the state. They will now be discussed at length.

Direct initiatives

Countless grassroots recollections of the Fifteen-Year War were produced thanks to top-down initiatives. The CCP regime attached great importance to education in the 'revolutionary tradition' throughout the period between 1949 and 1982. Fifteen-Year War veterans were great 'living teaching materials' in this regard. On certain special occasions, such as Fifteen-Year-War memorial days and school holidays, they were often invited to talk about their wartime experience in factories, schools and other such places, or were interviewed by students or newspaper reporters. Heroic wartime stories were often related alongside accounts of their sufferings.[37]

Nevertheless, at the centre of the top-down initiatives that encouraged grassroots war remembrance were activities relating to 'remembering bitterness' (*yiku* 忆苦) or 'speaking bitterness' (*suku* 诉苦). *Yiku* was widely used by the CCP regime as a political tool in various campaigns to attack the PRC's enemies who were alleged to have imposed great miseries on the Chinese people.[38] The specificities of bitterness and the target(s) of the attacks varied from campaign to campaign.[39] The general aim of encouraging Chinese people to 'remember bitterness' was to make them 'appreciate sweetness (*sitian* 思甜)' in the new, Communist China. However, the regime's specific aims of encouraging people to 'remember bitterness' differed from campaign to campaign.[40]

On Fifteen-Year-War related occasions, for instance, attacking the USA or Japan's conservative government was the main intention of the militarist-bashing campaigns, and attacking Lin Biao was the main aim of the campaigns criticising Lin's idea of 'Self-restraint and return to the rites' in 1974. On both occasions, victims of Japanese wartime atrocities were encouraged by the state apparatus to speak out about their suffering.[41] Organising farmers and workers in Nanjing to publicise their bitter past was also a typical state-initiated *yiku* activity. This initiative had several aims. One was to 'make staff contribute to the grain-and-steel-centred campaign of increasing production and practising thrift' which was advocated by the central government in the summer of 1960. Another aim was to 'make the staff establish the determination and braveness of facing up to as well as overcoming difficulties' – difficulties that were arguably mainly caused by the Great Chinese Famine and the increasingly disastrous Great Leap Forward campaign.[42]

Similarly, *yiku* was widely employed for the CCP regime's 'class struggle', which was re-emphasised by Mao after the Anti-rightist Campaign in China, and especially after the confrontation with Peng Dehuai in the Lushan Plenum in 1959. The Socialist Education Movement, which aimed at countering the Chinese people's class enemies, was carried out on a small scale after the tenth plenary session of the eighth CCP Central Committee Conference in September 1962.[43] Accordingly, *yiku* activities were organised by the CCP authorities nationwide. Wartime Japan, then an imperialist state, was an obvious target in this wave of *yiku* activities. This is because, together with the remnants of the KMT, the old 'three big mountains – imperialism, feudalism, bureaucratic capitalism', were still considered by Mao as exploiting classes that continued to exist in the PRC.[44] Furthermore, attacking imperialists was convenient, as the CCP officials' and intellectuals' opinions of the necessity of conducting domestic class struggle seemed to be divergent at the time. The idea of 'class reconciliation', which was contrary to Mao's domestic 'class struggle', was also popular.[45]

In Nanjing, organised 'remembering bitterness' activities first started to take place at the beginning of 1963. For instance, the Communist Youth League branch of a factory and a commune organised two 'class education' activities in January 1963. Both activities were kicked off by 'recollection and comparison' – many old workers and farmers talked of their suffering at the hands of the 'three big mountains' and their happy lives in the PRC. In one such testimony, a worker and CCP member, Zhou Maokui 周茂奎, recollected how he was tortured by the Japanese when he worked in Shandong Province during the war. Although he managed to escape, his 11-year-old son was ill during the period and eventually died because the family did not have enough money to see a doctor. It was observed that these recollections functioned 'like a smart key, which soon opened the sluice gate for the powerful current of the youths' class emotions'.[46] Taking advantage of the 40th anniversary of the Jinghan Railway Industrial Action (7 February 1923), Nanjing's *Xinhua Ribao* then started to solicit articles from older workers about their struggles with the 'three big mountains'. Between February and April 1963 many pieces appeared in the newspaper's special column 'Old workers talk about past and present (老工人今昔谈)'.[47] Several articles about Fifteen-Year-War themed stories were published. For example, a worker, Bai Shikui 白士奎, recollected his resistance against the Japanese army with his colleagues in a factory that had produced blankets and clothes for the Eighth Army.[48]

In May 1963 the first directive for the Socialist Education Movement was formally promulgated, and the campaign was carried out with vigour and vitality.[49] A mission to trace the history of the suppression of villages, schools, factories, streets, families and so forth was put into action from June 1963 onwards.[50] For example, the CCP Committee of Qishuyan Rolling Stock Plant, which was controlled by Britain, Japan and the KMT successively during the Republican era, organised army veterans, old cadres and old workers to talk about the plant's history of suffering to the staff in the factory. In addition, these testimonies were selected and published in a book entitled *A Locomotive in the Rainstorm*.[51] To support this effort, other platforms for demonstrating and circulating these grassroots histories were provided. For example, a 'Class education display' and a 'Display of the history of towns, villages and families' was organised on 10 August.[52]

Moreover, on 5 July 1963, *Xinhua Ribao* started to 'make a stormy sea stormier' when it started to solicit articles for another special column, 'Red genealogy' 红色家谱. The authors of the potential contributions were required to describe both the experiences of being oppressed in the past and the changes in the PRC, as well as to portray both the ugly outlook of the 'counter-revolutionary' classes and the faces of those supporting the resistance. The tragic-heroic narrative was what the newspaper was looking for. Furthermore, *Xinhua Ribao* required that all the stories should be real, with no exaggeration or fabrication. Every article should include the name(s) of those who could verify the story. This was very different from the approach during the Great Leap Forward.[53]

Thanks to this special column, several tragic-heroic and relatively objective recollections of encounters with the Japanese army could be read by the masses. For instance, an article entitled 'Story of Childhood' revealed how one day the author and his grandfather had tried to sell their calf in exchange for some groceries in the town, but ended up being beaten by Japanese soldiers who wanted to get the calf without paying. Luckily, they were saved by an Eighth Army soldier. Five years later, the author met the soldier again, joined the Eighth Army and became a messenger. Also, the wartime experience of Ren Ganting 任淦庭, an artist in a ceramic craft factory in Yixing, was published in the column by a reporter who interviewed him. Ren's description of the chaotic situation when the Japanese occupied Yixing city was recounted in the article, including stories of many buildings being destroyed by Japanese air raids following the spring of 1937, forcing people to leave the city. Ren also told the reporter that many teapot factories were occupied by the Japanese as blockhouses, so workers became jobless, including Ren himself, and he recollected one incident in which he was badly beaten by a Japanese soldier and lost consciousness in the street.[54]

'Remembering bitterness' activities, with 'class struggle' as the aim, continued after the Socialist Education Movement was unfolded in May 1964, and reached a climax during the Cultural Revolution. Imperial Japan was still often attacked in these grassroots activities.[55] Even people's time off on summer evenings was used for this purpose – various outdoor activities of 'remembering bitterness' were organised in such evenings during the Cultural Revolution.[56] Several memorials were built as class education bases in places which suffered from the atrocities committed by the Japanese army, such as the mass graves visited by Honda, and a monument in *sharentang* ('people-killing pond 杀人塘') in 1966 in Jianshanwei (the Japanese army landed here on 5 November 1937 and was alleged to have killed 1,015 Chinese).[57] In Nanjing, relics and remains from the War of Resistance period were carefully investigated and protected by the local cultural relics preservation committee as a site of revolutionary tradition education and class struggle education.[58]

The CCP regime also sponsored some research projects, which in turn produced several accounts of the Fifteen-Year War. For instance, in a speech in 1959, Zhou Enlai urged scholars to preserve research materials on Chinese history from the time of the Hundred Days Reform in 1898 to the establishment of the PRC in 1949. Zhou's advocacy led to the formation of the Committee on Historical Research Materials under the CPPCC and the Committee's branch offices in various provinces, which conducted an ongoing campaign throughout China to gather written and oral testimonies from people who had unique experiences in China between 1989 and 1949. With Zhou's patronage, numerous such materials have been collected and published as a 'Selection of Historical Materials 文史资料选辑' since then. Numerous testimonies related to the Fifteen-Year War were collected and published by the Committee's central and provincial offices. These include recollections about the key events of the Fifteen-Year War, such as the September 18th Incident, the Shanghai Incident and the Macro Polo Bridge Incident. There were also detailed accounts about Japanese atrocities, such as a recollection about how the Northeastern patriots revealed these atrocities to the League of Nations' investigation delegation. Similarly, Japan's wartime misdeeds in Anhui Province, such as constructing mass graves, forcing Chinese females to act as 'comfort women' and selling opium were included in the publication produced by the Anhui provincial branch office of the committee.[59]

What is more, this epic project had a clear political aim – to propitiate 'people whose class backgrounds were judged by the Party to be ideologically undesirable, even hostile, but whose support for the new regime was nonetheless considered helpful'.[60] Thus, wartime recollections of many ideologically controversial people, such as former KMT officials, were published by the Committee.[61] More interestingly, many of these recollections were not perfectly in line with the CCP's version of the Fifteen-Year-War memory, as I mentioned in Chapter 4. For instance, the recollections of former KMT generals Du Yuming 杜聿明 and Song Xilian 宋希濂 about the Chinese Expeditionary Army's operation in Yunnan and Burma were published.[62] Du's article objectively evaluated the army's sacrifices in resisting the Japanese, although it did blame Chiang Kai-Shek, the warlord in Yunnan and the 'arrogant' British 'imperialists' for the loss of the expeditionary army. An article by Mei Ruao (the judge of the IMTFE) about the Nanjing Massacre was also published by the Committee. In contrast to the standard statement at the time that foreigners co-operated with the Japanese to kill Chinese people during the massacre, it objectively evaluated their role in helping Nanjing citizens. Mei Ruao also tactfully criticised academic circles for not taking the Nanjing Massacre seriously enough and suggested that China should publish more works like Japan's 'Record of the A-bomb Disaster in Hiroshima' (広島原爆災害誌), which could introduce the Nanjing Massacre in a comprehensive way.[63]

As regards the arts, in general, as a part of 'revolutionary history subject matter', the Fifteen-Year-War theme was encouraged in the PRC's art and literary circles by the CCP regime between 1949 and 1982.[64] For instance, the War of Resistance theme was recommended by the Central Film Bureau's production plan between 1954 and 1957.[65] Accordingly, during this period, several films telling stories about the Fifteen-Year War were produced, such as *The Letter with Feathers* (鸡毛信 1954), *The Storm of South Island* (南岛风云 1955), *The Plains Guerrillas* (平原游击队 1955), *The Railway Guerrillas* (铁道游击队 1956), and *Breaking Through the Darkness* (冲破黎明前的黑暗 1956). Writers were also organised to write Fifteen-Year-War themed fiction and memoirs. Establishing committees that compiled martyrs' biographies, mentioned in the previous chapter, is one such example.[66] Also, a large number of wartime stories were written and published thanks to this kind of top-down initiative.[67] For example, in 1962 the Nanjing Municipal Federation of Literary and Art Circles organised some old cadres to write their memoirs about the 'revolutionary struggles' in Nanjing. The Federation initiated a series of activities in the beginning of 1962 to help these old cadres turn their recollections into a written form, such as holding meetings to listen to each other's recollections and to discuss the potential source material, and interviews with the old cadres. Some high quality memoirs related to the Fifteen-Year War were created, such as *An Underground Red Thread* 一根地下红线. This memoir, which was about the activities of the intelligence services who worked undercover to combat the Japanese, was written by Yan Jingcheng 严竟成, from Nanjing Normal College.[68]

Apart from being affected by the state's attitudes and stated-initiated campaigns, Fifteen-Year-War remembrance constructed by unofficial agents was also affected by some larger top-down factors, such as the overall political atmosphere in the PRC, the official interpretation of Fifteen-Year-War history, and the party's aesthetic guidelines.

Indirect impacts

The elite storytellers of the Fifteen-Year War, who were tightly controlled by the regime through both official and party-led unofficial units (such as the Ministry of Culture, the Ministry of Education, the All-China Federation of Literary and Art Circles, the Association of Chinese Historians and so forth), were particularly subject to the PRC's overall political atmosphere and the regime's attitude to intellectuals.[69] The CCP regime's approach to intellectuals was contradictory: it tried to stimulate their professional productivity at the same time as trying to harness them to the party's ideologies. This contradictory approach led to a policy that vacillated between periods of ideological and political relaxation and periods of repression.[70]

The periods when the regime relaxed its control over the activities of intellectuals during the Maoist era were: the period before 1951, when a campaign was launched by the new regime to re-orient intellectuals towards Marxism-Leninism; the time of the Hundred Flowers Campaign in 1957; the period of relative relaxation between 1961 and September 1962 sponsored by Liu

Shaoqi's faction to make up for the losses caused by the Great Leap Forward campaign; and the period after 1973 when Mao re-emphasised the spirit of 'One Hundred Flowers'.[71] During these times, intellectuals were 'granted some responsibilities and privileges in order to win their cooperation' in building the new PRC.[72]

After 1978, intellectuals were further liberated. Many Fifteen-Year-War themed works that were banned or forgotten in earlier years gradually reappeared.[73] For instance, the opera *Red Nose Joins the Army*, which was popular in the CCP's anti-Japanese base in Jiangsu Province around 1942, was performed again in 1980. Although the original script was lost, an operatic regiment of the PLA Military District in Nanjing organised some old cadres to produce a new script based on their recollections. The story was about how a young man with the nickname 'Red Nose' decided to join the New Fourth Army to fight against the Japanese, after witnessing Japanese misdeeds of 'raping, burning and killing, as well as forcing Chinese people to be their labourers/soldiers, and looting the Chinese people's food provisions in his hometown area'.[74] Aisin-Gioro Puyi's recollections of many events that happened in the Japanese-controlled puppet state of Manchukuo were also serialised in newspapers.[75] Moreover, to cater to the collective desire for knowledge in the arts and humanities, which had been belittled during the Cultural Revolution, newspapers and radio broadcasts started producing special columns and programmes to popularise this kind of knowledge. Stories about the history of the Fifteen-Year War were popular with these kinds of columns and programmes.[76]

During the periods of repression, the time that artists and scholars had available to carry out their professional work was squeezed or even taken away altogether, as intellectuals had to participate in various thought reform campaigns and many of them were purged from their professions. Moreover, artists and scholars did not dare to produce anything radical, in terms of aesthetic judgements, viewpoints that were in defiance of the party line and so forth. As a result, many Fifteen-Year-War themed works were 'a thousand pieces of the same tune'. What was worse, many previously produced works that 'stepped out of line' were affected during leftist political campaigns. For instance, the film *The Story of Liubao* (柳堡的故事 1957), which told of a love story between a New Fourth Army officer and a young woman in Liubao village during the War of Resistance, was heavily criticised during the Cultural Revolution. The film's 'crime' was that it followed Liu Shaoqi and his followers' 'reactionary theory of human nature'.[77] Historical studies were also jeopardised during the Cultural Revolution. 'Innuendo historiography' (*yinshe shixue* 映射史学), which was often employed in the CCP's factional struggles, became predominant. Furthermore, the history of the Fifteen-Year War was often distorted in order to declare the faction that lost power and influence guilty, such as in the cases of Tian Han and Lin Biao mentioned in Chapter 4. Similarly, Liu Shaoqi's alleged crime of 'advocating a philosophy of survival, appeasement, betrayal' was fabricated and used against him.[78]

A detailed account regarding the 'ebb and flow' of Nanda's research project and *Song of Youth* can illustrate the contextual influence on the elite storytellers of the Fifteen-Year War. *Diaocha* (调查, a research approach involving fieldwork and interviews), which was highly valued by Mao since before 1949, reached its golden age in the Great Leap Forward period. Historical *diaocha* projects were also conducted on an unprecedented scale. These projects were chosen, designed and sponsored by research institutions, which were always located in areas where major events in Chinese history had occurred, or where famous historical figures had lived.[79] It was within this atmosphere that Nanda's research project was initiated. Nevertheless, the failed plan to publish the project's manuscript was caused mainly by the contextual influence of the CCP regime.

According to Yoshida, it was the Chinese government that classified this manuscript because it 'did not welcome public focus on wartime weakness at a time when it was trying to build up national pride and strength among the people'.[80] However, as I have argued, the victimhood narrative of the war was not a problem in the PRC, as long as it could also be associated with something heroic. The victims' indomitable spirit is emphasised throughout this manuscript, which also has a whole chapter specially devoted to introducing the Nanjing people's resistance during the massacre.[81] Thus, Yoshida's explanation for the failure to publish the manuscript is not wholly convincing.

Another explanation was given by Gao Xingzu's students. According to Jing Shenghong 经盛鸿 and Sun Zhaiwei 孙宅巍, contemporary Chinese history, especially that part relating to the Republic of China, contained many areas that were off-limits, which rendered the subject risky for both scholars and publishers. For example, it was impossible to do research specifically on Chiang Kai-Shek or his army's resistance to Japan. Also, there were no relevant university courses on the history of the Republic of China. As a part of that history, some aspects of the Nanjing Massacre were off-limits in the early years of the PRC. Thus, the publisher did not want to take on the risk of publishing the manuscript, despite the fact that Gao and his colleagues tried to make it perfectly in harmony with the Party line (apart from foregrounding the indomitable spirit, it also condemned America's 'cooperation' with the Japanese in abusing Nanjing people, and emphasised the difference between the evil Japanese militarists and the kind Japanese people).[82]

Although I think this latter explanation is more convincing, more contextual information could make it more compelling. As I pointed out earlier, former KMT officials' accounts of the KMT's efforts of resistance were published by the Committee on Historical Research Materials under the CPPCC, which suggests that this kind of history was accepted at the time. However, the 10th Plenum in September 1962 changed the situation and contributed to the failure to publish the manuscript. The Plenum marked a shift from the relative relaxation of the previous period to intensified control over intellectuals, which might have damaged several relevant intellectuals and made the publishers more cautious. Moreover, the Plenum formally announced the necessity of 'class struggle' in China, which might have changed the regime's tolerant attitude to research involving resistance by the KMT. After the Plenum, the remnants of the KMT – as class enemies – were struggled with, rather than reconciled with. Nevertheless, since Gao passed away in 2001 the real reason why publication was turned down remains as a mystery.

One the other hand, the regime's contextual influence also affected *Song of Youth*. Thanks to the Hundred Flowers Campaign which was carried out to 'promote the flourishing of the arts and the progress of science' in 1956, this 'problematic' book was accepted for publication. Nevertheless, It was banned during the Cultural Revolution, due to the alleged 'crime' of 'building a stele and writing a biography for Liu Shaoqi and Peng Zhen' – but it then reappeared afterwards. Furthermore, the regime's contextual influence also affected Yang's work in a subtle and indirect way. Moreover, as an intellectual of this era, Yang's thoughts and beliefs were influenced unobtrusively and imperceptibly by the era in which she lived.[83]

For instance, the problems of *Song of Youth* pointed out by Yang's referee in 1955, and by the 'masses' in 1958, were more or less the same. Why was Yang not willing to revise the book in 1955, when this was vital for publication, but happy to do so voluntarily around 1960? Furthermore, many of Yang's readers thought the changes made in 1960 created serious flaws in the book and viewed these changes as compromises made in response to the political pressure at the time. Moreover, when Yang had the freedom to decide the content of her book after the Cultural Revolution, she insisted on including the added or revised parts from 1960 in a new edition of *Song of Youth* in 1977 and in successive editions.[84] Why did Yang do this? I argue that she did so because *Song of Youth* was always a product of 'self-expression', as Yang herself claimed. The 'self' had been transformed during the period between 1955 and 1960, from a petty bourgeois 'self' to a more ideologically correct 'self'. What had helped forward this self-transformation were two of the Party's campaigns: the anti-rightist campaign in 1958, and the Great Leap Forward, in which a 'mass line' was emphasised. Furthermore, this new 'self' of Yang was strengthened through the Socialist Education campaign, the Cultural Revolution, and so forth.

Also, the CCP's various interpretations of the Fifteen-Year War constrained the elite storytellers of the Fifteen-Year War. The USA and the KMT were often accused by the CCP of cooperating with the Japanese invasion during the war. Consequently, many 'memories' of US–Japanese/KMT–Japanese 'collusion' were created by certain non-official agents.[85] For instance, both the manuscript of the Nanda project and the article related to the Nanjing Massacre that was included in the Shanghai Normal University series condemned the Americans' loyal 'assistance' to the Japanese Imperial Army. The latter series also included many articles revealing how the KMT had suppressed the CCP's resistance activities during the war, implying that the KMT 'colluded' with the Japanese.[86]

Similarly, the CCP's leadership during the war was depicted in an excessively positive light in almost all works by non-official agents between 1949 and 1982. For instance, the Shanghai Normal University's series included articles which argued that the CCP's ability to resist the Japanese was superior to that of the KMT. And many pre-1949 productions that were circulated in the PRC 'revealed' the impotence, corruption and other negative sides of the KMT. For instance, many wartime songs accusing Chiang Kai-Shek's army of impotence were warmly welcomed in the PRC, such as the following:

> The Central Army [the KMT army] sleeps after being replete,
> When devils come, it retreats.
> The Eighth Army carries out guerrilla warfare,
> attacks the devils and makes their hearts and gall tremble with fear.[87]

The CCP's aesthetic guidelines mainly targeted artists. For instance, in 1958 Mao recommended a method for artistic creation that 'combines revolutionary realism with revolutionary romanticism' (革命现实主义与革命浪漫主义相结合), which soon replaced 'socialist realism' as the theoretical and aesthetic foundation for artistic creation in the PRC.[88] This method had a huge impact on the creation of Fifteen-Year-War themed novels and movies, which became increasingly romanticised, or 'illusionistic'. Take the characters in the films *Landmine Warfare* (地雷战 1962) and *Tunnel Warfare* (地道战 1965), and the novel *Little Soldier Zhangga* (小兵张嘎 1961) as examples: the Chinese protagonists are unrealistically heroic and intelligent, and the Japanese invaders are portrayed as ugly and stupid.[89] Also, in these artistic works, the achievements are always 'artistically' exaggerated, and it seems that the Japanese are always defeated by the Chinese guerrillas without much effort, when in reality the struggles were much more brutal. For instance, in reality, the Japanese Imperial Army responded to the tunnel warfare very well, through means such as poison-gassing the tunnels. There were instances when the tunnel warfare caused extraordinary numbers of causalities on the Chinese side (e.g. the Beitong Massacre 北疃惨案, which happened in a village in Hebei Province in May 1942).[90] After 1954, Jun Qing, a writer born in Shangdong Province in 1922, published a series of short stories on the subject of the war (including both the War of Resistance and the Civil War) during the 1940s on the Jiaodong Peninsula in his home province. It is argued that the perilous nature of life during these times was powerfully stressed in these stories. Plot lines involving death and savage torture were often used to stress the 'superhuman' will of the heroic characters.[91]

Also, the 'principle of three emphases', which was widely practised during the Cultural Revolution, gave birth to a batch of anti-Japanese heroes lacking in normal human feelings. For instance, the film *The Plains Guerrillas* appeared in three versions. In the 1950s, the leading character Li Xiangyang was portrayed as a deceitful and humorous anti-Japanese hero, who always applied unconventional methods to deal with the Japanese soldiers. However, influenced by the 'principle of three emphases', Li later became a standardised hero who frequently used 'quotations from Chairman Mao' during conversations.[92]

Compared to the elite storytellers, the grassroots storytellers of the Fifteen-Year War, who were 'mass' in character, were less subject to identification and control by the regime. Nevertheless, they were still subject to the CCP's regime's contextual influence. For example, during the Cultural Revolution, Li Xiuying, who testified on many public occasions as a survivor of the Nanjing Massacre, was seldom invited to speak about her experience. She was transferred to Guanyun, Jiangsu Province with her husband (who worked in the KMT's Telephone and Telegraph office before 1949) for about ten years. Meanwhile Jiang Genfu, another survivor of the Nanjing Massacre, continued to be invited to talk about the Japanese atrocities in the late 1960s and 1970s, as his class origins were considered to be positive.[93] Furthermore, the grassroots storytellers of the Fifteen-Year War were also subjected to a less obtrusive form of influence by the CCP regime. For instance, 'speaking bitterness' activities were sometimes carried out spontaneously within a family, at school and so forth when no political campaigns were being implemented.

At the same time, grassroots remembrance of the Fifteen-Year War also benefited from the CCP's contextual influence. For instance, thanks to Mao's belief in the power of the masses, grassroots remembrance of the Fifteen-Year War was not only prevalent but was also raised to a very high position in public discourse during the Maoist period. Furthermore, it was often intensely encouraged on an ad hoc basis during a number of the CCP regime's political movements. The regime's derogatory line regarding the KMT and Western foreigners, as well as the 'exaggerated' narrative style, were also adopted by the grassroots storytellers. In short, all three categories of non-official agent were subject to the contextual influence of the CCP.

* * *

Thanks to the CCP regime's supportive attitude, it was possible for Fifteen-Year-War themed arts, research and grassroots wartime memories to be circulated unimpeded in the PRC between 1949 and 1982. Furthermore, the regime initiated several activities to facilitate non-official agents' remembrance of the war. These activities inevitably combined non-official war memories with various forms of state propaganda, but nevertheless they also provided a good platform for those people who wished to speak out about their wartime experiences. Finally, the CCP regime also indirectly influenced the non-official agents of the Fifteen-Year War memory through other grander means. However, as powerful as the CCP regime was, it could not dictate all aspects of the process of creating war-themed arts, conducting research on the war and relating wartime experiences. Those aspects that were not controlled by the state will be dealt with in the next section.

Other influential aspects

The CCP regime's influence on unofficial agents of the Fifteen-Year War memory was omnipresent. However, there was one thing that the state could not dictate – the non-official agents' inward motivations with regard to sharing, creating art about and researching the topic of the war. For instance, if the farmers and workers in Nanjing kept silent about their traumatic wartime experiences, they would not be identified by the authorities, let alone invited to speak out at public meetings. Similarly, if the regime did not support the war-related narratives, it could not seal the mouths of everyone who wanted to tell others about the war.[94] This section of the chapter will mainly discuss these inward motivations. Also, the state had a limited voice as regards the works of these unofficial agents: namely, the details of their content, the language they used and so forth were influenced by other factors, which will also be dealt with in this chapter.

Motives

Survivors of wartime atrocities do not always share their traumatic experiences with others. According to one psychological study, if they decide to talk about the experience they are often inwardly motivated by different needs, such as to memorialise, to honour the past, to teach others to remember the facts, to respond to direct questions, to 'unload' and to engage in self-revelation.[95] Thus, similarly, when choosing to speak out about their stories of being cruelly treated by Imperial Japan, apart from the 'invitations' from the state in various top-down campaigns, the public testifiers must have been driven by these inward motives. For instance, ensuring that the Japanese soldiers who caused her such suffering would face the judgement of the law was such a motive for the Nanjing Massacre survivor Li Xiuying. Her husband recollected that Li was very excited when she was invited to testify at the Nanjing Tribunal. However, being disappointed with the treatment of the accused Japanese (they were provided with comfortable chairs and nice drinks as well as tobacco, while the witnesses did not have anywhere to sit) and the leniency of the tribunal, Li refused to testify anymore until the CCP took over Nanjing. In the PRC era, Li offered her testimony on most occasions when the past and present Japanese militarists were being attacked (apart from during the Cultural Revolution).[96] In 1999 she even sued Japanese rightists for making the accusation that her testimonies were fake.

Artists and scholars, as creators with their own conciousness, were not merely cultural tools of the CCP regime. They were also inwardly motivated to create Fifteen-Year-War themed works. The biggest motivation of this kind derived from the war itself. A close-up exploration of the experiences of the most 'hardcore' artists and scholars working on the subject of the Fifteen-Year War reveals that the war played a vital role in the lives of most of them. It was the wartime experience, which was engraved on their bones and heart, that sustained their spirits in regard to relating the war to others, even as a lifetime undertaking.[97] Also, it was the embodiment of their first-hand wartime experience that made their relating of the war inspirational, authentic and easily acceptable for people in the post-war era. What inwardly motivated testifiers to speak out about their first-hand wartime experiences (especially the traumatic ones), and what inwardly motivated artists and scholars to create a certain kind of memory of the war without presenting (or without fully and factually presenting) their wartime experience, was different yet similar.

The first such inward motivation was to respond to strong emotions, especially during wartime when resistance against the Japanese was a matter of prime importance, and numerous works reflecting the cruelty of the war and promoting Chinese people's morale were produced. The creators of these works felt the pain of witnessing their motherland being lost to the invaders and were inspired by the daily resistance of their countrymen and women. Their feelings and inspiration were raw, real and intense; thus, their works immediately resonated among the Chinese people during and after the war.[98] We can take as an example three resistance songs, which were also popular in the PRC:

> September 18, September 18, from that miserable moment, I have left my hometown and given up the endless treasure. Roaming, roaming …When can I go back to my homeland? …[99]

Whenever they sang this song, 'On Songhua River (松花江上)', people would feel the misery of losing the homeland. Zhang Hanhui 张寒晖 was motivated by the sad emotions prevailing among the roaming Northeastern soldiers (who were shifted to the area to fight the Communists) and Northeastern students in Xi'an after the September 18th Incident, to produce this famous wartime song. The crying of Northern women over their husbands' or sons' graves also inspired Zhang, who adapted their cries for the song's melody:[100]

> Look! Numerous mountains and valleys, solid walls like copper and iron, the beacon of resistance against Japan is burning on the Taihang Mountain … Listen! Mothers ask sons to fight with East Ocean [Japan], wives send husbands to the battlefield …[101]

When hearing 'On the Taihang Mountain (在太行山上)', one can see the epic picture of the whole nation united to resist the invader. It is said that Gui Taosheng 桂涛声 wrote the lyrics when he was working in the Taihang Mountain area. He was deeply impressed by the patriotic people he met there, who were active or were about to be active on the battlefield against the Japanese. Most of them were encouraged by their own mothers and wives:[102]

> The day of the War of Resistance has come! The Volunteer Army are fighting on the northeast front, the county's people are resisting in the back, march bravely, our Chinese army [the original line was 'our 29th

army was not alone'], aim straight at the enemy! Destroy them, destroy them! Charge! Cut the devil's head off with the broadsword! Kill![103]

Whenever a person hears this slightly 'brutal' and straightforward 'Dadao March', one's fighting spirit is naturally aroused. Mai Xin 麦新 produced this song just after the July 7th Incident. He was inspired by the heroic deeds of the broadsword unit of the 29th Corps, who fought against the Japanese. [104]

In the post-war era, the lyrics, melodies and tales behind these kinds of wartime songs were widespread. The wartime events, scenes and even emotions were brought back to the post-war Chinese people through the songs in an intense, but not artificial, way.[105]

The second inward motivation was to cherish the memory of the past. When the past is very beautiful or when the reality is too dull people easily become very nostalgic. For several people who had experienced the Fifteen-Year War, the war was the most exciting and meaningful time of their lives. When they were treated unfairly in the PRC, many people tended to retreat to their 'golden era' to find some comfort.[106] This motive can be found in Xu Guagyao's 徐光耀 writing of *Little Solider Zhang Ga*. In 1957 Xu was heavily criticised as a rightist and was required to 'shut himself up and ponder over his mistakes in seclusion'.[107] Depressed, Xu decided to write a story to distract himself. He wanted to write something happy and warm to drive the present dullness away. The first thing he thought of was a boy he had written about in another novel, *Fire in Plain* 平原烈火. When he tried to think about the sources to enrich the character, he said 'particularly, the eccentric little Eighth Army soldiers during the War of Resistance, in company with the smoke of gunpowder and gunfire, came to my mind with a beaming face'. His experience during the War of Resistance became the 'inexhaustible source' of the story.[108] According to Xu's own account, once he began writing, he started eating more, and sleeping more. When writing something exciting, he even started dancing in his flat.

Why did writing about the War of Resistance period have such a magical power? Xu revealed that it was because although the situation was extremely brutal during the war, the soldiers fought until their last drop of blood, 'not for promotion in office and becoming rich'. The masses also supported the soldiers, 'even if their houses were burned down and pots were broken, even if they had to be separated from their wives and children'.[109] Fighting for the same aim, people in the war supported each other, trusted each other and 'lived in the right and self-confident' way. This feeling indeed could drive away the dullness of the present reality – in which people exposed each others' 'crimes', and Xu himself was accused of acting unlawfully in relation to the party. Also, the war in Xu's memory was a bright and epic period, full of heroes and legendary deeds, such as attacking the enemy by using a disguised identity. Thus, although he was confined in his flat just like a prisoner in reality, he found that the excitement of recollecting and writing about the war allowed him to overcome him circumstances.

Moreover, people simply became more nostalgic as they got older. For example, Xu Deheng 許德珩, who founded the September 3rd Society (the name commemorates V-J Day), published an emotional poem for the 45th anniversary of the December 9th movement. He was 91 years old that year:

To save the nation from extinction, we drove out the enemy bandits,
To love my country, we recollect the respectful predecessors.
Sun and moon shine new lights, The old sky is replaced by the new.
I think about the past in the cold season of a year, I am old, still my aspiration is tenacious.[110]

Mourning relatives and friends who died during the war was another motive for creating war-themed works. For instance, Yang Kaizhi 杨开智 wrote an article to commemorate his daughter Yang Zhan 杨展, who was a known anti-Japanese martyr and the niece of another martyr – Mao's first wife.[111] He recollected two phases of his daughter's anti-Japanese activities. After the July 7th Incident, Yang Zhan organised several campaigns and activities, such as giving speeches, singing resistance songs and performing resistance dramas, to call for resistance against the Japanese in her high school in Changsha, Hunan Province. She and her fellow students also organised fundraising events in support of the soldiers on the front line, and publicised the importance of resistance among the masses around her school and in the countryside during holidays. In 1938, Yang Zhan started studying in a school in Yanan. In the summer of 1939 she followed a contingent of students and teachers in the Yanan area and set out for the front line at the Shanxi, Chahar and Hebei anti-Japanese base. As her father related it, the journey was very dangerous, as they had to break through several Japanese blockades. After they arrived at the base the situation became even worse. The contingent had to constantly move to avoid the mopping-up actions carried out by the Japanese. In autumn 1941, Yang fell from a cliff and died during an emergency blood transfusion after a stealth attack by a Japanese unit.

Similarly, Wu Hu 吴虎, a factory director in Nanjing who wrote several war-themed memoirs, also suggested that his dead comrades-in-arms were an important motivating factor for his writings:

I just started learning about literary creation. Nevertheless, I had had the idea of writing something for a long time. During the period of the revolutionary wars, I witnessed many close comrades-in-arms who fought for the undertaking of the party regardless of their personal safety, and sacrificed their lives one by one; I have also heard about many heroic deeds of revolutionary struggles from my seniors and other comrades-in-arms. The stories I saw and heard touched me deeply.[112]

Wu Hu also mentioned another reason that compelled him to write. He said that the deeds of the heroes and comrades-in arms were continuously inspiring for him: if he did not write them down, he felt 'an obligation of mine has not been fulfilled, my heart cannot be tranquil'. He also thought that if he published his pieces about these deeds, they could help educate the younger generations. This sense of the 'obligation to educate others' was another motive for people who worked on the subject of the Fifteen-Year War.

For instance, the Nanjing Massacre was not a politically ideal research area for a young scholar like Gao Xingzu. I suggest it was the obligation to ensure many more people knew about the Nanjing Massacre which impelled him, as an historian who had first-hand experience of the wartime devastation, to carry out the 1960 research project. Gao was born in 1928 in Changzhou, Jiangsu Province, an area that was devastated during the War of Resistance. The Japanese Imperial Army seized Changzhou on 29 November 1937, on their way to Nanjing. As a prelude to the occupation of Nanjing, several atrocities were committed by the Japanese soldiers in Changzhou. For instance, it was one of the settings of the notorious one-hundred-men killing contest.[113] What Gao had lost during the war was not only his homeland, but also his father and an uncle.[114] Furthermore, Gao's formative years were haunted by the horrors, hardships and pain experienced in his hometown and motherland, imposed by the Japanese Imperial Army. It was also suggested by some scholars that because these experiences had such a strong impact on Gao they imperceptibly but inexorably led him to gradually become a scholar with a strong academic interest Japan's wartime atrocities and a leading authority and 'educator' in the research field of the Nanjing Massacre.[115]

Mei Ruao (Mei Ju-ao)'s case may also exemplify this motive. On 19 March 1946, shouldering the whole country's hopes to make the Japanese 'atone for the blood debt', Mei went to Tokyo.[116] He had a dislike for the accused Japanese – even their names and faces could trigger unpleasant memories and outrage.[117] At the tribunal he learned of even more crimes committed by the Japanese during the Fifteen-Year War. Many times, he was shocked by the brutality of these crimes.[118] He tried his best to insist that the death penalty be handed out to twenty-eight convicted Japanese war criminals. However, many other war criminals escaped punishment.[119] Thus, when he heard about the revival of Japanese militarism, it was natural for Mei to be outraged. Some people suggested that Mei Ruao was a 'barometer' of Sino–Japanese relations in the 1950s and 1960s, as whenever bilateral relations were bad, he would be invited to write articles about Japanese wartime atrocities and the Tokyo tribunal. However, I argue that when he wrote such pieces it is possible he was also motivated by a felt obligation to ensure more people knew about what he had learned from the tribunal and the war.[120] Furthermore, in September 1962, Mei started writing a book about the Tokyo tribunal, at his own initiative. The writing was interrupted by the Cultural Revolution, and his manuscript – four chapters out of the planned seven – was even confiscated by the Red Guards as 'evidence of the crime'. Fortunately, Mei was able to get it back later on. However, the manuscript remained incomplete, as Mei died in 1973.[121]

Although I only have discussed four motives – responding to strong emotions, longing for the past, commemorating loved ones and an obligation to teach the facts – that impelled artists and academics to work on the Fifteen-Year War, there were many other such motives, such as using arts as means of healing for the survivors of war atrocities. Furthermore, individuals were normally driven by multiple motives.

Let me again take Yang Mo as an example. Longing for the past is evident in Yang Mo's writing of *Song of Youth*. The majority of her works were related to the war, as has been described: 'she was keen on writing about the eight-year War of Resistance, and then she wrote diligently, only about the period of the War of Resistance in her life, and did not write anything else (apart from some little occasional essays)'. Why was Yang so devoted to the wartime period? We can find a clue in her own comments:

> The life during the War of Resistance, that experience, becomes the most beautiful, blissful and unforgettable memory in my life. To recollect any time in my life before or after the war, is not comparable to the wartime life. I love the life during the war, I feel proud that I was lucky enough to be part of that life which was full of fighting spirit and was extremely rich and colourful.

Commemorating her dead comrades-in-arms also motivated Yang Mo to write about the war period. In her diary, notes and published pieces, there are plentiful records about the dark side of the war – the deaths of her friends and comrades. The place she worked during the war was close to Beijing and Tianjing, where the struggles with the Japanese were very fierce. She witnessed her comrades-in-arms being killed almost every day: for example, she saw one of her friend's heads hung on the city gate. This was really unbearable for Yang, as a sensitive and soft woman. She cried for her friends and comrades, dreamed about them, became ill with concern for them, and wrote many articles to commemorate them.[122] In addition, she also developed a habit of collecting biographies or materials about known or unknown martyrs.[123]

In addition, Yang Mo's son suggested another motivation for this writer of stories about the Fifteen-Year War: Yang's writings were also impelled by an artist's desire for self-expression:

> We went to live and work in production teams in the countryside [during the Cultural Revolution] for eight years; although most of the time was very ordinary, our desire to write about the period was so strong. My mother experienced the torment of the war and nearly died; one can well imagine the mingled sensations in her heart and her desire of expression. [124]

In short, grassroots individuals and elite unofficial agents were all influenced by their own subjective motivations when they decided to deal with and present publicly their wartime experiences. At the same time, the process of bringing the war back to the public was also influenced by factors that went beyond either these people's subjective motivations or the influence and control of the state.

Content and mutual influence

Immediately after the end of the Fifteen-Year War, from 1945 to 1949, around one-fifth – about thirty – of films produced were about the war. This was understandable, as the war was the most influential factor in Chinese people's lives, both during the war years and during the post-war period. However, it is strange that almost all of these films, which normally describe espionage and social life during the war, do not directly portray the battle-field. There are several reasons for the lack of battlefield action on the screen during the immediate post-war period: there were not enough funds for expensive battlefield scenes; Chinese film makers were traditionally good at indoor themes but not at producing films with big spectacles; and audiences rejected the 'realities' of war, and preferred entertaining content, like espionage, to the cruel realities of the battlefield. [125]

For other artists, scholars and grassroots people, their work and recollections were also influenced by similar factors to those discussed above, which were not controllable by themselves or the state.

For example, similar to film makers, writers of Fifteen-Year-War themed novels were influenced by a traditional characteristic of their profession – a tendency to be 'social historians'. For since as early as the 1930s, contemporary Chinese novelists had tended to infuse their fiction with an 'epic character' and to use their fiction to reveal the 'essence of history' or the 'spirit of the times', through introducing 'major historical events into narratives'. [126] As a result, it was normal to find page upon page of in-depth wartime background in novels of the Fifteen-Year War. Likewise, 'speaking bitterness' was also a tradition of both contemporary Chinese intellectuals and grassroots individuals. Although substantially employed by the CCP regime, 'speaking bitterness' was by no means a Communist invention; rather, it was a 'dominant narrative pattern of modern Chinese history' and was prevalent in post-war Taiwan as well. [127] Furthermore, the war-themed works and recollections were influenced by each other. This active borrowing of each other's ideas among the unofficial agents of the war memory will be explored in detail in this subsection.

The elite group's works were mutually influential. For instance, the narratives of the Fifteen-Year-War novels and films produced after 1949 largely reflect the popular academic discourses about the war at the time, like the people's war theory. Also, a large number of films and literary works were created after the Nanjing Massacre became a 'hotspot' of historical research in the PRC in the 1980s. In addition, many artists were inspired by other artists' Fifteen-Year-War works and decided to work them into other forms. The 'Yellow River Cantata' was adapted into a piano concerto in 1969 and a painting, 'The Guerrillas Are the Heroes in the Green Curtain of Tall Crops' (青纱帐里游击队员逞英豪 1977), was inspired by the lyrics of the cantata. Similarly, based on the song 'The Dadao March', a sculpture (1977) and an opera (1963) were created. Inspired by the film *Landmine Warfare*, a painting was created in 1964. Another typical example is the adaptations of 'The Five Warriors of Liangya', which was originally a newspaper article that appeared in 1941 and was subsequently made the basis of several literary works (e.g. in 1950 and 1978), a film, and an oil painting (1959).[128] Also, some artists' works were used in other artists' pieces. For instance, the resistance song 'Flower in May 五月的鲜花' was quoted in *Song of Youth* and was used in the film version of the novel.[129] With this kind of recycling, the popular wartime stories mediated by the original artists were known to every household in mainland China. More importantly, thanks to these adaptations, the lives of the popular Fifteen-Year-War themed arts were extended and endowed with new meanings by the interpretations of the adaptors.

Elite and grassroots works also influenced each other. For instance, the resistors in Anda, Heilongjiang Province, which suffered from Japanese biological warfare, initially only remembered their own losses and were unaware of the bigger picture. They remembered the existence of some weird facilities of the Japanese army in the area and some strange orders given by them: for example, around 15,000 primary school students were ordered to catch around 100,000 mice. The residents also knew about the atrocities committed by the Japanese army: for example, the Chinese labourers who helped build the facilities were killed and many Chinese froze to death.[130] Once these Japanese biological warfare atrocities were exposed systematically by experts via newspapers, radio and so forth, their memories were upgraded to another level: they started to narrate their own misforunes in connection with the bigger picture.

Moreover, there was an increasing similarity between elite and grassroots groups' descriptions of the behaviour of Japanese soldiers. For instance, given below are descriptions of how those soldiers molested and killed unyielding Chinese woman, the first in a literary work and the second in a speech given by a member of the Speech Group of Farmers and Workers in 1960:

> After seeing Caiying, these two devils immediately threw their torches away, grinned and shouted at her: 'Flower lady, flower lady …' Caiying bit the back of the right hand of a devil with all her might. That devil roared and loosed his hand. Caiying took the opportunity to escape towards the gate … The devil whose hand was bitten ran after her … held up the bayonet and aimed at the middle of Caiying's back.[131]

> The leader of a devils' squad raised a girl's hair with a bayonet. The girl gnashed her teeth, thrust out her chest, glared furiously at the devils, the leader of the devils' squad put up a smiling face like a ghost, 'Flower lady, the imperial army will give you nice preferential treatment.' He then wanted to touch the girl's face, and one could only hear a sound as if somebody was slapped on the face; the leader of the devils' squad ... fell back two steps ... the bayonet was stabbed into the girl's chest ...[132]

In a similar fashion, the images of Japanese soldiers in films and novels of the PRC era were always ugly and hideous. For example, in *Giant of Fire* (烈火金钢 1958), there were three Japanese characters: Cat-eyes Commander, who 'had two huge yellow eye balls', Mr Donkey, the corners of whose mouth would reach his ears when he started shouting, and Pig-Head Captain, with a head that looked like a pig. In *Little Soldier Zhang Ga*, the Japanese soldier who killed Zhangga's grandmother had a 'head that looked like round-bottomed wicker basket and eyes like a toad, with a few black facial hairs'.[133] Strikingly, in the recollections of the Speech Group of Farmers and Workers in Nanjing, the Japanese soldiers were also depicted as beasts with voices like the howls of wolves, with some variations. For example:

> Some devils swayed like a herd of beasts, laughed widely, walked out from the door, and ran quickly towards the houses of the neighbours in the east.
> These devils behaved like when flies saw some decayed meat, 'wa wa' they shouted and started to run after [it].
> The devil commander started shouting like a wolf, revealed his two dog's teeth, as if he wanted to eat people ...
> A Japanese devil, who had a full beard on the face and grew a few hairs on the chin, goggled his two dead-fish eyes and stuck out his demon's claw, which was covered by black hair ...
> I [a cart-driver] pulled a Japanese woman who was as fat as an old pig.[134]

The grassroots contributed to the elite's works as well. For instance, the Nanda project on the Nanjing Massacre drew on witness testimonies. Many artistic works which were based on real Fifteen-Year-War events also absorbed the grassroots memories about the events. For example, when adapting *The Plains Guerrillas* into a colour film, the scriptwriter A Jia 阿甲 met with the prototype of the leading character. During the meeting, this person told A Jia many wartime episodes, such as when he had managed to kidnap a Japanese officer's wife in order to exchange her for his own wife who had been kidnapped by the Japanese officer. A Jia found the episode very interesting and included it in the revised script.[135]

Similarly, grassroots memories also played a vital role in the film *Tunnel Warfare*. At the beginning of 1963, August First Film Studio was required to produce a 'revolutionary tradition educational film about the militia', which would reflect the people's war theory, and educate the masses about military knowledge. Relevant staff were sent to Hebei Province to collect source material through interviews. Although they tried very hard, the staff failed to create a script that was educative and entertaining at the same time. Soon, another team led by a veteran director, Ren Xudong 任旭东, embarked on an interview trip. The team spent several months and visited around twenty villages famous for their resistance activities during the war. Finally, Ren Xudong found his inspiration in Gaoping village. The team invited eleven villagers who had participated in tunnel warfare to recollect their experiences. The episodes told by the villagers, especially the one about Liu Shazi, who was the party secretary and leader of the Gaoping village militia, made a strong impression on Ren. Liu Shazi organised the villagers to start digging the tunnels and led them to successfully resist the Japanese attacks. Unfortunately, Liu was killed in action in 1945 when he was 29 years old. Consequently, Ren decided to create a story based on the tunnel warfare experience of Gaoping village. Two of the main characters – a party secretary and a leader of the militia – were based on Liu Shazi. The film was finished in 1966 and soon became very popular.[136] It is true to say that without the vivid recollections of the villagers *Tunnel Warfare* could not have achieved such popularity and might have ended up as a featureless 'military education film'. Sometimes, thanks to the popularity of these war-themed artistic works, the original grassroots memories which inspired them were also able to be widely recognised.[137]

In summary, artists, scholars and grassroots individuals were mutually influenced, and worked according to their own particular professional traditions, availability of funds, audience preferences, and so forth. Similar to the inward motivations, these influential factors were not dictated by the CCP regime.

* * *

Mainly through examining the three realms of remembrance of the Fifteen-Year War by unofficial agents, this chapter has argued that much pre-1982 Fifteen-Year-War remembrance was mediated by unofficial agents, and these unofficial agents were subject to the influence of the CCP regime, the many inner motivations of the agents themselves, and other elements in Chinese society. Even during the Maoist period, these people were not merely pawns who were ideologically manipulated by the CCP.

Furthermore, the KMT's wartime performance was also often denounced by unofficial agents in the pre-1982 PRC. Nevertheless, recollecting the KMT's involvement in the war in a relatively objective way was not completely taboo, and sometimes was even encouraged by the CCP regime. Similarly, a tragic-heroic tone was adopted by most unofficial agents when relating the war. Nonetheless, the misery of the war was also frequently employed by these artists, scholars and grassroots individuals.

Moreover, the memory of the war that was mediated by unofficial agents provides a perfect complement to the memory mediated by the central government (as discussed in Chapter 4). The war remembrance constructed by artists, scholars and grassroots testifiers – for instance through vivid reconstructions of the battlefield in war films, the detailed explanations of wartime events in academic writings, and the dramatic narratives of wartime atrocities related at mass meetings – was much more abundant, colourful and emotional than the simplified and insipid narratives of the war presented in the realms constructed by the central state.

Notes

1 Telephone interview, Duan (a participating student of the research project), 24 July 2013.

2 History Department, Nanjing University (ed.), *Riben diguozhuyi zai Nanjing de datusha* [The Japanese imperialists' massacre in Nanjing] (A restricted publication, 1979 edition) 南京大学历史系, 日本帝国主义在南京的大屠杀 (内部刊物, 1979). Unless cited separately, most of the information about the research project in this chapter is from this book. The 1979 edition was more or less similar to the edition of the 1960s.

3 A few testimonies gathered through the team's interview can be found in: Zhang Lianhong and Zhang Sheng (eds), *Nanjing Datusha shiliaoji 25 xingcunzhe koushu (shang)* [The historical materials of the Nanjing Massacre 25 survivors' testimonies] (Nanjing: Jiangsu renmin chubanshe, 2005) 张连红 张生编, 南京大屠杀史料集25 幸存者口述 (江苏人民出版社, 2005). The archives from the NMA, e.g. NMA-3-1-950, 'Guomindang shoudu difang fayuan jianchachu fengling diaocha dikou zuixing baogaoshu' [The KMT capital local court's report on the investigation of the crimes committed by the enemy 国民党首都地方法院检查处奉令调查敌寇罪行报告书]; from the NICA, e.g. NICA-1-35230 'Beihairende Kongsuwenjian' [Accusation by the victims 被害人的控诉文件] (the example given in the book was a testimony from a KMT POW) and NICA-1-35125, 'Bingjun shahai renmin' [Bacteria kills people 病菌杀害人民]; from the Nanjing Historical Material Sorting Office, e.g. an unpublished book 'Lunxianqu canzhuangji' [Record of the miserable situation in the occupied area volume 5 沦陷区惨状记 第5册].

4 E.g. *Shen Bao* 申报, *Dagong Bao* 大公报, *Tokyo Nichinichi Shinbun* 东京日日新闻, *Jiefang Ribao* 解放日报 and *Xinhua Ribao* 新华日报.

5 E.g. Harold John Timperley (Yang Ming, trans.), *Wairen muduzhi Rijun baoxing* [What war means: the Japanese atrocities in China] (Guomin chubanshe, 1938) 田伯烈 (杨明译), 外人目睹中之日军暴行 (国民出版社, 1938); Zhang Xiaolin (trans.), *Yuandong guoji junshi fating panjueshu* [Report of the International Military Tribunal for the Far East] (Chongqing: Wushiniandai chubanshe, 1953) 张效林译, 远东国际军事法庭判决书 (五十年代出版社, 1953); Anonymous, *Rijun baoxing huashi* [Picture history of Japanese atrocities] (Dahua chubanshe, 1946) 匿名, 日军暴行画史 (大华出版社, 1946); Du Chengxiang, Rikou baoxinglun [Survey of Japanese bandits' atrocities] (Shidai chubanshe, 1939) 杜呈详, 日寇暴行论 (时代出版社, 1939).

6 Liu mentioned that 1962 年 was the 25th anniversary of the Nanjing Massacre (according to my interview with Liu), but it is unclear whether this manuscript was produced for commemorative purposes.

7 This section is based on History Department, *Riben diguozhuyi zai Nanjing de datusha*.

8 History Department, *Riben diguozhuyi zai Nanjing de datusha*.

9   All information about the Speech Group is from NMA-6001-3-311 'Shehui zhuyi jiangyantuan cailiao' [Materials of the Socialist Speech Group 社会主义讲演团材料], 28 December 1960.

10 NMA-6001-3-311.

11 Unless cited separately, the information about Yang Mo in this chapter is based on: Lao Gui, *Muqing Yang Mo* [Mother Yang Mo] (Wuhan: Changjiang wenyi chubanshe, 2005) 老鬼, 母亲杨沫 (长江文艺出版社, 2005). This is a biography written by Yang's son Ma Bo (马波, Lao Gui is a pen name), based on Yang's dairies, articles and his own recollections of Yang Mo. He claimed people can see the true Yang Mo through this biography.

12 Yang's diary entry for 9 June 1951, Laogui, *Muqing Yang Mo.*

13 Laogui, *Muqing Yang Mo.*

14 According to Mao Zedong, 'Zai Yangan wenyi zuotanhui shangde jianghua' [Talks at the Yan'an Forum on Literature and Art 在延安文艺座谈会上的讲话], May 1942. The talks were treated as a 'Bible' for literature and art workers in the Maoist PRC.

15 Anonymous, 'Hongse qingchunde jiyi bianqian – "qingchun zhige" chuangzuo, yingxiang shihua' [The evolution of the memory of the Red Youth – history of the creation of 'Song of Youth' and its influence 红色青春的记忆变迁 – 《青春之歌》创作、影响史话]. www.chinawriter.com.cn/2011/2011-04-21/96633.html, 21 April 2011, date accessed, 10 March 2014.

16 Laogui, *Muqing Yangmo.*

17 Guo Kai, 'Lvetan dui Lin Daojing demiaoxie zhongde quedian' [Brief discussion about the weakness in the description of Lin Daojing], *China Youth*, 1959: www. xzbu.com/6/view-3371371.htm, date accessed, 16 March 2014 郭开, 略谈对林道静的描写中的缺点, 中国青年, 1959: 2.

18 Guo, 'Lvetan'; Laogui, *Muqin Yangmo*; Yang Mo, 'Epilogue' in *Song of Youth* (second edition) (Beijing: Renmin wenxue chubanshe, 1960) 杨沫, 后记, 青春之歌 (人民文学出版社, 1960).

19 See, Merle Goldman, 'The Party and the Intellectuals', and 'The Party and the Intellectuals: Phase Two', in R. MacFarquhar and J. Fairbank (eds), *Cambridge History of China Volume 14* (Cambridge: Press Syndicate of the University of Cambridge, 1989), pp. 218–253 and 432–463.

20 *Xinhua Ribao*: 'Guanggao' [Advertisement 广告], 2 July 1949 (Nanjing had already been under the CCP's control since April 1949); 'Qingzhu Wuyi laodongjie yingchu yingpian' [Films will be shown to celebrate the May 1st Labour Day 庆祝五一劳动节映出影片], 28 April 1979, the film was included in the list. *Xinhua Ribao*, 'Dianying "Yijiang Chunshui Xiangdongliu" guanhou' [电影一江春水向东流观后 Thoughts after watching the film *The Spring River Flows East*], 6 May 1979. Scholarly work on the PRC's Fifteen-Year War themed films before 1949, see, Jay Leyda, *Dianying* (Cambridge MA: MIT Press, 1972).

21 *Xinhua Ribao*: 'Guanggao Renminyinyuejia Xian Xinghai shishi sizhounian jinianyinyuehui' [Advertisement, commemorative concert for People's Musician Xian Xinghai, who had passed away four years ago 广告 人民音乐家 冼星海逝世四周年 纪念音乐会], 30 October 1949; 'Weidade renmin geshou Xian Xinghai daibiaozuo "Huanghe dahechang"' [Great People's Musician Xian Xinghai's masterpiece 'The Yellow River Cantata' 伟大的人民歌手冼星海代表作 '黄河大合唱'], 30 October 1949. *Nanjing Ribao*, advertisement for the performance of 'The Yellow River Cantata', 13 May 1956; Ma Ko, 'A Fighting Song is Born', *China Reconstructs*, 1963: 5. Yin Yen, 'Concerts Honor Two Pioneer Composers', *China Reconstructs*, 1976: 2. The anniversary of the death of another musician Nie Er 聂耳, the composer of 'March of the Volunteers' and many other resistance songs, was also commemorated regularly.

22 NMA-5063-2-214: 'Guanyu qingli zushutan lianhuanhua debaogao' [Report about rectifying rental outlets and comic books 关于清理租书摊连环画的报告], 14 June 1966. Film comic books such as *The Plain Guerrilla* and *Little Soldier Zhangga* were on the list.

23 Apart from the domestic newspapers and radio channels, articles introducing model operas can be found in PRC's propaganda magazines targeting foreigners as well: Anonymous, 'The Red Lantern, an example for New Peking Opera', *China Reconstructs*, 1965: 12; Anonymous, 'Selected Singing Passages from The Red Lantern (May 1970 script)', *China Reconstructs*, 1970: 9. Anonymous, 'Fighting on the Plains. A modern revolutionary Peking opera', *China Reconstructs*, 1974: 8. For a detailed account of the PRC's model operas, see, Paul Clark, *The Chinese Cultural Revolution* (Cambridge: Cambridge University Press, 2008).

24 Liu Dejun, *Kangri zhanzheng yanjiu shuping* [Review of the research on the War of Resistance against Japan] (Jinan: Qilu shushe, 2005) 刘德军, 抗日战争研究述评 (齐鲁书社, 2005).

25 Shanghai shifan daxue lishixi Zhongguo xiandaishi jiaoyanshi ziliaoshi, *Zhongguo xiandaishi ziliao xuanji disance (shang, zhong, xia) Kang Ri zhanzheng shiqi* [Selection of materials on Chinese contemporary history, volume 3 (1–3) War of Resistance period] (Shanghai shifan daxue lishixi Zhongguo xiandaishi jiaoyanshi ziliaoshi, 1978) 上海师范大学历史系中国现代史教研室资料室 编印, 中国现代史资料选辑 第三册 (上,中,下 抗日战争时期), 1978.

26 E.g. official documents (e.g. the KMT's 'Guiding Principle for War of Resistance and Construction of the Nation 抗战建国纲领 9 December 1937', 'The Third Konoe Statement 第三次近卫声明 22 December 1937' and the 'Potsdam Declaration 中美英三国促令日本投降之波茨坦公告 26 July 1945), articles written in the name of individuals (e.g. Chiang Kai-shek's 'China's Destiny 中国之命运', Wang Ming 王明's 'the Current Situation concerning the War of Resistance 目前抗战形式与如何坚持持久战争取抗战的最后胜利'), and the newspaper reports (e.g. *Jiefang Ribao*, 'Guogong kangzhan chengjide bijiao' [Comparing the KMT's and the CCP's achievements in the War of Resistance 国共两党抗战成绩的比较], 24 August 1943).

27 Scholarly work, e.g. Zhonghuarenmin zhengfu geminjunshi weiyuanhui, 'Guanyu kang Ri zhanzheng shiqi Zhongguo renmin jiefangjun de wuge tongji cailiao' [Five statistic documents about the PLA during the War of Resistance], *Xinhua yuebao*, 4 (1951) 中共人民政府人民革命军事委员会, 关于抗日战争时期中国人民解放军的五个统计材料, 新华月报, 4 (1951). Leader's speechs, e.g. *Renmin Ribao*, Nie Rongzhen 聂荣臻, 'Zhongguorenmin zenyang zhanshengle Riben faxisi qinlvezhe' [How the Chinese people defeated the Japanese fascist invader 中国人民怎样战胜了日本法西斯侵略者], 30 June 1951. Memoirs, e.g. *Yangcheng wanbao* 羊城晚报, Anonymous, 'Dawushan fan "saodang" dehuiyi' [Recall anti-mopping up in Dawushan 大悟山反"扫荡"的回忆], 1 September 1965.

28 It was originally published in *Xinhua Ribao* in 1951.

29 Jiefangjun Gequ xuanji bianji bu, *Kang Ri Zhanzheng gequ xuanji (1–4)* [Selection of songs of the War of Resistance (volumes 1–4)] (Beijing: Zhongguo qingnian chubanshe, 1957) 解放军歌曲选集编辑部, 抗日战争歌曲选集1–4 (中国青年出版社, 1957).

30 Zhongguo kexueyuan Jiangsu fenyuan wenxueyanjiusuo, *Jiangsu minge cankao* [Jiangsu folksong reference] (Nanjing: Zhongguo kexueyuan Jiangsu fenyuan wenxueyan jiusuo, 1958) 中国科学院江苏分院文学研究所编印, 江苏民歌参考资料 (中国科学院江苏分院文学研究所, 1958).

31 Liaoning, Jilin, Heilongjiang, Yanbian renmin chubanshe lianhe bianji, *Dongbei renmin kang Ri geyao xuan* [Selection of northeastern people's Anti-Japanese songs]

(Liaoning, Jilin, Heilongjiang,Yanbian renmin chubanshe lianhe bianji, 1959) 辽宁,吉林,黑龙江, 延边人民出版社联合 编辑出版, 东北人民抗日歌谣选, 1959.

32 Wang Shisan, Han Shutian, et al., *Chuzhong guowen diliuce* [Middle school Chinese, volume 6] (Xinhua shudian, 1980, 3rd edn) 王食三,韩书田等, 初中国文 第六册 (新华书店出版, 1950. 8.三版).

33 Renminjiaoyu chubanshe, *Chujizhongxue yuwen disice* [Middle school Chinese, volume 4] (Renmin jiaoyuchubanshe, 1955, 7th edn) 初级中学语文课本 第四册 (人民教育出版社编辑出版, 1955 第七版 [1952第一版]).

34 NMA-6002-3-130: 'Guanyu zai quanshi shaonian ertongzhong kaizhan "woai dushu" huodong detongzhi' [Announcement about organising 'I Love Reading Books' activity among children in the city 关于在全市少年儿童中开展 "我爱读 书" 活动的通知], 1958.

35 See, for example, Ma Ko, 'Songs play their part in revolution', *China Reconstructs*, 1965: 6; *Nanjing Ribao*: 'Gaochang geming gequ' [Sing revolutionary songs enthusiastically 高唱革命歌曲], 31 December 1960; *Xin Nanjing Ribao*,'-Woshi dachang geming gequ huodong bianji chengxiang' [Our city's activity of singing revolutionary historical songs spreads through cities and countries 我市 大唱革命历史歌曲活动遍及城乡], 8 May 1970; *Xinhua Ribao*, 'Nanjingshi juban gongren geyong dahui' [Nanjing organises workers' mass singing meeting 南京市举办工人歌咏大会], 30 September 1974; *Xinhua Ribao*, 'Geming gequ geyong hui' [Revolutionary songs singing meeting 革命歌曲歌咏会], 26 December 1976;'Woshi juxing shiershou geming gequ yanchanghui' [Our city organises concert of twelve revolutionary songs 我市举行十二首革命歌曲演唱会], 29 May 1980.

36 According to the lyrics of 'Sing about the cowhand Erxiao', written by Fang Bing 方冰. NMA-6002-3-188: 'Guanyu zai quanshi kaizhan dachang geming gexude qunzhong geyong huodong de yijian' [Opinion on organising a mass activity of singing revolutionary songs in the city 关于在全市开展大唱革命歌曲 的群众歌咏活动的意见], April 1962; 'Guanyu juban quanshi xuexiao geming gequ he shige langsong huibao yanchu de tongzhi' [Announcement on organising schools' performance of revolutionary songs and poetry reading in the city 关于举办全市学校 革命歌曲和诗歌朗诵汇报演出的通知], 7 November 1962.

37 See, for example, *Xinhua Ribao*, 'Hanjia shenghuo: fangwen laoertongtuan tuanyuan' [Life in winter holiday: visit old member of Children's Regiment 寒假生 活 访问老儿童团团员], 31 January 1963; *Xinhua Ribao*, 'Geming chuantong yuxinren'[Revolution tradition educate new generations 革命传统育新人], 21 March 1973; *Nanjing Ribao*, 'Baixiaqu juban zhuanti gushihui reqing gesong laoyibei gemingjia' [Baixiaqu organises story meeting and praises the old revolutionary generation 白下区举办专题故事会 热情歌颂老一辈革命家], 4 January 1979; *Xinhua Ribao*, 'Laohongjun laoganbu xiangqingnian jiang chuantong' [Old Red Army soldiers and old cadres talk about tradition to youths 老红军老 干部向青年讲传统], 2 May 1981.

38 'Speaking bitterness' was widely used before the foundation of the PRC. For the CCP's typical methods of encouraging Chinese people to 'speak bitterness', see, Jinchaji junqu zhengzhibu, *Suku fuchou* [Speak bitterness and take revenge] (Jinchaji junqu zhengzhibu, 1947) 晋察冀军区政治部, 诉苦复仇 (晋察冀军区政 治部, 1947). William Howard Hinton, *Fanshen: a documentary of revolution in a Chinese village* (London: Monthly Review Press, 1966); L. Rofel, *Other modernities: gendered yearnings in China after socialism* (Berkeley: University of California Press, 1999), p. 141; C. Berry, 'Speaking bitterness: history, media and nation in twentieth-century China', *Historiography East and West*, 2(1) (2004), 16–43.

39 Rofel, *Other modernities*, p. 140.

40 *Xinhua Ribao*: 'Cong jiushidai daoxinshidai: wodui Jiangnan shuinichang ershinian jingyande ganxiang' [From old era to new era: thoughts about my twenty-year

experience in the Jiangnan Cement Factory 从旧时代到新时代 – 我对江南水泥厂二十年经验的感想], 20 September 1954. The experience of being bullied by the Japanese was mentioned in this article.

41   E.g. *Xinhua Ribao*, 'Tongyi nanjingdatusha shimin yizhi fan Mei Kang Ri: Yongliya chang cengshou Rikou pohaide zhigong, juxing qiqi zuotan' [Painfully recall the Nanjing Massacre, all citizens opposite the US and resist Japanese: Yongliya factory's staff, who were suppressed, hold July 7th forum 痛忆南京大屠杀 市民一致反美抗日 – 永利铔厂曾受日寇迫害的职工, 举行七七座谈], 7 July 1949. *Xin Nanjing Ribao*, 'Wohentou le Suxiu Meidi' [I hate Soviet revisionists and American imperialists 我恨透了苏修,美帝], 31 May 1970.

42   See, NMA-6001-3-311 'Shehui zhuyi jiangyantuan cailiao'; *Renmin ribao*, 'Liji kaizhan yige yiliang, gang wei zhongxin de zengchan jieyue yundong' [Start a grain-and-steel-centred campaign of increasing production and practicing thrift immediately 立即开展一个以粮 钢为中心的增产节约运动], 18 August 1960.

43   Mao formally put 'to be sure not to forget class struggle 千万不要忘记阶级斗争' into a slogan, *Zhongguo gongchan dang xinwen* 中国共产党新闻, 'Yijieji douzheng weigang' [Class struggle as the guiding principal 以阶级斗争为纲]. http://cpc.people.com.cn/GB/64162/64170/4467349.html, date unknown, date accessed, 10 March 2014; Stuart R. Schram, 'Mao Tse-tung's thought from 1949 to 1976', in R. MacFarquhar and J. Fairbank (eds), *Cambridge History of China Volume 15* (Cambridge: Press Syndicate of the University of Cambridge, 1991), pp. 1–107. It was argued that the Tenth Plenum 'marked the beginning of Mao's effort to stop the criticism of his policies in the Great Leap Forward, see, Goldman, 'The party and the intellectuals'; and 'The socialist education movement', in Maurice Meisner, *Mao's China and after: a history of the People's Republic* (New York: Free Press, 1999).

44   In his speech on 6 April 1958 to the Hankou Conference, Schram, 'Mao Tse-tung's thought'.

45   Goldman, 'The party and the intellectuals'.

46   *Xinhua Ribao*, 'Tamen zenyangyong jieji guandian wuzhuang qingniande' [How they use the class theory to arm the youths 他们怎样用阶级观点武装青年的], 5 January 1963.

47   *Xinhua Ribao*, 'Benbao juban "laogongren jinxitan" zhengwen' [our newspaper solicits articles for 'Old workers talk about past and present' 本报举办 "老工人今昔谈" 征文], 2 February 1963; '"laogongren jinxitian" jieshuyu' [Summary of 'Old workers talk about past and present' "老工人今昔"谈结束语], 14 April 1963.

48   *Xinhua Ribao*, 'Zai dayouji de rizili' [The days of fighting as a guerrilla 在 打游击 的日子里], 2 March 1963.

49   Goldman, 'The party and the intellectuals'; Meisner, 'The socialist education movement'.

50   For example, three examples of relating family history to children were carried out in a section:*Xinhua Ribao*, 'Changjiang wuchanjieji jiashi jiaoyu zilv' [Always relating the proletarian family history to educate the children 常讲无产阶级家史教育子女], 20 June 1963.

51   *Xinhua Ribao*, 'Qijichang zuzhi "sanlao" dajiang "sanshi"' [Qishuyan rolling stock plant organised 'three olds' to relate enthusiastically 'three histories' 戚机厂组织"三老"大讲"三史"], 20 June 1963; '"Baoyu zhongde huo chetout" pingjia' [Review of 'A locomotive in the rainstorm'《暴风雨中的火车头》评价], 7 June 1963. The plant was controlled by the Japanese between 1937 and 1945.

52   *Xinhua Ribao*, 'Nanjing jiejie jiaoyu zhanlanhui', 10 August 1963; 'Ji Nanjingshi jiaoqu xiangshi, cunshi, jiashi zhanlan hui' [Record of the town history, village history and family history exhibition on the outskirts of Nanjing 记南京市郊区乡史, 村史, 家史展览会], 10 August 1963.

53 *Xinhua Ribao*, '"Hongse jiapu" zhengwen qishi' [Announcement of articles solicited for 'Red genealogy'《红色家谱》征文启示], 5 July 1963.

54 *Xinhua Ribao*, 'Tongnian de gushi' [Story of childhood 童年的故事], 10 August 1963; 'Baojiaode huabi' [Fully dipped painting brush 饱蘸的画笔], 30 August 1963.

55 See, for example, *Xinhua Ribao*, 'Yiku' [Recall the bitterness 忆苦], 24 November 1969; *Xin Nanjing Ribao*, 'Renzhen gaohao liangyi sancha' [seriously conduct 'two remember' and 'three investigate' 认真搞好两忆三查], 17 May 1970; *Xinhua Ribao*, 'Yiding buwang jiejiku' [Never forget the bitterness of class 一定不忘阶级苦], 18 December 1976.

56 *Xinhua Ribao*, 'Chenglianghui shang jiang geming gushi' [Relate revolutionary stories in the enjoy-the-cool party 乘凉晚会上讲革命故事], 29 July 1965; 'Yong duozhong wenyi xingshi zhanling chengliang zhendi' [Use various art and literature forms to occupy the enjoy-the-cool-battlefield 用多种文艺形式占领乘凉阵地], 3 August 1974. Most of stories told had 'comparison' parts.

57 Xiaohongliu 小红柳, 'Wuqi gushi' [Story of five seven 五七故事]. http://shzq.net/pjq/Print.asp?tid=5012, 7 May 2011, date accessed, 10 March 2014.

58 NMA-5063-2-215, 'Guanyu zhengli geming yizhi, yijicailiao,qingzhuanbao shiweizuzhibu yuyi shenchade baogao' [Report about forwarding the documents relating to revolutionary relics and remains to the municipal party committee 关于整理革命遗址 遗迹材料 请转报市委组织部予以审查的报告], 11 February 1966.

59 See, 'Records of the eight years when Huaihailu was occupied 淮南路沦陷八年琐记' and 'Records about Chuxian being occupied 滁县沦陷纪略', in Zhenxie Anhui wenshi ziliao yanjiu gongzuozu (ed.), *Anhui wenshi ziliao xuanji*.

60 By the mid-1980s, approximately a quarter (over a billion Chinese characters) of what had been collected in total had been published, Luke S. K. Kwong, 'Oral history in China: a preliminary review', *The Oral History Review*, 20 (1992), pp. 37–38.

61 See, for example, Jiang Guangnai, Cai Tingkai and Dai Ji 蒋光鼐 蔡廷锴 戴戟, 'Nineteenth Army recall the second Shanghai Incident 十九路军淞沪抗战回忆 volume 37', Zhang Zhizhong 张治中, 'The course of the Fifth Army's participation in the second Shanghai Incident 第五军参加淞沪抗日战役的经过 volume 37'.

62 Du Yuming 杜聿明, 'Talk about Chinese Expeditionary Army's operation against Japan in Burma 中国远征军入缅对日作战述略 volume 8'; Song Xilian 宋希濂, 'Chinese Expeditionary Army's training, consolidating and counterattack in west Yunnan 远征军在滇西的整训和反攻 volume 8'; Mei Ruao 梅汝璈, 'About Tani Hisao, Matsui Ishine and the Nanjing Massacre 关于谷寿夫、松井石根和南京大屠杀事件 volume 22'; Mei Ruao, 'Some additions and corrections to "the Nanjing Massacre" 关于《南京大屠杀事件》的几点补正 volume 34'.

63 Mei Ruao, 'About Tani Hisao, Matsui Ishine and the Nanjing Massacre'.

64 Page 120 in Hong Zicheng, *A history of contemporary Chinese literature* (Leiden: Brill, 2007).

65 Zhongyang dianyingju juben chuangzuo bianjibu 中央电影局剧本创作所编辑部, '1954–1957 nian dianying gushipian zhuti,ticai tishi caoan' [Draft recommendation for the themes, materials of the films 1954–1957 年电影故事片主题, 题材提示草案], 1953.

66 See, for example, Li Guangtao, *Huaiyin bashier lieshi* [Eighty-two martyrs in Huaiyin] (Nanjing: Jiangsu renmin chubanshe, 1960) 李广涛, 淮阴 八十二烈士 (江苏人民出版社, 1960) Nanjingshi wenhuaju chuangzuozu, *Yuhuatai geming lieshi gushi* [Revolutionary martyrs in Yuhuatai] (Nanjing: Jiangsu renmin chubanshe, 1978) 南京市文化局创作组, 雨花台革命烈士故事 (江苏人民出版社, 1978).

67   Poems, e.g. Cai Heng (1958). 'Jiangnan kangzhan dezange' [Glorious songs of War of Resistance in Jiangnan], *Yuhua*, 1958: 8 采蘅, 1958, 江南抗战的赞歌, 雨花, 1958: 8. Books, e.g. Liao Rongbiao and Zhang Fan, *Kangri defenghuo* [Flame of resisting the Japanese] (Beijing: Zhongguo qingnian chubanshe, 1958) 廖荣标, 张藩, 抗日的烽火 (中国青年出版社, 1958); Tonghua zhuanyuan gongshu wenjiao weisheng bangongshi, *Chang baishan kang Ri gushi* [Anti-Japanese stories in Changbai mountain] (Jilin renmin chubanshe, 1964) 通化专员公署文教卫生办公室编, 长白山抗日故事 (吉林人民出版社出版 1964); Zhenjiang junfenqu zhengzhibu, *Maoshan kang Ri douzheng gushi* [Stories of anti-Japanese struggles in Maoshan] (Nanjing: Jiangsu renmin chubanshe, 1979) 镇江军分区政治部编, 茅山抗日斗争故事 (江苏人民出版社, 1979). The Fifteen-Year War themed stories were also included in books of general 'heroes' stories', 'revolutionary stories', 'fighting stories', and the numbers of these kinds of books were huge. For instance, Shanghai wenhua chubanshe, *Geming lishi douzheng gushiji* [Collection of stories of struggles in revolutionary history] (Shanghai: Shanghai wenhua chubanshe, 1965) 上海文化出版社出版编辑, 革命历史斗争故事集, 1965.

68   NMA-6004-2-18: 'Laoganbu chuangzuo zongjiedeng' [Summary of old cadres' creations and so forth 老干部创作总结等], January–December 1962; NMA-6004-3-48: 'Wenyi jianbao laoganbu daxie huiyilu' [Bulletin of arts and literature 1: old cadres write memoirs enthusiastically 文艺简报 老干部大写回忆录], 16 January 1962. For other memoirs that appeared in Nanjing's local publications, see, Liao Zhenguo (a major-general), 'Lujiatan tongjian Rikou' [Japanese bandits annihilated mercilessly in Lujiatan], *Yuhua*, 1958: 8 少将廖振国, 卢家滩痛歼日寇, 雨花, 1958: 8; 'He Zhensheng, zai kang Ri de linghai shang' [On anti-Japanese territorial waters], *Yuhua*, 1958: 9 何振声, 在抗日的领海上, 雨花 1958: 9.

69   For more on the All-China Federation of Literary and Art Circles, see, Cyrill Birch, 'Literature under communism', in MacFarquhar and Fairbank (eds), *Cambridge History of China Volume 15,* pp. 743–815.

70   Goldman, 'The party and the intellectuals', p. 218.

71   Jin and Xun, 'Shiqinian shiqi'; Goldman, 'The party and the intellectuals', 'The party and the intellectuals: phase two'; Cyrill Birch, 'Literature under communism'.

72   Goldman, 'The party and the intellectuals', p. 218.

73   Anonymous, '"The East Is Red" – another suppressed film reappears', *China Reconstructs*, 1977: 8.

74   Jiangsusheng wenlian ziliaoshi, *Jiangsu geming genjudi wenyiziliao huibian* (internally circulated, 1983), p. 3 江苏省文联资料室编, 江苏革命根据地文艺资料汇编 (内部发行 1983); *Xinhua Ribao*, 'Geju "Hongbizi canjun" chongxin paiyan' [Opera 'Red Nose joins the army' is rehearsed again 歌剧《红鼻子参军重新排演], 5 October 1980.

75   *Xinhua Ribao*, 'Puyi houbansheng caifang sanji' [Interview, second half of the life of Puyi 溥仪后半生采访散记 (连载)], 4 April 1981; *Xinhua Ribao*, 'Zuzhi laoganbu zuanxie huiyilu' [Organising old cadres to write memoirs 组织老干部撰写回忆录], 10 August 1980. *Nanjing Ribao*, 'Cangben shizong shijian shimo' [Whole story of the Missing Kuramoto Incident 藏本失踪事件始末], 26 June 1982.

76   E.g.*Nanjing Ribao*, 'Xuexi: from jiuyiba dao yierjiu' [Learning: from September 18th to December 9th 学习 从九一八到一二九], 17 March 1982; 'Xuexi: Kang Ri zhanzheng de baofa' [Learning: outbreak of the War of Resistance 学习: 抗日战争的爆发], 29 April 1982; '"Qiqi shibian" yihoude Nanjing' [Nanjing after the July 7th Incident "七七事变"以后的南京], 10 July 1982.

77 *Nanjing Ribao*, 'Chedipipan Liu Shaoqi yihuo fandongde renxinglun' [Criticise Liu Shaoqi group's reactionary theory of human nature 彻底批判刘少奇一伙反动的人性论], 3 June 1971.

78 Kwong, 'Oral history in China', p. 39; Hughes, 'Japan in the politics of Chinese leadership legitimacy'.

79 Kwong, 'Oral history in China', pp. 32–33.

80 Yoshida, *The making of the 'Rape of Nanking'*.

81 The chapter's title was 'People who never surrender', written by a participating teacher, Zha Ruizhen 查瑞珍.

82 Zhao Shoucheng 赵守成. 'Gao Xingzu: Nanjing datusha yanjiu diyiren' [Gao Xingzu: the pre-eminent researcher of the Nanjing Massacre 高兴祖:南京大屠杀研究第一人]. www.js.xinhuanet.com/xin_wen_zhong_xin/2005-08/13/content_4874686.htm, 13 August 2005, date accessed, 10 March 2014; Interview, Sun.

83 Laogui, *Muqin Yang Mo*.

84 Yang Mo, 'Epilogue' in *Song of youth* (new edition) (Beijing: Shiyue wenyi chubanshe, 1991). 杨沫, 后记, 新版青春之歌 (北京十月文艺出版社, 1991).

85 See, for example, *Xinhua Ribao*, 'Meidi he Rikou doushi guizishou' [American imperialists and Japanese bandits were both enemies 美帝和日寇都是刽子手], 28 November 1950; '11qu xuanchuandui zai nanjiao yuhualu yanchu jietouju "Jiang Ri Wang Heliu"' [11th district's propaganda team performed a street drama 'Collaboration of Chiang, Wang and Japanese' 11区宣传队在南郊雨花路演出街头剧 '蒋日汪合流'], 7 July 1949.

86 For instance: 'The reactionaries within the KMT's crimes of damaging the anti-Japanese bases in the occupied areas 国民党内的反动派破坏敌后抗日根据地的罪行一斑', in Shanghai shifandaxue, *Zhongguo xiandaishi*.

87 'Dade guizi xindan han' [Attacks the devils and makes their hearts and gall tremble with fear 打得鬼子心胆寒] in Jiangsusheng minjian wenxue yanjiu hui (ed.), *Youle renma haoshuohua* [It would be easier if we had troops] (Nanjing: Jiangsu renmin chubanshe, 1965) 江苏省民间文学研究会编, 有了人马好说话 (江苏人民出版社, 1965).

88 Jin Danyuan and Xu Wenming, '"Shiqinian" shiqi "liangjiehe" sixiang jiqidui Zhongguo dianying de yingxiang' [the 'two combined' theory during the 'seventeen-year period' and its impact on Chinese films], *Yishu baijia*, 2 (2010), 13–18 金丹元,徐文明, 十七年时期的"两结合"思想及其对中国电影的影响,艺术百家, 2 (2010), 13–18.

89 Su Kui, 'Tan jianguo chuqi kang Ri ticai xiaoshuo yu dianying' [Talk about the anti-Japanese themed novels and films during the first years of the PRC], *Dianying wenxue*, 11 (2008) 苏奎, 谈建国初期抗日题材小说与电影, 电影文学, 11 (2008).

90 Anonymous, 'Beitong didao fangdu canan' [Tragedy of defending against chemical weaons in Beitong tunnel 北疃地道防毒惨案]. www.zainanlu.com/a/zhanzhengzainan/feichangguiwuqi/huaxuewuqi/642.html, 22 November 2011, date accessed, 10 March 2014; Yan Yan 燕雁, 'Didaozhan qishi hen canku' [Tunnel warfare actually was very cruel 地道战其实很残酷]. http://blog.sina.com.cn/s/blog_675b55c401019jgb.html, 21 April 2013, date accessed, 10 March 2014.

91 Hong, *A history of contemporary Chinese literature*, p. 130.

92 Liu Jialing, 'Pingyuan youjidui gushide zhengliu guocheng' [The distillation process of the story of 'The plains guerrillas'], *Shanghai wenxue*, 3 (2002), 70–73 刘嘉陵, 平原游击队故事的蒸馏过程, 上海文学, 3 (2002), 70–73.

93 Li Xiuying was not invited to testify during the Cultural Revolution period because her husband's previous experience was based on Liu's speculation, Interview, Liu.

94 Cyril Birch, 'Literature under communism', p. 745.

95   Sheryl Perlmutter Bowen and Juliet I. Spitzer, 'Survivors sometimes tell their stories: motives for sharing and motives for silence', in Johannes-Dieter Steinert and Inge Weber-Newth (eds), *Beyond camps and forced labour: current international research on survivors of Nazi persecution* (Proceedings of the first international multidisciplinary conference at the Imperial War Museum, London, 29–31 January 2003) (Osnabrvck, Germany: Secolo Verlag, 2005).

96   *Xinhua Ribao*, 'Yonggan wanqiangde Li Xiuying' [Brave Liu Xiuying 勇敢顽强 的李秀英], 23 February 1951. Xu, 'Nanjing datusha xingcunzhe de xinlulicheng'.

97   Quoting a scholar of Chinese literature, 'they were naturally willing to look back', p. 121 in Hong, *A history of contemporary Chinese literature*, p. 121.

98   For instance, *Nanjing Ribao*, 'Kan yinyuepian "Huanghe Dahechang"' [Watch the musical film *The Yellow River Cantata* 看音乐片 "黄河大合唱"], 25 May 1956; Anonymous, 'Fighting spirit in songs', *China Reconstructs*, 1966: 2.

99   Translated by the author.

100   Fan Yongqiang, Lu Honggen, He Kun, 'Shida jingdian kangzhan gequ' [Ten classic War of Resistance songs], *Hainan renda*, 12 (2006), 47 樊永强, 陆洪根, 何 坤,十大经典抗战歌曲, 海南人大, 12 (2006), 47.

101   Translated by the author.

102   Qi Yue 齐越, 'Zai Taihangshan shang wangshi xinti' [Re-mention the past of 'On the Taihang Mountain', '在太行山上' 往事新提]. http://news.ifeng.com/mil/his tory/detail_2011_02/14/4656318_0.shtml, 14 February 2011, date accessed 10 March 2014.

103   Translation from website.

104   Cao Xinxin, 'Kangzhan gequbeihou' [Behind classic War of Resistance songs], *Xiangchao*, 2005, 30–42 曹欣欣, 抗战经典歌曲背后, 湘潮, 2005, 30–42; Anonymous, 'Zui jiehende kangzhan gequ' [War of Resistance songs which can best vent one's hatred], *Wenshi bolan*, 8 (2009), 52 佚名,最解恨的抗战歌曲, 文史博 览, 8 (2009), 52.

105   For instance, the Dadao March was adapted into a local drama in Jiangsu province in the PRC, see, 'Jinxian' in Jiangsu renmin chubanshe, *Yancheng gemin gushiji* [Revolutionary stories in Yancheng county] (Nanjing: Jiangsu renmin chubanhe, 1972) 紧铉, 江苏人民出版社, 盐城县革命故事集 (江苏人民出版社, 1972). Also, the song and the story behind the song was also carried in the newspapers, see: *Xin Nanjing Ribao*, 'Dadaoxiang guizimen detoushang kanqu' [The Dadao March 大刀向鬼子们的头上砍去], 10 May 1970. It was also sung in various mass singing activities, e.g. *Xinhua Ribao*, 'Gemin gequ geyong hui'.

106   Some scholars also noticed this, see, 'A few writers sought to raise spirits under the current, arduous situation and used this as a trigger for memories of past events.' Hong, *A history of contemporary Chinese literature*, p. 122.

107   Xu Guangyao, '"Xiaobing Zhanggao" de qiyi chushi' [Unusual birth of 'Little Social Zhangga'] in Ma Qingshan (ed.) *Feitian 60nian diancang (woyuwenxuezhuan)* [Feitian, sixty years of book reservations (volume of 'Me and literature')] (Yinchuan: Gansu wenhua chuabnshe, 2010), pp. 100–103 徐光耀, '小 兵张嘎'的奇异出世, 马青山, 飞天 60年典藏 (我与文学卷) (甘肃文化出版社, 2010), pp. 100–103.

108   Xu Guangyao, '"Xiaobing Zhanggao"'

109   Xu Guangyao, '"Xiaobing Zhanggao"'. For a similar example of Sun Li and his War of Resistance themed work 'An initial record of a stormy situation 风云初 记', see, Hong, *A history of contemporary Chinese literature,* p. 133.

110   *Renmin ribao*, 'Yierjiu sishiwu zhounian' [45th anniversary of December 9 "一 二·九" 四十五周年], 9 December 1980.

111   *Renmin Ribao*, 'Huiyi nver Yang Zhan lieshi' [Recall daughter martyr Yang Zhan 回忆女儿杨展烈士], 17 September 1978. It also reflected the official line at the time, for example, it accused Zhang Chunqiao, a member of the Gang of

Four, of being the KMT's operative and indirectly contributing to Yang Zhan's death.

112 NMA-6004-1-9: 'Nanjingshi disanjie wenxueyishu gongzuozhe daibiaodahui chouban,zhaokai qingkuang' [Issues concerning preparing and convening the third conference of art and literature workers in Nanjing 南京市第三届文学艺术工作者代表大会筹备召开情况], January 1962. For the works of Wu, see, 'Wugong duiyuan zhiqi' [The wife of a member of the armed working team 武工队员之妻].

113 Gao Xingzu, 'Cong Riben ziliao kang Rijun zai Jiangsu Changzhou diqu debaoxing' [The Japanese army's atrocities in Changzhou area, Jiangsu, from the Japanese materials], *Minguo chunqiu*, 5 (1997) 高兴祖, 从日本资料看日军在江苏常州地区的暴行, 明国春秋, 5 (1997).

114 Zhao, 'Gao Xingzu: Nanjing datusha yanjiu diyiren'.

115 Zhao, 'Gao Xingzu'. For scholarly works of Gao, see: www.nj1937.org/List.asp?ID=2577, 25 June 2013, date accessed, 10 March 2014.

116 *Zhongyang Ribao*, 'Qingsuan xuezhai, Yuangdong guojifating shenpanguan Mei Ruao jinfei Dongjing' [Straighten out blood debt: the IMTFE judge Mei Ruao flies to Tokyo today 清算血债, 远东国际军事法庭审判官 梅汝璈 今飞东京], 19 March 1946.

117 Mei Ruao, dairy entry, 4 May 1946.

118 Mei Ruao, 'About Tani Hisao, Matsui Ishine and the Nanjing Massacre'.

119 Zhang Guogong 张国功, 'Zhongguo haidei zhengqi caidui' [China still needs to try to make a good showing 中国还得争气才对]. www.gmw.cn/02blqs/2005-08/07/content_311894.htm,7 August 2005, date accessed, 10 March 2014; Mei Changzhao, 'Bofu Mei Ruao jiushi' [Past events of uncle Mei Ruao], *Jinri mingliu*, 1995, 62–69 梅长钊,伯父梅汝璈旧事,今日名流, 1995:7, 62–69; Yang Furong 楊馥戎, 'Tangdi zhuiyi dongjing shenpan muhou' [Cousin recalls the backstage of the IMTFE 堂弟追忆东京审判幕后]. http://big5.huaxia.com/zhwh/whrw/2013/04/3307087.html, 24 April 2013, date accessed, 10 March 2014.

120 See, for example, Mei Ruao, 'About Tani Hisao, Matsui Ishine and the Nanjing Massacre'. For other occasions when Mei wrote articles, see: *Xinhua Ribao*, 'Meidi shangtu bihuxijun zhanfan faxuejia Mei Ruao yanyubochi' [American imperialists still want to cover-up the criminals who conducted the biological warfare, law expert Mei Ruao claimed seriously 美帝尚图庇护细菌战犯 法学家梅汝傲 严予驳斥], 11 February 1950; 'Mei Ruao zai *Renmin Ribao* shang zhuan wen chize Meiguo baobi Riben zhanfanzuixing' [Mei Ruao wrote an article in the People's Daily criticising the US cover-up of Japanese war crimes 梅如璈在人民日报上撰文 斥责美国包庇日本战犯罪行], 10 May 1951; 'Zaishijie heping lishihui tebiehuiyishang Mei Ruao fayan fandui Meiguo wuzhuang Riben' [At the special conference of the world peace committee, Mei Ruao gave a speech against American revisionism in Japan, 在世界和平理事会特别会议上 梅汝璈发言反对美国武装日本], 7 July 1952.

121 Mei Ruao, *Yuandong junshifating* [The IMTFE] (Beijing: Falv chubanshe, 1998) 梅汝璈 远东军事法庭 (法律出版社, 1998); Yang Ziyun, 'Mei Xiaoao yanzhongde fuqin Mei Ruao' [Mei Ruao, as a father, in the eyes of Mei Xiaoao], *Jianghuai fazhi*, 3 (2006), 13–15 杨子云, 梅小璈眼中的父亲梅汝璈, 江淮法制, 3 (2006), 13–15.

122 Such as, 'A small pocket watch 一只小怀表', 'Remember brother Xu Qing 忆哥哥许晴'.

123 Laogui, *Muqin Yang Mo*.

124 Laogui, *Muqin Yang Mo*.

125 Wang Chaoguang, 'Kang Ri zhanzheng lishide yingxiangjiyi – centered around the postwar Chinese films' [Memory of the War of Resistance against Japan in films – centred on the postwar Chinese films], *Xueshu yanjiu*, 6 (2005), 91–100 汪

朝光, 抗日战争历史的影像记忆- 以战后中国电影为中心, 学术研究 6 (2005), 91–100.

126   Hong, *A history of contemporary Chinese literature*, pp. 122–123.

127   Berry, 'Speaking bitterness: history, media and nation in twentieth-century China'.

128   Besides, the 1941 report was included in a school textbook and a monument was built on the mountain peak from where the warriors jumped.

129   'Flower in May' was produced four years after the September 18th incident, to praise the anti-Japanese martyrs, criticise the capitulationist clique and ultimately call for the Chinese people's resistance.

130   *Xinhua Ribao*, 'Dongbei mudu Rikou zhizao xijun jumin fennu kongsu Riben zhanfan wanezuixing' [Residents in Northeast who witnessed Japanese bandits producing bacteria angrily accuse Japanese war criminals of their crimes 东北目睹日寇制造细菌居民 愤怒控诉日本战犯万恶罪行], 6 February 1950.

131   'Sanjin Luhuacun' [Enter Luhua village three times 三进芦花村] in Zhenjiang junfenqu zhengzhibu (ed.), *Maoshan kang Ri gushi*, 194–200.

132   NMA-6001-3-311.

133   Su, 'Tan jianguo chuqi kang Ri ticai xiaoshuo yu dianying'.

134   NMA-6001-3-311.

135   Xing Ye, '"Pingyuan youjidui" xiugaiji' [Story of revising 'The plains guerrillas'], *Bainianchao*, 5 (1999), 74–77 刑野, 平原游击队修改记, 百年潮, 5 (1999), 74–77.

136   Wu Weiman, 'Tamen yongyuan shizanminbing' [They are our militiamen forever], *Zhongguo minbing*, 8 (2005), 8–10 吴维满, 他们永远是咱民兵, 中国民兵, 8 (2005), 8–10; Yuan Chengliang, 'Dianying "didaozhan" danshengji' [The birth of the film 'Tunnel Warfare'], *Dangshi tiandi*, 2 (2006), 39–41 袁成亮, 电影地道战诞生记, 党史天地, 2 (2006), 39–41. According to Yuan, within three years the film was duplicated 2,800 times.

137   E.g. Kao Chen-Feng, 'How we fought with tunnel warfare', *China Reconstructs*, 1970: 11; Chao Shou-Fu and Yu Hua-Hu, 'National militia heroes', and 'Recollections of mine warfare', *China Reconstructs*, 1970: 9.

6   Conclusion

The Fifteen-Year War was remembered well in mainland China between 1945 and 1982. Prior to 1982, confined by the international and domestic context, central and local official authorities, unofficial agents and first-tier agents interacted to shape remembrance of the war. The origin of the problematic aspects of China's remembrance of the Fifteen-Year War lies in the pre-1982 period. During the immediate post-war period between 1945 and 1949, the Fifteen-Year War was an unavoidable subject in almost every aspect of life, from the practical side – such as reconstruction, war crimes trials, compensation claims, etc. – to the spiritual side – such as commemorating the martyrs, watching cinema films about the war and so forth. Remembrance of the war was also of great import in the PRC. Although the scale of remembrance was not as large as nowadays, it was large enough to invalidate the argument of a pre-1982 'generous amnesia'. This book has provided evidence to invalidate the three explanations which are given in the existing literature to support that argument.

Chapter 2 showed that although the CCP regime was eager for friendship with 'Japanese people' in general, and with the Japanese government during certain periods, remembrance of the Fifteen-Year War and Japanese wartime atrocities was not troublesome, thanks to the CCP regime's distinction between Japanese militarists and Japanese people. Chapter 3 indicated that despite the CCP–KMT rivalry regarding commemoration of the war's martyrs, the war and some battles fought by the KMT were remembered in most periods of the PRC (although the KMT elements became increasingly controversial after the 1960s). Chapter 4 suggested that the suffering at the hands of wartime Japan was also not a taboo topic in the pre-1982 PRC, as a victimhood narrative was useful to serve as a foil to the heroic resistance narrative and was desirable on some occasions in local communities. Chapter 5 also found that unofficial recollections of the KMT's involvement in the war were tolerated in the PRC to some extent, such as Du Yuming's article, and that a victimhood narrative existed in the realms constructed by unofficial agents, such as speeches delivered in 'speaking bitterness' activities.

In the PRC, remembrance of the Fifteen-Year War was affected by the CCP regime's changing relations with other foreign powers. For instance, when Sino–Japanese inter-governmental relations were bad, Japanese militarist-bashing activities were intensified; after the Sino–Soviet split, the CCP regime started putting a greater emphasis on the Chinese people's role in winning the War of Resistance. The nature of the international environment between 1949 and 1982, such as the rise of the international anti-imperialist movement and the Cold War in East Asia, also influenced the PRC's remembrance of the war. Parallel to this, war remembrance was also affected by the PRC's domestic situation. The most vital influential domestic event was the Cultural Revolution, during which glorification of martyrs, commemoration of the war on memorial days, presentation of the war in textbooks and museums, and relating of the war by artists, scholars and grassroots testifiers was seriously interrupted. Nevertheless, the core of the war remembrance itself stayed relatively intact from between 1949 and 1982, and both the central as well as local CCP authorities, non-official social agents and individuals who told their wartime stories on private occasions (first-tier agents) were the custodians of that remembrance.

The discussion of the main body of this book was largely from the perspective of the central and local CCP authorities. The CCP regime's mature stance as to how to remember the Fifteen-Year War in its diplomatic conduct towards Japan was that remembering the war was a condition for developing friendship with Japan. Accordingly, the regime launched numerous Japanese militarist-bashing activities whenever the Sino–Japanese inter-governmental relationship was bad and was not shy to raise the topic of the war when the relationship was good (Chapter 2). Also, because the central CCP regime *had to* (Chapter 3) and *wanted to* (Chapter 4) embrace remembrance of the war it organised numerous remembrance activities, such as honouring its martyrs in the Babaoshan Revolutionary Cemetery, and presenting the war in its national history museums. The essence of the war remembrance promoted by the central CCP regime was of a tragic-heroic resistance that took place under the CCP's leadership.

Moreover, for the CCP regime, Fifteen-Year-War remembrance was a valuable resource for constructing the PRC's national past and ultimately the PRC's present national identity.[1] For instance, the practice of denouncing Westerners and praising the Soviet Union's performance in the war was used to nurture a socialist identity in the PRC. Moreover, the wartime period was not only indispensable in school history textbooks, but also when introducing a city's or a person's 'life story'. Although, most of the time, the war was treated as just one part of the CCP's history or of China's revolutionary history in these national realms of war or other symbols, it was no doubt the most essential part, as all the war memorial days, as well as the national anthem, were related to it.

Nanjing was used as an example to illustrate the local dimension of the PRC's remembrance of the Fifteen-Year War. In general, the local CCP authorities were extensions of the centre, in terms of the various war remembrance activities initiated by the latter. For instance, the Japanese militarist-bashing campaigns launched by the centre took place in every corner of the PRC, and local museums adapted the national museums' narrative of the war. In terms of the content of the local memory, which was especially dealt with in Chapter 4, the remembrance of places that were not directly involved in the war was more or less the same as the national remembrance of the war. However, in places directly involved, it was the local wartime memories that thrived the most, as long as these memories were not contradictory to the national memory. Some of the distinctive local memories were drawn into the national narrative of the war and became known nationwide, such as the memory of *wanrenken* and the memory of tunnel warfare.

The perspective of non-official agents also runs throughout the book (e.g. the families as well as comrades-in-arms of the Fifteen-Year War martyrs who publicised the martyrs' deeds in order to get them recognised), and was especially dealt with in Chapter 5. These non-official agents, inwardly motivated by several factors, also played an important role in shaping the PRC's remembrance of the war, and their activities of relating the war were supported and facilitated by the regime. Such remembrance was much more detailed, emotional and colourful than that constructed by the state.

The voices of first-tier agents have occasionally emerged in the book as well (although they were not dealt with extensively). Not being subject to public scrutiny, first-tier agents' remembrance was very diverse and personal. For example, one of my interviewees, who was born in Langzhong, was a survivor of the devastating Langzhong air raid. Nevertheless, what he told me about was not how brutal the Japanese air force was, but his lucky experience as a three-month-old baby: he was left by his parents alone (they having fled to the countryside) in bed during the air raid; nevertheless, he survived, while many people, houses nearby and even the gate of his home was destroyed by the bombs. Another interviewee, whose mother was born in a little village in Yixing, Jiangsu Province, related his mother's story: Japanese soldiers once came to her village and asked for eggs, chickens and women. The villagers resented these soldiers very much. However, his mother, who was a little girl at the time, did not. This was because the chicken in her household was not confiscated (it flew away) and the soldiers gave her some sweets. Other interviewees also told stories of Japanese soldiers who were kind to children.[2]

Occasionally, the wartime episodes, the recounting of which was not socially encouraged at the time, were passed down to the next generation through these first-tier agents, such as the experience of fleeing in a cowardly way (without offering any resistance at all), the rumours about women who were raped by the Japanese soldiers and bore their children, as well as affection for some Japanese soldiers who treated Chinese children well.[3]

To what extent did the Chinese people accept the war remembrance articulated by the agents? Answering this question would involve empirical research that is beyond the scope of this book, and which would also be hugely challenging to undertake. Still, I assume that most of the war remembrance produced by the state, unofficial social agents and first-tier agents was accepted among Chinese people, based on the responses from my interviewees to the question: Did you experience any artistic activities related to the Fifteen-Year War before 1982? Most of them had enjoyed Fifteen-Year-War themed arts during the period. Reading stories in the *xiaoren shu* (小人书 a kind of book for children) was commonplace. At the time, children liked to spend time in book rental stores, where they would read these kinds of books to kill time.[4] After watching films about the war, discussing their plots was also commonplace. Boys even played variations of a game called 'beating the devils' after seeing such war films as *The Little Soldier Zhangga* and *The Letter With Feathers.* [5] Moreover, the interviewees could clearly remember singing the resistance songs, like 'The Dadao March' and 'On Songhua River', in their music classes or on other occasions.[6] Some could not stop themselves singing them during the interviews. One story, 'Little Hero Yulai' (小英雄雨来), which was also included in several textbooks published between 1949 and 1982, was often mentioned by many interviewees.[7]

Nevertheless, Chinese people accepted the memories articulated by the official, non-official and first-tier agents differently. As a result, although situated in a similar context – that of the Communist PRC – one citizen's remembrance would not be the same as another's. For people who did not have first-hand wartime experience, their memory of the Fifteen-Year War relied on the contents of the secondary memories that they received. Different people received different combinations of secondary memories of the war, depending on their education levels (e.g. those who were unable to attend school might not be able to learn about the war as presented in the text-books), locations (e.g. people who lived in rural areas had less chance to attend exhibitions related to the war), and accidental aspects (e.g. a novel would normally have more detailed descriptions of Japanese atrocities than a film version of the same story, so those who read the novel might have a more vivid idea of enemy atrocities than those who saw the movie). On the other hand, the memories of people who experienced the war would overlap with memories articulated by other agents. How these people remember the war in the PRC era would depend on the content of their first-hand memory as well as the secondary memory of the war they received, and on the process of the 'overlapping'.

How was the Fifteen-Year War remembered in China and how did this remembrance evolve before the 1982 Textbook Incident? What was the relationship between national and local war remembrance activities before 1982? How did the official and non-official agents interact with each other to shape remembrance of the war before 1982?

Overall, remembrance of the Fifteen-Year War was prevalent in China before 1982. However, in the PRC, as the war was remembered differently from person to person and from place to place, the compromised term 'collective remembrance' is still too general to describe how the war was remembered. Nevertheless, although the content of the war memory was various it was not conflicted and it could be unified under several major tags: the memory of heroic resistance, the memory of suffering at the hands of the Japanese invaders, and non-mainstream memories (such as Emperor Puyi's recollections about his collaboration with the Japanese and several memories articulated by first-tier agents). This was because, generally speaking, Chinese people's wartime experience, as well as their way of viewing the war – that it was a war of resistance against the oppression imposed by a foreign invader – were ultimately similar.

In the PRC, although the external and internal atmosphere had an impact on remembrance of the Fifteen-Year War, the core part of the war memory actually did not evolve that much. The core part of the national memory promoted by the central CCP regime, as reflected in school history textbooks and national history museums, was a series of wartime events that justified the its leadership during the war. The core part of the war memory in localities was the national memory plus those memories that thrived in the local areas; and the core part of an individual's war memories was the superimposition of the national, local and individual memory, as I argued previously. As long as it was in harmony with the national memory, the local wartime experience could be remembered without being suppressed from above. But local memories also formed the foundation of the national memories. In terms of the interaction between official and non-official agents in shaping the Fifteen-Year War memory in the PRC, the latter were confined, but were generally supported by the former, and offset the former's insufficiencies (i.e. lack of details, of emotional content, and so forth).

The CCP-sponsored patriotic campaigns around 1982 indeed contributed to making Chinese war remembrance more problematic. These patriotic campaigns have made the Fifteen-Year War, and especially the War of Resistance period, further stand out as the most profound conflict in Chinese contemporary history, mainly because 'in this war China could claim its first complete victory against foreign invaders'. At the same time, a sense of Chinese victimhood was explicitly promoted by these campaigns;[8] thus they have contributed to make the war an even more distorted symbol of an extremely heroic, yet at the same time miserable, past.

Nevertheless, these patriotic campaigns were not the progenitors of problematic aspects of Chinese war remembrance (exaggerating the heroic resistance and the prevalence of the victimhood narrative), which was formed through the joint efforts of the CCP central and local authorities, unofficial agents and ordinary Chinese people before 1982. The PRC's war remembrance after 1982 is a relatively natural continuation of that before 1982. The Fifteen-Year War was an issue in China's relations with Japan before 1982 and has continued to be thereafter. In the domestic sphere, for instance, Imperial Japan was referred to as one of the foreign evils in the class education that took place during the Maoist period, and then it became a villain in the patriotic education sponsored by Mao's successors. We can see a striking similarity between class education and patriotic education: Japan, as a member of the group of former imperialists, has always been a convenient and shared 'other' that can be blamed whenever there is a split in the PRC and whenever the regime wants to bring other former KMT personnel and other 'problematic' classes under the same umbrellla.

* * *

In 1972, Tada's wish to achieve a true Sino–Japanese reconciliation through the apology by Prime Minister Tanaka as a representative of Japanese people in the Sino–Japanese negotiations was doomed from the start. This is because the difference between the Chinese and Japanese in terms of remembrance of the Fifteen-Year War at the time made it impossible for the two countries to reach an agreement on the sincerity of that apology. The Chinese remembered the war well, not only as a heroic national victory, but also as a time of suffering imposed on them by Imperial Japan. The latter remembrance was particularly prevalent around the negotiation period, as the militarist-bashing campaign was carried out until July 1972. As regards the Japanese side, generally, apart from some progressives, the war remembrance of most Japanese people – including those ordinary people who suffered from historical amnesia, those who had an inward-looking victim mentality, and those nationalists or revisionists – was problematic for the Chinese. At the time of the 1972 negotiations, according to Tada, there was a tendency in Japan to disrespect or downplay the meaning of the Fifteen-Year War, and, due to the country's economic success, that part of its population who were only interested in their own private lives, or did not know much about the war, or did not feel responsibility for it, had increased.

In such a context, how could Tanaka, as a head of a conservative government and representative of the majority of Japanese people, wholeheartedly make an apology that satisfied the Chinese side? Furthermore, it was difficult for the Chinese to genuinely accept Tanaka's 'insincere apology' (by Chinese standards) and the Japanese way of remembering the war, which was illustrated by the confrontation with the Japanese delegation over the problematic phrase 'causing trouble'.

If it is not managed appropriately, or if it is manipulated, the differences between the Chinese and Japanese war remembrance can escalate into clashes. A 'clash' may take the form of an emotional outburst or a diplomatic conflict, and may be on an individual or a national level. These outbursts can be destructive when the history problem is combined with other current bilateral conflicts, which has become a routine phenomenon. For example, the Chinese protest over Japan's wish to purchase the disputed Diaoyu/Senkaku Islands in July 2012, escalated twice that year: around August 15th (the anniversary of the end of the Fifteen-Year War in 1945) and September 18th (the anniversary of Japan's invasion of Manchuria in 1931).

The confrontation over the phrase 'causing trouble' was one such clash. There were similar clashes before the 1972 negotiations, such as the Chinese cadres' discomfort when their Japanese guests casually used words like '*shina*'.

The 1972 normalisation failed to lead to a Sino–Japanese post-war reconciliation mainly because the negotiations did not truly deal with the difference between the two countries' war remembrance, but rather shelved it for pragmatic reasons. Furthermore, the 1972 normalisation signalled the gradual ending of the Cold War structure in East Asia. Similarly to Europe, the Cold War not only split East Asia into two camps, but also blocked a 'shared war memory' in the region, as each nation had independently developed its own version of war memory. Thus, liberated from Cold War politics, the encounters between Chinese and Japanese war remembrance, previously confined within national borders, have grown significantly since 1972.[9] However, this defrosting process of war remembrance, unlike that of their Eastern and Western European counterparts, has led to increasing clashes between China and Japan, due to a lack of effective initiatives to narrow the gap between the two war remembrances, as well as several deliberate manipulations by the governments of the two countries.

Thus, these conflicts continued to occur after 1972, and much more frequently; examples are the Chinese criticism of the revisionist moves carried out by the Japanese organisation *Seirankai* in 1974; the Textbook Incident in 1982; the controversy centred around Prime Minister Nakasone's first official visit to the Yasukuni Shrine in 1985, and so forth. For the Chinese side, the 1982 Textbook Incident was just like any clash in earlier periods. The Chinese media continued to insist on the distinction between the good Japanese and bad militarists/revisionists, and was not willing to escalate the incident. For instance, there were newspaper stories that talked about how some good Japanese visitors in Nanjing had criticised a handful of people in the Ministry of Education for causing the Textbook Incident, and that most Japanese did not agree with the latter's action.[10] It was the 1985 Yasukuni Shrine controversy that changed the nature of the development of the Sino–Japanese history problem. This was because, according to Kosuge, an official visit to a place that was dedicated to worshipping Japanese war criminals by the head of the Japanese state who was elected by the majority of Japanese people severely challenged the foundation of the CCP regime's post-war conduct towards Japan – the distinction between a handful of Japanese militarists and the majority of the Japanese people.[11]

Is there any method that can solve the Sino–Japanese history problem – that is, avoid the confrontation between Chinese and Japanese war remembrance? The mutual misunderstandings between the two countries, as I mentioned in the Preface, make any resolution of these problems extremely complicated. Thus, the first step to solving the history problem is, in my opinion, to narrow this gap in the two countries' perceptions: to understand correctly the true situation regarding the history problem in China and Japan, and especially to understand objectively how the problem was formed. As Fujiwara commented:

the issue here is not to decide which way of remembering the war is right, but to calmly make sure what is the war memory which is considered by each party concerned as normal, to what extent the behaviours based on this war memory are constrained historically, and to what extent these behaviours are different from each other. It is because disputes reflecting bias are arising everywhere after confronting different ways of remembering the war that it is necessary to look at the origins of these memories objectively.[12]

Indeed, clashing is not necessarily a bad thing: it could be a golden opportunity for the two countries to face up to the problems of their war remembrance and to tackle these problems together. Unfortunately, China and Japan have missed several such opportunities, and they have made the problems even more intense throughout the post-war period. If the Chinese and Japanese had tried to calmly look at each other's war remembrance and to understand the historical context in which this remembrance was formed, then the wartime history would not have been the cause of such problems between the two countries. This book's contribution to solving the history problem thus lies in its examination and presentation of the historical settings that nurtured the Chinese and Japanese remembrance of the war.

Notes

1 For the connection between a nation's past and its present identity, see, Dittmer and Kim, *China's quest for national identity*; Ann Low-Beer, *School history, national history and the issue of national identity* (Birmingham: University of Birmingham, 2003); Dennis Walder, 'Literature, memory and nation', in Clive Emsley (ed.), *War, culture and memory* (Buckingham: The Open University, 2003).
2 Interview, Chen and Chen's wife, Nanjing Massacre Memorial, 13 May 2012.
3 Interview, Duan.
4 Interview, Zhang and Luo; Interview, Lv.
5 Interview, Zuo, Nanjing Massacre Memorial, 13 May 2012.
6 Interview, Mu, Nanjing University Sports Ground, 8 May 2012. Mu learned how to sing 'Yellow River Cantata' and 'On Songhu River' and 'Dadao March' in the music class. Interview, Zhang and Luo.
7 See, 'Xiaoyingxiong Yulai' [Little Hero Yulai 小英雄雨来] in Beijingshifan daxue zhongwenxi putong jiaoyu gaige xiaozu (ed.), *Yuwen dibace* [Chinese volume 8] (Renmin jiaoyu chubanshe, 1960), pp. 90–98 北京师范大学中文系普通教育改革小组,语文第八册 (人民教育出版社出版, 1960).
8 He Yinan, 'Remembering and forgetting the war', p. 58.
9 S. M. Jager and R. Mitter, *Ruptured histories: war, memory, and the post-Cold War in Asia* (Cambridge, MA: Harvard University Press, 2007), p. 2. The book argues that the Cold War was not ended in 1989 in East Asia; the 'post-Cold War … was 'a particular historical process that occurred with the definitive end of a bifurcated Asia' after 1972 when China and Japan normalised their relationship.
10 See, for example, *Nanjing Ribao*, 'Zai Ning lvyoude bufen Riben youke zhize Riben wenbusheng cuangai qinhua lishi' [Some Japanese visitors in Nanjing accuse Japanese Ministry of Education, Science and Culture (MESC) of distorting history of invading China 在宁旅游的部分日本游客 指责日本文部省篡改侵华历史], 12 August 1982; 'Ribao yaoqiu wenbusheng qingtingguoji shang piping' [Japanese

newspaper asks the MESC to listen to the international criticisms 日报要求文部省倾听国际上批判], 27 July 1982.

11 Kosuge, Sengo wakai.
12 Fujiwara, *Sensou wo kioku*, p. 39.

Bibliography

Primary sources

Archival materials

Nanjing Municipal Archives, PRC

NMA-5003, files of the Nanjing Municipal Government.
NMA-5012, files of the Nanjing Municipal Bureau of Civil Affairs.
NMA-5063, files of the Nanjing Municipal Bureau of Culture.
NMA-6002, files of the Communist Youth League Committee of Nanjing.
NMA-6001, files of the Nanjing Municipal Federation of Trade Unions.
NMA-6004, files of the Nanjing Municipal Federation of Literary and Art Circles.
NMA-9080, files relating to the Yuhuatai Martyrs' Cemetery in Nanjing.

Jiangsu Provincial Archives, PRC

JPA-4007, files of the Jiangsu Provincial Department of Civil Affairs.

Central Archives, PRC

Files relating to the national anthem and the Revolutionary Museum of the PRC.

The National Archives, UK

Files relating to foreigners' cemeteries in Shanghai.

Hiroshima Municipal Archives, Japan

Files relating to the August 6 commemoration in Hiroshima.

National Archives Administration, Taiwan

Files relating to the Fifteen-Year-War commemoration in Taiwan.

NHK's War Testimony Archives

www.nhk.or.jp/shogenarchives/kioku/, date accessed, 10 March 2014.

Newspapers

Asahi Shinbun, Tokyo, Japan.
Nanjing Ribao, Nanjing, PRC.
Renmin Ribao, Beijing, PRC.
Xin Nanjing Ribao, Nanjing, PRC.
Xinhua Ribao, Nanjing, PRC.
Yomiuri Shinbun, Tokyo, Japan.
Zhongyang Ribao, Nanjing, ROC.

Journals

China Pictorial, Beijing, PRC.
China Reconstructs, Beijing, PRC.

Interviews

Interview, Chen and Chen's wife, Nanjing Massacre Memorial, 13 May 2012.
Interview, Duan, Nanjing Massacre Memorial Hall, 13 May 2012.
Telephone interview, Duan (a participating student of the Nanda research project), 24 July 2013.
Interview, Liu, Liu's office in the Nanjing Massacre Memorial, 11 June 2012.
Interview, Lv (born in Langzhong in 1941, moved to Nanjing in 1961), Gulou Park, 12 May 2012.
Interview, Mu, Nanjing University Sports Ground, 8 May 2012.
Interview, Sun, Sun's home in Nanjing, 22 June 2012.
Interview, Wang, Nanjing Municipal Library, 30 June 2012.
Interview, Yu, Nanjing Municipal Archives, 19 June 2012.
Interview, Zhang, Zhang's office in Nanjing, 21 June 2012.
Interview, Zhang and Luo (husband born in 1957 and wife born in 1958, Nanjing), Nanjing Municipal Library, 30 June 2012.
Interview, Zhu (born in Nanjing in 1957), Gulou Park, 12 May 2012.
Interview, Zuo, Nanjing Massacre Memorial, 13 May 2012.

School history and Chinese language textbooks

Beijingshifan daxue zhongwenxi putong jiaoyu gaige xiaozu (ed.), *Yuwen dibace* [Chinese, volume 8] (Renmin jiaoyu chubanshe, 1960) 北京师范大学中文系普通教育改革小组,语文第八册 (人民教育出版社出版, 1960).
Beijing shifan daxue zhongwenxi putongjiaoyu gaige xiaozu (ed.), *Yuwen dijiuce* [Chinese, volume 9] (Renmin jiaoyu chubanshe, 1960) 北京师范大学中文系普通教育改革小组编, 语文第九册 (人民教育出版社出版, 1960).
Beijing shifan daxue zhongwenxi putongjiaoyu gaige xiaozu (ed.), *Yuwen dishice* [Chinese, volume 10] (Renmin jiaoyu chubanshe, 1960) 北京师范大学中文系普通教育改革小组编, 语文第十册 (人民教育出版社出版, 1960).
Beijingshi jiaoyuju zhongxiaoxue jiaocai bianshenchu, *Beijingshi gaojixiaoxue shiyongkeben Lishi xiace* [Beijing municipal senior primary school trial textbook, history, volume 2 (Beijing chubanshe, 1961) 北京市教育局中小学教材编审处, 北京市高级小学试用课本 历史 下册 北京出版社出版, 1961.

Beijingshi jiaoyuju zhongxiaoxue jiaocai bianxiezu (ed.), *Beijingshi zhongxue keben yuwen diqice* [Beijing municipal school textbook, Chinese, volume 7] (Beijing: Beijing Renmin Chubanshe, 1972) 北京市教育局中小学教材编写组, 北京市中学课本语文 第七册 (北京人民出版社出版, 1972).

Beijingshi jiaoyuju jiaocai bianxiezu, *Beijingshi zhongxue shiyong keben lishi disance shangce* [Beijing municipal high school trial textbook, history, volume 3, issue 1] (Renmin jiaoyu chubanshe, 1973) 北京市教育局教材编写组,北京市中学试用课本历史第三册 (上册) (人民教育出版社, 1973).

Liaoningsheng zhongxiao xue jiaocai bianxiezu, *Liaoning sheng zhongxue shiyong keben Zhongguo lishi xiandaibufen* [Liaoning Provincial High School trial textbook, Chinese history, contemporary part] (Liaoning renmin chubanshe, 1977) 辽宁省中小学教材编写组, 辽宁省中学试用课本 中国历史 现代部分(辽宁人民出版社, 1977).

Ma, Jingwu and Li, Gengxu, *Gaoji xiaoxue keben lishi disice* [Senior primary school textbook, history, volume 4] (Renmin jiaoyu chubanshe, 1957) 马精武 李赓序, 高级小学课本 历史 第四册 (人民教育出版社出版, 1957).

Renminjiaoyu chubanshe (ed.), *Chujizhongxue yuwen dierce* [Middle school Chinese textbook volume 2] (Renmin jiaoyu chubanshe, 1952), pp. 122–126 初级中学语文课本 第二册 (人民教育出版社编辑出版, 1952).

Renmenjiaoyu chubanshe (ed.), *Chujizhongxue Yuwen keben diyice* [Middle school Chinese textbook volume 1] (Renmin jiaoyu chubanshe, 1953), pp. 48–54 初级中学语文课本 第一册 (人民教育出版社编辑出版, 1953).

Renminjiaoyu chubanshe (ed.), *Chujizhongxue yuwen disice* [Middle school Chinese volume 4] (Renmin jiaoyu chubanshe, 1955, 7th edn) 初级中学语文课本 第四册 (人民教育出版社编辑出版, 1955 第七版 [1952第一版]).

Renming jiaoyu chubanshe, *Gaoji zhongxue keben shijie jindai xiandaishi xiace* [Senior high school textbook, world modern and contemporary history, volume 2] (Renmin jiaoyu chubanshe, 1958) 人民教育出版社, 高级中学课本 世界近代现代史 下册 (人民教育出版社, 1958).

Renminjiaoyu chubanshe, *chujizhongxue keben zhongguo lishi disice jiaoxue cankaoshu* [Junior high school textbook, Chinese history, volume 4, teaching reference book] (Renmin jiaoyu chubanshe, 1959), 人民教育出版社, 初级中学课本 中国历史 第四册 教学参考书 (人民教育出版社, 1959).

Renminjiaoyu chubanshe, *Gaoji zhongxue keben zhongguo xiandaishi* [Senior high school textbook, Chinese contemporary history] (Renmin jiaoyu chubanshe, 1960) 人民教育出版社, 高级中学课本 中国现代史 (人民教育出版社, 1960).

Renminjiaoyu chubanshe, *Gaoji zhongxue keben zhongguo xiandaishi* [Senior high school textbook, Chinese contemporary history] (Renmin jiaoyu chubanshe, 1964, 3rd edn) 人民教育出版社, 高级中学课本 中国现代史 (人民教育出版社, 1964).

Shanghai jiaoyu chubanshe, *Gaozhong zhongguo xiandaishi jiaoxue cankaoshu xiace* [Senior high school Chinese contemporary history teaching reference book, volume 2] (Shanghai jiaoyu chubanshe, 1960) 上海教育出版社, 高中中国现代史 教学参考书 下册 (上海教育出版社, 1960第一版).

Wang, Shisan, Han, Shutian, et al., *Chuzhong guowen diliuce* [Middle school Chinese volume 6] (Xinhua shudian, 1980, 3rd edn) 王食三,韩书田等, 初中国文 第六册 (新华书店出版, 1950. 8.三版).

Wang, Yi and Xu, Yishi, *Guoyu cidian disice* [A Chinese dictionary, volume 4] (Beijing: Shangwu yinshuguan, 1948) 汪怡, 徐一士等编, 国语辞典 第4册 (商务印书馆, 1948).

Yao, Yongbin and Su, Shoutong, *Chujizhongxue zhongguo lishi disice* [Junior high school textbook, Chinese history, volume 4] (Renmin jiaoyu chubanshe, 1956) 姚涌彬 苏寿桐, 初级中学课本 中国历史 第四册 (人民教育出版社, 1956).

Yao, Yongbin and Su, Shoutong, *Chujizhongxue zhongguo lishi disice* [Junior high school textbook, Chinese history, volume 4] (Renmin jiaoyu chubanshe, 1963, 7th edn) 姚涌彬 苏寿桐, 初级中学课本 中国历史 第四册 (人民教育出版社, 1963).

Publications relating to Fifteen-Year-War themed arts and research

History Department, Nanjing University (ed.), *Riben diguozhuyi zai Nanjing de datusha* [The Japanese Imperialists' Massacre in Nanjing] (A restricted publication, 1979 edn) 南京大学历史系, 日本帝国主义在南京的大屠杀 (内部刊物, 1979).

Jiangsu renminchubanshe, *Yancheng gemin gushiji* [Revolutionary stories in Yancheng county] (Nanjing: Jiangsu renmin chubanhe, 1972) 江苏人民出版社, 盐城县革命故事集 (江苏人民出版社, 1972).

Jiangsusheng minjian wenxue yanjiuhui, *Jiangsu gemin geyao* [Jiangsu revolution songs] (Nanjing: Jiangsu renmin chubanshe, 1965) 江苏省民间文学研究会, 江苏革命歌谣 (江苏人民出版社, 1965).

Jiangsusheng minjian wenxue yanjiu hui (ed.), *Youle renma haoshuohua* [It would be easier if we had troops] (Nanjing: Jiangsu renmin chubanshe, 1965) 江苏省民间文学研究会编, 有了人马好说话 (江苏人民出版社, 1965).

Jiangsusheng wenlian ziliaoshi, *Jiangsu geming genjudi wenyiziliao huibian* (Internally circulated, 1983) 江苏省文联资料室编, 江苏革命根据地文艺资料汇编 (内部发行, 1983).

Jiefangjun Gequ xuanji bianji bu, *Kang Ri Zhanzheng gequ xuanji (1–4)* [Selection of songs of the War of Resistance, vols 1–4)] (Beijing: Zhongguo qingnian chubanshe, 1957) 解放军歌曲选集编辑部, 抗日战争歌曲选集1–4 (中国青年出版社, 1957).

Kangri yingxiong gushixuan [Selective stories of anti-Japanese heroes] (Baoding: Baoding diqu renmin chubanshe, 1959) 保定地区人民出版社编辑出版, 抗日英雄故事选, 1959.

Li, Guangtao, *Huaiyin bashier lieshi* [Eighty-two martyrs in Huaiyin] (Nanjing: Jiangsu renmin chubanshe, 1960) 李广涛,淮阴 八十二烈士 (江苏人民出版社, 1960).

Liao, Rongbiao and Zhang, Fan, *Kangri defenghuo* [The flame of resisting the Japanese] (Beijing: Zhongguo qingnian chubanshe, 1958) 廖荣标, 张藩, 抗日的烽火 (中国青年出版社, 1958).

Liaoning, Jilin, Heilongjiang,Yanbian renmin chubanshe lianhe bianji, *Dongbei renmin kang Ri geyao xuan* [Selection of northeastern people's anti-Japanese songs] (Liaoning, Jilin, Heilongjiang: Yanbian renmin chubanshe lianhe bianji, 1959) 辽宁, 吉林,黑龙江, 延边人民出版社联合 编辑出版, 东北人民抗日歌谣选, 1959.

Nanjingshi wenhuaju chuangzuozu, *Yuhuatai geming lieshi gushi* [Revolutionary martyrs' story in Yuhuatai] (Nanjing: Jiangsu renmin chubanshe, 1978) 南京市文化局创作组, 雨花台革命烈士故事 (江苏人民出版社, 1978).

Ren, Gong, *Yang Jingyu degushi* [Yang Jingyu's story] (Shanghai: Shanghai renmin chubanshe, 1977) 任功, 杨靖宇的故事 (上海人民出版社, 1977).

Shanghai shifan daxue lishixi Zhongguo xiandaishi jiaoyanshi ziliaoshi, *Zhongguo xiandaishi ziliao xuanji disance (shang, zhong, xia) Kang Ri zhanzheng shiqi* [Selection of materials on contemporary Chinese history, volume 3 (1–3), War of Resistance period] (Shanghai shifan daxue lishixi zhongguo xiandaishi jiaoyanshi ziliaoshi, 1978) 上海师范大学历史系中国现代史教研室资料室 编印, 中国现代史资料选辑 第三册 (上,中,下 抗日战争时期, 1978).

Shanghai wenhua chubanshe, *Geming lishi douzheng gushiji* [Collection of stories of struggles in revolutionary history] (Shanghai: Shanghai wenhua chubanshe, 1965) 上海文化出版社出版编辑, 革命历史斗争故事集, 1965.

Shanghai wenyi chubanshe, *Kangzhan geyao* [War of Resistance songs] (Shanghai: Shanghai wenyi chubanshe, 1960) 上海文艺出版社, 抗日歌谣 (上海文艺出版社, 1960).

Shi, Ying, *Ji Hongchang* (Tianjing: Tianjing renmin chubanshe, 1978) (1st edn 1960), 石英, 吉鸿昌 (天津人民出版社, 1978).

Tonghua zhuanyuan gongshu wenjiao weisheng bangongshi, *Chang baishan kang Ri gushi* [Anti-Japanese stories from Changbai mountain] (Jilin renmin chubanshe, 1964) 通化专员公署文教卫生办公室编,长白山抗日故事 (吉林人民出版社出版, 1964).

Wang, Jinbao and Qi, Zhaolin, *Changbaishan kang Ri lianjun geyao* [Songs of Changbhai Mountain's United Anti-Japanese Army] (Shanghai: Shanghai wenyi chubanshe, 1959) 王金宝, 齐兆麟,长白山抗日联军歌谣 (上海文艺出版社, 1959).

Xiao, Hai, *Zhandou zai zhedong* [Fighting in the east of Zhejiang province] (Hangzhou: Zhejiang renmin chubanshe, 1959) 啸海, 战斗在浙东 (浙江人民出版社出版, 1959).

Yinyue chubanshe bianjibu, *Kangzhan gequ xuan* [Selection of War of Resistance songs] (Beijing: Yinyue chubanshe, 1958) 音乐出版社编辑部, 抗战歌曲选 (音乐出版社, 1958).

Zhenjiang junfenqu zhengzhibu, *Maoshan kang Ri douzheng gushi* [Stories of anti-Japanese struggles in Maoshan] (Nanjing: Jiangsu renmin chubanshe, 1979) 镇江军分区政治部编, 茅山抗日斗争故事 (江苏人民出版社, 1979).

Zhongguo kexueyuan jiangsu fenyuan wenxueyanjiusuo, *Jiangsu minge cankao* [Jiangsu folksong reference book] (Nanjing: Zhongguo kexueyuan Jiangsu fenyuan wenxueyan jiusuo, 1958) 中国科学院江苏分院文学研究所编印, 江苏民歌参考资料 (中国科学院江苏分院文学研究所, 1958).

Zhongguo minjian gequ jicheng 'Jiangsu juan' bianjiweiyuanhui, *Zhongguo minjian gequ jicheng jiangsujuan (1–5)* [Chinese folksongs compendium, Jiangsu, vols 1–5] (Nanjing: Zhongguo minjian gequ jicheng 'Jiangsu juan' bianjiweiyuanhui, 1982) 中国民国歌曲集成《江苏卷》编辑委员会 编印, 中国民间歌曲集成 江苏卷 (1–5), 1982.

Zhongguo yinyuejia xiehui Jiangsu fenhui, *Kang ri zhanzheng gequ xuan* [Selection of War of Resistance songs] (Nanjing: Jiangsu renmin chubanshe, 1965) 中国音乐家协会江苏分会编,抗日战争歌曲选 (江苏人民出版社出版, 1965).

Zhongyang yinyue xueyuan yanjiubu, *Zhongguo gemin minge xuan* [Selection of Chinese revolutionary folksongs] (Shanghai: Yanye shudian, 1953) 中央音乐学院研究部, 中国革命民歌选 (万页书店, 1953).

Secondary materials

Anonymous, 'Rokoukyou kengaku imawa heiwa sonomono' [Trip to Marco Polo Bridge 盧溝橋見學 今は平和そのもの], *Yomiuri Shinbun*, 25 September 1972.

Anonymous, 'Zui jiehende kangzhan gequ' [War of Resistance songs which can most vent one's hatred], *Wenshi bolan*, 8 (2009), 52 佚名,最解恨的抗战歌曲, 文史博览, 2009:8, 52.

Anonymous, 'Hongse qingchunde jiyi bianqian – "qingchun zhige" chuangzuo, ying-xiang shihua' [The evolution of the memory of the Red Youth – history of creating 'Song of Youth' and its influence 红色青春的记忆变迁 – 《青春之歌》创作、影响史话]. www.chinawriter.com.cn/2011/2011-04-21/96633.html, 21 April 2011, date accessed, 10 March 2014.

Anonymous, 'Beitong didao fangdu canan' [Tragedy of defending against chemical weaons in Beitong tunnel 北瞳地道防毒惨案]. www.zainanlu.com/a/zhanzhengza inan/feichangguiwuqi/huaxuewuqi/642.html, 22 November 20111, date accessed, 10 March 2014.

Anonymous, 'Ba Qingzheng 巴清正'. http://lov.vac.gov.tw/Protection/Content.aspx?i= 151&c=5&e=&p=8, date unknown, date accessed, 9 March 2014.

Anonymous, 'Ba Qingzheng Jinianguan' [Ba Qingzheng Memorial 巴清正纪念馆]. http://cn.netor.com/m/box201005/m104949.asp, 17 May 2010, date accessed, 8 March 2014.

Anonymous, *Jiangsusheng difangzhi* [Gazetteer of Jiangsu Province 江苏省地方志]. www.jssdfz.com/, date unknown, date accessed, 9 March 2014.

Anonymous, 'Nanjing datusha cengshi yanjiu jinqu beizhongguo chedi yiwang 35 nian' [The Nanjing Massacre used to be the academic forbidden zone, and had been completely forgotten in China for 35 years 南京大屠杀曾是研究禁区 被中国彻底遗忘35年]. www.hottx.net/history/lsmw/201012/73592.html, 13 December 2010, date accessed, 10 March 2014.

Anonymous, 'Sanshinian,youyide jianzheng – Hangzhou Qifu youhao sanshi zhou-nian' [30 years, witness of frierndship – Hangzhou and Gifu establish friendship for 30 years 30年,友谊的见证 – 杭州岐阜缔结友好30周年]. http://z.hangzhou. com.cn/ 09yhszfh/content/2009-10/14/content_2825432.htm, 14 October 2009, date accessed, 8 March 2014.

Anonymous, 'Watashi to Chuugoku' [Me and China 私と中国]. http://homepage3. nifty.com/harakicindexotolith/dexchugoku.html#ryokou, 26 March 2006, date accessed, 10 March 2014.

Anonymous, 'Woguo sheli Zhongguorenmin kangRizhanzheng shengli jinianri he Nanjing datusha sinanzhe goujia gongjiri' [China set up the National Memorial Day of the Victory in the Chinese Peoples's War of Resistance against Japanese Aggression and the National Public Memorial Day for the Victims of the Nanjing Massacre 我国设立中国人民抗日战争胜利纪念日和南京大屠杀死难者国家公祭日 2014年02月27日]. www.gov.cn/jrzg/2014-02/27/content_2624727.htm, 27 February 2014, date accessed, 22 August 2016.

Askew, David, 'Westerners in Occupied Nanking: December 1937 to February 1938', in Bob T. Wakabayashi (ed.), *The Nanking Atrocity 1937–1938. Complicating the Picture* (Oxford, New York: Berghahn Books, 2007), 227–248.

Assmann, Jan, 'Collective Memory and Cultural Identity', *New German Crtique*, 65 (1995), 125–133.

Bailey, Paul, *Postwar Japan: 1945 to the Present* (Oxford: Blackwell, 1996).

Bannister, Nonna, *The Secret Holocaust Diaries: The Untold Story of Nonna Bannister* (Carol Stream: Tyndale House Publishers, 2010).

Barnighausen, Till, 'Data Generated in Japan's Biowarfare Experiments on Human Victims in China, 1932–1945, and the Ethics of Using Them', in Jing Bao Nie, Nanyan Guo, Mark Selden, and Arthur Kleinman (eds), *Japan's Wartime Medical Atrocities: Comparative Inquiries in Science, History, and Ethics* (London: Routle-dge, 2010), pp. 81–107.

Beal, Tim, Nozaki, Yoshiko and Yang, Jian, 'Ghosts of the Past: The Japanese History Textbook Controversy', *New Zealand Journal of Asian Studies*, 3(2001), 177–188.

Berry, Chris, 'Speaking Bitterness: History, Media and Nation in Twentieth Century China', *Historiography East and West*, 2(2004).

Biess, Frank and Moeller, Robert G., *Histories of the Aftermath: The Legacies of the Second World War in Europe* (New York: Berghahn Books, 2010).

Birch, Cyrill, 'Literature Under Communism', in R. MacFarquhar and J. Fairbank (eds), *Cambridge History of China Volume 15* (Cambridge: The Press Syndicate of the University of Cambridge, 1991), pp. 743–815.

Bird, Kai and Lifschultz, Lawrence, *Hiroshima's Shadow* (Stony Creek: Pamphleteer's Press, 1993).

Bonnell, Victoria E., 'The Use of Theory, Concepts and Comparison in Historical Sociology', *Comparative Studies in Society and History*, 22(1980), 156–173.

Bowen, Sheryl Perlmutter and Spitzer, Juliet I., 'Survivors Sometimes Tell Their Stories: Motives for Sharing and Motives for Silence', in Johannes-Dieter Steinert and Inge Weber-Newth (eds), *Beyond Camps and Forced Labour: Current International Research on Survivors of Nazi Persecution* (Proceedings of the first international multidisciplinary conference at the Imperial War Museum, London, 29–31 January 2003) (Osnabrvck: Secolo Verlag, 2005).

Boyle, John H. *China and Japan at War, 1937–1945: The Politics of Collaboration* (Stanford, CA: Stanford University Press, 1972).

Bracke, Maud Anne, 'From Politics to Nostalgia: The Transformation of War Memories in France during the 1960s–1970s', *European History Quarterly*, 41(2011), 5–24.

Brackman, Arnold C., *The Other Nuremberg: The Untold Story of the Tokyo War Crimes Trials* (London: Collins, 1989).

Brook, Timothy, *Documents of the Rape of Nanking* (Ann Arbor:University of Michigan Press, 1999).

Brook, Timothy, 'Chinese Collaboration in Nanking', in Bob T. Wakabayashi (ed.), *The Nanking Atrocity 1937–1938. Complicating the Picture* (Oxford and New York: Berghahn Books, 2007), pp. 196–227.

Brook, Timothy, *Collaboation: Japanese Agents and Local Elites in Wartime China* (Cambridge, MA: Harvard University Press, 2005).

Bunker, Gerald E., *The Peace Conspiracy: Wang Ching-wei and the China war, 1937–1941* (Cambridge, MA: Harvard University Press, 1972).

Cai, Chengxi, 'Hongdong Beijingde diyici Riben shangpin zhanlanhui' [The first sensational Japanese merchandise exhibition in Beijing], *Zonghen*, 2002, 38–41 蔡成喜, 轰动北京的第一次日本商品展览会, 纵横, 2002, 38–41.

Callahan, William A., *China: the Pessoptimist Nation* (Oxford: Oxford University Press, 2010).

Cao, Xinxin, 'Kangzhan gequbeihou' [Behind classic War of Resistance songs], *Xiangchao*, 2005, 30–42 曹欣欣, 抗战经典歌曲背后, 湘潮, 2005, 30–42.

Casses, Antonio and Roling, B. V. A., *The Tokyo Trial and Beyond: Reflections of a Peacemonger* (Cambridge: Polity, 1993).

Cave, Peter, 'Japanese Colonialism and the Asia-Pacific War in Japan's History Textbooks: Changing Representations and Their Causes', *Modern Asian Studies*, 47 (2013), 542–580.

Cesarani, David, 'Lacking in Convictions: British War Crimes Policy and National Memory of the Second World War', in Martin Evans and Ken Lunn (eds), *War and Memory in the Twentieth Century* (Oxford: Berg, 1997), pp. 27–42.

Chan, Che-po and Bridges, Brian, 'China, Japan and the Clash of Nationalisms', *Asian Perspective*, 30(2006), 127–158.

Chang, Iris, *The Rape of Nanking: The Forgotten Holocaust of World War II* (New York: Basic Books, 1997).

Chanlett-Avery, Emma and Nanto, Dick K., *The Rise of China and Its Effect on Taiwan, Japan, and South Korea: U.S. Policy Choices.* CRS Report for Congress, 2006.

Chen, Xubin 谌旭彬, 'Guojun kang Ri lieshi daiyu bianqian' [The changes in the treatment of the KMT's anti-Japanese martyrs 国军抗日烈士待遇变迁]. http://view. news.qq.com/zt2013/gjkrls/index.htm, 12 April 2013, date accessed 9 March 2014.

Chen, Xubin 谌旭彬, 'Guogegeci chenfu' [Ups and downs of lyrics of the national anthem 国歌歌词沉浮]. http://news.qq.com/zt2011/ghgcd013/, date unknown, date accessed 16 March 2014.

Chen, Xubin 谌旭彬, 'Fansi bashinian "jiuyiba" jinianshi' [Reflect on the eighty-year commemorative history of 'September 18th' 反思八十年'九一八'纪念史]. http:// view.news.qq.com/zt2012/jyb/index.htm, 18 September 2012, date accessed 10 March 2014.

Clark, Paul, *The Chinese Cultural Revolution* (Cambridge: Cambridge University Press, 2008).

Chiang, Kai-shek, 'Jiang Jieshi shengliri yanshuo quanwen (3 September 1945)' [Chiang Kai-shek's speech on the victory day] , in Hunan Zhijiang xianzhi bangongshi (ed.), *Kangzhan shengli shouxiang* [Receiving the surrender after winning the War of Resistance] (Zhijiang: Internally circulated materials, 2002) 湖南芷江县志办公室, 蒋介石胜利日演说全文 抗战胜利受降 (内部资料, 2002).

Chuugoku shinbunsha, *Hiroshima no kiroku* [Hiroshima's record] (Hiroshima: Chuugoku shinbunsha, 1986) 中国新聞社, ヒロシマの記録 (中国新聞社, 1986).

Chuugoku Shinbusha, NHK, *NHK to Chuugoku shinbun no genbaku houdou* [NHK and Chuugoku news reports about atomic bombing] (NHK, 2003) 中国新聞社, NHK, NHKと中国新聞の原爆報道 (NHK, 2003).

Collier, David, 'The Comparative Method', in A. W. Finifter (ed.), *Political Science: The State of the Discipline II* (Washington, DC: American Political Science Association, 1993), pp. 105–119.

Conrad, Sebastian, 'Entangled Memories: Versions of the Past in Germany and Japan, 1945–2001', *Journal of Contemporary History*, 38(2003), 85–99.

Cumings, Bruce, 'Japan's Position in the World System', in A. Gordon (ed.), *Postwar Japan as History* (Berkeley: University of California Press, 1993), pp. 34–64.

Deng, Xiaoping, *Dengxiaoping wenxuan* [Selected works of Deng Xiaoping] vol. 2 (Beijing: Renminchubanshe, 1994) 邓小平, 邓小平文选 第二卷, (人民出版社, 1994).

Denton, Kirk A., 'Horror and Atrocity: Memory of Japanese Imperialism', in LeeChing Kwan and YangGuobin (eds), *Re-envisioning the Chinese Revolution* (Palo Alto, CA: Stanford University Press, 2007), pp. 245–286.

Diamant, Neil J., 'Between Martyrdom and Mischief: The Political and Social Predicament of CCP War Widows and Veterans, 1949–66', in Diana Lary and Stephen Mackinnon (eds), *Scars of War: The Impact of Warfare on Modern China* (UBC Press, 2001), pp. 162–189.

Diamant, Neil J., 'Conspicuous Silence: Veterans and the Depoliticisation of War Memory in China', *Modern Asian Studies*, 45(2001), 431–461.

Diamant, Neil J., *Embattled Glory: Veterans, Military Families, and the Politics of Patriotism in China (1949–2007)* (Lanham, MD: Rowman & Littlefield, 2010).

Dittmer, Lowell and Kim, Samuel S. (eds), *China's Quest For National Identity* (Syracuse, NY: Cornell University Press, 1993).

Dower, John W., *Embracing Defeat: Japan in the Aftermath of World War II* (London: Penguin, 2000).

Dower, John W., 'The Bombed: Hiroshimas and Nagasakis in Japanese Memory', in Michael J. Hogan (ed.), *Hiroshima in History and Memory* (Cambridge: Cambridge University Press, 1996), pp. 116–143.

Duara, Prasenjit, 'Nationalism in East Asia', *History Compass*, 4(2006), 407–427.

Dajiang, Jiansanlang and Weng, Jiahui (trans.), *Guandao Zhaji* [Hiroshima note] (Beijing: Zhongguo guangbo chubanshe, 2009) 大江健三郎,翁家惠译, 广岛札记 (中国广播出版社, 2009).

Ells, Mark D. V., 'Nanjing, China'. www.historynet.com/nanjing-china.htm, 14 July 2009, date accessed, 15 June 2014.

Endo, Kyoon, 'Bukkyou kouryuu tsuuji,nicchu yuukouni jinryoku' [Devotes himself to Sino–Japanese friendship, through Buddhism], *Watashi to Chuugoku*, 2009: www.jcfa-net.gr.jp/watashi/2009/090815.html, date accessed, 16 March 2014 遠藤教温, 仏教交流通じ 日中友好に尽力, 私と中国 2009.

Evans, Martin and Lunn, Ken (eds), *War and Memory in the Twentieth Century* (Oxford: Berg, 1997).

Eykholt, Mark, 'Aggression, Victimisation, and Chinese Historiography of the Nanjing Massacre', in Joshua A. Fogel (ed.), *The Nanking Massacre in History and Historiography* (London: University of California Press, 2000), 11–70.

Fan, Ning and Chen, Jianzhong 樊宁 程建中, 'Guomin gemingjun dishijiulu jun, diwujun wuming yingxiong jinianbei' [Monument to the unknown heroes of the 5th Corps and 19th Corps, National Revolutionary Army 国民革命军第十九路军、第五军无名英雄纪念碑]. www.hoplite.cn/templates/gjzlc0020.html, date unknown, date accessed, 9 March 2014.

Fan, Yongqiang, Lu, Honggen and He, Kun, 'Shida jingdian kangzhan gequ' [Ten classic War of Resistance songs], *Hainan renda*, 12(2006), 47 樊永强, 陆洪根, 何坤, 十大经典抗战歌曲, 海南人大, 2006:12, 47.

Fang, Chengzhi, 'Jianguo chuqi zhongxiaoxue jiaokeshu de biange' [The transformation of the Primary and Secondary School Textbook in the Early Period after the founding of New China], *Journal of Educational Science of Hunan Normal University*, 6(2007), 13–28 方成智, 建国初期中小学教科书的变革, 湖南师范大学教育科学学报, 2007:6, 13–28.

Fang, June 方军, 'Ba Dai Anlan jiangjun beihuiguode erbaishi baisui laobing' [One-hundred-year-old veteran who carried General Dai Anlan back to China on his back 把戴安澜将军背回国的二百师百岁老兵]. http://news.ifeng.com/history/special/zhongguoyuanzhengjun/200903/0305_5741_1046780.shtml, 5 March 2009, date accessed, 6 March 2014.

Fogel, Joshua A. (reviewer), '*Interpreting History in Sino–Japanese Relations: A Case Study in Political Decision Making*, by Caroline Rose. Nissan Institute/Routledge, London, 1998. xviii, 253 pages', *Journal of Japanese Studies*, 26(2000), 518.

Fogel, Joshua A. (ed.), *The Nanking Massacre in History and Historiography* (London: University of California Press, 2000).

Fogel, Joshua A., 'Introduction', in Joshua A. Fogel (ed.), *The Nanking Massacre in History and Historiography* (London: University of California Press, 2000), pp. 1–11.

Fogel, Joshua A., 'The Nanking Atrocity and Chinese Historical Memory', in Bob T. Wakabayashi (ed.), *The Nanking Atrocity 1937–1938. Complicating the Picture* (Oxford, New York: Berghahn Books, 2007), pp. 267–285.

Fujiwara, Akira, 'The Nanking Atrocity: An interpretive overview', in Bob T. Wakabayashi (ed.), *The Nanking Atrocity 1937–1938. Complicating the Picture* (Oxford, New York: Berghahn Books, 2007), pp. 29–57.

Fujiwara, Kiichi, *Sensou wo kiokusuru: Hiroshima, Horokousuto to genzai* [Remember the war, Hiroshima, Holocaust and the present] (Tokyo: Koudansha gendai shinsho, 2001) 藤原帰一, 戦争を記憶する 広島 ホロコーストと現在 (講談社現代新書, 2001).

Funingke 福宁客, 'Mao Zedong weihe pishi xiufu Dai Li mu' [Why Mao Zedong ordered the repair of Dai Li's grave 毛泽东为何批示修复戴笠墓]. http://fn01.i.sohu.com/blog/view/258182837.htm, 21 March 2013, date accessed, 9 March 2014.

Gao, Fanfu 高凡夫, 'Bunengyong ganqing daiti zhengce – Zhong Ri fujiaoqian Zhongguo zhengfu duiminzhongde shuifu jiaoyu' [Chinese government persuades and educates Chinese people before Sino–Japanese normalisation 不能用感情代替政策 – 中日复交前中国政府对民众的说服教育]. www.iccs.cn/contents/610/13339_3.html, 31 October 2012, date accessed, 16 March 2014.

Gao, Xingzu, 'Cong Riben ziliao kan Rijun zai Jiangsu Changzhou diqu debaoxing' [Japanese army's atrocities in Changzhou area, Jiangsu, from the Japanese materials], *Minguo chunqiu*, 5(1997) 高兴祖, 从日本资料看日军在江苏常州地区的暴行', 明国春秋, 1997:5.

Gluck, Carol, 'The Past in the Present', in Andrew Gordon (ed.), *Postwar Japan as History* (Berkeley: University of California Press, 1993).

Gold, Hal, *Japan's Wartime Human Experimentation Program: Unit 731 Testimony* (North Clarendon: Tuttle Publishing, 1996).

Goldman, Merle, 'The Party and the Intellectuals', in R. MacFarquhar and J. Fairbank (eds), *Cambridge History of China Volume 14* (Cambridge: Press Syndicate of the University of Cambridge, 1989), pp. 218–253.

Goldman, Merle, 'The Party and the Intellectuals: Phase Two', in R. MacFarquhar and J. Fairbank (eds), *Cambridge History of China Volume 14* (Cambridge: Press Syndicate of the University of Cambridge, 1989), pp. 432–463.

Gordon, Andrew, *Postwar Japan as History* (Berkeley: University of California Press, 1993).

Gregor, Neil, *Haunted City: Nuremberg and the Nazi Past* (New Haven, CT: Yale University Press, 2008).

Guo, Kai, 'Lvetan dui Lin Daojing demiaoxie zhongde quedian' [Brief discussion about the weakness in the description of Lin Daojing], *China Youth*, 2(1959). www.xzbu.com/6/view-3371371.htm, date accessed, 16 March 2014 郭开, 略谈对林道静的描写中的缺点, 中国青年, 1959:2.

Guan, Zhihao, 'Kawaranu yonjuunen noyoujyou' [Friendship that has lasted for forty years], *Jinmin Chuugoku*, 2005. www.peoplechina.com.cn/maindoc/html/teji/200508/teji-5.htm, date accessed, 16 March 2014 关志豪, 变わらぬ四十年の友情, 人民中国, 2005.

Harris, Sheldon, *Japanese Biological Warfare Experiments and Other Atrocities in Manchuria, 1932–1945, and the Subsequent United States Cover-Up: A Preliminary Assessment* (Dordrecht: Kluwer Academic, 1991).

Hane, Mikiso, *Eastern Phoenix: Japan since 1945* (Oxford: Westview Press, 1996).

Harrison, Henrietta, 'Martyrs and Militarism in Early Republican China', *Twentieth Century China*, 23(1998), 41–70.

Hasegawa, Tsuyoshi (ed.), *Cold War in East Asia* (Washington, DC: Woodrow Wilson Center Press, 2011).

Hasegawa, Tsuyoshi and Togo, Kazuhiko, *East Asia's Haunted Present: Historical Memories and the Resurgence of Nationalism* (Westport, CT: Praeger, 2008).

He, Yinan, 'Remembering and Forgetting the War: Elite Mythmaking, Mass Reaction, and Sino–Japanese Relations, 1950–2006', *History and Memory*, 19(2007), 43–74.

He, Yinan, 'Ripe for Cooperation or Rivalry? Commerce, Realpolitik, and War Memory in Contemporary Sino–Japanese Relations', *Asian Security*, 4(2008), 162–197.

He, Yinan, *The Search for Reconciliation: Sino–Japanese and German–Polish Relations since World War II* (Cambridge: Cambridge University Press, 2009).

Hersey, John, *Hiroshima* (London: Penguin Books, 1985).

Hicks, George, *The Comfort Women: Japan's Brutal Regime of Enforced Prostitution in the Second World War* (New York: W. W. Norton, 2011).

Higashinakano, Shudo, *The Nanking Massacre: Fact versus Fiction: A Historian's Quest for the Truth* (Tokyo: Sekai Shuppan, 2005).

Hinton, William Howard, *Fanshen: A Documentary of Revolution in a Chinese Village* (London: Monthly Review Press, 1966).

Hiroshima ken, *Genbaku sanjyunen* [Atomic bombing: thirty years] (Hiroshima ken, 1981) 広島県, 原爆三十年 (広島県, 1981).

Hiroshima toongaku iinkai, *Hiroshima to Ongaku* [Hiroshima and music] (Tokyo: Choubunsha, 2006) 「ヒロシマと音楽」委員会, ヒロシマと音楽 (汐文社, 2006).

Honda, Katsuichi, *Chuugoku No Tabi* [Travels in China] (Tokyo: Asahi Shinbunsha, 1981) 本多勝一, 中国の旅 (朝日新聞社, 1981).

Hong, Zicheng, *A History of Contemporary Chinese Literature* (Leiden: Brill, 2007).

Hu, Changfang, 'Yong sheng ming baohu Peng Xuefeng yigude Liyaba' [Li the mute who sacrificed his life to protect the remains of Peng Xuefeng], *Dangshi wenhui*, 9 (2012), 62–63 胡昌方, 用生命保护彭雪枫遗骨的李哑巴, 党史文汇, 9(2012), 62–63.

Huang, Tzu-chin, 'Chiang Kai-shek in East Asia: The Origins of the Policy of Magnanimity toward Japan after World War II', *Journal of Institute of Modern History, Academia Sinica*, 45(2004), 143–194 黃自進 抗戰結束前後蔣介石對日態度 「以德報怨」真相的探討 中央研究院近代史研究所集刊, 45(2004), 143–194.

Hughes, Christopher R., 'Japan in the Politics of Chinese Leadership Legitimacy: Recent Developments in Historical Perspective', *Japan Forum*, 20(2008), 245–266.

Hung, Chang-tai, 'The Cult of the Red Martyr: Politics of Commemoration in China', *Journal of Contemporary History*, 43(2008), 279–304.

Ide, Kanako, 'The Debate on Patriotic Education in Post-World War II Japan', *Educational Philosophy and Theory*, 41(2009), 441–452.

Ienaga, Saburo, *Senso sekinin* [War responsibility] (Tokyo: Iwanami shoten, 2005) 家永三郎, 戦争責任 (岩波書店, 2005).

Ijiri, Hidenori, 'Sino–Japanese Controversy since the 1972 Diplomatic Normalisation', *The China Quarterly*, 124(1990), 639–661.

Ikei, Masaru, *Nihon gaikoushi gaisetsu* [An outline of Japanese diplomatic history] (Tokyo: Keiou gijyukudaigaku shuppankai, 2002) 池井優, 日本外交史概説 (慶応義塾大学出版会, 2002).

Iriye, Akira, 'Sino–Japan relations 1945–1990', *The China Quarterly*, 124(1990), 624–638.

Ishida, Takeshi, *Kioku to boukyakuno seijigaku – douka seisaku, sensou sekinin, shuugouteki kioku* [Politics of remembering and forgetting – assimilation policy, war responsibility and collective memory] (Tokyo: Akashi shoten, 2000) 石田雄, 記憶と忘却の政治学 – 同化政策 戦争責任 集合的記憶 (明石書店, 2000).

Israel, John, 'The December 9th Movement: A Case Study in Chinese Communist Historiography', *The China Quarterly*, 23(1965), 140–169.

Israel, John, 'The December 9th Movement', *The China Quarterly*, 27(1966), 166–167.

Jager, Sheila Miyoshi, and Mitter, Rana, *Ruptured Histories: War, Memory, and the Post-Cold War in Asia* (Cambridge, MA: Harvard University Press, 2007).

Ji, Pengfei, 'Yinshui buwangjuejinren' [Don't forget the well-diggers when you drink from this well] in AnJianshe (ed.), *Zhou enlai zuihoudesuiyue* [Last days of Zhou Enlai] (Beijing: Zhongyangwenxian chubanshe, 1995), p. 289) 姬鹏飞, 饮水不忘掘井人, 安建设(ed.) 周恩来最后的岁月(北京, 中央文献出版社, 1995).

Jin, Danyuan and Xu, Wenming, '"Shiqinian" shiqi "liangjiehe" sixiang jiqidui Zhongguo dianying de yingxiang' [The 'two combined' theory during the 'seventeen-year period' and its impact on Chinese films], *Yishu baijia*, 2(2010), 13–18 金丹元,徐文明, 十七年"时期的"两结合"思想及其对中国电影的影响,艺术百家, 2(2010), 13–18.

Jinchaji junqu zhengzhibu, *Suku fuchou* [Speak bitterness and take revenge] (Jinchaji junqu zhengzhibu, 1947) 晋察冀军区政治部, 诉苦复仇 (晋察冀军区政治部, 1947).

Jinteng, Zhaoer and Luo, Jianzhong, 'Mei Su Ri sanguo dui "731 budui" de yanjiu zhuangkuang' [The research of the US, USSR and Japan on 'Unit 731'], *Wuling xuebao*, 35(2010), 53–55 近藤昭二 ,罗建忠, 美苏日三国对"731部队"的研究状况, 武陵学报 35(2010), 53–55.

Johnson, Chalmers, 'The Patterns of Japanese Relations with China, 1952–1982', *Pacific Affairs*, 59(1986), 402–428.

Kasahara, Tokushi, *Nankin jiken ronsoushi* [History of Nanjing incident debate] (Tokyo: Heibonsha, 2007) 笠原十九司, 南京事件論争史 (平凡社, 2007).

Kansteiner, Wulf, 'Finding Meaning in Memory: A Methodological Critique of Memory Studies', *History and Theory*, 41(2002), 179–197.

Kau, Michael Y. M. and Marsh, Susan H., *China in the Era of Deng Xiaoping: A Decade of Reform* (New York: M. E.Sharpe, 1993).

Kawamura, Kazuyuki, 'Chuugoku no heiwa kinenkan' [Chinese peace memorials] in *Seikaino heiwa hakubutsukan* [Peace museums of the world] (Tokyo: Nihon zusho sentai, 1995) 川村一之, 中国の平和記念館, 世界の平和博物館 (日本図書センター, 1995).

Kosaka, Masataka, *A History of Postwar Japan* (Tokyo: Kodansha International, 1972).

Kidd, William and Murdoch, Brian, *Memory and Memorials: The Commemorative Century* (Farnham: Ashgate Publishing, 2004).

Kosakai, Yoshiteru, *Hiroshima tokuhon* [Hiroshima textbook] (Hiroshima heiwa bunka sentai, 1995) 小堺吉光, ヒロシマ読本 (広島平和文化センター, 1995).

Kushner, Barak, 'Nationality and Nostalgia: The Manipulation of Memory in Japan, Taiwan and China since 1990', *International History Review*, 29(2007), 709–944.

Kushner, Barak, 'Pawns of Empire: Postwar Taiwan, Japan and the Dilemma of War Crimes', *Japanese Studies*, 30(2010), 111–133.

Kushner, Tony, '"I Want to Go On Living after My Death": The Memory of Anne Frank' in Martin Evans and Ken Lunn (eds), *War and Memory in the Twentieth Century* (Oxford: Berg, 1997), pp. 3–25.

Kuwajiro, Mizuta, *Genbaku wo yomu* [Read atomic bombing] (Tokyo: Koudansha, 1982) 水田九八二郎, 原爆を読む (講談社, 1982).

Kwong, Luke S. K., 'Oral History in China: A Preliminary Review', *The Oral History Review*, 20(1992), 23–50.

Kyridis, A., Mavrikou, A., Zagkos, C., Golia, P., Vamvakidou, I. and Fotopoulos, N., 'Nationalism through State-Constructed Symbols: The Case of National Anthems', *International Journal of Interdisciplinary Social Science*, 4(2009), 244.

Lagrou, Pieter, 'Victims of Genocide and National Memory: Belgium, France and the Netherlands 1945–1965', *Past and Present*, 154(1997), 181–222.

Lebow, Richard Ned and Kansteiner, Wulf, *The Politics of Memory in Postwar Europe* (Durham, NC: Duke University Press, 2006).

Lan, Xuehua, 'Kangzhan shiqi guomin zhengfu de junren youfu anzhi zhidu pingshu' [Review of the KMT's policy of giving preferable treatment and compensation to military personnel], *Changchun shifanxueyuan xuebao*, 28(2009), 63–68 兰雪花, 抗战时期国民政府的军人优抚安置制度评述, 长春师范学院学报 28(2009), 63–68.

Lao, Gui, *Muqing Yang Mo* [Mother Yang Mo] (Wuhan: Changjiang wenyi chubanshe, 2005) 老鬼, 母亲杨沫 (长江文艺出版社, 2005).

Lei, Shenghong, 'Guogegeci congfeizhi qudai daohuifu de quzhelicheng' [The vicissitudes of the lyrics of the national anthem from being banned, replaced and recovered], *Dangshi bolan*, 2008, 17–18 雷声宏, 国歌歌词从废止, 取代到恢复的曲折历程, 党史博览, 2008, 17–18.

Lei, Yi, 'Qu Qiubai yuanan bushiyu sirenbang depohai' [Qu Qiubai's case of injustice did not start from the persecution of 'gang of four'], *Wenshi cankao*, 2010. http://news.ifeng.com/history/zhongguoxiandaishi/detail_2012_09/10/17483072_0.shtml, date accessed, 16 March 2014 雷颐, 瞿秋白冤案不始于四人帮的迫害, 文史参考, 2010:10.

Levin, Mark, 'Case Comment: Nishimatsu Construction Co. v. Song Jixiao et al., Supreme Court of Japan (2d Petty Bench), April 27, 2007, and Ko Hanako et al. v. Japan, Supreme Court of Japan (1st Petty Bench), April 27, 2007', *American Journal of International Law*, 102(2008), 1–6.

Leyda, Jay, *Dianying* (Cambridge, MA: MIT Press, 1972).

Li, Fushan, 'Wocanyu zhenxun Riben zhanfan shimo' [The story of how I participated in investigating and interrogating Japanese war crimals], *Dangshi bolan*, 2008. http://dangshi.people.com.cn/GB/85039/12826451.html, date accessed, 16 March 2014 李甫山, 我参与侦讯日本战犯始末, 党史博览, 2008.

Li, Mengwen and Jin, Shuang, *Wuhan huizhan: Baowei Dawuhan* [The battle of Wuhan: defend the great Wuhan] (Beijing: Tuanjie chubanshe, 2005) 李梦文, 金爽, 武汉会战: 保卫大武汉 (团结出版社, 2005).

Li, Xiang, 'Kangzhan shiqi guomin zhengfu qianghua junren fuxu zhidu yuanyin zhifenxi' [Analysis of the reasons why the KMT government strengthened its policy of compensating to military personnel during the War of Resistance period], *Junshi lishi*, 1(2008), 18–21. 李翔, 抗战时期国民政府强化军人抚恤制度原因之分析, 军事历史 2008, 18–21.

Li, Xiang (2008), 'Kangzhan shiqi guominzhengfu lujun fuxu jigou chutan' [Exploration of the KMT's ways of consoling and compensation the army during the War of Resistance period], *Kang Ri zhanzheng yanjiu*, 1(2008), 82–109 李翔, 抗战时期国民政府陆军抚恤机构初探, 抗日战争研究, 1(2008), 82–109.

Liu, Dejun, *Kangri zhanzheng yanjiu shuping* [Review of the research on the War of Resistance against Japan] (Jinan: Qilu shushe, 2005) 刘德军, 抗日战争研究述评 (齐鲁书社, 2005).

Lipkin, Zwia *Useless to the State: 'Social Problems' and Social Engineering in Nationalist Nanjing, 1927–1937* (Cambridge, MA: Harvard University Press, 2006).

Liu, Jialing, 'Pingyuan youjidui gushide zhengliu guocheng' [The distillation process of the story of 'The Plains Guerrillas], *Shanghai wenxue*, 3(2002), 70–73 刘嘉陵, 平原游击队故事的蒸馏过程, 上海文学, 3(2002), 70–73.

Liu, Jianping, *Zhanhou Zhong Ri guanxi 'buzhengchang' lishide guocheng yujiegou* [Sino–Japanese relations after World War II: abnormal historical process and construction] (Beijing: Shehui kexue wenxian chubanshe, 2010) 刘建平, 战后中日关系"不正常"历史的过程与结构 (社会科学文献出版社, 2010).

Liu, Yanjun, 'Guominzhengfu dui nanjingdatusha deshenpan shideyouguan Nanjingbaoxing deshehuijiyi deyisheng cheng' [The KMT government's trial of the Nanjing Massacre give birth to the social memory about the Nanjing Massacare], *Nanjing datushashi yanjiu*, 2002, 117–120 刘燕军, 国民政府对南京大屠杀案的审判使得有关南京暴行的社会记忆得以生成, 南京大屠杀史研究, 2002, 117–120.

Liu, Yanjun, 'Nanjing datushade lishijiyi' [The historical memory of the Nanjing Massacare], *Kangri zhanzheng yanjiu*, 2009, 5–22 刘燕军, 南京大屠杀的历史记忆, 抗日战争研究, 2009, 5–22.

Low-Beer, Ann, *School History, National History and the Issue of National Identity* (University of Birmingham Press, 2003).

Lu, Zhicheng, 'Chen Dengke de liangjian yian' [Two motions of Chen Dengke], *Jianghuai wenshi*, 5(2006), 127–131 陆志成, 陈登科的两件议案, 江淮文史, 5(2006), 127–131.

Luo, Pingfei, 'Jianguoqian Zhongguo gongchandang junren fuxu youdai jituiyi anzhi zhengce yanjiu' [A study of the CPC's policy on pensions, favored treatment and demobilisation placement for servicemen before the founding of New China], *Zhonggong dangshi yanjiu*, 6(2005), 73–78. 罗平飞, 建国前中国共产党军人抚恤优待及退役安置政策研究, 中共党史研究, 6(2005), 73–78.

Ma, Ming, 'Taiyuan shenpan Riben zhanfan baodaode huiyi' [Memoir of reporting the Taiyuan military tribunal], *Xinwen caibian*, 1966, 43–44 马明, 太原审判日本战犯报道的回忆, 新闻采编, 1966, 43–44.

Maruki, Shun and Maruki, Iri, *'Genbaku no zu'* [Atomic bombing panel] (Tokyo: Komine shoten, 2000) 丸木位里,丸木俊, 原爆の図 普及版完本 (小峰書店, 2000).

Materials, *Materials on the Trial of Former Servicemen of the Japanese Army Charged with Manufacturing and Employing Bacteriological Weapons* (Moscow: Foreign Languages Publishing House, 1950).

Mei, Changzhao, 'Bofu Mei Ruao jiushi' [Past articles of uncle Mei Ruao], *Jinri mingliu*, 7(1995), 62–69 梅长钊,伯父梅汝璈旧事', 今日名流, 7(1995), 62–69.

Mei, Ruao, *Yuandong junshifating* [The IMTFE] (Beijing: Falv chubanshe, 1998) 梅汝璈 远东军事法庭 (法律出版社, 1998).

McCargo, Duncan, *Contemporary Japan* (Basingstoke: Palgrave Macmillan, 2004).

McDougall, Gay J., *Contemporary Forms of Slavery: Systematic Rape, Sexual Slavery and Slavery-like Practices During Armed Conflict* (New York: Office of the United Nations High Commissioner for Human Rights, 1998).

Meisner, Maurice, *Mao's China and After: A History of the People's Republic* (New York: Free Press, 1999).

Minzhenbu fagui bangongshi, *Zhonghua renmin gongheguo minzheng gongzuo wenjian huibian (1949–1999)* [Compilation of the documents of the PRC's civil affairs department] (Beijing: Zhongguo fazhi chubanshe, 2001) 民政部法规办公室, 中华人民共和国民政工作文件汇编 (中国法制出版社, 2001).

Mitsui, Hideko, 'The Politics of National Atonement and Narrations of War', *Inter-Asia Cultural Studies*, 9(2008), 47–61.

Mitter, Rana, 'Behind the Scenes at the Museum: Nationalism, History and Memory in the Beijing War of Resistance Museum, 1987–1997', *The China Quarterly*, 161 (2000), 279–293.

Mitter, Rana, 'Old Ghosts, New Memories: China's Changing War History in the Era of post-Mao Politics', *Journal of Contemporary History*, 38(2003), 117–131.

Mitter, Rana and Moore, Aaron W., 'China in World War II, 1937–1945: Experience, Memory, and Legacy', *Modern Asian Studies*, 45(2011), 225–240.

Moore, Aaron William, 'The Problem of Changing Language Communities: Veterans and Memory Writing in China, Taiwan, and Japan', *Modern Asian Studies*, 45 (2001), 399–429.

Mvller, Jan-Werner, *Memory and Power in Post-War Europe: Studies in the Presence of the Past* (Cambridge: Cambridge University Press, 2002).

Musgrove, Charles , *China's Contested Capital: Architecture, Ritual, and Response in Nanjing* (Hong Kong University Press, 2013).

Naka, Hisao, *Sengo Nihonno nakano 'sensou'* ['War' within postwar Japan] (Kyoto: Seikai shisousha, 2004) 中久郎, 戦後日本のなかの「戦争」(世界思想社, 2004).

Nakamura, Masanori, *Sengoshi* [Postwar history] (Tokyo: Iwanami shoten, 2005) 中村政則, 戦後史 (岩波書店 2005).

Nanjing difangzhi bianzuan weiyuanhui bangongshi, *Nanjing jianzhi* [Brief history of Nanjing] (Nanjing: Jiangsu guji chubanshe, 1986) 南京市地方志编纂委员会办公室, 南京简志 (江苏古籍出版社出版, 1986).

Nanjing difangzhi bianzuan weiyuanhui, *Nanjing jianzhi zhi* [Gazetteer of Nanjing's administrative development] (Shenzhen: Haitian chubanshe, 1994) 南京市地方志编纂委员会, 南京建置志 (海天出版社, 1994).

Nanjing difangzhi bianzuan weiyuanhui, *Nanking minzheng zhi* [Gazetteer of Nanjing civil affairs] (Shen Zhen: Haitian chubanshe, 1994) 南京地方志编纂委员会, 南京民政志 (海天出版社, 1994).

NHK Shuzaihan, *Shuu Onlai no ketsudan* [Zhou Enlai's determination] (Tokyo: Nihon housou kyokai, 1993), p. 149. NHK 取材班, 周恩来の決断 (日本放送協会, 1993).

Nie, Jing-Bao, 'On the Altar of Nationalism and the Nation-state: Japan's Wartime Medical Atrocities, the American Cover-up, and Postwar Chinese Responses', in Jing Bao Nie, Nanyan Guo, Mark Selden and Arthur Kleinman (eds), *Japan's Wartime Medical Atrocities: Comparative Inquiries in Science, History, and Ethics* (London: Routledge, 2010), 123–139.

Niu, Jun, *Zhonghua renmin gongheguo duiwai guanxi shigailun (1949–2000)* [An introduction to the PRC's international relations] (Beijing: Beijingdaxue chubanshe, 2010) 牛军, 中华人民共和国对外关系史概论(1949–2000) (北京大学出版社, 2010).

Niven, Bill and Paver, Chloe, *Memorisalisation in Germany since 1945* (Basingstoke: Palgrave Macmillan, 2010).

Nobuko, Kosuge, *Sengo wakai* (Tokyo: Chuukou shinsho, 2005) 小菅信子, 戦後和解 (中公新書, 2005).

Nozaki, Yoshiko, *War Memory, Nationalism and Education in Postwar Japan, 1945–2007: The Japanese History Textbook Controversy and Ienaga Saburo's Court Challenges* (London: Routledge, 2008).

Okuda, Hiroko, *Genbaku no kioku* [Memory of atomic bombing] (Keio gijyuku daigaku chuppankai, 2010) 奥田博子, 原爆の記憶 (慶応義塾大学出版会, 2010).

Poupard, James and Miller, Linda, 'History of Biological Warfare: Catapults to Capsomeres', *Annals of the New York Academy of Sciences*, 666(1992), 9–20.

Pyle, B. Kenneth, 'Japan Besieged. The Textbook Controversy: Introduction', *Journal of Japanese Studies*, 9(1983), 297–300.

Qi, Yue 齐越, 'Zai Taihangshan shang wangshi xinti' [Re-mention the past of 'On the Taihang Mountain', '在太行山上' 往事新提]. http://news.ifeng.com/mil/history/deta il_2011_02/14/4656318_0.shtml, 14 February 2011, date accessed 10 March 2014.

Qin, Xiaoyi (ed.), *Xian zongtong Jianggong sixiangyanlun zongji* [Compilation of Chiang Kai Shek's thoughts and speeches] (Unpublished source, 1982) 秦孝仪, 先总统蒋公思想言论总集 (未出版资料, 1982).

Reilly, James, 'China's History Activists and the War of Resistance Against Japan: History in the Making', *Asian Survey*, 19(2004), 276–294.

Reilly, James, 'Remember History, Not Hatred: Collective Remembrance of China's War of Resistance to Japan', *Modern Asian Studies*, 45(2011), 463–490.

Rofel, Lisa, *Other Modernities: Gendered Yearnings in China after Socliaism* (Berkeley: University of California Press, 1999).

Rose, Caroline, *Interpreting History in Sino–Japanese Relations: A Case Study in Political Decision-making* (London: Routledge, 1998).

Rose, Caroline, 'Patriotism Is not Taboo: Nationalism in China and Japan and Implications for Sino–Japanese Relations', *Japan Forum*, 12(2001), 169–181.

Rosenfeld, Gavriel and Jaskot, Paul B., *Beyond Berlin: Twelve German Cities Confront the Nazi Past* (Ann Arbor: University of Michigan Press, 2008).

Schram, Stuart R., 'Mao Tse-tung's Thought from 1949 to 1976', in R. MacFarquhar and J. Fairbank (eds), *Cambridge History of China Volume 15* (Cambridge: The Press Syndicate of the University of Cambridge, 1991), 1–107.

Seaton, Philip A., *Japan's Contested War Memories: The 'Memory Rifts' in Historical Consciousness of World War II* (London: Routledge, 2007).

Sekizawa, Mayumi (ed.), *Sensou kiokuron: boukyaku, henyou shoshite keishou* [War memory: forget, change and inherit] (Kyoto: Shouwadou, 2010) 関沢まゆみ,戦争記憶論 – 忘却、変容そして継承 (昭和堂, 2010).

Selden, Kyoko and Selden, Mark, *The Atomic Bomb: Voices from Hiroshima and Nagasaki* (The East Gate Book, 1989).

Senjin, Zhuangnei, 'Renmin shizenyang duidai taiyangqide', in Baigenzilang (ed.) and Fang, Guizhi (trans.), *Zhanhou Ri Zhong maoyishi* (Liaoning Renmin chubanshe, 1988), pp. 52–55 森井庄内 人们是怎样对待太阳旗的, 白根滋郎 and 方桂芝[译], 战后日中贸易史 (辽宁人民出版社, 1988), 52–55.

Seraphim, Franziska, *War Memory and Social Politics in Japan, 1945–2005* (Cambridge MA and London: Harvard University Press, 2006).

Sewell, H. William, 'Marc Bloch and the Logic of Comparative History', *History and Theory*, 6(1969), 211.

Shen, Yang, 'Guomin zhengfu kangzhan shiqi junshi youfu pingxi' [Review of the KMT's manoeuvres of giving preferable treatment and compensation to military personnel during the War of Resistance period], *Kang Ri zhanzheng yanjiu*, 2008, 123–135. 沈阳, 国民政府抗战时期军事优抚评析, 抗日战争研究, 2008, 123–135.

Shen, Zhihua, 'Zhong Su zai 1958 niande guanxi weihe jiangdao bingdian' [Why Sino–Soviet relations fell below freezing point in 1958], *Wenshitiandi*, 7(2013). www. faobserver.com/Newsinfo.aspx?id=9270, date accessed, 16 March 2014 沈志华, 中苏在1958年的关系为何降到冰点, 文史天地 2013:7.

Shen, Zui, *Shen Zui huiyi zuopin quanji* [Collection of Shen Zui's recollective articles] (Beijing: Jiuzhou tushu chubanshe, 1998) 沈醉, 沈醉回忆作品全集 (九洲图书出版社, 1998).

Shi, Ou and Li, Xin, 'Xin Zhongguo 60 nian zhongxiaoxue jiaocai jianshe zhi tanxi' [Research on the development of Chinese and secondary textbooks over sixty years], *Journal of Educational Science of Hunan Normal University*, 8(2009), 5–10. 石鸥, 李新, 新中国60年中小学教材建设之探析, 湖南师范大学教育科学学报 8 (2009), 5–10.

Shi, Zhen, 'Wengehou gaihuan guogegeci shimo' [The whole story about the changes to the lyrics of the national anthem after the Cultural Revolution], *Wuhan wenshiziliao*, 10(2004), 38 史真, "文革"后改换国歌歌词始末, 武汉文史资料 10(2004), 38.

Shijiezhishi chubanshe (ed.), *Ribenwenti wenjian huibian* (1) [Compilation of documents of Japanese issue] (Beijing: Shijiezhishi chubanshe, 1955) 世界知识出版社, 日本问题文件汇编 (1) (世界知识出版社, 1955).

Shijie zhishi chubanshe (ed.), *Riben wenti wenjian huibian* (2) [Compilation of documents of Japanese issue] (Beijing: Shijiezhishi chubanshe, 1958) 世界知识出版社, 日本问题文件汇编(2) (世界知识出版社, 1958).

Shijiezhishi chubanshe (ed.), *Riben wenti wenjian huibian* (3) [Compilation of documents of Japanese issue] (Beijing: Shijiezhish chubanshe, 1961) 世界知识出版社, 日本问题文件汇编(3) (世界知识出版社, 1961).

Shijiezhishi chubanshe, *Shijie zhishi cidian* [World knowledge dictionary] (Beijing: Shijiezhishi chubanshe, 1950) 世界知识出版社, 世界知识辞典 (世界知识出版社, 1950).

Sihong xian renmin zhengfu 泗洪县龙集镇人民政府, 'Yingshan Lieshi lingyuan jianjie' [Brief introduction to the Yingshan Martyrs' Cemetery Park 应山烈士陵园情况简介]. www.longji.gov.cn/whly/yslsly/130.aspx, 15 June 2012, date accessed, 9 March 2014.

Snow, Edgar, 'December 9th Movement', *The China Quarterly*, 26(1966), 171–176.

Su, Kui, 'Tan jianguo chuqi kang Ri ticai xiaoshuo yu dianying' [Talk about the anti-Japanese themed novels and films during the first years of the PRC], *Dianying wenxue*, 11(2008), 61–64 苏奎, 谈建国初期抗日题材小说与电影, 电影文学, 11 (2008), 61–64.

Su, Zhiliang, *Weianfu yanjiu* [Research on comfort women] (Shanghai: Shanghai shudian chubanshe, 2000) 苏智良, 慰安妇研究 (上海书店出版社, 2000).

Sun, Ge, 'Nicchuu sensou – kanjyou to kiokuno kouzu' [Sino–Japanese war: compilation of sentiments and memories], *Sekai*, 673(2000), 158–170 孫歌, 日中戰爭 – 感情と記憶の構図,世界, 673(2000), 158–170.

Sun, Ge 孙歌, 'Zhong Ri chuanmei zhongde zhanzheng jiyi' [The war memory in Chinese and Japanese media 中日传媒中的战争记忆]. www.frchina.net/data/personArticle.php?id=126, November 2003, date accessed, 8 March 2014.

Sun, Pinghua, *Zhong Ri youhao suixianglu* [Memoirs of Sino–Japanese friendship] (Shenyang: Liaoningrenmin chubanshe, 2009), p. 8 孙平化, 中日友好随想录 (辽宁人民出版社, 2009).

Sun, Zhaiwei, 'Lun Guo Gong liangdang dui Nanjing datusha degongshi' [A survey of common perceptions of the Nanjing Massacre by the KMT and the CCP], *Republican Archives*, 2(2005), 105–109 孙宅巍, 论国共两党对南京大屠杀的共识, 民国档案, 2(2005), 105–109.

Tachibana, Seiitsu, 'The Quest for a Peace Culture: The A-bomb Survivors' Long Struggle and the New Movement for Redressing Foreign Victims of Japan's War', *Diplomatic History*, 19(1995), 329–346.

Tanaka, Hiroshi, 'Kyouiku houki kaisei nimiru "aikokushin kyouiku"' [Review 'patriotic education' from the perspective of changing education law], *Ryuukyuu daigaku kyouiku gakubu kiyou*, 76(2010), 67–76 田中洋, 教育法規改正にみる「愛国心教育」, 琉球大学教育学部紀要, 76(2010), 67–76.

Tanaka, Yuki, *Japan's Comfort Women: Sexual Slavery and Prostitution during World War II and the US Occupation* (London: Routledge, 2002).

Tang, Baolin, 'Liu Shaoqi yu yierjiuyundong dezhuanzhe' [Liu Shaoqi and the turning point of the December 9th Movement], *Jindaishi yanjiu*, 3(1988), 195–211 唐宝林, 刘少奇与一二九运动的转折, 近代史研究, 3(1988), 195–211.

Tokushi, Kasahara, 'Massacres outside Nanking City', in Bob T. Wakabayashi (ed.), *The Nanking Atrocity 1937–1938. Complicating the Picture* (Oxford, New York: Berghahn Books, 2007), pp. 57–70.

Tori, Tami, *Han Nichide Iki Nobiru Chuugoku Kou Takumin no sensou* (Soushisha, 2004) 鳥居民,「反日」で生きのびる中国 江沢民の戦争 (草思社, 2004).

Treat, John Whittier, *Writing Ground Zero: Japanese Literature and the Atomic Bomb* (Chicago: University of Chicago Press, 1995).

Tsuneishi, Keiichi, 'Unit 731 and the Japanese Imperial Army's Biological Warfare Program'. www.japanfocus.org/-Tsuneishi-Keiichi/2194, date unknown, date accessed, 16 March 2014.

Tsuneishi, Keiichi, 'Nanasanichi butai no bourei – teigenjiken zaidokuku' [Departed soul of Unit 731 – re-read the Imperial Bank Incident], *Gendai shisou*, 33(2005), 154–160 常石敬一, 七三一部隊の亡霊 – 帝銀事件再読, 現代思想, 33(2005), 154–160.

Vietor, Richard H. K., 'Japan: Deficits, Demography, and Deflation', *Harvard Business School Case*, 2005.

Wakabayashi, Bob T. (ed.), *The Nanking Atrocity 1937–1938. Complicating the Picture* (Oxford, New York: Berghahn Books, 2007).

Wakabayashi, Bob Tadashi, 'The Nanking 100-Man Killing Contest Debate, 1971–75', in Bob T. Wakabayashi (ed.), *The Nanking Atrocity 1937–1938. Complicating the Picture* (Oxford, New York: Berghahn Books, 2007), pp. 149–155.

Walder, Dennis, 'Literature, Memory and Nation', in Clive Emsley (ed.), *War, Culture and Memory* (Milton Keynes: The Open University Press, 2003).

Waldron, Arthur, 'China's New Remembering of World War II: The Case of Zhang Zizhong', *Modern Asian Studies*, 30(1996), 945–978.

Wang, Suzy, 'Medicine-related War Crimes Trials and Post War Politics and Ethics: The Unresolved Case of Unit 731, Japan's Bio-warfare Program', in Jing Bao Nie, Nanyan Guo, Mark Selden and Arthur Kleinman (eds), *Japan's Wartime Medical Atrocities: Comparative Inquiries in Science, History, and Ethics* (London: Routledge, 2010), pp. 32–59.

Wang, Chaoguang, 'Kang Ri zhanzheng lishide yingxiangjiyi-centered around the postwar Chinese films' [The memory of the War of Resistance against Japan in films – centred around the postwar Chinese films], *Xueshu yanjiu*, 6(2005), 91–100 汪朝光, 抗日战争历史的影像记忆- 以战后中国电影为中心, 学术研究, 6(2005), 91–100.

Wang, Junyan, *Zhong Ri guanxi juejingren: ji sishiwuwei Zhong Ri youhaode xianqu* [Well-diggers of Sino–Japanese relationship: 45 forerunners of Sino–Japanese friendship] (Beijing: Shijiezhishi chubanshe, 2010) 王俊彦, 中日关系掘井人:记45位中日友好的先驱 (世界知识出版社, 2010).

Wang, Zheng, 'National Humiliation, History Education, and the Politics of History Memory: Patriotic Education Campaign in China', *International Studies Quarterly*, 52(2008), 783–806.

Wang, Zheng, *Never Forget National Humiliation: Historical Memory in Chinese Politics and Foreign Relations* (New York: Columbia University Press, 2012).

White, Gordon, 'The Politics of Demobilised Soldiers from Liberation to Cultural Revolution', *The China Quarterly*, 82(1980), 181–213.

Whitehead, Anne, *Memory* (London: Routledge, 2009).

Wickert, Erwin, *The Good German of Nanking: The diaries of Jone Rabe* (London: Abacus, 2000).

Winter, Jay and Sivan, Emmanuel (eds), *War and Remembrance in the Twentieth Century* (Cambridge: Cambridge University Press, 1999).

Wolfe, Thomas C., 'Past as Present, Myth, or History? Discourses of Time and the Great Fatherland War', in Richard Lebow and Wulf Kansteiner (eds), *The Politics of Memory in Postwar Europe* (Durham, NC: Duke University Press, 2006), pp. 249–283.

Working, Russell, 'The Trial of Unit 731'. www.japantimes.co.jp/opinion/2001/06/05/commentary/the-trial-of-unit-731/#.UxomUKXNXkw, June 2001, date accessed, 6 March 2014.

Wu, Beiguang 吴北光, 'Jiducangsang guogede dansheng ji beihou xianwei renzhi de gushi' [Inside story of the birth of the national anthem 几度沧桑 国歌的诞生及背后鲜为人知的故事]. www.gov.cn/test/2006-02/27/content_211883.htm, 27 February 2006, date accessed, 6 March 2014.

Wu, Weiman, 'Tamen yongyuan shizanminbing' [They are our militiamen forever], *Zhongguo minbing*, 8(2005), 8–10 吴维满, 他们永远是咱民兵, 中国民兵, 8(2005), 8–10.

Wu, Xuewen, *Fengyuyinqing wosuo jinglide Zhong Ri guanxi* [The Sino–Japanese relationship I experienced] (Beijing: Shijiezhishi chubanshe, 2002) 吴学文, 风雨阴晴, 我所经历的中日关系 (世界知识出版社, 2002).

Xiaohongliu 小红柳, 'Wuqi gushi' [Story of Five Seven 五七故事]. http://shzq.net/pjq/Print.asp?tid=5012, 7 May 2011, date accessed, 10 March 2014.

Xie, Miao, 'Zhongguo gongchandang de fuxu zhengce yanjiu' [Research on the CCP's policy of consolation and compensation (1949–1966)] (Shandong shifan daxue, master's dissertation, 2010) 谢苗, 中国共产党的抚恤政策研究 (1949–1966) (山东师范大学, 硕士论文, 2010).

Xing, Ye, '"Pingyuan youjidui" xiugaiji' [The story of revising 'The Plains Guerrillas'], *Bainianchao*, 5(1999), 74–77 刑野, 平原游击队修改记, 百年潮, 5(1999), 74–77.

Xu, Guangyao, '"Xiaobing Zhanggao" de qiyi chushi' [Unusual birth of 'Little Social Zhangga'] in MaQingshan (ed.), *Feitian 60nian diancang (woyuwenxuezhuan)* [Feitian, 60 years of book reservations (volume of 'Me and literature')] (Yinchuan: Gansu wenhua chubanshe, 2010), pp. 100–103 徐光耀, '小兵张嘎'的奇异出世, 马青山, 飞天 60年典藏 (我与文学卷) (甘肃文化出版社, 2010), pp. 100–103.

Xu, Qiufang, *Jibiandiyicheng de xuese jiyi: tengchong kangzhan jianzhenglu* [The border city's memory with blood color: eyewitness of the War of Resistance in Tengchong] (Wuhan: Wuhandaxue chubanshe, 2003)许秋芳, 极边第一城的血色记忆: 腾冲抗战见证录 武汉大学出版社2003).

Xu, Rongsheng and Lin, Chengxi, *Guomindang kongjun kangzhan shilu* [Record of the KMT Air Force's War of Resistance 国民党空军抗战实录] (Zhongguo dangan chubanshe, 1994).

Xu, Shuhong, 'Kongjuyu jiyi – Nanjing datusha xingcunzhe dexinlu licheng' [Fear and memory – the psychological process of the Nanjing Massacre survivors] in WangJin and XuLei (eds) *Chuangshangde lishi Nanjing datusha yuzhanshi Zhongguo shehui* (Nanjing: Nanjing shifandaxue chubanshe, 2005), 63–102 许书宏, 恐惧与记忆 – 南京大屠杀幸存者的心路历程, 王瑾, 徐蕾 创伤的历史 – 南京大屠杀与战时中国社会 (南京师范大学出版社, 2005), 63–102.

Yamamoto, Masahiro, *Nanking: Aanatomy of an Atrocity* (Westport, CT: Praeger, 2000).

Yan, Yan 燕雁, 'Didaozhan qishi hen canku' [Tunnel warfare actually was very cruel 地道战其实很残酷]. http://blog.sina.com.cn/s/blog_675b55c401019jgb.html, 21 April 2013, date accessed, 10 March 2014.

Yang, An, 'Fuqin Yang Xiaolu degushi: "Hengyang kangzhan jiniancheng" jianshe shimo' [My father Yang Xiaolu's story: the whole story of developing 'Hengyang, War of Resistance memorial city'], *Wenshi cankao*, 2010. www.people.com.cn/GB/198221/198819/198849/12412595.html, date accessed, 14 March 2014 杨安, 父亲杨晓麓的故事"衡阳抗战纪念城"建设始末, 文史参考, 2010.

Yang, Daqing, 'The Challenges of the Nanjing Massacre: Reflections on Historical Inquiry', in Joshua A. Fogel (ed.), *The Nanking Massacre in History and Historiography* (London: University of California Press, 2000), pp. 133–181.

Yang, Daqing, 'Mirror of the Future or the History Card? Understanding the 'History Problem'", in Marie Söderbergthe (ed.), *Chinese–Japanese Relations in the Twenty-first Century: Complementarity and Conflict* (London: Routledge, 2002), pp. 10–31.

Yang, Fang, 'Guojiabowuguan qiaoranbianhua: cong gemingmiankong dao shechipin zhanshi' [Quiet change of the National Museum of China: from the face of revolution to the exhibition of luxurious goods], *Zhongguo guojia bowuguan meizhou kuaixun*, 25(2011), 4–8 杨芳, 国家博物馆悄然变化:从革命面孔到奢侈品展示, 中国国家博物馆 每周快讯, 25(2011), 4–8.

Yang, Furong 楊馥戎, 'Tangdi zhuiyi dongjing shenpan muhou' [Cousin, recall the backstage of the IMTFE 堂弟追忆东京审判幕后]. http://big5.huaxia.com/zhwh/whrw/2013/04/3307087.html, 24 April 2013, date accessed, 10 March 2014.

Zhengxie Anhui wenshi ziliao yanjiu gongzuozu, *Anhui wenshi ziliao xuanji* [Selection of materials about Anhui's history] (Hefei: Anhui renmin chubanshe, 1964) (政协安徽文史资料研究工作组, 安徽文史资料选辑, 安徽人民出版社, 1964).

Yang, Mo, 'Epilogue' in *Song of Youth* (2nd edn) (Beijing: Renmin wenxue chubanshe, 1960) 杨沫, 后记, 青春之歌 (人民文学出版社, 1960).

Yang, Mo, 'Epilogue', in *Song of Youth* (new edition) (Beijing: Shiyue wenyi chubanshe, 1991). 杨沫, 后记, 新版青春之歌 (北京十月文艺出版社, 1991).

Yang, Ziyun, 'Mei Xiaoao yanzhongde fuqin Mei Ruao' [Mei Ruao, as a father, in the eyes of Mei Xiaoao], *Jianghuai fazhi*, 3(2006), 13–15 杨子云, 梅小璈眼中的父亲梅汝璈, 江淮法制, 3(2006), 13–15.

Yim, Kwan Ha, *China since Mao* (London: Macmillan, 1980).

Yoneyama, Lisa, *Hiroshima Traces: Time, Space, and the Dialectics of Memory* (Berkeley and London: University of California Press, 1999).

Yoshida, Takashi, 'A Battle over History: The Nanjing Massacre in Japan' in Joshua A. Fogel (ed.), *The Nanking Massacre in History and Historiography* (London: University of California Press, 2000), pp. 70–133.

Yoshida, Takashi, *The Making of the 'Rape of Nanking': History and Memory in Japan, China and the United States* (Oxford: Oxford University Press, 2006).

Yoshimi, Yoshiaki, *Comfort Women: Sexual Slavery in the Japanese Military during World War II* (New York: Columbia University Press, 2000).

Yudin, Boris G., 'Research on Humans at the Khabarovsk War Crimes Trial: A Historical and Ethical Examination', in Jing Bao Nie, Nanyan Guo, Mark Selden, and Arthur Kleinman (eds), *Japan's Wartime Medical Atrocities: Comparative Inquiries in Science, History, and Ethics* (London: Routledge, 2010), pp. 59–79.

Yu, Feng 于峰, 'Yuhuatai kangzhan jinianta yiji chencang jumin xiaoqu' [The ruins of the monument commemorating the War of Resistance are hidden in a resistance area 雨花台抗战纪念塔遗迹深藏居民小区].   http://news.163.com   12/0707/00/85P711N400014AED.html, 7 July 2012, date accessed, 9 March 2014.

Yuan, Chengliang, 'Dianying "didaozhan" danshengji' [The birth of the film 'Tunnel Warfare'], *Dangshi tiandi*, 2(2006), 39–41 袁成亮, 电影地道战诞生记, 党史天地, 2 (2006), 39–41.

Yuan, Chengyi, *Fenghuo suiyue zhongde jiyi: Zhejiang Kang Ri zhanzheng koushu fangtan* [Memory during the war period: testimonies and interviews about the War of Resistance in Zhejiang Province] (Beijing: Beijing tushuguan chubanshe, 2007) 袁成毅, 烽火岁月中的记忆: 浙江抗日战争口述访谈 北京图书馆出版社, 2007.

Zhang, Guogong 张国功, 'Zhongguo haidei zhengqi caidui' [China still needs to try to make a good showing 中国还得争气才对]. www.gmw.cn/02blqs/2005-08/07/content_311894.htm, 7 August 2005, date accessed, 10 March 2014.

Zhang, Kaiyuan, *Eyewitnesses to Massacre* (New Haven, CT: Yale Divinity School Library, 2001).

Zhang, Lianhong and Zhang, Sheng (eds), *Nanjing Datusha shiliaoji 25 xingcunzhe koushu* [The historical materials of the Nanjing Massacre 25: survivors' testimonies] (Nanjing: Jiangsu renmin chubanshe, 2005) 张连红 张生编, 南京大屠杀史料集25, 幸存者口述 (江苏人民出版社, 2005).

Zhang, Lianhong, 'Nanjing datusha xingcunzhe deriji yuhuiyi' [The dairies and remembrance of the Nanjing Massacre survivors], *Kangri zhanzheng yanjiu*, 2005, 172–176 张连红, 南京大屠杀幸存者的日记与回忆, 抗日战争研究, 2005, 172–176.

Zhang, Lili, *Xin Zhongguo yu Riben guanxishi (1949–2010)* [History of relations between new China and Japan] (Shanghai: Shanghai renmin chubanshe, 2011) 张历历, 新中国与日本关系史 (1949–2010) (上海人民出版社, 2011).

Zhang, Limin, *Jiyide kedu: Dongzong de kangzhan suiyue* [The mark of memory: Dongzong's period of War of Resistance] (Beijing: Qunzhong chubanshe, 2006) 张黎明,记忆的刻度:东纵的抗战岁月 (群众出版社, 2006).

Zhao, Quangsheng, *Interpreting Chinese Foreign Policy: The Micro–macro Linkage Approach* (Oxford: Oxford University Press, 1996).

Zhao, Suisheng, 'A State-led Nationalism: The Patriotic Education Campaign in Post-Tiananmen China', *Communist and Post-Communist Studies*, 31(1998), 287–302.

Zhang, Xiangshan, 'Zhong Ri fujiao tanpanhuigu' [Review the negotiation on Sino–Japanese normalisation] *Riben xuekan*, 1998. http://xuewen.cnki.net/CJFD-REED801.001.html, date accessed, 16 March 2014 张香山, 中日复交谈判回顾, 日本学刊, 1998.

Zhang, Zhenglong, *Zhanzheng Jiyi* [War memory] (Chongqing: Chongqing chubanshe, 2010) 张正隆, 战争记忆 (重庆出版社, 2010).

Zhao, Cuisheng and Pan, Hong, 'Junren shehui baozhang zhidu tanwei' [Explore the policy of military personnel's social indemnification], *Wujing Xueyuan xuebao*, 6 (2001), 69–73. 赵翠生,潘红, 军人社会保障制度探微, 武警学院学报, 6(2001), 69–73.

Zhang, Shaozhe, Kang, Xianshu and Huang, Xiaochun, 'Chuugoku' [China], in Tetsu Nakamura (ed.), *Higashi Ajia no rekishi kyoukasyou wa dou kakareteiruka* [How the history textbooks have been written in East Asia] (Tokyo: Nihon hyouronsya, 2004) 張紹哲,康賢淑,黃孝春, 中国, 中村哲, 東アジアの歴史教科書はどう書かれているか (日本評論社, 2004).

Zhao, Shoucheng 赵守成, 'Gao Xingzu: Nanjing datusha yanjiu diyiren' [Gao Xingzu: the pre-eminent researcher of the Nanjing Massacre 高兴祖:南京大屠杀研究第一

人]. www.js.xinhuanet.com/xin_wen_zhong_xin/2005-08/13/content_4874686.htm, 13 August 2005, date accessed, 10 March 2014.

Zhonggong zhongyang wenxianyanjiushi, *Mao Zedong zhuan* [Biography of Mao Zedong] (Beijing: Zhongyang wenxian chubanshe, 2003) 中共中央文献研究室, 毛泽东传(1949–1976) (中央文献出版社, 2003).

Zhonggong zhaoqing shiwei dangshi yanjiushi 中共肇庆市委党史研究室, 'Qiqijianguo jinianbei' [July 7 cenotaph of the War of Resistance and nation-building 七七抗战建国纪念碑]. http://ds.zhaoqing.gov.cn/xqds/sh/201204/t20120409_ 153391.html, 9 April 2012, date accessed, 10 March 2014.

Zhonggong zhongyang wenxian yanjiushi, *Zhou enlai nianpu (1949–1976)* [Chronicle of Zhou Enlai's life] (Beijing: Zhongyangwenxian chubanshe, 2007) 中共中央文献研究室, 周恩来年谱 (1949–1976) (中央文献出版社, 2007).

Zhongguo gongchan dang xinwen 中国共产党新闻, 'Yijieji douzheng weigang' [Class struggle as the guiding principal 以阶级斗争为纲]. http://cpc.people.com.cn/GB/64162/64170/4467349.html, date unknown, date accessed, 10 March 2014.

Zhongguo geming bowuguan, *Zhongguo geming bowuguan cangpinxuan* [Selections from the collection of the Museum of the Chinese Revolution] (Beijing: Wenwu chubanshe, 2003) 中国革命博物馆, 中国革命博物馆藏品选 (文物出版社, 2003).

Zhongguo guomindang zhongyangzhixing weiyuanhui xuanchuanbu, *Qiqijinian zongcai wengao huibian* [Compilation of the president's statements on commemorating July 7] (Zhongguo guomindang zhixingweiyuanhui xuanchuanbu, 1942) 中国国民党中央执行委员会宣传部, 七七纪念总裁文告汇编 (中国国民党中央执行委员会宣传部, 1942).

Zhongguo renmin junshi bowuguan, *Zhongguo junshi bowuguan wenwujianshang* [Appreciate the period pieces of the Chinese Museum of the Military] (Shanghai: Shanghai renmin chubanshe, 2006) 中国人民军事博物馆, 中国军事博物馆文物鉴赏 (上海人民出版社, 2006).

Zhonghua renmin gongheguo waijiaobu and Zhonggong Zhongyang wenxian yanjiushi, *Mao Zedong waijiao wenxuan* [Selected diplomatic works of Mao Zedong] (Zhongyang wenxian chubanshe, 1994) 中华人民共和国外交部 中共中央文献研究室 (1994). 毛泽东外交文选, 中央文献出版社.

Zhonghua renmin gongheguo waijiaobu and Zhonggong zhongyang wenxian yanjiushi, *Zhou Enlai waijiao wenxuan* [Selected diplomatic works of Zhou Enlai] (Zhongyangwenxian chubanshe, 1990) 中华人民共和国外交部 中共中央文献研究室, 周恩来外交文选 (中央文献出版社, 1990).

Zhou, Shiyu and Li, Bengong, *Youfu baozhang* [Consolation, compensation and indemnification] (Zhongguo shehui chubanshe, 1996), pp. 7–8 周士禹, 李本公, 优抚保障 (中国社会出版社, 1996).

Index